INVESTITURE

Investiture

Royal Ceremony and National Identity
in Wales, 1911–1969

JOHN S. ELLIS

UNIVERSITY OF WALES PRESS
CARDIFF
2008

© John S. Ellis, 2008

All rights reserved. No part of this book may be reproduced, stored in a retrieval system, or transmitted, in any form or by any means, electronic, mechanical, photocopying, recording or otherwise, without clearance from the University of Wales Press, 10 Columbus Walk, Brigantine Place, Cardiff, CF10 4UP.
www.uwp.co.uk

British Library Cataloguing-in-Publication Data

A catalogue record for this book is available from the British Library.

ISBN 978-0-7083-2000-6

The right of John S. Ellis to be identified as author of this work has been asserted by him in accordance with sections 77 and 78 of the Copyright, Designs and Patents Act 1988.

Printed in Great Britain by CPI Antony Rowe, Wiltshire

To my family, on both sides of the Atlantic
I fy nheulu, ar ddwy ochr yr Atlantig

Contents

Acknowledgements ix
List of abbreviations xi

Part 1   Introduction 1
Pageantry in the face of the sun 3
The investiture and invented tradition 9

Part 2   A ceremony for Wales: The 1911 Investiture 19
1   Welsh nationalism and the Liberal Party 21
2   *Iuxta morem* – according to custom 37
3   The 'invention' of the investiture 49
4   The prince and the *gwerin* 67
5   Reconciling the Celt 91
6   The red dragon and the red flag 115
7   Recessional 125

Part 3   Pomp, perspex and protest: The 1969 Investiture 131
8   'Let's Go!' Labour and Wales 133
9   Reinventing the investiture 145
10   The investiture and 'The Way Ahead' 163
11   We'll keep a welcome? 189
12   *Bradwyr* and extremists 245
13   Whither the prince? 303

CONTENTS

Conclusion	317
Select bibliography	323
Index	335

Acknowledgements

I gratefully acknowledge the support of many individuals and institutions that have contributed to this study.

I would like to thank the staff of the National Library of Wales, the College of Arms, the Public Records Office, and the British Library from whose collections the research for this study is primarily based. In particular, I would like to acknowledge Gwynant Phillips of the National Library of Wales, for his generosity, invaluable aid and reliable support in response to my many questions and requests and for his friendship and company during my many research expeditions to Aberystwyth.

I am grateful for the financial support without which this study would not have been possible. Assistance was provided by the Fulbright Program, the University of Michigan's Horace H. Rackham School of Graduate Studies, and the University of Michigan Flint Office of Research. I am grateful for the encouragement and support of my colleagues in the Department of History at the University of Michigan Flint and for the instruction and opportunities provided by Boston College and the University of Wales, Aberystwyth.

I acknowledge the kind permission of the College of Arms to quote from their archives and to Tegwyn Jones for the use of his political cartoons in this work. For permission to use material that first appeared in their journals, I am grateful to the editors of the *Welsh History Review* and the *North American Journal of British Studies* and its publisher the University of Chicago Press. I would like to thank the staff at the University of Wales Press for their interest in this project and kind assistance in bringing it to fruition.

Dr Paul O'Leary and Dr Peter Weiler were critical sources of feedback and guidance during the initial phase of my research and they have remained valued mentors and friends. I would

ACKNOWLEDGEMENTS

like to thank Dr Melinda Gray, Martha Davies and Dr Huw Griffiths for their assistance with translations of Welsh-language material at various stages of the project. I am indebted to Merfyn and Eunice Phillips and the whole Phillips clan of Aberystwyth who provided valued companionship and a home away from home during my long stays in Wales while conducting research for this book. Finally, I would like to acknowledge the dedication and patience of my wife, Karen, who has provided the foundation of love and support upon which my work is built.

Abbreviations

CA	College of Arms, London
NLW	National Library of Wales, Aberystwyth
PRO	Public Record Office, Kew

Part 1

Introduction

Pageantry in the face of the sun

> Pageantry is true or false according to the meaning we put into it, the substance that lies behind it. The only use we can make of ancient pageantry in an age that has outgrown its first feudal intentions is to find a new vacancy and set into it a meaning and a soul that shall be consonant with our civilization, the spirit of our age and the temper of our creed.

Daily Telegraph on the 1911 Investiture, 14 July 1911.

> Newspapers, admittedly, are sometimes mistaken as to their readers' opinions but perhaps the success of royal occasions is measured not by what people feel but by what they, or their newspapers, say that they feel.

Welsh Office memorandum on the 1969 Investiture, August 1967.[1]

On 13 July 1911, a new Prince of Wales was proclaimed amidst medieval battlements and the fanfare of trumpets. For the first time in almost 200 years, the monarch formally bestowed this title upon the heir apparent to the British Crown in a ceremony that ritually dressed, or invested, him in princely robes and regalia. Taking place in a magnificent medieval fortress in north Wales, it was a breathtaking and romantic Edwardian pageant evoking the ancient history and culture of the principality. At the climax of the ceremony and in line with an apocryphal medieval legend, the newly proclaimed and invested prince was to be 'presented' by his father to his people – the people of Wales.

The day began with the Royal Family leaving their yacht anchored in Holyhead harbour and embarking on a special train heading for Caernarfon, where the ceremony of the investiture was to take place. Contrary to fears of rain, the day was bright and sunny, the warmest in 1911. The train took its

---

[1] Memorandum, R. E. Davies, 25 August 1967, 1.0.I 1969 Investiture of the Prince of Wales, College of Arms, London.

royal passengers, including King George V, Queen Mary, Princess Mary, the Duke of Connaught and Prince Edward, to a train station at Griffith's Crossing, just outside the historic town. Although the coronation had taken place less than a month before, the events of this day were not to centre on King George V but on the young figure of Prince Edward, at 17 the eldest son of the Royal Family and the heir to the throne of the United Kingdom. As the Royal Family left the train, a military band struck up 'God Save the King' and then 'God Bless the Prince of Wales', the first of many times the songs would be paired in Caernarfon that day. Under the gaze of the crowd assembled on the hill overlooking the station, the Royal Family was taken to their waiting coaches and horses. The prince was first to set off for the castle, his coach surrounded by a mounted detachment of the Denbighshire Yeomanry. Forty minutes later and escorted by a troop of 150 mounted Life Guards, three other coaches bearing King George V and his retinue proceeded across town, winding their way through the narrow streets. 12,400 soldiers, standing shoulder width apart, lined the length of the two and a half mile route. Behind the soldiers, the crowds of onlookers grew denser as the procession neared the castle, filling the square below the battlements to capacity. Some 250,000 spectators reputedly gathered in the small town to cheer the prince.[2]

After receiving a loyalty address in the town square from the people of Caernarfon, the prince passed through the castle gates to the sound of gunfire and trumpets, his banner unfurling high above the towers. Watched eagerly by the 12,000 invited guests seated around the castle walls, the prince walked through the courtyard preceded by the robed bards of the Gorsedd of the National Eisteddfod of Wales and accompanied by a formal procession of Welsh MPs, mayors, lords, and military officers. The prince entered the Chamberlain's Tower to prepare for the ceremony. After the King and his retinue arrived, the Constable of Caernarfon Castle ritually unlocked the castle gates for the monarch's entrance. The prince's banner was replaced with that of the King to the sound of a twenty one gun salute. Accompanied by a procession of Lords Lieutenant,

[2] *Sun*, 1 July 1969.

High Sheriffs, peers, clerics, government dignitaries, palace officials and heralds, the King and Queen joined Liberal Prime Minister H. H. Asquith and members of his Cabinet on a canopy covered dais sheltering the royal thrones in the midst of the upper courtyard.

From his throne, the King summoned the prince. Preceded by Welsh lords and heralds bearing the robes and insignia of his title and followed by officers of the Welsh military regiments, a procession led the prince to the dais. There, the Letters Patent creating the title were read by Home Secretary Winston Churchill, while the King duly invested the prince with the mantle, sword, coronet, ring and golden rod of the Prince of Wales. Following the prince's act of homage, the reading of a loyalty address from the people of Wales, and a religious service, the King led the prince to a platform overlooking the town square from the Queen's Gate. To the blast of trumpets, the King presented the people with their new prince. The sea of spectators below roared, greeting their prince by singing the Welsh national anthem, 'Hen Wlad Fy Nhadau' (Land of My Fathers). Perched atop the battlements, a popular choral conductor waved the musical efforts of the throng to a passionate crescendo. The King led the prince away to be presented again to the people assembled at the King's Gate and then once more for those whose seats were obstructed from viewing the ceremony within the lower courtyard. With the ceremony ended, the royal party filed out of the castle, climbed into their carriages and returned to the special train heading for Holyhead, the royal yacht and a well deserved rest for an exhausted prince. After a brief three-day tour of north and mid Wales, the Royal Family returned to more familiar surroundings in London. On that sunny day in July, not only had a new prince been invested, a new tradition had been created for Wales.

Over fifty years later, the trumpets atop the battlements of Caernarfon Castle sounded once more. On 1 July 1969, some sixteen years after her own coronation, Queen Elizabeth II invested her twenty-one-year-old son Charles as Prince of Wales. Prince Phillip, the Queen Mother, Princess Anne and Princess Margaret were on hand at the dais. Labour Prime Minister Harold Wilson and members of his Cabinet were joined by a collection of foreign dignitaries, including former

US President Herbert Hoover and the daughter of US President Richard Nixon. With royal processions, the reading of the letters patent, the bestowal of insignia, the swearing of fealty, the presentations of the prince and the greeting of the people of Wales, the programme was much like it was in 1911. The character of the 1969 Investiture, however, was substantially different. Rather than a visit of a few days, this ceremony was the climax of a prolonged state celebration of Welsh culture and identity. It began with a series of royal visits and affiliated events more than a year before the ceremony took place, included a six-week term of study for the prince at the University of Wales, Aberystwyth, and ended with an intensive four-week post-investiture tour of the principality. Unlike the minimal utterances accorded to Prince Edward in 1911, the 1969 Investiture assigned Prince Charles a substantial speaking role, much of it in the Welsh language. In place of the medieval-like tent that had sheltered the ceremony in 1911, a magnificent transparent plastic canopy hovered majestically over the dais and gave the rite a futuristic aura. Rather than accompanied by courtiers as in 1911, the prince was joined in his carriage by the occupier of the newly created post of the Secretary of State for Wales. Instead of Edwardian lords and soldiers dressed in robes and scarlet uniforms, the prince was supported in his procession by a troop of Welsh youth sharply outfitted in stylish blazers. With a television audience of 500 million, the 1969 Investiture was undoubtedly the most globally recognized event in Welsh history.

Yet, there were differences between the two ceremonies that were cause for concern. Both the pomp and the crowds in 1969 were noticeably diminished. Compared to the 250,000 that were thought to have cheered the prince in 1911, the 90,000 people assembled in the streets in 1969 were somewhat of a disappointment. The martial splendour of the event was also noticeably curtailed, with only about one-fifth of the soldiers in the street that had been employed in 1911. With dignitaries being duly searched upon entering the castle, security was far more apparent than it had been in 1911, and for good cause. Although the crowd in the streets was overwhelmingly enthusiastic in its welcome of the royals, from within its midst came a few rude gestures and an apple thrown at the Queen's carriage.

More ominously, the twenty-one-gun salute announcing the arrival of the Queen ended with the hostile boom of a bomb detonating in a nearby wood. The 1969 Investiture was destined to be a more raucous affair than its predecessor. Yet, both events perfectly reflected the tenor and times of the Welsh nation for which it was performed.

The investiture and invented tradition

This study seeks to explore the Investiture of the Prince of Wales as an 'invented tradition'. Eric Hobsbawm has argued that 'traditions' which appear to be old are often of quite recent origin. The need for such invention is greater in times of social stress and rapid change, when old social and political relationships are disrupted and new ones must be established. Traditions and those that employ them serve to support these new relationships by symbolizing social cohesion and group membership, legitimizing institutions and relations of authority, and inculcating a certain system of beliefs, values and behaviour.[1] Through the participation of the masses, these festivals of national regeneration symbolically re-establish order at a time of change and restore a sense of community and continuity to a fragmented society. Ceremonies define, model and communicate social relations in order to promote, legitimize and internalize those relations. In other words, public ritual not only involves the embodiment of power relations, but actually seeks to propagate them.[2]

Royal ceremonies became the major patriotic celebrations of a modernizing British society. This expansion of royal ceremonial occurred between 1870 and 1914 when Europe was being transformed from a predominately rural and agrarian society into a primarily urban and industrial one. This was a period of stark political change as the expansion of democracy empowered larger and larger sections of the middle and working classes. Through royal celebrations, the nation was thus imagined and unified. The declining political power of the

---

[1] Eric Hobsbawm, 'Introduction: Inventing Traditions', Eric Hobsbawm and Terrence Ranger (eds), *The Invention of Tradition* (Cambridge, 1983), pp. 1–14.
[2] Catherine Bell, *Ritual Theory, Ritual Practice* (Oxford, 1992), p. 82; David I. Kertzer, *Ritual, Politics and Power* (London and New Haven, 1988), p. 95.

monarchy and the landed elite corresponded to the rise of their symbolic power as the embodiment of the nation.[3]

In his pioneering work on nationalism, Benedict Anderson has defined nations as 'imagined communities', invented or forged through symbols, images and other forms of ideological and creative work.[4] According to this view, nations do not create states and nationalism; it is the state and nationalism that creates the nation.[5] Applying this approach, Linda Colley has argued that British national identity was forged by 1837 through an overarching Protestantism grounded in military hostilities with Catholic France.[6] However, national identity is inherently open to debate and contestation. It must be constantly made and remade as political and social circumstances change. The power of Protestantism and anti-French sentiment as a basis for British national unity had weakened by the twentieth century. Therefore, royal ceremony would have to be dynamic in its representation of a national identity that was itself subject to flux. The symbolic qualities of the Crown were also subject to change depending on the geographic, cultural and social perspective from which it was observed.

Nowhere in Britain were the effects of social and political change in the nineteenth and mid-twentieth centuries more pronounced than in Wales. Yet, with a few notable exceptions, the study of royal ceremony has largely focused on London and its vicinity.[7] This study helps redress the scholarship on royal

---

[3] Paul Ward, *Britishness Since 1870* (London and New York, 2004), pp. 14–36; William Kuhn, *Democratic Royalism; The Transformation of the British Monarchy, 1861–1914* (New York, 1996); David Cannadine, 'The Context, Performance and Meaning of Ritual: The British Monarchy and the Invention of Tradition, c.1820–1977,' in Hobsbawm and Ranger (eds), *Invention of Tradition*, pp. 101–8; Ilse Hayden, *Symbol and Privilege: The Ritual Context of British Royalty* (Tuscon, 1987); Tom Nairn, *The Enchanted Glass* (London, 1988).
[4] Benedict Anderson, *Imagined Communities: Reflections on the Origin and Spread of Nationalism* (London, 1991).
[5] E. J. Hobsbawm, *Nations and Nationalism Since 1780* (New York, 1990), p. 10.
[6] See Linda Colley, *Britons: Forging the Nation 1707–1837* (New Haven and London, 1992).
[7] For writing on the monarchy and modern Wales, see Ted Rowlands,

ceremony by moving it from the centre to the periphery of the British state. From this location, royal evocations of national identity and unity become far more problematic as the monarchy is forced to explicitly address the essentially multinational context of their realm. What happens to the meaning of the British monarchy when it leaves the English centre and crosses into the Celtic periphery? How does royal ceremony define and contest the relationship between ethnicity, nationality and the state when it takes place amongst a potentially problematic group like the Welsh? How are internal social and cultural divisions within the periphery represented, addressed and reconciled in such ceremonial? How are the relationships and the constellations of identity reflected by these ceremonies formed, contested and changed over time? This study will seek to answer these questions by exploring royal ceremony and the public reaction to them through the Investiture of the Prince of Wales.

While exploring the investiture as an 'invented tradition', this study builds upon scholarship that challenges and revises Hobsbawm's original concept.[8] Critics have argued against Hobsbawm's narrow identification of the invention of tradition, associating it with anti-democratic attempts by the political right to manipulate and stupefy the masses. They have questioned Hobsbawm's notion of the rigidity of invented tradition and its supposedly inherent projection of a conservative, essentially unchanging society. Critics have also objected

Something Must Be Done: South Wales vs Whitehall 1921–1951 (Merthyr Tydfil, 2000); Hywel Teifi Edwards and E. G. Millward, *Jiwbili y Fam Wen Fawr: Fictoria, 1887–1897* (Llandysul, 2002); John Davies, 'Victoria and Victorian Wales', in Geraint H. Jenkins and J. Beverley Smith (eds), *Politics and Society in Wales, 1840–1922* (Cardiff, 1988), pp. 7–28; for a parallel approach focused on Ireland, see James Loughlin, *The British Monarchy and Ireland 1800 to the Present* (Cambridge, 2007); James H. Murphy, *Abject Loyalty: Nationalism and Monarchy in Ireland During the Reign of Queen Victoria* (Washington DC, 2001); S. Paseta, 'Nationalist Responses to Two Royal Visits to Ireland, 1900 and 1903', *Irish Historical Studies*, 124 (1999), 488–504.

[8] For the historiography of 'invented traditions', see Stephen Vlastos, 'Tradition Past/Present Culture and Modern Japanese History', in Stephen Vlastos (ed.), *Mirror of Modernity: Invented Traditions of Modern Japan* (California, 1998), pp. 1–12; Kuhn, pp. 1–14.

to a corresponding agenda that is fixated on the debunking of the bogus and revealing the anti-democratic origins of invented traditions. As this study will show, the investitures of 1911 and 1969 had meaningful historical precedents, were not purely the product of the traditional elite and certainly cannot be characterized as projects of the political right alone. Indeed, in the form of the Liberal Party in 1911 and the Labour Party in 1969, the main agents in the investiture's creation and implementation were left of the political centre. Far from anti-democratic in tone, the ceremonies were infused with an ideology that William Kuhn has termed 'democratic royalism'. Through the investitures, the monarchy actually sought to demonstrate that it 'was not opposed, but crucial to the success of an expanded democracy'.[9] It is true that certain aspects of the investiture involved depictions of the essential and unchanging nature of the Welsh and the Welsh past, but the timelessness of such images was paired with representations of a dynamic nation, in the midst of transformation in the present and looking forward to the promise of the future. Indeed, the investitures of 1911 and 1969 were predicated upon and, to a large degree, in celebration of change.

Despite these revisions, the term 'invented traditions' is still a valid and useful term of analysis. It emphasizes that traditions are not merely observed but are objects of agency, involving creative, political, intellectual and artistic activity. Rather than inherited, traditions are actively 'chosen'.[10] The organizers of the investitures and the public that they sought to engage were highly conscious of the agency and choice implicit in the holding of the ceremony. A vehicle to affirm and communicate cultural and political beliefs, the investiture was regarded as deeply meaningful not only by those who organized the event but also by those who opposed it. There was a recognition that the meaning of the ceremony was not inherent but would be constructed through a discourse between the organizers, the media and the public. Organizers were only too aware that they held no monopoly over the investiture's construction, and that oppositional groups could contest the nature and meaning of the ceremony toward their own ends.

[9] Kuhn, pp. 12–13.
[10] Vlastos, p. 12.

THE INVESTITURE AND INVENTED TRADITION

Following the work of anthropologist Clifford Geertz, students of the monarchy have argued that the meanings of royal ceremonies can be ascertained by setting them within their historical context through a process of 'thick description' of the social, political and cultural milieu within which they are preformed. When studying the rituals and ceremonies of invented tradition, the object of analysis shifts away from the meaning of symbols to the conditions under which symbols become meaningful.[11] According to Stephen Vlastos, the study of 'invented traditions' should go beyond the effort to debunk their origins to answer 'How, by whom, under what circumstances, and to what social and political effect are certain practices and ideas formulated, institutionalized and propagated as tradition?'[12] As Hobsbawm recognized, invented traditions can be treated as a kind of historical evidence, symptoms and indicators of problems which might not otherwise be recognized, and of developments which are otherwise difficult to identify and date.[13]

Rather than merely establishing the ersatz nature of the investiture, this study explores the construction and contestation of the ceremony's meaning and its relationship to national identity in modern Wales. Attempting to interpret the meanings and significance of the ceremonies, the development of the 1911 and 1969 investitures are traced and located within the political, social, cultural and economic context of Wales in the early and mid-twentieth century. The relationship between the royal ceremonies, the framework of Welsh politics and the articulation of Welsh national identity can help us explore the political culture of Wales at formative times in its modern history and in its relationship with the United Kingdom. This relationship will be examined not only through the origins, personalities, form and content of the ceremonies themselves, but through the reporting, commentary, poetry, literature, images, and material culture that connected the ceremonies to their political and cultural context. By unravelling the discourse of national identity at the foundation of these ceremonies, this study seeks to

---

[11] Bell, p. 39; Hayden, pp. 1–13; Cannadine, pp. 101–8; Clifford Geertz, *The Interpretation of Cultures* (New York, 1973), pp. 3–32.
[12] Vlastos, p. 5.
[13] Hobsbawm, p. 12.

establish the 1911 and 1969 Investitures as important aspects of the political culture of Wales.[14]

In addition to a broad range of newspapers, journals and ephemera, this study makes use of government documents, personal papers and the archives of the College of Arms, the institutional guardian of royal ritual and symbolism. To a large degree, the 1969 Investiture can be reconstructed in far better detail than that of 1911 because of its richer documentation. As the organizers of the 1969 Investiture discovered to their chagrin, the planning records of the 1911 Investiture are not available for study. Relatively little about the 1911 Investiture exists in government documents, the Royal Archives, the personal papers of the Earl Marshal or the archives of the College of Arms. The scarcity of documentation is largely due to the fact that the ceremony was planned and implemented by an ad hoc committee organized outside the usual structure of royal ceremonial or the ministries of state. But even searches of the personal papers of the main figures involved in this committee have proved fruitless. In all likelihood, the planning documents and records of the 1911 Investiture were intentionally and systematically destroyed to safeguard their contents. In the absence of such documentation, the 1911 Investiture must largely be reconstructed from published sources and scattered references in personal papers and memoirs. Although limited, these sources provide important clues on the investiture's origins and creation. They certainly provide a rich vein for understanding the construction and contestation of the meaning of the investiture in 1911. Fortunately, documentation for the 1969 Investiture is much more extensive. Although still organized by means of an ad-hoc committee, the efforts of that committee were effectively housed within the Welsh Office and the College of Arms, bodies which kept extensive records of the deliberations, decisions and actions connected to the planning of the ceremony. The author has not had access to material on

[14] Ronald P. Formisano, 'The Concept of Political Culture', *Journal of Interdisciplinary History*, 31 (winter 2001), 393–426; David Howarth and Yannis Stavrakakis, 'Introducing Discourse Theory and Political Analysis', in David Howarth, Aletta J. Norval and Yannis Stavrakakis (eds), *Discourse Theory and Political Analysis: Identities, Hegemonies and Social Change* (Manchester and New York, 2000).

the 1969 Investiture kept at the Royal Archives. When such access is made available in the future, it will no doubt be possible to discuss in more detail the reactions, motives and actions of the royal family and Crown. This information will be particularly useful in regards to the Palace's public relations efforts connected to the investiture. While the more personal responses of the royal family largely fall outside the scope of this study, the Crown's key contributions and some hint of royal thinking in regards to the ceremony can be effectively traced through government documents and published sources. It is worth noting as well that the availability of media commentary on the 1969 Investiture is also more extensive than that of 1911, both in terms of volume and diversity of form, especially in regard to television, film and other aspects of mass media.

Far from being nothing but a simple royal diversion or an empty spectacle, the 1911 and 1969 Investitures were imbued with deep and conflicting meanings that reflected fissures within Welsh and British political culture. The ceremonies occurred at times of overwhelming political support for a single political party in Wales yet they were conducted against a rich backdrop of social, cultural and political conflict. The 1911 ceremony occurred at the height of Liberal ascendancy in Wales but it took place in the midst of a political maelstrom that questioned the very basis of the British constitution and the nature of the British state. At the same time, violent industrial conflict turned south Wales into a cockpit of class struggle, giving voice to an increasingly radical socialist movement demanding a fundamental reconfiguration of British society. The ceremony of 1969, on the other hand, was held at the zenith of Labour Party dominance in Wales. However, here too the investiture was conducted in a heady atmosphere. Iconoclastic youth culture, decolonization, and deindustrialization set the stage for the royal ceremony. The social agony of the coal field's decline was matched by the virulence of the student-led Welsh-language movement, the electoral breakthrough of Plaid Cymru and the threat of Welsh paramilitary violence. In these contentious political and social environments, differing groups contested the meaning of the investiture and its articulation of Welsh national identity. Consequently, supporters and opponents of the investiture projected competing assumptions about the underlying relationship between Wales and the United Kingdom. This study examines the role of the Crown, government and political parties who supported the investitures but it equally explores the response of those who opposed and constructed rival meanings for the ceremonies.

This study is divided into two parts, devoted to the 1911 and 1969 Investitures respectively. With particular attention to the relationship between Welsh nationalism and the Liberal Party, Chapter 1 reviews the political, cultural and social background of Edwardian Wales. Chapter 2 examines the historical precedents and models for the revival of the investiture ceremony in modern times. Chapter 3 identifies the individuals, organization and process involved in the origins and reinvention of the investiture in 1911. Chapter 4 analyses the meaning of the 1911 Investiture in relationship to patterns of class reconciliation and conflict within Welsh society. Chapter 5 explores how the 1911 Investiture was used to articulate Welsh national identity in the context of the British state and empire. Chapter 6 considers how opposition to the 1911 Investiture by socialists in south Wales helped crystallize conflicting 'centralist' and 'devolutionist' traditions within the Labour Party in Wales. Chapter 7 provides a summary of political and cultural developments in Wales following the 1911 Investiture and the changing context in which the Welsh nation was imagined. In Part 2, Chapter 8 examines the political hegemony of the Labour Party in Wales in the mid-twentieth century, its identity as the 'Party of Wales' and the challenges posed to it by a reconstructed Welsh nationalism. With emphasis on the role of the Welsh Office and the Labour Party, Chapter 9 explores the events, personalities, institutions and process by which the investiture was reconstructed for performance in the 1960s. Chapter 10 analyses the 1969 Investiture as an aspect of the political culture and policy of the Labour Party in Wales. Chapter 11 identifies the opponents of the 1969 Investiture, describes the anti-investiture campaign and details the state's response to its increasing security concerns. Chapter 12 analyses the competing meanings attributed to the investiture by

THE INVESTITURE AND INVENTED TRADITION

supporters and opponents and how this contest reflected conflicting definitions of Welsh and British national identities. Chapter 13 examines developments within Welsh political culture since the investiture and the relationship between the prince and the principality since 1969. The book concludes with a comparison of the discourse provoked by the ceremonies in 1911 and 1969 and how that discourse highlights the fault lines within Welsh national identity.

Part 2

A ceremony for Wales: The 1911 Investiture

1
Welsh nationalism and the Liberal Party

Reporting on the 1911 Investiture, the *Manchester Guardian* wrote: 'The national distinctiveness and separateness of Wales is a thing so completely accepted by Englishmen that it may seem hardly worth labouring the point.'[1] Yet this had not always been the case. The very notion of the existence of a Welsh nation was highly contested in the Victorian period. Like Italy before Mazzini, Wales was often regarded as a mere geographic expression, devoid of a national life or institutions. The denial of Welsh nationhood corresponded with the popular Victorian view that equated Britishness with Englishness. Contrary to the multinational, Protestant identity posited for the British nation in the eighteenth and early nineteenth centuries, by the 1880s the United Kingdom was generally held to be one, essentially English nation-state founded upon the Anglo-Saxon institutions of monarchy, Parliament and the established Anglican Church. The nation was integrated through its Anglo-Saxon racial identity, traditional ruling class, English language and literature, and the ancient universities of Oxford and Cambridge. While Irish Protestants and Lowland Scots could be embraced as a branch of the Anglo-Saxon race, the Welsh, Irish and Highland Scots were regarded as members of an inherently inferior 'Celtic' race. Racially incapable of self-responsibility in religious or civic affairs, the destiny of the Celts was to be guided and ruled by a paternal England. Rather than foundations of nationhood, differences of culture and identity were to be relegated as simple 'local colour' ultimately consigned to be absorbed by a dominant English culture and nation.[2]

[1] *Manchester Guardian*, 14 July 1911.
[2] John S. Ellis, 'Celt Versus Teuton: Race, Character and British National Identity, 1850–1918', *Irish German Studies*, (2001/2002), 13–27;

The Victorian Conservative Party became closely associated with this vision of an essentially homogeneous Anglo-Saxon nation-state. As the champion of the landed classes, the established Anglican Church and the hallowed British constitution, the Conservative Party sought to slow down the pace and scale of democratization and social change. Opposing demands for the disestablishment of the Church in Wales and for some form of self-government or 'home rule' in Ireland, they argued that recognition of the Celtic 'nations' worked against the progress and evolution of the nation-state and, therefore, of civilization itself. They insisted that the ethnic integration and centralization of the United Kingdom was an essential component of the British constitution and a fundamental factor in Britain's rise to global power. Consequently, Conservatives regarded official or constitutional recognition of distinct nations within the United Kingdom as corrosive to the very basis of British nationhood and empire. The term 'British' was merely a contrived word, indicative only of the absorption of the Irish, Scots and Welsh into an essentially English national polity.[3]

In the Conservative perspective, national unity within the confines of the British Isles was imperative, for if England could not secure the basis of its own nation-state how could it govern successfully abroad? For Conservatives and even some imperially minded Liberals, the centralization and unity of the British state were the foundations and model for a wider imperial unity. Articulated by Disraeli in 1870 and reasserted by Joseph Chamberlain and other imperial ideologues around the turn of the century, the empire was seen as a global extension of the English nation-state, united by race, religion, culture and a common destiny.[4] As John Robert Seeley argued

    Murray G. H. Pittock, *Celtic Identity and the British Image* (Manchester, 2000): Murray G. H. Pittock, *Inventing and Resisting Britain: Cultural Identities in Britain and Ireland, 1685–1789* (New York, 1997); Hugh MacDougall, *Racial Myth in English History* (Hanover, 1982).

[3] Hugh Cunningham, 'The Conservative Party and Patriotism', in Robert Colls and Phillip Dodd (eds), *Englishness; Politics and Culture 1880–1920* (London, 1986), p. 294; Bill Schwarz, 'Politics and Rhetoric in the Age of Mass Culture', *History Workshop Journal*, 46, (1998), 131–2, 137–9.

[4] Wolfgang Mock, 'The Function of Race in Imperialist Ideologies: The

in his seminal work, *The Expansion of England*, the English nation-state was like an organism that must expand or die.[5] Conversely, the expansion of an Anglo-Saxon empire would force the inferior peoples and nations to give way to the forward march of progress and evolution. According to Sir Charles Dilke, the subjugation of 'cheap races' under the triumphant rise of 'Saxondom' was 'not only a law of nature, but a blessing to mankind'.[6]

Initially, the Welsh were far less problematic to the idea of a unitary British nation-state than the Irish or the Scots. Although the eighteenth century produced some notable Welsh radicals and a formidable cultural institution in the form of the Eisteddfod, there were no Welsh equivalents of the Scottish Jacobite or Irish republican movements to seriously disturb the repose of the English nation-state. As Prys Morgan has written, the Welsh were seen by the English as 'too few, too poor and too weak to be threatening'.[7] In 1770, Wales could be dismissed as a rural backwater with a half a million inhabitants, only one eighth of the population of Ireland. The great majority of the Welsh population was Welsh speaking, but Welsh-language print culture had yet to develop into a mass media. In the realm of religion, the great majority of the Welsh people remained within the fold of the official, state-established form of Anglican Protestantism. Rather than being actively excluded, as were the Catholic Irish, or actively reconciled, as were the Presbyterian Scots, the Welsh were simply ignored by their more powerful English neighbours before 1830.

Wales, however, became increasingly problematic to the British state as the nineteenth century wore on. By 1850, a social, economic and cultural revolution had fundamentally

Example of Joseph Chamberlain', in Paul Kennedy and Anthony Nicholls (eds), *Nationalist and Racialist Movements in Britain and Germany Before 1914* (Oxford, 1981); H. John Field, *Toward a Programme of Imperial Life: The British Empire at the Turn of the Century* (Westport, 1982).

[5] As quoted in Field, pp. 45–6.
[6] As quoted in MacDougall, p. 99.
[7] Prys Morgan, 'Early Victorian Wales and its Crisis of Identity', in Laurence Brockliss and David Eastwood (eds), *A Union of Multiple Identities: The British Isles, c.1750–1850* (Manchester and New York, 1997), p. 94.

altered the nature of Welsh society. From a sparsely populated, rural and agrarian 'province of England', Wales grew into one of the British Empire's foremost industrial centres.[8] The rising metallurgical and mining industries transformed the landscape, especially in south and north-eastern Wales. Increasingly drawn to the new urban centres from the Welsh countryside, the population of Wales doubled by 1850 to over one million and continued to grow at a rapid pace. Industrialization had transformed Welsh from a spoken language of a forgotten peasantry to an urban language of print culture utilized by dozens of journals and newspapers, many of them radical and nationalist in political tone.[9] Seriously undermining the façade of British Protestant unity, the religion of Wales had also undergone a revolution. Closely associated with the Welsh language and culture, a distinctively Welsh form of nonconformity had lured approximately 80 per cent of worshippers in Wales away from the Anglican Church. These rudimentary changes were accompanied by a spate of violent industrial and rural disturbances. The Scotch Cattle riots, the Merthyr Rising, the Newport Rising and the Rebecca Riots ensured that Wales could no longer be safely ignored by the British state. To safeguard against these disturbances, for a period south Wales in effect became the most heavily militarized zone in early nineteenth-century Britain.[10]

In Victorian Wales, social and economic conflicts were inextricably intertwined with issues of cultural and national identity. From the nonconformist point of view, the cultural division of Wales was sharply defined in terms of an 'alien' aristocratic class of landlords and a 'native' peasantry. The landed gentry and aristocracy of Wales were largely English speaking and Anglican, while the Welsh middle and working

[8] Gwyn A. Williams, 'Imperial Wales', in Gwyn A. Williams, *The Welsh and their History* (London, 1980), pp. 171–86.
[9] Aled Gruffydd Jones, *Press, Politics and Society: A History of Journalism in Wales* (Cardiff, 1993).
[10] Gwyn A. Williams, *When Was Wales?* (London, 1985), p. 196; Prys Morgan, 'Early Victorian Wales', pp. 93–107; Gwyn A. Williams, *The Merthyr Rising* (London, 1978); Ivor Wilks, *South Wales and the Rising of 1839* (Llandysul, 1989); David Williams, *The Rebecca Riots* (Cardiff, 1955); Pat Molloy, *And They Blessed Rebecca* (Llandysul, 1983).

classes were overwhelmingly Welsh speaking and nonconformist. These ethnic divisions were replicated in the industry of early nineteenth-century Wales, where the capitalist class largely hailed from England while the workers were gathered from the surrounding Welsh countryside. Although recent scholarship has stressed the political need for landlord sensitivity to the concerns and opinions of their unenfranchised tenants, the electorate largely consisted of the landed classes who consequently dominated local and national politics in the early Victorian period.[11] The British state protected the religion of the Anglican minority as the established Church. This entailed numerous privileges for the state sponsored Church, including a monopoly over state-funded education and control of parish burial grounds. Most controversially, the state compelled people of all religions to pay the tithe to the Anglican Church.

Events at mid-century further embittered the ethnic divisions within Welsh society. Largely composed of English and Anglican members, a parliamentary commission of 1847 identified the continued dominance of the Welsh language and the growing influence of religious nonconformity as the primary causes for disturbance, backwardness and sexual immorality in Wales. In an act of blatant cultural chauvinism, the commissioners recommended that the school system be used to root out and destroy the Welsh language. Denounced by the Welsh as the 'Treason of the Blue Books', this 'national insult' served as a catalyst for an acute sense of national resentment. The national response to the Blue Books consequently became a rallying point and reference for the construction of a distinct national identity based on the Welsh-language culture of nonconformist Wales.[12] After 1870, agricultural depression

---

[11] For an interesting challenge to the more standard interpretation of landlord political dominance in the early Victorian period, see Matthew Cragoe, *Culture, Politics and National Identity in Wales 1832–1886* (Oxford, 2004).

[12] Gwyneth Tyson Roberts, *The Language of the Blue Books: The Perfect Instrument of Empire* (Cardiff, 1998); Gwyneth Tyson Roberts, '"Under the Hatches" English Parliamentary Commissioners' views of the people and language of mid-nineteenth century Wales', in Bill Schwartz (ed.), *The Expansion of England: Race, Ethnicity and Cultural History* (London, 1996), pp. 171–98; Prys Morgan, 'The

ensured the continuation of the conflict between 'alien' landlords and 'native' farmers and exacerbated a sense of Welsh national grievance.

In these conditions, a populist form of ethnic nationalism found fertile ground in Wales. The Welsh middle and working classes became 'natural' allies in their struggle against an oppressive and alien class of landlords, bishops and Tory brewers. An espirit de corps was forged through the struggles of Welsh nonconformity and, by extension, through the aspirations of the Welsh nation. A growing and interconnected sense of national consciousness and class alliance informed and linked demands for franchise, land and educational reform, temperance legislation, the disestablishment of the Anglican Church, the reorganization of local government and even some form of parliamentary Welsh home rule. Welsh nonconformity and the idea of the Welsh as a classless people effectively created a political language which tied cultural characteristics to ideas of social equality, the economic well-being of the community and the aspirations of the Welsh nation.[13] Denied by the Conservative and Anglo-Saxonist vision of British national identity, the foremost task for Welsh nationalism was the assertion that the Welsh nation did in fact exist and was a valid community of political opinion deserving legal and constitutional recognition. Rather than the creation of a separate Welsh nation-state, Welsh nationalism aspired to the recognition of the Welsh nation within a multinational British state. Although more limited than the demand for national separation, such a demand was regarded by Conservatives as highly radical and even dangerous to the integrity of the unitary British state.

If populism provided the Welsh nationalist movements with its spirit, the growth of democratic politics in the second half of the century gave it strength. The Reform Act of 1867 extended

Gwerin of Wales – Myth and Reality', in I. Hume and W. T. R. Pryce (eds), *The Welsh and their Country* (Swansea, 1986), pp. 134–52.

[13] Peter Stead, 'The language of Edwardian politics', in David Smith (ed.), *A People and a Proletariat* (London, 1980) pp. 148–65; Paul O'Leary, 'The Languages of Patriotism in Wales, 1840–1880', in Geraint H. Jenkins (ed.), *The Welsh Language and its Social Domains, 1801–1911* (Cardiff, 2000) pp. 534–60.

the franchise to selected members of the Welsh middle and working classes. For the first time, the populist alliance of Welsh nationalism could make its voice heard in an election. Instances in 1868 where Welsh tenant farmers were summarily evicted for voting contrary to the wishes of their landlords were heavily publicized and helped to inflame public opinion and spur on the growth of Welsh nationalism. The series of nineteenth-century reform acts expanded the electorate across the United Kingdom and collectively transferred the location of political power away from the landed gentry and into the hands of a much larger section of society. This served to enhance the political power of nationalism in Wales and to link it with the broader process of democratization.

In the election booth, Welsh nationalists closely allied themselves to the Liberal Party. In many ways, the British based Liberal Party was uniquely qualified to represent Welsh nationalist populism in the political arena. The removal of aristocratic privilege and the opening of careers to the common man formed the unifying themes that integrated a broad range of causes stemming from nonconformist grievances, desire for moral improvement and concern for the welfare of the working class. If the nonconformist regions of northern England and the Midlands lent their support to Victorian Liberalism, such support was all the more emphatic in Wales, where class and religious conflict were tied to ethnic division and popular nationalism. Welsh issues, however, were initially ignored or marginalized by the Liberal Party in favour of issues thought to be more central to British politics. In the late nineteenth century, political developments within the party outside of Wales and the development of party organization within Wales helped Welsh Liberals demand the attention of their party.

W. E. Gladstone's support of Irish disestablishment in 1869 and his subsequent decision to support Irish Home Rule in 1886 led to the Liberal Party's ideological recognition of Irish, and by extension, Welsh nationhood. Rejecting the Conservative's Anglocentric vision of Britishness, the Liberals under Gladstone held that the United Kingdom was a multinational state composed of the distinct and equally valuable national traditions and cultures of England, Ireland, Scotland and Wales. Nothing but injustice and ill feeling had been accomplished through past attempts to impose English cultural and institutional dominance on these nations. Recognizing their national identities and addressing their sense of national grievance, the Liberals proposed to remove the 'alien' institutions imposed upon Ireland and Wales and thus restore the heartfelt loyalty of the Celtic fringe to the British state. In this way, the Gladstonian tradition sought to reconcile Irish and Welsh national identities with a new, wider and stronger sense of British patriotism based on equality and mutual self-respect.[14] The same principles applied to Gladstone's vision of an empire based on goodwill, common consent and voluntaryism. Playing down the Anglocentric bonds of race and religion in favour of the 'silken ties of love and affection', Gladstone argued that the diverse peoples of the colonies should be allowed the maximum amount of freedom to develop their own sense of nationhood. The United Kingdom was thus seen as a multinational state at the heart of a voluntary, multinational empire.

From a more pragmatic political point of view, the subsequent Liberal split over Irish Home Rule placed the Liberal Party in a clear position of electoral dependence on the 'Celtic fringe', consequently magnifying the influence of Welsh Liberal politicians within the party. This influence was further strengthened by Stuart Rendel's development of a specifically Welsh national party organization within the Liberal Party, known as the 'Welsh Parliamentary Party', and the subsequent formation of regional Liberal associations in north and south Wales. Through these organizations, Welsh Liberals were provided a platform to more effectively discuss, coordinate and promote policy on Welsh national issues within the Liberal Party's official programme.[15]

Led by radical Welsh Liberals like Thomas Edward Ellis and David Lloyd George, Welsh nationalism took on a more aggressive tone from 1886. Welsh nationalist sentiment was

[14] Alan O'Day, 'Irish Home Rule and Liberalism,' in Alan O'Day (ed.), *The Edwardian Age: Conflict and Stability 1900–1914* (London and Basingstoke, 1979); George D. Boyce, 'Marginal Britons,' in Colls and Dodd, pp. 230–53.

[15] Graham V. Nelmes, 'Stuart Rendel and Welsh Liberal Political Organization in the Late Nineteenth Century', *Welsh History Review*, 9 (1978/79), 468–85.

fuelled by the confidence inspired by the phenomenal industrial growth of the south Wales coal and shipping industries, largely owned by a new class of native, Welsh-speaking industrialists. The expanding industries of Wales helped support a population of over two million by 1900. The mining valleys provided the main source of coal not only to the United Kingdom but also to the empire beyond. The rising spirit of Welsh nationalism resulted in concrete political gains. The Welsh Sunday Closing Act of 1881, which closed the pubs on Sundays in recognition of the temperance sentiments of Welsh nonconformity, was the first piece of legislation since the Act of Union of 1536 officially to recognize Wales as an entity legally distinct from England. Buoyed by the popular and at times violent resistance of the so-called 'Tithe War' of the 1880s, the Welsh Liberals used parliamentary politics to push through legislation addressing the issues of tithe, education, temperance and land reform in Wales. Heavily infused with nationalist ideology, a fabric of Welsh institutional identity was woven through the creation of the University of Wales (1896), the National Library of Wales (1905) and the National Museum of Wales (1905). During the 1890s, *Cymru Fydd*, the Welsh home rule movement led by David Lloyd George, became very popular in the north and west. The primary emphasis of Welsh nationalism, however, was never on home rule but rather on the demand for the disestablishment of the Anglican Church in Wales. The Liberals introduced Welsh disestablishment Bills in 1894 and 1895, only to have them stalled by the opposition of the Conservative dominated House of Lords, withdrawn and ultimately halted by the fall of the Liberal government.

The 1895 general election ushered in a decade of Conservative rule in the United Kingdom. Epitomized by the imperial ambitions of Foreign Secretary Joseph Chamberlain, the 1895–1906 Conservative government promulgated a 'New Imperialism' characterized by imperial expansion, centralization, cultural uniformity and military might abroad and Anglocentric hubris and staunch opposition to Irish and Welsh nationalism at home. As their increasingly bellicose foreign policy found popular support during the late 1890s, the Conservatives seemed to have succeeded in converting the English nation-state to their own militant and aggressive spirit of imperial nationalism. With Gladstone's retirement in 1893, a section of the Liberal Party even rejected the traditional Liberal programme of imperial voluntarism, Irish home rule and Welsh disestablishment in support of the Conservatives' seemingly more popular imperial rhetoric. With this dissension in the Liberal ranks, the Boer War of 1899–1902 represented the climax of the Conservative national and imperial vision. The Conservatives argued that the overwhelming force of the British Empire must be brought to bear on what was characterized as a racial struggle for dominance with the Boers. Only total victory and the complete subjugation of the enemy would resolve the conflict. The government appeared committed to a policy in which 'Freedom as a nationality will never again be enjoyed by the Boers'.[16] Looking forward to postwar reconstruction, the Conservatives projected an image of an Anglicized South Africa, colonized and transformed by an influx of men of the Anglo-Saxon race.

Although the Boer War was initially popular amongst the British public, it provided a platform for the remnants of Gladstonian Liberalism to rearticulate their alternative sense of Britishness. For these 'Pro-Boers', the Conservative's prosecution of the war was a crime against the principle of nationality that would ultimately weaken the bonds of empire no matter the military outcome. Instead, they argued, the Boers should be reconciled with the empire by demonstrating 'what respect is to be shown for their sense of nationality, their love of their flag and of their country.'[17] To the Pro-Boers, the war presented the empire with a simple choice between the doomed policy of force and the moral policy of national reconciliation and recognition. The barbaric subordination of small nations was a theme that resonated for Welsh and Irish opponents of the war who saw echoes of their own history in the British treatment of the Boers. Although actually divided in its attitudes to the war, Wales had acquired a reputation as a 'nation of Pro-Boers'. Led by the vigorous advocacy of David Lloyd George, opposition to the war seemed at least to reflect the opinion of Welsh language and nonconformist Wales. As the war dragged on and its popularity

[16] *Hansard's Parliamentary Debates*, 4th ser., vol. 101 (1902), col. 530.
[17] *Hansard's Parliamentary Debates*, 4th ser., vol. 89 (1901), col. 525.

began to fade, the criticism and alternative imperial vision of the Liberals increasingly found support in the United Kingdom as a whole.[18]

Despite the Conservative dominance and Liberal disruption of the 1890s, it is important to note the relative political success of Welsh nationalism during the late Victorian period. Nationalism had already vanquished the political ascendancy of the 'alien' Anglican elite that it had been called into existence to oppose. Welsh Liberals had secured control of local government through the democratically elected county councils established by the Local Government Act of 1888. Welsh politics was now dominated by a political hegemony practically unknown elsewhere in the United Kingdom, comparable only perhaps with southern Ireland. In the 1906 general election, not one Conservative was returned for a Welsh constituency. The Welsh Liberals controlled thirty-two out of thirty-four parliamentary seats, the few seats outside of their hold falling to the representatives of a newly independent Labour Party. At both the local and national level, Welsh Liberalism enjoyed overwhelming dominance as the political voice of the Welsh nation.

However, cracks in the populist-nationalist alliance in Wales were already becoming apparent by the turn of the century. The Welsh home rule movement of *Cymru Fydd* faltered on the hostility of Welsh industrialists who sought to protect their close connections to capital in London and opposed the growth of working class power that the proposed home rule parliament would entail.[19] A growing rift between the middle class leadership and the working class supporters of the nationalist movement was becoming more and more evident. Much of the nationalist programme concerned the interests of bourgeois farmers to the neglect of the working class concerns of agricultural labourers and urban workers. With the defeat of their common aristocratic foes, the nationalist alliance began to

[18] John S. Ellis, 'The "Methods of Barbarism" and the "Rights of Small Nations": War Propaganda and British Pluralism', *Albion*, 30(1) (spring 1998), 49–75.

[19] Emyr W. Williams, 'Liberalism in Wales and the politics of Welsh Home Rule 1886–1910', *Bulletin of the Board of Celtic Studies*, 37 (1980), 191–207.

drift apart. Consequently, the labour movement in Wales increasingly defined its demands in opposition to the interests of a new, native Welsh social elite.

The socially integrative force of nationalist populism was thus under growing strain at a time of growing class consciousness in Wales. The increasingly competitive global coal market resulted in the amalgamation of the industry into huge, impersonal combines alienated from a labour force conditioned to a more direct and personal relationship with employers. The coalmine owners' desire to shore up profits in the face of growing competition by cutting production costs resulted in strident disputes over wages and the safety of working conditions. Class division was exacerbated by the coalfield's seemingly insatiable demand for labour, bringing an enormous influx of working class English immigrants to the valleys of south Wales. These English miners brought with them both their language and a far more militant vision of class relations. The model of class cooperation inherent in the populist ideal and the national leadership of the Welsh middle class were effectively challenged. Although Welsh was still the majority language of the principality in 1900, the melding of immigrant and native in the coal valleys was producing a new English-speaking culture in industrial south Wales, a culture as distinctly working class in consciousness as it was Welsh in outlook. A new generation of Welsh labour leaders advocated class conflict rather than cooperation and some even began to contemplate the violent overthrow of capitalism. In 1900, Merthyr Tydfil elected James Keir Hardie as their MP, a constituency which he would serve until his death in 1915. A Scotsman, former coal miner, journalist and trade unionist, Hardie was a socialist firebrand and the founder of the newly created Labour Party. The year 1911 was to be one of intense social conflict in south Wales. Miners of the Rhondda and Swansea valleys, the dock workers and seamen of Cardiff and the national railway workers were all engaged in bitter and sometimes violent strikes. The populist alliance of Welsh middle and working classes was increasingly undermined by working class militancy.

However, interpretations that see Welsh political nationalism in a state of advanced decay following the failure of the

Cymru Fydd movement in 1896 overstate their case. Despite the growth of working class politics, questions of religion and nationality continued to be the dominant issues in Welsh elections. In all, Welsh nationalists maintained a tight grip on their political power during the Edwardian period. Any loss of momentum was primarily due to the nearly complete realization of the political agenda of Welsh nationalism and the correspondingly conservative character of its outlook. It was in this context that David Lloyd George turned his attention away from a purely Welsh agenda to broader, British-based issues of social reform. When Lloyd George assumed a cabinet position in the Liberal government of 1906–14, he did so secure in the knowledge that the forces of Welsh nonconformist nationalism now virtually controlled the political, cultural, social and economic life of Wales. Welsh political nationalism had worked splendidly and, by all appearances, was advancing from a position of strength at the turn of the century. All that remained of the nationalist programme was its much sought after capstone: Welsh disestablishment. Disestablishment became a symbolic fetish of nationalist victory, the crowning achievement that would signify the realization of Welsh nationhood. With the election of the Liberals in 1906, this goal finally seemed within reach and by 1914 disestablishment would pass through Parliament and be placed on the statue book. Rather than a time of stagnation or collapse, the Edwardian period should be seen as contemporaries saw it – a period of triumph for the nationalist movement in Wales. No longer could Welsh nationality be simply denied, ignored or suppressed as it had been in the past. In many ways, the Welsh nation was now an established fact whose existence the British state would be forced to address and reconcile.

The 1906–14 Liberal government pursued a policy of constitutional reform that promised to transform the nature of the British state and empire. Initially led by former war critic Henry Campbell-Bannerman, the Liberal government featured several prominent Pro-Boers in its cabinet, including David Lloyd George. As one of the first items on their agenda, the Liberals repealed several of the Conservative's repressive policies in South Africa and granted the Afrikaner colonies self-government under the British Crown in 1907. In 1910, the colonies joined together in a Union of South Africa whose constitution recognized the British monarch as the head of state. As anti-British hostility seemingly dissolved among the Boers, Prime Minister Louis Botha, a former general of the hostile Boer army, became a warm advocate of the benefits of imperial membership. The Liberal policy in South Africa seemed to provide a wise precedent for future recognition of the principle of nationality within the empire.

Meanwhile, as Chancellor of the Exchequer, David Lloyd George proposed that the wealthy be taxed to fund old age pensions in the so-called People's Budget of 1909. Fuelled by Lloyd George's own scathing and levelling rhetoric, the budget was widely perceived as an attack on the British landed classes. Consequently, its passage was blocked by the veto power of the aristocratic and Conservative dominated House of Lords. Faced with this defiance, the Liberal government resolved to confront the House of Lords and clearly establish the legislative supremacy of the House of Commons. In 1910, the government introduced its Parliament Bill seeking to curb the Lords' power, reducing its veto to a mere ability to delay the final passage of legislation. The Conservatives were apoplectic, framing the measure as a frontal assault on the integrity of the British constitution to be opposed by any means necessary. The Liberals threatened that the Lords' obstruction of the Bill would result in a showdown involving the King. Armed with a democratic mandate, the government promised to call upon King Edward VII to create enough new peers to stack the deck in the House of Lords in the Liberals' favour, a prospect regarded with horror by the Conservatives and Crown alike.

The controversy over the House of Lords stirred up other constitutional whirlwinds. Having been consistently blocked in the past through the Lords' veto, legislation for Welsh disestablishment and Irish home rule stood anxiously waiting in the wings. The debt for Welsh and Irish support of the Liberal Party was now due and the new Prime Minister, H. H. Asquith, duly promised action on the Bills once the struggle over the House of Lords was resolved. Entailing clear and constitutional recognition of the existence of distinct nationalities within the British state, the passage of these Bills promised to fundamentally transform the nature of the United Kingdom along the lines of the Liberals' imperial policy of national recognition and reconciliation. Wales would achieve something like parity with Ireland in having its nationhood recognized through the disestablishment of the Church in Wales. Furthermore, the Liberals would phrase their commitment to Irish home rule as the first step in a process of 'home rule all around' that would eventually be expanded to include some form of Welsh self-government. Of course, all of this stimulated further expressions of anger and dismay from the Conservatives. The rhetoric of political debate became increasingly polarized and violent.

Just as the Liberal government was pushing toward a final confrontation with the power of the House of Lords, King Edward VII died. The coronation of George V took place in these uncertain and contentious times. If ever there was a period of social and political change that called for the cohesive and stabilizing effects of 'invented traditions', it was during the summer of 1911 when the very nature of the British state was on the verge of transformation.

2
Iuxta morem – *according to custom*

Although often cited as bearing the hallmark of sham tradition, the Investiture of the Prince of Wales had historical, material and discursive antecedents. Rather than simply debunking the bogus antiquity and establishing the modern origins of 'invented traditions', more recent scholarship has emphasized that traditions are rarely manufactured completely from whole cloth. Precedent and perceptions of history underlie the power and legitimacy of tradition. As William Kuhn has argued, those who organized royal ceremony 'altered and adjusted traditions, they did not invent them'.[1] Reversing Hobsbawm's equation, so-called 'invented traditions' are now believed to have foundations of demonstrable precedent, albeit coloured and informed by contemporary envisioning of the historical past. For most traditions, 'genealogies, if not origins, can be found'.[2] Historical sources, antique precedents and contemporary ceremonial models helped inform the reconstruction and performance of the investiture in a modern and modernizing Wales.

The nineteenth-century transformation of the social, economic and political basis of Welsh society required institutional and ceremonial recognition. Such recognition would not only celebrate the achievements of the Welsh nation but also provide a sense of stability to the new society that had been forged. Pageantry and ceremony became more pronounced in Welsh national life, leading to a reinvigoration of the National Eisteddfod of Wales and the affiliated pageantry of the bards and druids of the Gorsedd. The leeks, daffodils, dragons and other symbols of Welsh nationality achieved an established

---

[1] William Kuhn, Democratic Royalism: The Transformation of the British Monarchy, 1861–1914 (New York, 1996), p. 13.
[2] Miriam Silverberg, 'The Café Waitress Serving Modern Japan', in Vlastos, p. 211.

status and 'HenWlad Fy Nhadau' was recognized as the Welsh national anthem. The celebration of St David's Day as a Welsh patriotic holiday was institutionalized in the nation's schools. Children observed the day by participating in patriotic recitals and dressing up in the 'traditional' female costume of shawl, skirt and tall beaver felt hat. In 1909, the highly popular National Pageant in Cardiff was held. A massive outdoor theatrical extravaganza, the pageant played out the history of the principality with a costumed cast of hundreds to sold-out audiences seated in grandstands.[3]

The culmination of this dramatic development of institutions and ceremonies in Wales, the 1911 Investiture was the grandest of Welsh national pageants. It would encompass within its embrace all of the symbolism, institutions and pageantry that had preceded it. It was a Welsh ceremony which surpassed all others, for it was not only a ceremony of the emergent nation but a ceremony of the British state, featuring no less a cast than the Royal Family itself. As David Cannadine has demonstrated, the Edwardian period was a golden age for royal ceremonial in which the monarchy enjoyed a new popularity. Ideologically removed from the great political transformations of British society, the monarchy provided a sense of continuity and consensus through a sense of cultivated anachronism. The monarchy was the focus of a host of updated traditions, spurred on by international competition in displays of public pageantry that paralleled the international competition of a new formal imperialism.[4] An 'invented tradition' in many respects, the 1911 Investiture could, however, be described just as accurately as a revival of an ancient ceremony.

Historically, the investiture was born of the circumstances surrounding the creation of the first English Prince of Wales in 1301. The English conquest of Wales, the termination of the native line of Welsh princes, and the re-establishment of the principality of Wales under King Edward I loomed large in

[3] Dai Smith, *Aneurin Bevan and the World of South Wales* (Cardiff, 1993) pp. 45–66; Dai Smith, *Wales! Wales?* (London, 1984) pp. 28–54; Hywel Teifi Edwards, 'Pasiant Cenedlaethol Caerdydd 1909', *Codi'r Hen Wiad Yn Ei Hôl* (Swansea, 1989) pp. 239–80.

[4] Cannadine, 'Context, Performance and Meaning of Ritual', pp. 120–32.

the ceremony's background. Originally, the term 'prince' signified the ruler of a small state, or 'principality'. The title 'Prince of Wales' thus referred to the ruler of a nominally united Wales, albeit under the feudal overlordship of the King of England. This title was first realized by Llywelyn 'the Great' in 1205 but his realm fell apart following his death. His grandson, Llywelyn ap Gruffydd, would restore the legacy of the principality, expand its borders, and increasingly assert its independence. Following the precedent of his grandfather and pressing home a temporary diplomatic advantage over the King of England, Llywelyn's claim to the title 'Prince of Wales' was recognized by King Henry III in 1267. Llywelyn gradually asserted more and more sovereignty over his principality, setting up the framework of a nascent independent Welsh state. Upon the death of Henry III, he defied calls to do homage to Edward I, the newly crowned King of England. In the late thirteenth century, King Edward I and Prince Llywelyn 'the Last' waged a desperate armed struggle for regnal supremacy over Wales. On 11 December 1282, an English soldier killed Prince Llywelyn near the town of Cilmery. When his identity was recognized, the prince's head was cut off and publicly displayed upon a spike on the Tower of London. In mockery of Llywelyn's pretensions to sovereignty, its brow was adorned with a crown of ivy. Llywelyn's brother Dafydd continued the struggle for some months afterward, but was captured by fellow Welshmen, turned over to the king's forces and executed as a traitor to the Crown in October 1283. In the aftermath, the immediate line of the Prince of Wales was snuffed out, the children of Llywelyn and Dafydd being locked in prisons, confined in nunneries and dying childless. Edward transferred the prince's lands directly to himself as the personal holdings of the Crown. He recast the administration of Wales along English lines in the Statue of Rhuddlun and consolidated his hold on the principality with what would become the greatest campaign of castle building in Europe. Chief amongst these fortresses was Caernarfon Castle. Protecting the new administrative capital of Edward's conquered principality, the castle was constructed with symbolism recalling Caernarfon's historic role as an outpost of the Roman Empire. Its many coloured fortifications were in imitation of those of Constantinople and redolent of the vision of Welsh folk hero Mascen Wledig. Among its battlements were placed the stone eagle totems of imperial Rome. As these walls were under construction in 1284, Edward sent for his pregnant wife to join him in the town. There, she gave birth to a son, Edward of Caernarfon – eventually to be crowned King Edward II. When his elder brother died only a few months after his birth, the infant became the heir apparent to the throne. In a later ceremony held at Lincoln in 1301, King Edward I bestowed the title of his slain foe upon his 17-year-old son and heir. By doing so, Edward reasserted the existence of the Principality of Wales while attaching in perpetuity the princely title directly to the Crown of England. By re-establishing a Principality of Wales under the royal prerogative, Edward attempted to reconcile Welsh opinion by maintaining Wales as an entity distinct from England. At the same time, the creation of his son as Prince of Wales provided a suitably safe focus of loyalty for Welsh nobles and chieftains, many of whom would be critical to raising Welsh troops for Edward's armies. Embraced as a popular figure amongst these members of the Welsh ruling class, Edward of Caernarfon thus became the first English Prince of Wales and the Crown lands that made up the principality were duly bestowed upon him.

Since Edward of Caernarfon took the title in 1301, tradition has dictated that the heir apparent to the English throne bear the title of Prince of Wales. Twenty-one heirs to the throne have held the title to date.[5] The succession to the title is not automatic, but is 'created' by the personal prerogative of the monarch through the issuance of Letters Patent. At such times as it is vacant, the title reverts back to and is absorbed by the Crown. With some notable exceptions, the general custom was to bestow the title upon the heir apparent shortly after either the birth of the prince or the accession of the monarch to the throne. Initially, the title of Prince of Wales was actually tied to the governance and revenues of the principality and signified the legal existence of Wales as an entity separate from but subordinate to the Kingdom of England. Under a series of reforms between 1536 and 1543 collectively known as the Acts

[5] For further details on the historical background to the creation and investiture of the Princes of Wales, see Francis Jones, *The Princes and Principality of Wales* (Cardiff, 1969), pp. 113–57.

of Union, Henry VIII incorporated the governance and law of Wales into that of a united English realm. The authority of the prince over his principality was effectively eliminated. George II was the last prince to be granted the revenues of Wales in the early eighteenth century. After him, the title's last material bonds to the principality were severed.[6] The title subsequently became an honorary one, bereft of any state function, legal immunities or revenues and increasingly distant from any connection to the principality that provided its name.

The 'creation' of the Prince of Wales was quite distinct from the ceremony of investiture, where the prince was ceremonially dressed, or 'invested', with the symbols and regalia of his title. This too has authentic medieval origins.[7] Although Edward of Caernarfon may very well have observed the rite at Lincoln, the earliest record of the Investiture of the Prince of Wales dates to 1343 when Edward, the 'Black Prince', is said to have been invested in a form established *Iuxta morem* – according to custom. The ceremony was intermittently observed in conjunction with the creation of the Princes of Wales thereafter, some twelve of the twenty-one English princes having been invested. Seemingly based on the ritual performed for the creation of an earl, the fullest early description of a Prince of Wales's investiture was written in 1610 in connection with Prince Henry, son of James I. This description includes almost all the basic ritual elements for the ceremony, including the entrance of the king's procession and the enthroning of the king; the subsequent entrance of the prince's procession bearing the insignia of his title and letters patent; the identification of the prince's insignia as a mantle, sword, coronet, ring and rod; the kneeling of the prince, the reading of the letters patent and the investing of the prince at the hands of the monarch; the oath of fealty; the ritual departure of the king's procession followed by that of the prince; and subsequent public processions and rejoicing. Before 1911, the rite of investiture was primarily performed in London as a parliamentary affair in front of the Lords and Commons. The public ceremony fell into abeyance after 1616,

[6] Press Information – The Prince of Wales, BD 67/52, PRO.
[7] Stewart Gordon, *Robes and Honour: The Medieval World of Investiture* (Basingstoke, 2000).

the last investiture before 1911 occurring as a private ceremony of the Hanoverian court in 1714. As the title lost its feudal responsibilities and privileges, the ceremony ceased to have any direct affiliation to Wales or the Welsh per se and focused rather on the figure of the Prince of Wales simply as the heir-apparent to the English Crown.

Nevertheless, the organizers of the 1911 Investiture could draw upon a distinct and well established Welsh royalist tradition.[8] As Paul O'Leary has argued, 'loyalty' was a keyword in Welsh patriotic discourse of the nineteenth century. In contrast to the more unruly Irish, any separatist tendencies inherent in Welsh nationalism were supposedly countered by a special Welsh attachment to the Crown and a pronounced loyalty to the state.[9] Members of the Royal Family were frequently the subject of celebration in bardic competitions. Royal births, marriages, deaths and jubilees produced volumes of adulatory verse in the Victorian and Edwardian Welsh press. Unsurprisingly, the Prince of Wales was regarded by the Welsh as uniquely their own. Indeed, following the Cymmrodorion's adoption of the badge in 1751, the heraldic ostrich feathers and coronet of the Prince of Wales became an icon of Wales itself. Employed widely by pubs, civic and sporting organizations in Wales, the prince's icon was most notably adopted by the Welsh Rugby Union upon its foundation in 1881. However, Welsh royalism did not concentrate solely on the heir to the throne. There was great interest in establishing Welsh roots for the royal lineage in general. Describing Queen Victoria as 'Boadicea rediviva – our Buddug the Second', John Williams ab Ithel memorably proclaimed at the 1853 Abergavenny Eisteddfod that the Welsh had more right to claim the Queen than their English friends for there was 'a larger quantity of Celtic than of Saxon blood flowing through her royal veins'.[10] Despite the apparent adulation of the Welsh

[8] For Victorian Welsh royalism, see Hywel Teifi Edwards and E. G. Millward, *Jiwbili y Fam Wen Fawr: Fictoria 1887–1897* (Llandysul, 2002); John Davies, 'Victoria and Victorian Wales', in Geraint H. Jenkins and J. Beverley Smith (eds), *Politics and Society in Wales, 1840–1922* (Cardiff, 1988), pp. 7–28.

[9] O'Leary, 'The Languages of Patriotism', pp. 544–6.

[10] As quoted in Davies, 'Victoria and Victorian Wales', p. 14.

for royalty, the interest was not mutual. Indeed, the chief Welsh criticism of the monarchy was the charge of neglect. Even if the monarchy often seemed aloof, the Welsh were eager to seize royal attention. Opportunities for Welsh artists to perform for royalty such as those garnered by John Thomas, Queen Victoria's Royal Harpist, and the Treorchy choir's victorious invitation to sing at Windsor Castle were regarded as causes for national pride and celebration.[11] Even with little encouragement or participation from the royals themselves, the Welsh were highly active and creative in fostering royal connections to the principality.

As medieval monarchs and princes tended to concern themselves with Wales as a necessary consequence of martial recruiting or campaigning, royal connections to the principality were heavily associated with Welsh military service to the Crown. In fact, one longstanding literary convention conflates the history of the Welsh people after 1282 with the Welsh soldiers who fought by the side of the medieval English Princes of Wales. Chief among them were the Welsh bowmen who fought under the Black Prince at Crécy (1346) and with Henry V at Agincourt (1415).[12] The leek was worn on St David's Day in commemoration of Crécy, where, in the words of Shakespeare, 'the Welshmen did good service in a garden where leeks did grow'.[13] It was also at Crécy that the Prince of Wales is supposed to have adopted as his own device the heraldic badge of the slain blind king of Bohemia, with its coronet, ostrich plumes and 'Ich Dien' (I Serve) motto.[14] The ostrich feather device was thus thought to have a special

---

[11] For the Treorchy Choir, see Gareth Williams, *Valleys of Song: Music and Society in Wales 1840–1914* (Cardiff, 1998), 125–30.

[12] Prys T. J. Morgan, 'The Clouds of Witnesses: The Welsh Historical Tradition', in R. Brinley Jones (ed.), *Anatomy of Wales* (Peterston-Super-Ely, 1972), p. 24. This tradition continued during the Victorian period right to more recent popular histories. See Wynford Vaughan Thomas, *The Princes of Wales* (Kingswood, 1982); John Miles, *Princes and People: A Story of Wales* (Llandysul, 1969).

[13] William Shakespeare, 'Henry V', in *The Complete Works of William Shakespeare* (New York, 1936), p. 585.

[14] Arguing that the Crécy story is mere legend, Francis Jones claims that the ostrich feathers are in fact a traditional heraldic motif of the Royal Family that gradually became attached to the heir apparent rather than to the title of the Prince of Wales per se; see Francis Jones, pp. 178–84.

meaning when attached to the Welsh military regiments and militias that bore its insignia.

A second major foundation for a Welsh royalist tradition lay in the Welsh lineage and connections of Henry VII, the founder of the Tudor dynasty. Although the depth of Henry Tudor's Welshness and the degree to which his dynasty improved conditions in Wales is debated by scholars today, the coming of the Tudors to the throne was traditionally seen as an unqualified triumph and blessing for the people of Wales. Henry VII was cast as the direct descendent of the native Welsh princes, the heir of Cadwaladr, the last Welsh king to rule all Britain. Hailed as the 'son of prophecy' foretold by the bards, Henry Tudor would restore Britain to the hands of the Welsh. Landing and raising an army in Wales, Henry fought under the red dragon banner and secured the English Crown with his victory at Bosworth (1485). Fully aware of their own Welsh roots and grateful for the assistance of their Welsh allies, the Tudors are said to have bestowed upon Wales marks of special favour in court, a reformed and more just government in the Act of Union, and the blessings of the Reformation in the form of the Welsh translation of the Bible. In a historiographical tradition dating back to the sixteenth century and extending through the Edwardian period, Henry's victory at Bosworth represents nothing less than the fulfilment of Welsh bardic prophecy, the undoing of the conquest of Wales and the ultimate climax of Welsh history.[15] Through the Tudors, the genealogy of the British Royal Family was thus traced to the 'Welsh' Tudors and through them back to the ancient Welsh princes themselves.

In more peaceful, modern times, examples of direct royal associations with the principality are harder to find. Royal visits to Wales were sparse and often tangential. In the eighteenth century, there were no royal visits to the principality at all. Things improved somewhat during the nineteenth century, but royal visits to Wales were still far and few between. They were often conducted as a stopover on the way to more purposeful visits to Ireland or as a brief detour on the familiar route to

---

[15] Morgan, 'Clouds of Witnesses', 26–8; David Rees, *The Son of Prophecy: Henry Tudor's Road to Bosworth* (London, 1985); J. Gwynfor Jones, *Wales and the Tudor State: Government, Religious Change and the Social Order, 1534–1603* (Cardiff, 1989).

Balmoral in Scotland. Important exceptions occurred with Princess Victoria's three-month visit to Anglesey in 1832, Prince Edward's opening of a new dock in Swansea in 1881 and his three-day visit to Wales in 1894. Through these occasions, the standard elements of Victorian royal ceremony – royal receptions, patronage of local institutions, the opening of public works and buildings, carriage processions, military displays and the presentation and acceptance of loyalty addresses – were adapted into a specifically Welsh context and idiom. An important royal connection to Wales was also formed through royal patronage of the Eisteddfod. In 1832, the Beaumaris Eisteddfod received the patronage of Princess Victoria, who awarded the prizes to the winning competitors. Following a brief visit to the National Eisteddfod in London in 1887, Prince Edward attended the National Eisteddfod in Caernarfon in 1894 and was made a member of the Gorsedd of Bards.

The most direct model for a distinctly Welsh royal ceremony was provided by the installation of the prince as Chancellor of the University of Wales. This ceremony would anticipate many of the themes of the 1911 Investiture. Amongst much pomp and pageantry, the university court installed Prince Edward as the first Chancellor at Aberystwyth in 1896. The university itself was hailed as the Welsh nation's first great national institution, so its opening would be no mere academic rite. The ceremony was meant to project and reaffirm the connection between the prince, people and nation of Wales. The public speeches and press commentary on the event established the ceremony as a national affair, celebrating the distinct achievements and culture of Wales through the union of its university and its prince. 'If ceremonial is ever to hold a place and take part in the life and thoughts of a nation', Lord Rendel wrote, 'then the Installation of the Prince of Wales as first Chancellor of its infant university should draw the eyes and hearts of the entire people of Wales'.[16] There could be no mistaking the national flavour of the event. Witnessed by an assembly of representatives of Welsh national life, the ceremony was gilded with the Welsh language, choirs, and the iconography of Welsh nationhood. The university was represented as the very embodiment of the Welsh nation's genius

[16] *Young Wales,* June 1896.

and traditions. Its establishment was hailed as a national coming of age, an awakening of national self-consciousness, greater national organization and, in the estimation of some enthusiastic nationalists, a step towards self-government. Much was made of the democratic and popular basis of the 'people's college' in Aberystwyth and the unification of the nation behind its educational ideals. Through the ceremony, the Prince of Wales once more assumed his destined role as the symbolic leader of the Welsh nation. As the noted Liberal nationalist, Llewelyn Williams, wrote: 'The sight of the Prince placing himself formally and publicly at the head of the national movement in the Principality was one that might have roused the dullest imagination.'[17] Through poetry and prose, the names of the ancient native princes were invoked and called upon to witness the return of the prince to his principality. Foreshadowing 1911, Lord Rendel said the ceremony marked a transition towards 'closer and happier and more just relations between England and Wales, and the formal admission of Wales into its full inheritance and field of action in the Empire and the world at large'.[18] Following Edward's accession to the throne, the honour of being chancellor was bestowed in 1902 on George as the Prince of Wales in a ceremony of similar magnitude and spectacle conducted at the new university campus in Bangor. Significantly, the 1902 ceremony featured a royal visit to the town of Caernarfon where commentators often recounted the story of the historic and mythical connections between its castle and the prince's title.[19]

---

[17] Ibid., July 1896.
[18] For the university movement and installation ceremonies, see: *Cambrian News*, 26 June 1896; *Young Wales*, June, July 1896, May 1902; *Carnarvon and Denbigh Herald*, 9 May 1902; Geraint H. Jenkins, *The University of Wales: An Illustrated History* (Cardiff, 1993); J. Gwynn Williams, *The University Movement in Wales* (Cardiff, 1993).
[19] Although the legend is assuredly false in its details, the demands of the Welsh chieftains bear some resemblance to a communication sent to Edward I by the followers of Llywelyn ap Gruffydd in 1282. The Welsh nobility vowed that they would refuse homage to 'any stranger as they are wholly unacquainted with his language, his way of life and his laws'; see John Davies, *A History of Wales* (London, 1990), p. 159.

IUXTA MOREM – ACCORDING TO CUSTOM

A legend first recorded in David Powel's *Historie of Cambria* in 1584 provided a crucial ingredient in the connection between the Prince of Wales and Caernarfon Castle. As the tale would have it, the Welsh chieftains feared that King Edward I would impose upon them an English overlord following the conquest of Wales. They demanded that any new Prince of Wales be of their own country, that he speak not a word of English and that he bear an unblemished reputation. King Edward summoned the chieftains to his new castle in Caernarfon where from the battlements he presented their new prince in the form of his infant son – born of their own country, speaking no English and bearing an unsullied reputation. Although the apocryphal nature of the tale was recognized, the legend became a colourful addition to the tradition of Welsh royalism and provided a key model for the shape of the 1911 Investiture.

Rather than merely the product of the Edwardian imagination, the investiture of the Prince of Wales has an authentic historical past. Through history and venerable legend, the ceremony was tied to the medieval English conquest of Wales, the construction of Caernarfon Castle and the creation of the first English Prince of Wales in 1301. Although it was primarily a ceremony of the court with little reference to the principality of Wales, the investiture itself has been irregularly observed since at least 1343. Its revival in 1911 after a long period of disuse occurred as the crescendo of a wave of institutional and ceremonial recognition of an emerging, dynamic and confident Welsh nation. Both past and present associations between Wales and the monarchy were plundered and employed in the investiture's introduction to Welsh national life. In seeking to create a royal ceremony that was distinctly Welsh in imagery and patriotic sentiment, the organizers of the ceremony could draw upon a rich melange of the ceremony's history, models of contemporary ceremonial, and a strong Welsh royalist tradition.

3
The 'invention' of the investiture

Despite its ancient precedents, it is fair to identify the 1911 Investiture of the Prince of Wales as part of the wave of 'invented traditions' which swept Europe in the nineteenth and early twentieth centuries. Much of the ceremony was new, created in the heady atmosphere of Edwardian Britain as an appendage to the coronation celebrations of George V in 1911. Following an absence of nearly one hundred years, the ceremony had to be re-established and recreated to serve new purposes. Although other investitures had been performed in the past, this investiture was to be different. For the first time, a Prince of Wales was to be invested on Welsh soil. There has been a general consensus giving credit (or blame) for the creation of the ceremony to the genius of David Lloyd George, then the Chancellor of the Exchequer. While occasional credit is given to the Bishop of St Asaph, Welsh historians, biographers and historians of the British monarchy have all accepted the primacy of Lloyd George's role in the ceremony's instigation and subsequent creation.[1] The Investiture of 1911 has been equated with a piece of political opportunism instigated,

[1] Don M. Creiger, *Bounder from Wales: Lloyd George's Career before the First World War* (Columbia and London, 1976), pp. 169–70; W. Watkin Davies, *Lloyd George 1863–1914* (London, 1939), pp. 380–1; J. Hugh Edwards, *The Life of David Lloyd George with a Short History of the Welsh People* (London, 1918), p. 185; Bentley Birkenhoff Gilbert, *David Lloyd George: A Political Life: The Architect of Change 1863–1912* (London, 1987), pp. 446–7; John Grigg, *Lloyd George: The People's Champion 1902–1911* (London, 1978), pp. 303–4; Kenneth O. Morgan, *Rebirth of a Nation: Wales 1880–1980* (Oxford, 1981), p. 124; Tom Nairn, *The Enchanted Glass: Britain and its Monarchy* (London, 1988), pp. 220–3; Dai Smith, *Wales! Wales?* (London, 1985), p. 50; Gwyn A. Williams, *When Was Wales?* (London, 1985), p. 221.

invented and organized by Britain's foremost political opportunist.

Although there is no doubt that David Lloyd George was involved in the 1911 Investiture, the widespread belief in the primacy of his role over-simplifies the process by which the investiture ceremony was created, ignores the sources of its creation and distorts its meaning. Owen Rhoscomyl, a soldier, novelist and Welsh nationalist, first publicly raised the idea of reviving the investiture, advocating that the ceremony be held in Cardiff. As Rhoscomyl's suggestion developed into a popular movement, an influential committee of Welsh public men, including David Lloyd George and the Bishop of St Asaph, seized control of the project and pressed for the investiture to be located within Lloyd George's parliamentary constituency in Caernarfon. A fierce debate ensued between the towns. This debate was of secondary importance, for control of the ceremony was already firmly in the hands of the small committee of Welshmen. Although Lloyd George was a prominent member of this committee, he was not necessarily the dominant force. Both the Bishop of St Asaph and Lord Plymouth seem to have played equally crucial roles. The 1911 Investiture developed in a process marked with conflict and must be set within the context of Edwardian Welsh nationalism.

Who first conceived of and presented the King with the idea of reviving the investiture ceremony is far from clear. David Lloyd George, the Bishop of St Asaph and Owen Rhoscomyl have all laid claim to the honour but their respective claims are based on testimony that lacks the support of corroborating evidence. In the absence of such evidence, there is no reason to suppose that David Lloyd George's claims are any more valid than those of the bishop or the soldier. It is clear, however, that all three played important roles in the invention of the investiture and that their background and claims are worth examining in detail.

David Lloyd George, who would subsequently climb to the very peak of political power and success as the prime minister who 'won the war' between 1916 and 1918, was already an icon in Wales in 1911. Born in Manchester but brought up a Welsh-speaking Welshman in the rural northern village of

Llanystumdwy, he had risen to prominence in the 1890s as a Liberal backbencher representing Caernarfon Boroughs. With inspiring oratory, he established himself as a champion of Welsh nonconformity and nationalism and as a scourge of inherited privilege, the landed gentry and the established Church. His continued rise to power as one of the few Welshmen to obtain a cabinet position and then his appointment in 1908 as the Chancellor of the Exchequer ensured him deification in Wales as a native son and Welshman par excellence. With levelling rhetoric that many regarded as inflammatory, Lloyd George confronted the British landowning class in his famous Limehouse speech and in his 1909 'People's Budget'. This alarmed the British elite, while further endearing him to the common people of Wales. Despite his increasing concentration on wider, British-based issues of social reform, Lloyd George's presence remained central to all Welsh affairs. The Investiture of 1911 was no exception.

Although he remained silent on the subject throughout his life, the case for David Lloyd George's role in the origins of the investiture was certainly made during the period of the 1911 Investiture itself. In August 1910, a 'well informed correspondent' from *the South Wales Daily News* announced:

> I am able, on high authority, to make public a fact that has been hitherto only been known by a few. On the death of the late King, it will be remembered that Mr. Lloyd George, who was motoring under the blue skies of Italy, hurried back to London. With the sole exception of Mr. Churchill, he was the first Cabinet Minister who had audience with the new King after his accession to the vacant throne . . . he took the occasion to assure King George that there was not a spot in the whole of his wide dominions where he could count upon such deep devotion and fervid loyalties as in the little land of Wales. And in the train of that assurance Mr. Lloyd George ventured to express his fervent hope that his Majesty could see his way to agree to the investiture of the young Prince of Wales on Welsh soil after the manner of ancient usage. Such a ceremony, declared Mr. Lloyd George, would give immense joy to the Welsh people, and it would help to form a new link between the Throne and the little land of the harp and the feathers. His Majesty not only readily acquiesced in the suggestion, but thanked the Chancellor for so happy a suggestion.[2]

[2] *South Wales Daily News*, 26 August 1910.

This scenario was soon attached to the claims of the Corporation of Caernarfon, which maintained that it had originally suggested the idea of holding the investiture in the form of a unanimous resolution upon the death of Queen Victoria. Having been entrusted by the town council to deliver the resolution in 1900, Lloyd George presumably reiterated the suggestion during his meeting with the King in 1910.[3] There is, however, no independent evidence to verify either of these stories and there exists cause for doubt. In a letter to his wife in May 1910, Lloyd George gave a rather detailed account of his first visit with George V, citing the fact that he was among the first ministers to receive an audience and describing intimate conversations with the new King about his departed father and the current political crisis over the House of Lords. Nowhere does he mention the idea of the investiture having been raised or discussed.[4] This is not to say that Lloyd George failed to recognize the benefits such an event could provide. In a 1908 letter to his brother, Lloyd George made a cryptic reference to some kind of event pairing Caernarfon Castle with the Prince of Wales:

> I am inclined to think a good deal of the idea of pulling the Prince of Wales into Carnarvon Castle although I see Uncle Lloyd is getting violently opposed to it. It will please the Carnarvon folk to have them think I can serve them unselfishly.[5]

This evidence demonstrates that Lloyd George saw the princely title and its connection to the history of Carnarvon as an effective means of gratifying his constituents and attracting royal attention to the borough. It falls short, however, in proving Lloyd George's supposedly instrumental role in instigating the investiture.

Most historians who identify David Lloyd George as the originator and 'stage manager' of the event cite the 1951 memoirs of the Duke of Windsor, the former Prince of Wales who was invested in 1911. The Duke flatly states that Lloyd

[3] *Carnarvon & Denbigh Herald*, 9 September 1910
[4] Lloyd George to Margaret Lloyd George, 9 May 1910, Lloyd George MSS 20429C, NLW.
[5] David Lloyd George to William George, 30 October 1908, William George Papers 2126, NLW.

George proposed to his father that the ceremony of investiture 'be transformed into a spectacular Welsh pageant'.[6] The Duke's testimony, however, is not unequivocal. Although the central object of the 1911 ceremony, it appears that the young prince had little access to or knowledge of the discussions concerning the investiture's origins or planning. It is apparent that he was informed of the decisions regarding the ceremony rather than being meaningfully consulted. This is clearly demonstrated in the prince's ineffectual revolt against the investiture costume, a fantastic affair of white silk breeches, purple mantle and surcoat of velvet edged with ermine. When presented with the design that the organizers had concocted, he called it a 'preposterous rig' and refused to wear it. Significantly, it was his mother, not the investiture organizers, who discussed the matter with him and convinced him to don the garment. Indeed, the only person involved in the investiture project that Prince Edward had any regular contact with was David Lloyd George, and that was in the minister's occasional capacity as a Welsh-language tutor to the prince.[7] Given the warmth of the relationship that developed between them stemming from those lessons, it is no wonder that the Duke of Windsor would, in recollection, fall into Lloyd George's camp over the matter of who first presented the idea of holding the ceremony. In 1969, the Duke further speculated on Lloyd George's motivation for supposedly inventing the investiture, believing that he was scheming to inject some of the popularity of the Royal Family into his radical image.[8] This has been echoed by Lloyd George biographer John Griggs, who wrote that: 'By stage-managing the Investiture he could make a harmless gesture to those elements in society which had been most affronted by his words and deeds.'[9] While providing some insight into the possible motivations for Lloyd George's personal involvement in the investiture, such statements do not establish his primacy as an organizer or stage manager of the ceremony.

[6] Edward Windsor, *A King's Story: The Memoirs of H. R. H. The Duke of Windsor K.G.* (London, 1951), pp. 78–9.
[7] Ibid.
[8] *Daily Express*, 26 June 1969.
[9] Grigg, pp. 303–4.

Destined to become the first Anglican Archbishop of Wales, A. G. Edwards was born in a rural Welsh village of Llanymawddwy, Merioneth, and was fluent in the Welsh language. Becoming the Bishop of St Asaph in 1889, he earned a reputation as the leading figure in the defence against the campaign to disestablish the Anglican Church in Wales. Consequently, he became a noted and formidable critic of Welsh nonconformist nationalism. Like Lloyd George, Edwards was a controversial and outspoken advocate that would in later years display a talent for compromise. Although Edwards and Lloyd George were the fiercest of political opponents in the 1890s, this spirit of compromise and consensus led to the formation of a rather unexpected friendship with David Lloyd George after the turn of the century. It also informed Edwards's hopes to reconcile the image of the Anglican Church in Wales with Welsh national sympathies.[10]

A. G. Edwards states in his 1927 memoirs that the idea of holding an investiture in Wales actually stemmed from a suggestion made to him by the Empress Frederick of Germany while he was preaching at Balmoral Castle in 1893. He claimed that the death of King Edward and the impending coronation of George V prompted him to revisit the idea in 1910. Edwards states that at his behest the Archbishop of Canterbury successfully approached the new King with the proposition of reviving the investiture. It was thus only after the informal consent of the monarch had been given to the scheme that David Lloyd George became actively involved.[11] Although Edwards's story was enough to convince no less a scholar than Francis Jones, there is no evidence to support these claims beyond Edwards's own published recollections.

Owen Rhoscomyl's background contrasts in many ways with that of Lloyd George and the Bishop of St Asaph. He was born in 1863 to an English father and Welsh mother as Robert

---

[10] Kenneth O. Morgan, *Freedom or Sacrilege: A History of the Campaign for Welsh Disestablishment* (Penarth, 1966), pp. 16–17; Neil Purvey Tyler, 'Lloyd George, the Bishop of St Asaph and the Disestablishment Controversy', in Judith Loades (ed.), *The Life and Times of David Lloyd George* (Bangor, 1991), p. 154; *The Dictionary of Welsh Biography down to 1945* (London, 1959), p. 184.

[11] Archbishop of Wales, *Memories* (London, 1927), pp. 242–5.

Scoufield Mill in Southport, Merseyside. He was brought up in Flintshire by his Welsh grandmother who, through her tales of Llywelyn the Last, Owain Glyndŵr and the distant Welsh past, instilled in him the romantic Welsh patriotism which characterized so much of his life. He seems to have had some knowledge of Welsh but he would primarily speak and would exclusively write in English. At the age of fifteen, he left Wales for a life of adventure as a stowaway on a ship bound for America. He found employment as a cowboy in the days of the American 'Wild West' and then actively served as a soldier for the United States and British armies. Adopting the name 'Arthur Owen Vaughan', he became a hero during the Boer War as a scout. It was in South Africa that he married an Afrikaner woman, reputedly absconding with her from her village and observing the marriage ceremony while under fire. Returning to Wales with his wife after the war and eventually settling in Cardiff, Rhoscomyl was an uncommon, even unlikely, Welsh nationalist. Rather than being a Welsh insider seeking a place in the wider society of imperial Britain like Lloyd George and Edwards, Rhoscomyl was a consummate outsider seeking his place within the smaller world of Welsh Wales. In a rather straight-laced nonconformist Wales, his habits and manners were 'aggressively American' and he held an antagonistic attitude towards organized religion.[12] Transplanted from her native Africa to Wales, his wife seems to have been ostracized from community life and may have suffered an emotional breakdown, temporarily fleeing back to her people in South Africa before being retrieved by her husband. Rhoscomyl was hardly a typical Welsh nationalist, yet his friend J. Glyn Davies, Professor of Welsh at Liverpool University, could write that Rhoscomyl was 'the only thorough paced, out and out Welsh patriot I have ever met . . . the very name "Cymru" was sacred to him; put up that symbol and all the sordidness and meanness that one finds in Wales as in all countries faded clean out of his vision'.[13]

[12] Edward James to Gwilym Roberts, 3 March 1952, Gwion Davies Donation 1971, NLW.
[13] J. Glyn Davies, 'Owen Rhoscomyl – A Tribute by the Man who Knew Him Best', unpublished typescript, p. 6, Olwen Vaughan Donation 1977, NLW.

INVESTITURE

A heroic figure in his own right, Rhoscomyl's major contribution to Welsh nationalism was through his writing. He wrote the script for the Cardiff National Pageant in 1909 and a number of romantic adventure novels featuring Welsh characters and themes in the vein of G. A. Henty. As a scholar, he was primarily involved in the construction of elaborate genealogies of the Welsh princes and gentry. These were used in his two historical books, *Flame-Bearers of Welsh History* (1905) and *The Matter of Wales* (1913). Although the former was popular and widely used as a school textbook, neither work was very well received by academic historians. In addition to his full-length works, Rhoscomyl was an avid commentator on Welsh nationalism in newspapers and journals. He championed a variety of causes and projects designed to build the stature of Wales within the empire, including the establishment of an Order of St David, a Prince's Privy Council for Wales, regiments of Welsh Guards and cavalry, and the foundation of a Welsh national theatre.[14] It was the investiture, however, that took pride of place in Rhoscomyl's fertile and vivid imagination.

In September 1910, Owen Rhoscomyl claimed that the idea to locate the investiture in Wales first came to him while convalescing in north Wales in the late 1880s. On a visit to Caernarfon Castle, Rhoscomyl viewed the castle's 'birth chamber', and determined that 'each new Prince of Wales, from that time forth, should begin by being invested with all the ancient and stately rites of the days when Wales was feared and not neglected'. He supposedly published his idea immediately in a letter to 'some small sheet of news printed in the region' under the nom de plume of Cymro. According to Rhoscomyl, his military duties in South Africa prevented him from pressing the idea at the time of Edward's coronation. Following the death of King Edward, however, he sent the idea to the press 'on the first day when such a thing could decently be printed'.[15] In an article published the day after the investiture and subtitled 'Honour to Whom it is Due', the *Western Mail* vouched for Rhoscomyl's account and gave him full credit for the origins of

[14] *Western Mail*, 14 July 1969.
[15] *Western Mail*, 10 September 1910.

56

the ceremony.¹⁶ In 1952, Edward James, a confidant of Rhoscomyl who served as the London correspondent for the *Western Mail* in 1911, refuted the Duke of Windsor's recent revelations regarding Lloyd George's key role in the ceremony and provided details of Rhoscomyl's attempts to revive the investiture. James described Rhoscomyl's efforts to get 'people in high places to take up his audacious idea'. He reportedly found the Bishop of St Asaph to be unsympathetic and Lloyd George regarded the scheme as mad. After a series of rebuffs, Rhoscomyl turned to Lord Howard de Walden, an amateur medievalist and dramatist who would subsequently become Rhoscomyl's patron and friend. Lord Howard de Walden was intrigued and communicated the idea to his uncle, the Duke of Norfolk, who as the Earl Marshal was nominally in charge of royal ceremonial. Sufficiently impressed, the Duke was said to have taken Rhoscomyl to the palace for a personal audience with the King. The King too was impressed with the idea. According to James:

> The King's pleasure was made known, and the people who had turned down Vaughan as a madman tumbled over each other in the scrum for places in the show . . . As for the Bishop of St Asaph's recollections of what happened, those who knew him best knew that he had a remarkable gift for remembering things that had never happened. Tom Ellis regarded him as a byeword for willful inaccuracy.¹⁷

James's account ends with an admission that Rhoscomyl never publicly pressed his claim or wrote down the details of what had happened in his private audience with the King. Perhaps fearing any embarrassment for the King, he entrusted Edward James and Lord Howard de Walden to keep the information confidential. Once again, we are left with interesting and plausible yet unverified claims. However, it is worth noting the cryptic reference Rhoscomyl made in the columns of the *South Wales Daily News* in August 1910. Refuting the paper's contention that it was Lloyd George who had first presented the idea to the King, Rhoscomyl indicated that he had 'direct

---

¹⁶ *Western Mail*, 13 July 1911.
¹⁷ Edward James to Gwilym Roberts, 3 March 1952, Mr Gwion Davies Donation 1971, NLW.

evidence to prove that your correspondent is wrong' and wrote: 'It did not seem to occur to your correspondent that the one with whom the final decision rests cannot be deceived as to who was first to suggest the investiture. And that one is the only one who counts.'[18]

Although the identity of the first person to present the idea of reviving the ceremony to the King may be unknowable, Owen Rhoscomyl was definitely the first to introduce the idea to the public. On 24 May 1910, Owen Rhoscomyl published an article in the *Western Mail* entitled 'The Next Prince of Wales; A Solemn Investiture Suggestion'. This was the first time the idea of reviving the investiture in connection with the Coronation of King George V had ever been publicly espoused. Rhoscomyl's romantic character was entirely consistent with being the source of the investiture in a way that Lloyd George, the hammer of the gentry, and the Bishop of St Asaph, a critic of Welsh nationalism, never could be. His writing was imbued with the same sense of pageantry and ceremony that characterized the event. J. Glyn Davies wrote; 'Rhoscomyl had his very soul in pageantry'.[19] All of his work emphasized 'Rhwysg', the spectacle and pomp of Welsh history, which revolved around the glory of the ancient princes. One acquaintance commented:

> ... it was this 'Rhwysg' – that of the Welsh Princes of medieval Wales – which always appealed to him, stirring his imagination. My first impression of him was of a medieval Cymro [Welshman], happy to be about the Court of Arthur, or seated among the Knights of the Round Table. Daringly earnest, he was a Knight Errant, here, there and everywhere, and at all seasons, alert for the glory and prestige of Wales, seeming to me at times ready to exchange the so-called democracy of the Principality for the prowess and glamour of the Princes.[20]

Rhoscomyl, however, was not motivated simply for the sake of pageantry. The event was firmly set in the context of modern industrial Wales. He would later write:

---

[18] *South Wales Daily News*, 27 August 1910.
[19] J. Glyn Davies, p. 5.
[20] Ifano Jones, unpublished typescript, p. 4, Olwen Vaughan Donation 1977, NLW.

THE 'INVENTION' OF THE INVESTITURE

> it was no cloudy eagerness for a 'show' which first moved the matter, neither was it, in the slightest degree any more mooning after the "picturesque in the past". It was in fact as a practical help in the problems most pressing in the Wales of today that the call for the Investiture was raised.[21]

Not only did Rhoscomyl advocate the ceremony's revival but he outlined the form which the ceremony should take. First, the actual ritual of investiture should follow the ancient precedents as established by the investiture ceremony of Harry of Monmouth in 1399. Secondly, the ceremony should be 'a celebration of the things that bear most weight and carry most pause in the life of Wales today'. He felt there would be 'no lack of heart stirring symbolism in a ceremony conducted on truly national lines'.[22] His vision included the participation of the Gorsedd of Bards and he would later suggest that the ceremony, after the practices of the ancient druids and the modern Gorsedd of Bards, should be held outside 'in the face of the sun'.[23] Thirdly, the ceremony should feature the presentation of the Prince of Wales to the people of his Principality 'where in the crowning of George V, it comes to the oath of allegiance from Princes, peers and prelates, each in their degree, we could substitute the very race itself in the investiture of his son'.[24] Although Rhoscomyl suggested other details that would never be realized, the actual form adopted by the ceremony in 1911 would heavily bear his imprint. The final ceremony differed significantly from Rhoscomyl's vision, however, in that he thought the investiture should be held at Cardiff.

Rhoscomyl's suggestion was received with great enthusiasm in Cardiff. The Lord Mayor and Cymmrodorion of Cardiff gave their vocal support and a lively discussion of the idea appeared in the columns of the *Western Mail*. On 3 June 1910, Rhoscomyl held a public meeting in Cardiff under the auspices of the Lord Mayor to discuss the matter. A national movement for reviving the investiture ceremony was inaugurated.[25] The idea attracted the interest of the principality at large. Other

[21] *Western Mail*, 15 August 1910.
[22] Ibid., 24 May 1910.
[23] Ibid., 11 June 1910.
[24] Ibid., 24 May 1910.
[25] Ibid., 25 May 1910, 31 May 1910 and 13 July 1911.

towns began to announce their desire to host the event. Caernarfon, Bangor, Carmarthen, Shrewsbury – all scrambled for the honour. With tongue in cheek, even the Welsh-Americans of Scranton, Pennsylvania put forth a bid. These challengers were not taken seriously by the champions of Cardiff, who patronizingly considered the claims of their rivals only as an indication of the widespread support for holding such a ceremony. On the birthday of Prince Edward in June 1910, the *Western Mail* was able to proclaim that: 'it seems clear that if Wales unitedly desires it, the proclamation of the Prince will take place in Wales, probably next year.'[26]

The movement to revive the ceremony, led by Owen Rhoscomyl and the *Western Mail*, continued to gather momentum. Then, on 30 July, it was publicly announced that an 'influential committee' had been formed to advance the issue independently of the Cardiff-based movement. The committee was rumoured to consist of a group of Welsh notables including David Lloyd George, the Bishop of St Asaph, Lord Plymouth, Lord Tredegar, Lord Cawdor, the Wesleyan minister the Revd Cadfan Davies and the Chairman of the Welsh Parliamentary Party, Sir Alfred Thomas. It was also intimated that the Committee favoured Caernarfon over Cardiff as the site of the ceremony.[27]

This revelation produced a bitter public debate. The proponents of Cardiff felt as if the investiture was being stolen out from underneath them and reacted with anger and dismay. Owen Rhoscomyl, John Chappell (Lord Mayor of Cardiff) and J. L. Wheatley (Cardiff Town Clerk) were the principal defenders of Cardiff's claim not only to the investiture but to the city's status as the informal capital of Wales and the civic centre of Welsh nationhood. Possibly advised by the 'influential committee' to take a low profile, the mayor of Caernarfon declined to take part in what he described as an 'unwise and unseemly brawl'.[28] Such scruples, however, were not held by the mayor's close associate and former mayor, Myrddin Evans, who argued stridently in the press on Caernarfon's behalf.

[26] Ibid., 11 June 1910.
[27] Ibid., 30 July 1910.
[28] Ibid., 25 August 1910.

Despite a spirited debate between the towns in August and September 1910, neither the defenders of Cardiff nor the advocates of Caernarfon would play much of a role in the selection of the site. With its privileged access to the corridors of power, it seems that the 'influential committee' seized the ceremony for themselves and excluded all others from participation at a relatively early stage of the ceremony's preparation. It was their vision of the Welsh nation that ultimately prevailed in the ceremony. The character of the project changed from that of a popular campaign conducted through the Welsh press to a closed and private affair directed by a small group of the Welsh political and social elite. This committee monopolized the issue of the investiture's revival through the secrecy of its own activities, the ambiguity of its membership, its official silence and its frequent warnings against 'unseemly brawls'. Conducted through the London papers and the London correspondents of the Welsh press, the committee cautioned others not to upset the sensitive scheme through unwanted interference or by arousing controversy. It was best to leave it all to the committee. When Rhoscomyl, the Lord Mayor and the Town Clerk of Cardiff continued to push their claims, one correspondent wrote angrily:

> Many weeks ago, when the question of the Investiture was first mooted, I ventured to point out that any serious division of opinion amongst the people of Wales – I said nothing then of unseemly wranglings as to the towns which might submit their claims to the honour – would act prejudicially, and might have the effect of depriving Wales of the ceremony altogether. There is unfortunately ground for believing that the danger I then apprehended has become a very serious one. If the Principality is to be honoured, this and that town must be content with laying their claims before the proper authorities in a loyal and becoming manner.[29]

Rhoscomyl was quick to respond, asking a poignant question:

> Who and what are the 'proper authorities' of which such mystery is made by those who lecture us? The whole mischief in this case has come of our having been awfully warned time and time again from behind the clouds that 'those who have the matter in hand' desired so and so on pain of so and so. Our answer is 'Who are they?' The

[29] *Manchester Guardian*, 29 August 1910.

inquisition and the caucus are equally out of place in a matter so fraught with so fair a day for the land we love as this matter of the Investiture. 'Fair and Open', that is all we want.[30]

A 'prominent public man of south Wales' went further, claiming that the secrecy shrouding the committee's proceedings and their endeavour to carry matters to a conclusion before the public could learn what was being done was scarcely in keeping with the nature of the ceremony. 'Why secrecy?', he asked: 'Due reticence as to detail is one thing; but complete silence whilst the interests of a section are being advanced to an accomplished fact is something quite different.'[31] The King's official consent to hold the ceremony was announced on 9 September 1910 during Lloyd George's attendance as a 'Minister in Waiting' at Balmoral Castle. The press was informed in a telegram that 'Acting upon the unanimous recommendation of a representative and influential committee, His Majesty has approved of the ceremony taking place at Carnarvon Castle during the month of July next'.[32] In the spirit of national unity, Cardiff was quick to accept the disappointing news and to offer its support to Caernarfon. Rhoscomyl sent a telegram to the Mayor of Caernarfon congratulating the town and asking in bardic tones 'A oes heddwch?' (Is there peace?)[33]

Despite the apparent triumph of Caernarfon town council, the matter of the investiture was to be kept strictly in the hands of what came to be called the 'National Committee'. The official responsibility for carrying out the investiture rested with the Earl Marshal (the Duke of Norfolk), the Lord Great Chamberlain (Earl Carrington), and the Secretary of the Office of Works (Sir Schomberg McDonnel). However, the settlement of 'purely Welsh questions' was left to the Committee.[34] In effect, these 'Welsh questions' would actually encompass the great majority of the form and content of the ceremony. Most of the substantive matters regarding the nature of the ceremony

[30] Ibid., 1 September 1910.
[31] *South Wales Daily News*, 27 August 1910.
[32] *Western Mail*, 9 September 1910.
[33] Rhoscomyl to Mayor, 9 September 1910, correspondence regarding the Investiture 1911, records and papers of the Borough of Caernarfon Gwynedd Record Office, Caernarfon.
[34] Archbishop of Wales, p. 247.

was thus in the hands of the National Committee while its mechanics and implementation were left to an established committee composed of hereditary officers, royal ministers and civil servants. These duties were largely folded into their work on the coronation. It is worth noting that the Office of Works was primarily engaged with the restoration and preparation of Caernarfon Castle while the Earl Marshal played only a token, symbolic role.[35] Although its cost is difficult to determine, apparently no expense was spared for the 1911 Investiture. Generous government outlay was heavily supplemented by public subscription. 'The investiture only comes once every 600 years,' opined Lloyd George, 'so we must not get frightened at the expense.'[36]

At some point, the membership of the 'influential committee' was expanded and informally renamed the 'National Committee'. The bishop of St Asaph explained in his memoirs that: 'The arrangements for the Investiture were beset with many novel problems, and it was clear that the committee to solve these problems must be representative of all classes in Wales. With that end in view the committee was enlarged and well and wisely balanced.'[37] In addition to the original seven members, the National Committee eventually included the Mayors of Caernarfon, Aberystwyth and Bangor, Welsh MPs W. G. Ormesby-Gore, Sir Herbert Roberts and W. F. Roth, Lord Kenyon, Sir Vincent Evans, R. M. Thomas, the Lord-Lieutenants of the Welsh counties, the four Welsh bishops, the heads of the four main nonconformist denominations of Wales and the chairmen and clerks of the county councils of Wales and Monmouthsire.[38] This, however, seems to have been simply a cosmetic alteration designed to give the false appearance of a representative committee. In fact, substantive decisions were left to a smaller group which, with the addition of

---

[35] In arguing that the committee that organized the investiture excluded politicians and was composed of Civil Service and Royal Household officials, William Kuhn has mistakenly overlooked the existence of the far more substantive National Committee, which operated outside of the usual channels of royal ceremonial; see Kuhn, 133.

[36] David Lloyd George to William George, 27 April 1911, William George Papers 2470, NLW.

[37] Archbishop of Wales, p. 246.

[38] *North Wales Chronicle*, 24 March 1911.

Conservative MP W. G. Ormesby-Gore, was confined to the original cabal of influential men. Following the official declaration of the royal consent, the basic framework of the investiture appears to have been worked out in two meetings attended by this small group. At the third meeting, the enlarged membership was presented with these plans as a fait accompli. It appears that the full committee acted only as a rubber stamp for the decisions of this inner core. It was decided at this third meeting that local investiture committees should be established in each county. The National Committee, however, maintained a tight grip on the investiture's control, giving strict guidance to the local committees on everything from whom to invite to what the guests should wear at the ceremony.[39]

Despite changes to make it appear more representative, the National Committee continued to operate in a manner shrouded in secrecy and surrounded by controversy. Once the National Committee became official, its meetings and attendance were announced but the proceedings were strictly 'private and confidential'. In April 1911, the committee became the object of criticism during prime minister's questions in Parliament. Clement Edwards, MP for Glamorgan East, asked Prime Minister Asquith to reveal who was responsible for the creation of the National Committee and on what basis the membership was selected. He then informed the prime minister of the dissatisfaction with the formation and methods of the committee, warning of the likelihood of grave friction and dissension within the Welsh nation. Prime Minister Asquith indicated that the composition of the committee was the result of 'informal arrangements' and reiterated his confidence in its operations.[40] Lloyd George answered the charge more fully in a carefully orchestrated 'spontaneous' talk delivered to the investiture choir. No doubt, the speech was directed equally to the reporters in attendance. Earlier that week, local resentment was surfacing over the Office of Works' measures to keep the preparations in the castle private through the erection of blinds. With dramatic flair, Lloyd George arrived on the scene

[39] Ibid.
[40] *Hansard's Parliamentary Debates*, 5th ser., vol. 24 (1911), cols. 429–430.

and ordered the blinds removed. That night in Caernarfon Castle after the choir's rehearsal he said:

> We do not want to keep anything secret. We want everybody to know what is being done so that we can carry the nation with us. There has been a complaint with reference to the National Committee. You cannot put everybody on the Committee. There are two millions of people in Wales, and you can't put them all on the committee.[41]

However, this did little to allay suspicion of the National Committee. Resentment was soon being directed at the local investiture committees and other organizations connected with the ceremony. The *North Wales Chronicle* wrote:

> Why all this mystery should surround everything pertaining to the deliberations, not only of the National Committee, but also of every other body having any official, or quasi-official connection with the Investiture, surpasses comprehension. Following the example of the National Committee, the Carnarvon Town Council, when it has any little detail connected to the Investiture to discuss, declares with becoming gravity, that 'the Council will now sit in committee' as though the peace of Europe depended upon the secrecy of its counsels.[42]

Because of the private and secret nature of the committee's proceedings, it is difficult to assess the role of the different individuals involved. However, the fragmentary evidence suggests that Lloyd George was not the dominant presence. Lord Plymouth, the Lord Lieutenant of Glamorgan, chaired the committee. As a leader of the Welsh Territorial Defense Association, a patron of the arts and a former Commissioner of Works, Plymouth was singularly qualified to direct the planning of the investiture.[43] The Bishop of St Asaph also seemed to play a key role, being a prominent member on the subcommittees on the investiture ritual and regalia, the religious service and the writing of the Loyalty Address of the Welsh people. Lloyd George, on the other hand, ceased to attend the meetings of the committee after the basic framework of the ceremony had been established. During much of that time, Lloyd George was recovering from a serious throat ailment. He was also kept

[41] *North Wales Chronicle*, 21 April 1911.
[42] Ibid., 16 June 1911.
[43] *Western Mail*, 8 March 1923.

extremely busy contending with the difficult passage of his controversial National Insurance Act.[44] His supposed attention to every detail in connection with the investiture is highly unlikely. It is far more probable that Lloyd George was less the creator and stage-manager of the 1911 Investiture and more a popular figure-head, legitimizing through his presence the activities of a controversial committee.

The invention of the 1911 Investiture of the Prince of Wales was the result of a complicated and controversial process. Owen Rhoscomyl was the first publicly to present the idea and to lay out the major characteristics of the ceremony, advocating that it should be held in Cardiff. Rather than the originator and stage manager of the ceremony, David Lloyd George seems to have been more a co-conspirator who assisted an 'influential committee' in hijacking the movement to revive the investiture and took steps to ensure that the ceremony would be transferred to Caernarfon. The formation of this committee provoked a bitter public debate between the advocates of Caernarfon and Cardiff, but the committee that would end up planning the investiture was a closed, private affair. The final form of the 1911 Investiture thus expressed a view of Welsh national identity formulated by a handful of the Welsh elite, comprising members of the Welsh gentry and Church as well as Liberal politicians and nonconformists.

---

[44] Creiger, pp. 163–86, 263–4.

4
The prince and the gwerin[1]

First and foremost, the 1911 Investiture was a celebration of Welsh nationhood. The trappings and symbolism of Welsh nationality pervaded the ceremony. The ritual act of investing the prince with his regalia took place under a canopy surmounted by the image of St David. The thrones and regalia were comprised of entwined Welsh dragons and daffodils. The work of the acclaimed sculptor Goscombe John, the crown, ring sword, brooch and rod were created by a Welsh artist from Welsh gold produced by Welsh miners.[2] With very few exceptions, most notably the royal family itself, the participants and audience were drawn from the population of Wales.[3] The druids of the Gorsedd of Bards led the prince's procession and a mixed Welsh choir – the women dressed in traditional tall beaver hats and shawls – sang out the anthems and hymns of a triumphant Welsh nation. The Welsh national anthem, 'Hen Wlad fy Nhadau', filled the air as the new prince was presented to his people.

In its evocation of the Welsh nation, the 1911 Investiture was obliged to define Welsh national identity in the political and social context of its time. Scholarship on Victorian Welsh national identity has frequently focused on the image of the '*gwerin*'. According to this image, the common people of Wales formed a classless and nonconformist 'folk', pitted against the wealth and power of the landed gentry and established Anglican Church. The Welsh middle and working classes were

---

[1] Material for this chapter first appeared in John S. Ellis, 'The Prince and the Dragon: Welsh National Identity and the 1911 Investiture of the Prince of Wales', *Welsh History Review*, 18 (1996), 272–94.
[2] *Daily Telegraph*, 13 July 1911.
[3] W. Ormesby-Gore, 'The Investiture of the Prince of Wales', *Wales: A National Magazine*, (July 1911), p. 150.

imagined to be fused through a common struggle and nonconformist religion. Ideally, the Welsh middle class was rooted in the working class and served as the natural leaders of a democratic and populist nation. Although this image could be projected onto an industrial setting, it was primarily based on a romantic vision of rural Welsh society. Being Welsh speaking, the *gwerin* was dedicated to the Welsh arts of poetry and song. They were a traditional people, addicted to the past, generally poor but industrious, committed to self-help and education, religious, peace-loving, sober and respectable. In contrast to the alien Church and gentry, the *gwerin* was thought to be wholly Welsh in speech and character.[4]

The *gwerin*, however, was not the only image of Welsh nationality in the Edwardian period. A distinct sense of Welshness had been created by the urban middle class of Cardiff. Their view of Welsh nationality had some important elements in common with the *gwerin* motif. It was originally based on a populist struggle pitting the middle and working classes against aristocratic urban landowners and the established Anglican Church. Cardiff in the nineteenth century was marked by conflict between this populist alliance and the economic and political dominance of the Marquess of Bute, the major landowner in the town. Cardiff also shared the *gwerin*'s enthusiasm for the traditional Welsh arts of poetry and song and revelled in the national symbols and aspirations of a reborn Welsh nation.[5] Like London, Cardiff was in the process of building all the grand trappings of a capital city. As London built her ceremonial way along the Mall, Cardiff was developing a ceremonial centre of its own in Cathays Park. The

[4] Paul O'Leary, 'The Languages of Patriotism in Wales, 1840–1880', in Geraint H. Jenkins (ed.), *The Welsh Language and its Social Domains* (Cardiff, 2000), pp. 534–60; Prys Morgan, 'The Gwerin of Wales – Myth and Reality', in *The Welsh and their Country* (Swansea, 1986), pp. 134–50; David Smith, *Wales! Wales?* (London, 1984), pp. 28–55; Gwyn A. Williams, *When Was Wales?* (London, 1985), pp. 234–41.

[5] John Davies, 'Aristocratic Town-makers and the Coal Metropolis: The Marquesses of Bute and the Growth of Cardiff, 1776 to 1947', in David Cannadine (ed.), *Patricians, Power and Politics in Nineteenth Century Towns* (New York, 1982), pp. 18–58; Neil Evans, 'The Welsh Victorian city: Middle Class and Civic and National Consciousness in Cardiff, 1850–1914', *Welsh History Review*, 12(3) (1985), 350–87.

complex included widened boulevards, refurbished castle, and magnificent civic buildings baroquely decorated with glowering Welsh dragons and the heroes of the Welsh past.[6]

Cardiff's sense of Welshness, however, was based on a notably different foundation than that of the *gwerin*. The city's thriving international export trade in coal attracted people to Cardiff from all over Britain, the empire and the world. Between 1861 and 1911, the population of Glamorgan county increased by 253 per cent.[7] By 1871, Cardiff had become the largest town in Wales. The census of 1911 revealed an increasingly cosmopolitan population unrivalled by any other Welsh town.[8] Such growth, urbanization and cosmopolitanism could not be encapsulated by the rural and Welsh-speaking ideal of the *gwerin*. Therefore, the middle class of Cardiff, many of whom were immigrants themselves, developed their own definition of Welshness that equated national pride with civic and commercial achievement. In their view, Welshness could embrace the contributions of immigrants and native Welshman alike.[9]

During August and early September 1910, the vigorous 'battle of the sites' between Cardiff and Caernarfon over where to locate the investiture highlighted a deeper conflict over the national identity of Wales. The terms of the debate over the investiture between the towns was already well established. Similar battles had been fought with other towns over the location of the University of Wales at the end of the nineteenth century and then again over the National Library and Museum in the early years of the twentieth century. In these debates, Cardiff flaunted its wealth, civic buildings, commercial power and population, held up its contributions to Welsh institutions and nationalism and trumpeted its status as the unofficial capital of Wales. In comparison, the rest of Wales seemed insular and parochial. These claims were received with jeers by Cardiff's rivals who insisted on the non-Welsh character of

[6] Evans, 'Welsh Victorian city', 380–83; Cannandine, 'Context, Performance and Meaning of Ritual', 127–8.
[7] M. J. Daunton, *Coal Metropolis: Cardiff 1870–1914* (London, 1977), p. 11.
[8] Neil Evans, 'Welsh Victorian City', 352.
[9] Ibid., 350–87.

Cardiff's cosmopolitan population and ridiculed the dominance of the English language in the so-called Welsh capital.[10] The debate over the investiture proceeded along similar lines.

On 11 August 1910, J. L. Wheatley established Cardiff's case in the *Western Mail*.[11] 'Carnarvon', he proclaimed, 'was beneath comparison with Cardiff, for the future of Wales and the Welsh people lies not around Carnarvon, but in the valleys of old Siluria'.[12] He stated that Cardiff's hinterland was steadily draining the rest of Wales of her manhood. 'Now three fourths of the population of Wales lay within a forty five mile radius of the city', he triumphantly proclaimed. Cardiff was on the forefront of advanced democracy and Welsh nationalism, absorbing an enormous influx of strangers into Welsh life while housing more Welsh speakers in total than Caernarfon could ever hope to muster. Wheatley then turned to Cardiff's transportation systems, parks and civic buildings, proclaiming Cathays Park, with its space for over a million spectators, as the only place in Wales where the event could really take on a national character. Finally, Wheatley asserted the status of Cardiff as the great Welsh metropolis, the unofficial capital of Wales and the only logical setting for the investiture.

After similar statements by the Lord Mayor of Cardiff appeared in the Welsh and London papers, the former Mayor of Caernarfon confronted the idea of Cardiff as the font of Welsh nationhood. Myrddin Evans attacked such pretensions by raising the spectre of the British League, an organization founded in 1906 to fight compulsory Welsh-language courses in Cardiff's schools:

> We have no British League in Carnarvon. The deliberations of our councils and public bodies are frequently carried on in the vernacular; 97 percent of us are Welsh speaking; Welsh is a compulsory subject in our schools. In fact, our town is now what it always has been, the home of Welsh nationalism, the real capital of Wales.[13]

One writer dismissed Cardiff's supposed Welshness, saying that while the Welsh language could occasionally be heard in

[10] Ibid., 370–4.
[11] *Western Mail*, 11 August 1910.
[12] Ibid.
[13] *Manchester Guardian*, 22 August 1910.

its streets, so could Chinese and possibly even Hotentot.[14] A common refrain in the debate was that the north should be considered first, as its language was still intact, its people less mixed and, therefore, its nationalism was of a stronger and more rooted strain.[15]

Advocates of Cardiff defended the city's cosmopolitanism and attempted to reconcile it with Welsh patriotism. Owen Rhoscomyl asserted: 'the man who is living in Wales, no matter where he was born, is a Cymro and the call is upon him to do what he can for Wales, as much as it is on the man whose blood ran red on every sod of it, from the veins of the misty generations of his ancestors...'[16] Wheatley, born and raised in England, stated that far from weakening Cardiff's Welshness, its cosmopolitanism had attracted the best brains of other races and, fired by the Welsh spirit of the town, changed them into an active force for Welsh nationalism.[17]

Cardiff was also attacked on the grounds of its un-Welsh materialism. The *Holyhead Chronicle* stated that Cardiff was exuberantly nationalist, as long as it paid to be so. He equated Cardiff's vaunted democracy with a plutocracy of the wealthy commercial class, able to outspend any other Welsh town and crush their rivals with the sheer weight of its expenditure.[18] The glory and spectacle of an investiture held in Cathays Park, Cardiff's temple of civic virtue, was likened to a crass performance of Buffalo Bill's Wild West Show in which the prince stood in for the red Indians.[19] 'Thank Goodness', wrote a correspondent to the *Manchester Guardian*, 'there are certain things even in this mercenary age which the "almighty dollar" is unable to purchase'.[20]

The debate over the 'battle of the sites' reflected two very different visions of Wales and Welshness. One vision was wholly compatible with the *gwerin* image, based on a rural ideal of small, homogeneous Welsh-speaking villages and

[14] *Holyhead Chronicle*, 26 August 1910.
[15] *Manchester Guardian*, 24 August 1910.
[16] *Western Mail*, 15 August 1910.
[17] Ibid., 25 August 1910.
[18] *Holyhead Chronicle*, 26 August 1910
[19] Ibid.
[20] *Manchester Guardian*, 24 August 1910.

towns. Caernarfon, in the extreme north and west of Wales, was represented as the epitome of that image. This ideal was exclusive, rejecting immigrants to Wales or those who did not speak Welsh. Foreign and Anglicizing influences were thought to corrupt and diminish Welsh nationality. Nowhere were these forces more rampant than in the urban crucible of Cardiff. The commercial power of the city and the glory of its civic buildings translated into a very un-Welsh display of vulgar ostentation and materialism. Welshness was not to be judged on such factors as wealth, power and size but on purity of language, race and nonconformist ideals. In marked contrast, Welshness as espoused by Cardiff's middle class was essentially inclusive. While respect was paid to the importance of the Welsh language, religious values and literature, these were not the only considerations. The strength of Welsh patriotism was to be judged by the ability of an individual or a town to advance the Welsh nation in the modern world, to serve the Welsh people and to further the glory of Wales within the British Empire. With immigrants flowing in from England and other foreign lands, it was the job of Welsh nationalism to produce Welshmen.

Caernarfon's ultimate victory in the 'battle of the sites' seemed to be a vindication of the traditional image of the *gwerin* and a rejection of the cosmopolitan and urban Welshness of Cardiff. To some extent, this was reflected by the symbolism and commentary of the investiture. The setting of the investiture in Caernarfon certainly helped foster a vision of the Welsh as a rural people. In souvenir programs and newspaper commentaries covering the event, much was made of the surrounding scenery of mountains, sea and farmland. 'Their soul must be sought in the mountains, not in the towns', wrote the *Daily Chronicle*.[21] In the quaint, medieval walled town of Caernarfon, the Welsh nation was called back to a simpler time in its history before King Coal and the Bute Docks. Within the cloistered walls of the castle, the modern world was kept well at bay. To ensure the proper atmosphere, Caernarfon's own signs of industrial and commercial activity – namely, the industrial slate docks – were carefully cleared and hidden from

[21] *Daily Chronicle*, 14 July 1911.

view for the duration of the ceremony. In contrast to the fanciful Victorian reconstruction of Cardiff Castle, Caernarfon Castle was hailed as a public monument 'without a touch of modernity or sham antiquity'.[22] Even the electric lights introduced to the castle for the event were disguised as wrought iron torches.[23] It was a setting steeped in tradition for a nation supposedly addicted to the past.

In the face of the increasingly English-speaking industrial community, Wales was depicted as a Welsh-speaking nation, the revival of its language leading it to recover 'more and more the full consciousness of its ancient self'.[24] The ceremony was conducted both in Welsh and English but it was the Welsh language that attracted the most attention. The *Standard* reported that: 'Welsh was the language of ceremony, of the folk songs and the anthems that the choir rendered so beautifully; of the address from the Welsh people presented to the Prince – aye, and of the Prince's reply.'[25] The investiture regalia and souvenir medals were inscribed 'Iorwerth Tywysog Cymru' (Edward Prince of Wales).[26] Even the Prince's motto, 'Ich Dien' (German for 'I serve'), was commonly Welshified to 'Eich Dyn' (Your Man).[27] *Baner ac Amserau Cymru* enthused: 'We cannot help rejoicing in the good fortune in this tribute to our language and our nation.'[28]

The traditional Welsh-language arts of poetry, song and literature were a major focus of the 1911 Investiture. Investiture commentary defined these arts as the very core of Welshness. Reams of poetry in Welsh and English dedicated to the prince's investiture flooded the newspapers, periodicals, souvenir booklets and broadsheets of the summer of 1911. As one poet exclaimed:

[22] *The Times*, 12 July 1911.
[23] Anon., *The Investiture of H. R. H. The Prince of Wales at Carnarvon: Handbook and Official Programme of Festivities* (Liverpool, 1911), p. 27.
[24] *Daily Telegraph*, 14 July 1911.
[25] *Standard*, 14 July 1911.
[26] *Daily Telegraph*, 13 July 1911; Anon., *Investiture of H. R. H. The Princes of Wales: Medals and Souvenirs Designed & Manufactured by Fattorini & Sons Ltd* (Bradford, 1911), p. 27.
[27] *Holyhead Chronicle*, 13 July 1911.
[28] *Baner ac Amserau Cymru*, 8 July 1911.

> Dywysog mwyn Cymru, boed nefoedd a llawr,
> Yn dirion iawn wrthyt, yn darian bob awr;[29]
>
> Dear Prince of Wales, let the heavens and the earth,
> Be fully loyal to you, a shield every hour.

The artistic traditions and institutions of Wales were represented at the ceremony by the Gorsedd of Bards of the National Eisteddfod of Wales. The bards were decked out especially for the occasion in new silk robes and led the prince's procession into the castle. Above all else, Welsh choral music was celebrated and portrayed as a national characteristic of the Welsh nation. 'Môr o gân yw Cymru i gyd' (All Wales is a sea of song) proclaimed Prince Edward to the adoring assembly.[30] In Caernarfon, the entire week of the investiture was filled with concert events featuring Welsh choral music and penillion, a traditional form of group singing accompanied by the harp.[31] The choir took pride of place in the ceremony and was given an honoured position directly behind the dais on which the Prince was to be invested. In the official portrait of the 1911 Investiture, painted by Welsh artist Christopher Williams, the choir and Gorsedd loom large in the background, the symbolic presence of the Welsh nation witnessing and blessing the ceremony. 'Poetry and Music', declared the *Evening Standard*, 'are not playthings to this nation, but necessities of a harmonious existence'.[32]

In opposition to growing class tension, the ceremony celebrated the democratic and populist character of the *gwerin*. W. Llewelyn Williams, MP for Carmarthen, felt assured that the investiture would better reflect the growth of democracy than the precedent bound coronation.[33] The mayors, chairmen of the county councils and the MPs for Wales marched in the prince's procession.[34] The populism of the Welsh nation was

---

[29] Abraham H. Thomas, 'Urddwisgiad ei uchelder Brenhinol Tywysog Cymru yn Nghaernarfon, 1911', leaflet, 1911.
[30] *Daily Telegraph*, 14 July 1911.
[31] *Handbook and Official Programme*, pp. 37, 45, 47, 49, 51.
[32] *Evening Standard*, 13 July 1911.
[33] *Morning Leader*, 12 July 1911
[34] Anon, *Ceremonial to be observed at the Investiture of his Royal Highness the Prince of Wales, K.G., July 1911* (London, 1911), p. 3.

apparent in the ceremony, both in the inclusion of a loyalty address from the 'People of Wales' and in the climax of the ceremony, the presentation of the prince from the Queen's Gate to the cheering crowds below. The long progress from Griffith's Crossing through the streets of Caernarfon afforded the common people a glimpse of the royal show. Inside the lower bailey of the castle, obstructed from an actual view of the investiture but enjoying the spectacle of the processions and presentations, sat a 'representative' cross section of the Welsh nation including 'the humblest of his Majesty's subjects'.[35]

The greatest symbol of Welsh democracy and populism was David Lloyd George himself. For many, the rise of the Welsh nation was embodied in his career. W. Llewelyn Williams described him as the inspirer and leader of the new Welsh democracy. 'He will be clad in the resplendent uniform of a Minister of the Crown', Williams wrote, 'but the crowds who will gather together from the wilds of Eryri in their homespun garments will recognize in him one of themselves, the youth who was bred in a poor cottage not far from the castle of which he is now Constable'.[36] Lloyd George carefully balanced his desire not to upstage the Royal Family with maintaining a high profile at the ceremony as a symbol of Welsh populism.[37] His arrival at the castle was an occasion for wild cheering. After the crowds had assembled inside the castle walls, Lloyd George made a circuit of the grounds. Ostensibly, this was to make a last inspection of the preparations in his capacity as Constable of Caernarfon Castle. That task, however, was safely in the hands of the Office of Works. Lloyd George's public circuit really served to underscore his presence at the event and provided an opportunity for him to bask in the praise of the spectators.[38] His official role in the ceremony was highly symbolic. As the royal procession approached, Lloyd George stood in court dress at the locked doors of the castle with keys in hand, ready to allow the entrance of the sovereign.[39] This

[35] *Daily Mail*, 13 July 1911.
[36] *Morning Leader*, 12 July 1911.
[37] Bentley Brinkerhoff Gilbert, *David Lloyd George: A Political Life: The Architect of Change, 1863–1914* (London, 1987), p. 446.
[38] *South Wales Daily News*, 14 July 1911; *Daily Telegraph*, 14 July 1911.
[39] *Daily Telegraph*, 14 July 1911.

image of David Lloyd George standing at the gate of the castle as the guardian of the Welsh nation, the keeper of the keys to the people's heart, proved to be very popular and was later sold to eager members of the *gwerin* as a picture postcard.[40] After the ceremony's conclusion, his exit from the castle was fully exploited by the politician to publicize his presence. His car was mobbed by an adoring crowd as it slowly made its way through the streets of Caernarfon.[41]

As a symbol of the people and democracy of Wales, Lloyd George was deliberately associated with the ceremony and the prince. The insistence in some newspapers at the time on crediting him with the origins and stage management of the ceremony takes on a new meaning in this context. His teaching of a few Welsh phrases to the prince for the ceremony was widely publicized as was his dramatic announcement in the House of Commons that he had to leave a debate on his National Insurance Bill early in order to take part in the investiture of 'my Prince'.[42] In fact, the Welsh politician was so closely linked to the ceremony that sometimes it became unclear who was actually being invested. Investiture commentary described Lloyd George in both laudatory and whimsical terms as a new Glyndŵr, a reincarnation of Llywelyn the Last and the uncrowned King of the Welsh.[43] The Conservative *Bystander* sourly wrote: 'It is now understood that the Investiture of Mr. David Lloyd George as Dictator will take place at Carnarvon.'[44]

In defining the Welsh nation, the 1911 Investiture ceremony drew on a number of the important elements of the image of the *gwerin*. The language, arts, democracy and populism of Wales all played their part. Other elements, however, contradicted the idea of the *gwerin*. After all, most of the members of

[40] 'The Investiture of the Prince of Wales at Carnarvon Castle: Constable of the Castle Mr. Lloyd George waiting to receive the Prince of Wales', postcard, PG 2354/118 1014, NLW.
[41] *Daily Telegraph*, 14 July 1911.
[42] *Baner at Amserau Cymru*, 8 July 1911; *Llais Llafur* 8 July 1911.
[43] Anon, 'Welsh Leaders – The Rt. Hon, David Lloyd George', *Wales: A National Magazine* (May 1911), p. 1; *Daily Telegraph*, 14 July 1911; *Carnarvon & Denbigh Herald*, 30 September 1910.
[44] *Spectator*, September 1910, quoted in *Carnarvon & Denbigh Herald*, 23 September 1910.

the National Committee which organized the investiture ceremony were drawn from outside that section of the Welsh population that was embraced by the image. Of the seven original members of the National Committee, three were members of the Welsh gentry and one was a bishop of the Anglican Church.[45] In fact, Anglicanism and aristocracy were pronounced features of the investiture.

Religion was a conspicuous and somewhat problematic element in the 1911 Investiture. Standing to the right of the dais on which the prince was to be invested were representatives of the four major denominations of Welsh nonconformity. Standing with them were the four Anglican bishops of Wales, a Roman Catholic bishop, and a local Anglican vicar and nonconformist minister from Caernarfon.[46] The religious service itself was conducted by two bishops of the Anglican Church and two ministers of nonconformity. Some hailed this triumphantly as state recognition of the status of nonconformity in Wales. *Y Tyst*, the Congregationalist newspaper, exclaimed that the investiture was a feather in the cap of nonconformity and that the ceremony would never have taken place if the bishops and the lords had been left to their own devices.[47] Other nonconformist papers, however, were hesitant to discuss the role of religion in the ceremony. Those who praised the investiture did so in terms general to Welsh nationality and avoided the religious question.[48] Others displayed a complete indifference to the investiture or criticized it on its materialism and its irrelevance to matters of the faith.[49] 'There is not a meaning in the world to the Investiture of the Prince of Wales', the Wesleyan *Gwyliedydd Newydd* declared. It advised its readers to direct their loyalty to a higher prince in the form of Jesus Christ.[50]

The reluctance of the Welsh nonconformist press to dwell on the issue of religion in the investiture is understandable because the service was in fact dominated by the Anglican Church.

[45] *Western Mail*, 30 July 1911.
[46] *South Wales Daily News*, 14 July 1911.
[47] *Y Tyst*, 9 July 1911
[48] *Y Goleuad*, 12 July 1911; *Baner ac Amserau Cymru*, 19 July 1911.
[49] *Seren Cymru*, 14 July 1911.
[50] *Gwyliedydd Newydd*, 18 July 1911.

INVESTITURE

Under the supervision of the Archbishop of Canterbury, the bishop of St Asaph was largely responsible for the service's content and arrangements.[51] Although the number of ministers performing the service were equally divided by denomination, the nonconformist ministers were confined to leading the choir and reading the lesson, roles typically played by laymen in Anglican services. The prayers and the benediction, on the other hand, remained firmly in the hands of the ordained priesthood of the established Church.[52] It even appears that there was pressure applied on the nonconformist ministers attending the ceremony to wear vestments. One of them actually chose to do so for the first time in his career.[53]

While symbols of Welsh democracy abounded, the Welsh gentry and aristocracy were equally evident in the investiture ceremony. In the prince's procession, Lord Kenyon and the Earl of Plymouth walked in positions of honour on either side of the prince.[54] Guarding the Chamberlain's Tower, in which the Prince prepared for the actual ritual, Sir Marteine Lloyd and Sir Herbert Lloyd Watkin Williams-Wynn stood as standard bearers representing the baronets of south and north Wales respectively.[55] Marching in the king's procession were the assembled peers of Wales, and occupying the central role of bearing the insignia and regalia of the investiture ritual were the 'representatives of the greatest Welsh families'.[56] The stands on which the audience was seated were ornately decorated with the heraldic shields not only of the king and prince, but of the twenty-seven aristocratic families and the six great lordships of the principality.[57]

If the image of the Welsh nation presented at the 1911 Investiture was the traditional *gwerin* motif, it was a *gwerin* which could scarcely be recognized. Here was a Welsh nation that proudly embraced the participation of both the established Church and the peerage. The rural ideal, the Welsh

[51] *North Wales Chronicle*, 19 May 1911.
[52] *Ceremonial*, pp. 14–18.
[53] *North Wales Chronicle*, 30 June 1911; *South Wales Daily News*, 14 July 1911.
[54] *Ceremonial*, p. 4.
[55] Ormesby-Gore, p. 149; *Ceremonial*, p. 4.
[56] *South Wales Daily News*, 14 July 1911; *Ceremonial*, pp. 7–8.
[57] *The Times*, 12 July 1911.

language and arts, even the idea of Welsh democracy and populism were relatively uncontentious issues in Edwardian Wales. The opposition to gentry and Church, however, was the fundamental characteristic which gave definition and cohesion to the image of the gwerin. This characteristic of Welshness was omitted from the vision of Welsh nationality expressed by the 1911 Investiture. Such a conception of Wales, however, was not without its precedents.

One source for the acceptance of the gentry as a part of Welsh national life came from the inclusive sense of Welsh nationality cultivated in the city of Cardiff. The growth and development of Britain's cities often pitted the local landowner against city corporations dominated by a civic-minded middle class in disputes regarding property rights and incorporation. With the decline of aristocratic political power, reconciliation between these corporations and the gentry were occurring throughout Britain in the form of the appointment of local aristocrats as ornamental mayors.[58] In Cardiff, however, the division between aristocracy and the middle class was also associated with Welsh nationalism. The appointment of the Marquess of Bute as Mayor of Cardiff in 1890 reconciled him not only to the city, but to the nation as well. With his political power destroyed, the Marquess was transformed into a symbolic figure-head, Cardiff's foremost citizen associated with the city's and, by extension, the Welsh nation's cultural and social aspirations.[59] Although the ceremony rejected many elements of Cardiff's sense of national identity, the investiture reflected its inclusive embrace of the landed elite and its emphasis on national service.

Welsh cultural and educational institutions provided an important precedent for an alternative vision of the Welsh nation which included the gentry. The aristocracy of Wales had

---

[58] David Cannadine, *The Decline and Fall of the British Aristocracy* (New Haven and London, 1990), pp. 559–72.
[59] Evans, 'The Welsh Victorian City', pp. 363–4; John Davies, 'Aristocratic town-makers and the Coal Metropolis: The Marquesses of Bute and the Growth of Cardiff, 1776 to 1947', in David Cannadine (ed.), *Patricians, Power and Politics in Nineteenth Century Towns* (New York, 1982), p. 55.

long been supporters of the National Eisteddfod. Such aristocrats as Lord Aberdare and Lord Tredegar served as honorary Presidents of the Day while others donated money for prizes.[60] Lord Mostyn, the Prince's mantle bearer at the investiture, was particularly associated with patronage of the Welsh arts and National Eisteddfod.[61] The much remarked upon new robes that the Gorsedd of Bards received for the investiture were designed and purchased by a committee which included Lord Mostyn, Lord Aberdare, Canon Edwards, Lady Cowell-Steppes and Lady St David's.[62] The prevalent role of Welsh arts and institutions in the investiture itself served to underscore aristocratic involvement in national life.

Like the arts, the university movement in Wales had also encouraged the participation of the gentry. Since its establishment in 1893, the federal University of Wales was a symbol of popular achievement and national status. Support for the university transcended political and sectarian barriers. The University College of North Wales in Bangor had many connections with the squirearchy of north Wales, particularly with Lord Kenyon; at Aberystwyth, the 'people's college' founded according to a popular myth on the subscriptions of the poor, evoked images of Welsh populism. Together with the University College of South Wales and Monmouthshire in Cardiff, the constituent colleges of the University of Wales were powerful symbols of national unity and purpose.[63] Of course, the British monarchy had fully embraced the non-divisive nature of the university movement through the prince's acceptance of the university's chancellorship.[64] The 1911 Investiture symbolically reaffirmed the links between the monarchy and Welsh educational movements. E. H. Griffiths and Lord Kenyon (principal and president respectively of the University College of North Wales) marched in the prince's

[60] David Ian Allsobrook, *Music for Wales: Walford Davies and the National Council of Music 1918–1941* (Cardiff, 1992), p. 22.
[61] *Holyhead Chronicle*, 16 June 1911.
[62] Ibid., 12 May 1911.
[63] Kenneth O. Morgan, *Rebirth of a Nation: Wales, 1880–1980* (Oxford, 1981), pp. 106–10.
[64] W. Lewis Jones, 'Royalty and the University of Wales', *Wales: A National Magazine* (July 1911), pp. 128–9.

procession.⁶⁵ After the investiture, the tour through Wales took the royal family to Bangor for the opening of the new college buildings and then on to Aberystwyth for the laying of the foundation stone of the National Library of Wales.⁶⁶

The investiture ceremony highlighted the aspects of Welsh life in which the participation of the aristocracy and gentry were pronounced and traditional. On this basis, the Welsh gentry attempted to develop a fresh image and a new function as decorative and symbolic leaders of a resurgent Welsh nation. They defined themselves as leaders dedicated to the social and cultural aspirations of Wales, committed to public service and the well-being of the Welsh people. In the investiture ceremony, the Prince served as a symbolic representative of the Welsh aristocracy. The Prince's motto 'Ich Dien' was taken as their own. The *Western Mail*'s words on the importance of the Prince's dedication to the Welsh nation applied equally to the Welsh aristocrat:

> ... the hereditary right of princes becomes contemptible and perilous unless it is accompanied and graced by moral exaltation and a profound devotion to the people's welfare. Rank and power are an excrescence, a sore, a disease, unless regulated by the sublime principle which the founder of Christianity has enshrined in the sentence, 'Whosoever will be chief among you, let him be your servant'.⁶⁷

The Church had also been pursuing a policy of reconciling itself with the spirit of Welsh nationalism since the 1880s. Rejecting the appellation of an 'alien church', the Anglican Church argued that it had been a force working to preserve Welsh culture throughout history. In 1897, the Church appointed Bishop John Owens, a cleric of undeniable Welsh ethnicity, to the See of St David's as a conciliatory gesture.⁶⁸

---

⁶⁵ *Ceremonial*, p. 3.
⁶⁶ *Wales and her Prince*, pp. 10–14.
⁶⁷ *Western Mail*, 14 July 1911.
⁶⁸ Kenneth O. Morgan, *Freedom or Sacrilege? A History of the Campaign for Welsh Disestablishment* (Penarth, 1966), pp. 14–15; Paul O'Leary, 'Religion, Nationality and Politics: Disestablishment in Ireland and Wales, 1868–1914', in John R. Guy and W. G. Neely, *Contrasts and Comparisons: Studies in Irish and Welsh Church History* (Cardiff, 1999), pp. 104–6.

INVESTITURE

The 1911 Investiture proved to be a perfect vehicle to further the Welsh credentials of the Anglican Church. In reviewing the lessons taught by the ceremony, the Anglican paper *Y Llan a'r Dywysogaeth* wrote:

> How many Welshmen are ministers in the English King's Government? And yet, they belong to Wales not a bit less. The only example where an official is seen as losing his nationality is when he is a man appointed a Bishop or a Priest in the Church. But the idea is so foolish and so contrary to that felt in every other circle of our relationship to England, that it won't be long before common sense makes the foolishness of this talk too obvious even to the most stupid.[69]

This new vision of the Welsh nation can only be understood in light of the increasingly beleaguered nature of the old Victorian establishment and the growing conservatism of the forces of Welsh nationalism during the Edwardian period. With the Local Government Act of 1888, the death knell for squirearchy in Wales had sounded. The nonconformist middle class had not only secured control of parliamentary representation through the Liberal Party in Wales but enjoyed power on a local basis through the newly established county councils. By 1911, like the British aristocracy in general, the Welsh gentry had come to accept the rising tide of democracy and the decline in their political precedence.[70] New developments, however, were threatening to wipe away their authority all together. In London, the House of Lords was under assault and Welsh disestablishment stood waiting impatiently but confidently in the wings.

David Cannadine has described how the British aristocracy, having abandoned their attempts to impose their will politically, tried to protect their social position by redefining their role in society and by reconstructing the nature of their social prestige. At the same time as the political might of the gentry waned, occasions of pomp and ceremony were becoming more and more pronounced in British society. This resulted in a growth in the numbers and importance of ceremonial and

---

[69] In translation from the original Welsh: *Y Llan a'r Dywysogaeth*, 13 July 1911.
[70] Canadine, *Decline of the British Aristocracy*, pp. 557–9.

ornamental roles, positions which the aristocracy was uniquely able and eager to fill.[71] But before the Welsh aristocracy could participate in this reconstruction of their social prestige, they first had to reconcile themselves with the ascendant power of Welsh nationalism.

With the monopoly of the gentry's power broken, the Welsh nonconformist middle class turned to secure their own political dominance. In doing so, the nonconformist elite was transformed from a radical group dedicated to achieving equality of status through fundamental political change to a socially conservative force working to preserve their power and to maintain the status quo.[72] This was proving to be difficult in an industrialized Wales increasingly characterized by class conflict, a development clearly demonstrated in the industrial disputes in the Rhondda. Starting in November 1910 and continuing right through the investiture summer of 1911, the dispute flared into violence with the Tonypandy riots. From the fighting with Captain Lindsay's Glamorgan Constabulary at the Cambrian Combine collieries, the altercation spread into the village itself. Dai Smith has described the subsequent orgy of window breaking and shop looting that took place as a form of working class protest, an attack against the new middle class hegemony of Wales.[73] Winston Churchill, the Liberal Home Secretary, felt obliged to restore order and the British Army was called in to clear the streets of Tonypandy. At the centre of this storm was D. A. Thomas, the Welsh-speaking industrialist, leader of the Cambrian Combine and a leading light in the agitation for Welsh disestablishment. Clearly, nonconformity could no longer bind the Welsh working class to middle class leadership. Social order was breaking down and the old radical nonconformist causes began to weigh heavy around the neck of a new elite struggling to maintain order in a new Wales. The ideal of the *gwerin* had cracked. A new vision was needed. It was under these circumstances that the aristocracy and Church were seen as potential allies by a struggling Welsh middle class.

[71] Ibid., pp. 557–605.
[72] Emyr W. Williams, 'Liberalism in Wales and the Politics of Welsh Home Rule 1886–1910', *Bulletin of the Board of Celtic Studies* 37 (1980), 191–207.
[73] Smith, *Wales! Wales?*, pp. 55–97.

Wealthy, influential and prestigious but deprived of the political power which they had once monopolized, the Welsh aristocracy and gentry could be relied upon to help restore order and stability to Welsh society.

The issues which had been a source of antagonism between the populist Welsh nation and the gentry were gradually fading. Welsh farmers were becoming more concerned with the economic and scientific issues of farming than with the eroded power of squirearchy. While on the surface the old divisive issue of disestablishment still raged, the radicals of nonconformity were beginning to lose their hold on the passions of the populace. The rhetoric of those who continued to fight for disestablishment was becoming increasingly nostalgic in tone, harking back to the days of the evictions of the 1860s and the Tithe War of the 1880s when the *gwerin* stood firm in the midst of its oppression.[74] Behind the scenes, efforts were being made to resolve the issue amicably. A. G. Edwards and David Lloyd George played a dominant role in attempts at forming a compromise between the Church and nonconformity.[75] Through the investiture, the Bishop of St Asaph and the Chancellor of the Exchequer also cooperated in forging a new vision of the Welsh nation that emphasized unity rather than division, solidarity rather than conflict.

The essential element in the 1911 Investiture was the idea of national unity. At a time of religious and political controversy, the nation was described as speaking in one voice in greeting its prince. Comparisons were made, linking the role of the young prince with that of the Welsh princes of old who forged a unified nation from the bickering tribes of Wales.[76] The Bishop of St Asaph wrote in his 1927 memoirs:

---

[74] Morgan, *Freedom or Sacrilege*, pp. 21, 32–3; Neil Evans, '"A Nation in a Nutshell": The Swansea Disestablishment Demonstration of 1912 and the Political Culture of Edwardian Wales', in R. R. Davies and Geraint H. Jenkins (eds), *From Medieval to Modern Wales* (Cardiff, 2004).

[75] Neil Purfvey-Tyler, 'Lloyd George, the Bishop of St Asaph and the Disestablishment Controversy', in Judith Loades (ed.), *The Life and Times of David Lloyd George* (Bangor, 1991), pp. 153–61.

[76] Owen Rhoscomyl, *The Book of the Investiture* (Cardiff, 1911), p. 4.

THE PRINCE AND THE *GWERIN*

> Historically, the title Prince of Wales was an outward and audible sign that Wales was a united national entity and not a congeries of petty princedoms always at war with one another. The year 1910 opened upon a bitterly divided Wales. Politics were at a white heat, but there were foreshadowings of better things. Behind all these divisions the idea of nationality had gained in power and in clearness of conception. No longer could it be said to rest upon a unity of antipathies. The mean antipathies and the old hatreds, more tribal than human, must cease, unless Wales was forever to remain divided, impotent, and ridiculous.[77]

The compliant Edwardian press treated all divisions of class, religion and politics as being swept aside by the tidal wave of enthusiasm that accompanied this celebration of Welsh national identity. 'That, of course', commented one writer, 'is altogether as it should be, a proof that the nation, whatever its opinions may be on matters of faith and policy, is one in its determination to permit no domestic differences to wreck its essential solidarity'.[78]

The division between the gentry, Church, chapel, middle and working classes were obvious ones that the 1911 Investiture sought to address, but the ceremony was also concerned with the increasing regional division of Wales. The acidic debate between Cardiff and Caernarfon over the site of the investiture had done much to poison relations between a rural north and the industrial south of Wales. However, once the announcement was made in favour of Caernarfon, the press of south Wales was willing to sacrifice its pride on the altar of national unity. Caernarfon, which only two days before had been characterized by a J. M. Staniforth cartoon in the *Western Mail* as a rather thin and flea-bitten cur standing in the way of the mighty bull of Cardiff, was now portrayed as a classical goddess shaking the hand of sister Cardiff under the affectionate gaze of Dame Wales and a wildly exuberant dragon.[79] The *Western Mail* wrote:

> The beauteous and romantic North may be trusted to strain every nerve to make the ceremony a brilliant success, and to that end the

[77] A. B. Edwards, *Memories* (London, 1927), pp. 243–4.
[78] *Newcastle Chronicle*, 13 July 1911.
[79] *Western Mail*, 8 September 1910.

North will be loyally aided by the South, for a matter like this there is no longer North or South, but a united Wales, eager to do honour to her Prince.[80]

Yet the divisions in Edwardian Welsh society were apparent even in this ceremony of national unity. Despite the sentiments and claims of the press, the 1911 Investiture portrayed a regionally divided nation. Although south Wales was represented by her MPs, peers and members of local government and the Lord Mayor of Cardiff was even given a distinctive position in the Prince's Procession, north Wales had a far more prominent position in the ceremony. The choir was drawn exclusively from the north and spectators within and outside the castle consisted mainly of the northern Welsh.[81] The royal investiture tour never went to south Wales and enthusiasm for the event there was, not surprisingly, muted. The southern Welsh counties could not give away all the tickets allotted them by the National Committee so the surplus was turned over to the north.[82] The local investiture celebrations in the south were quiet affairs, town and county councils choosing to concentrate more on the coronation festivities of the previous month.[83]

Class division was equally evident in the ceremony. The sound of breaking glass in the streets of the Rhondda could not be drowned out by the music of the military bands and choirs in Caernarfon. The contrast between the spectacles of the strike in south Wales and the investiture ceremony in the north was plain to see. The Conservative *North Wales Chronicle* satirically suggested that, in keeping with the national character of the event, an interesting detachment in the royal procession might be 'a selection of miners from Tonypandy carrying the weapons with which they "hammered" the Metropolitan Police'.[84] Ironically, Winston Churchill, the man who sent the army into Tonypandy, played a prominent role in the investiture ceremony in his capacity as Home Secretary. Standing to

[80] *Western Mail*, 9 September 1910.
[81] Anon., *Illustrated Programme of the Investiture of the Prince of Wales* (Carnarvon, 1911), p. 15.
[82] *North Wales Chronicle*, 2 June 1911.
[83] *Western Mail*, 8 July 1911.
[84] *North Wales Chronicle*, 26 May 1911.

the right of the king, it was Churchill who read the letters patent as the Prince was invested.[85]

In the face of social conflict, the meaning of the 1911 Investiture was irrelevant or suspect to many leaders of the Welsh working class. *Llais Llafur* (Labour's Voice) wrote of the miners' attitude to the Investiture:

> In the coal mining areas where the gwerin are left alone by the aristocracy and the pomp of the palaces and the daily life of the aristocracy is unknown, the people are not so servile and subservient. Although there is not much democracy and next to nothing of opposition to the crown, there is one thing that is growing and that is the unwillingness to accept things as they are. Socialism has never grown like it is now growing in the coalfield. While the North takes a holiday to worship the King and Prince, it is the things that tend to directly change the nature of society that are important in the South.[86]

Using Tonypandy as an example, James Keir Hardie, the Independent Labour Party MP for Merthyr Tydfil, stated that the primary object of the Liberal and Conservative parties was to keep the working class from realizing the extent of its oppression. To this end, the government used 'Coronations and Investitures as an offshoot to Captain Lindsay and Winston Churchill.'[87]

Echoes of the strike could not be muffled, even in the ceremony itself. It was planned that Sir John Rhys, the celebrated Oxford professor of Celtic studies and principal of Jesus College, would read the loyal address from the Welsh people supported by the Revd E. Rees, the Archdruid of the Gorsedd of Bards, and William 'Mabon' Abraham, Lib-Lab MP for Rhondda West. 'What a picture is here presented!', exclaimed one writer: 'The son of a peasant reading an address of loyal welcome to the Prince, and being supported on either hand by two working colliers!'[88] In the event, one collier never appeared. Through the *Merthyr Pioineer*, Keir Hardie publicly warned Abraham against participating, especially at a time when 'the gaunt spectre of hunger is haunting fifty thousand of

[85] *Ceremonial*, p. 12.
[86] In translation from the original Welsh: *Llais Llafur*, 22 July 1911.
[87] *Merthyr Pioneer*, 13 May 1911.
[88] *North Wales Chronicle*, 30 June 1911.

his constituents and neighbours night and day in the Rhondda Valley'.[89] The otherwise moderate and conciliatory Mabon had to walk away from the ceremony. All of the Welsh MPs were asked to march in the Prince's Procession and their names were even printed in the official programme.[90] However, only one out of the five Lib-Lab and independent Labour MPs attended the event.[91] On a list of local celebrations being held in south Wales, the *Western Mail* reported: 'In the Rhondda the industrial dispute overshadows everything, and no public rejoicings will be held.'[92]

In many respects, the 1911 Investiture of the Prince of Wales was a manifestation of the growing conservatism of Welsh nationalism in the tumultuous Edwardian period. The investiture borrowed elements from the *gwerin* motif but did not conform to it. It reflected a set of ideals of Welsh nationality which served to unite a beleaguered upper class searching for a new role in the nation with a Welsh nonconformist and middle class elite seeking to buttress its own position as the new establishment of Wales. In the face of increasing social conflict manifest in the bitter coal strike in the Rhondda, the investiture presented an image of Wales as a united nation. In doing so, the investiture and its definition of the Welsh nation embraced the gentry and the established Church, effectively undermining the populist basis of the *gwerin* myth. Preaching the importance of national solidarity, it could unify the upper and middle classes largely under Liberal auspices but found the working class increasingly estranged. The Welsh working class, still a radical force struggling for fundamental political and social change, found little in the message of the 1911 Investiture which related to them or their aspirations. This reflected the growing isolation of the Welsh working class and the breakdown of Welsh nationalist populism. Historians such as Gwyn A. Williams, Dai Smith and Peter Stead have argued that the obsolete image of the *gwerin*, propped up by the Welsh middle

[89] *Merthyr Pioneer*, 1 July 1911.
[90] *Ceremonial*, p. 3.
[91] John Williams, MP for Gower, was the only Lib-Lab and Labour Party MP to attend the 1911 Investiture; *South Wales Daily News*, 14 July 1911.
[92] *Western Mail*, 6 July 1911.

class during the Edwardian period, collapsed under the pressure of class conflict during the inter-war years.[93] The Investiture of 1911, however, suggests that the populist image of the *gwerin* had been substantially dismantled by the Welsh middle class themselves before the First World War. Rather than being reinforced by the ceremony, the image of the *gwerin* was undermined by the socially conservative vision of Welsh nationality which the investiture attempted to express.

---

[93] Dai Smith, *Wales! Wales?*, pp. 28–54; Peter Stead, 'The Language of Edwardian Politics', in David Smith (ed.), *A People and a Proletariat* (London, 1980), pp. 148–65; Gwyn A. Williams, *When Was Wales?*, pp. 234–51.

5
Reconciling the Celt[1]

Although the 1911 Investiture was a celebration of Welsh nationality and culture, it had broader implications. Such unequivocal state recognition of Welsh nationhood compelled a re-examination of the nature of the British nation, state and empire. In the Victorian period, it seemed as if there was little common ground or room for compromise between the Conservative and Liberal notions of nationality. However, the 1911 Investiture found at least tacit support from the Conservatives. Indeed, royal participation in the event would seem to indicate that state recognition of Welsh nationhood had ceased to be controversial by the Edwardian period. The investiture attempted to redefine Wales's relationship to the other nations of the United Kingdom, to the British state and to the British Empire beyond. In doing so, it reflected an emerging consensus concerning the nature of the United Kingdom and the British Empire, a consensus taking its form from the Liberal idea of constructing a more solid union through the recognition of its multinational nature. Crucially, however, the exact form of this recognition was left open to negotiation.

Regarding the 1911 Investiture as an event whose importance extended beyond Wales, the press publicized it widely throughout the United Kingdom and British Empire. To speed accounts of the event across the British world, organizers erected telegraph offices at the site of the ceremony. The railways established special express trains equipped with dark rooms to run stories, photographs and cinema film of the event from Caernarfon directly to London. The investiture had the rare honour of being one of the very first royal ceremonies to

---

[1] The material in this chapter first appeared in John S. Ellis, 'Reconciling the Celt: Identity, Empire and the 1911 Investiture of the Prince of Wales', *Journal of British Studies*, 37 (1998), 391–418.

have bits of its pageantry filmed by the new technology of motion picture cameras. Along with the structure and form of the ceremony itself, the imagery, rhetoric and narrative of such reporting explicitly connected the ceremony to the coronation of George V and specifically articulated the relationship between Britain, Wales and the Celtic peoples of the United Kingdom.

The newspaper commentary on the investiture ceremony produced a colourful image of Wales's relationship with England as one rooted in the battles and oppression of the past. Investiture commentary avoided direct confrontation with the Anglocentric vision of an English nation-state by projecting this modern conflict back to the romantic and warlike days of the Middle Ages. A soldier by profession, Owen Rhoscomyl did not spare the gore in his description of the Welsh past which he saw as culminating in the investiture's revival:

> The battles and the slaughters of a thousand years are at the root of it. The fire and sword and ravage of the thousand thronging armies that swore to wipe out this scanty folk from the roll of the nations faded into baffledness in the glory of this act and fact of tomorrow. I look back and back across the ages, and at last I see them come in ravening hosts ... red fronted and bannered in flame, panting to leave no last thing alive that bore the hated name of Cymro (Welshman). Fierce and raging, I hear them shake the heavens with oaths that they will kill and kill till none remain this time. At last, I see the Cymry standing to the shock, see them still fighting on deathlessly, resolute to be Cymry, to dream their own dreams and to live their own lives, indomitable that Cymru shall be Cymru still.[2]

The holding of the investiture signified the final victory of the Welsh nation over English attempts to exterminate its nationality and culture. *Y Tyst* gloated over the 1911 Investiture, claiming that: 'It shows that we have won the day over the English and have conquered totally their cruel attempt and traditional policy to weaken and destroy Welsh nationality.' Somewhat darkly, it added: 'We have at last grasped the sword from our enemy and buried it in his own heart.'[3]

Journalists often depicted Caernarfon Castle, built by the medieval conqueror of Wales, as a means of subjugating and

[2] *Western Mail*, 13 July 1911.
[3] Translated from the original Welsh: *Y Tyst*, 9 July 1911.

exterminating the national spirit. Yet it was a fitting site for a national celebration because it stood as a tribute to the fierce tenacity of the Welsh people.[4] It served as a monument to the fact that, despite the animosity of their English neighbour and the ravages of history, the Welsh nation had survived. As one commentator put it: 'The old castle of the Oppressor is in its ruins; the national spirit is stronger than ever it was before.'[5]

While symbolizing the oppression of the past, Caernarfon Castle was also a symbol of the transformation from strife and war to harmony and concord. Images of the castle as the seat of oppression were often paired with those celebrating the site where the Prince of Wales was first presented to the Welsh chieftains. King Edward's presentation of his heir as the Prince of Wales was hailed as a stroke of master statesmanship, a gesture of reconciliation at a time of armed hostility between the English and Welsh. It was the place where peace was established and a new unity forged:[6]

> Hen Castell Caernarfon, lle claddwyd y cledd
> Lle tarddodd hyd heddyw ffynonau o hedd;
> Daeth Cymru a Lloeger i heddwch parhaus,
> Rhowd terfyn ar ryfel a thrais.[7]

> Old Caernarfon Castle, where the sword was buried
> Source of the fountains of peace to our own day;
> Wales and England found continuing peace,
> War and violence were ended

Presentations of King Edward I alternated between his image as the ruthless conqueror who had built the castle and as the bringer of peace who presented his newborn son from the castle battlements in order to placate and conciliate the Welsh nation.[8]

Once characterized by bloodshed and oppression, the relationship between England and Wales was now flowering into a

[4] *Morning Leader*, 12 July 1911; *Manchester Guardian*, 22 August 1910.
[5] *Morning Leader*, 12 July 1911.
[6] *Daily Telegraph*, 14 July 1911; *The Times*, 14 July 1911.
[7] Abraham H. Thomas, 'Urddwisgiad ei uchelder Brfeninol Twysog Cymru yn Nghaernarfon, 1911', (Llansamlet, 1911).
[8] *South Wales Daily News*, 14 July 1911; *Daily Telegraph*, 14 July 1911.

new kinship of mutual understanding and affection. In the words of one poet:

> If torrents, once, of blood
> Turned Menai's ebb to flood
> Arvon's swift streams today with laughter run;
> The old Druidic Isle,
> As with a tear-lit smile,
> Home to Penmynydd calls her royal son.[9]

Writers described the ancient enemies, Saxon and Celt, as being inseparably joined in hearts and voices in hailing the Prince.[10] Beriah Gwynfe Evans's Welsh-language drama, *Glyndŵr: Tywysog Cymru – The Welsh Historical Investiture Play*, reflected the central theme of oppression and reconciliation. The play, centring on the medieval rebellion of the patriotic Welsh hero Owain Glyndŵr, was especially commissioned for the investiture, received royal patronage, and was performed in the castle the day after the ceremony. It received enough attention to merit a later production in London, a very rare occurrence for a play entirely in the Welsh language. In the drama, Evans explained that the character of Henry IV represented the 'older policy of repression and oppression which drove the whole nation into irreconcilable hostility and left for centuries a rankling sense of injustice in the nation's heart'. Henry V, however, was meant to represent the 'more statesmanlike policy of generous recognition', which made it possible for Glyndŵr's men to faithfully follow the English King to the victorious battlefield of Agincourt.[11]

To many romantic observers of the investiture, the blood of the Royal Family itself embodied the reconciliation of the English and Welsh. The ceremony paid special attention to the monarchy's connection to Wales, emphasizing the Royal Family's descent from the House of Tudor. Investiture commentators never tired of reminding their readers of the fact that

[9] H. Elvet Lewis, 'Ode: The Prince of Wales' Investiture', *Wales: A National Magazine* (July 1911), p. 115.
[10] *South Wales Daily News*, 14 July 1911; *Daily Telegraph*, 14 July 1911.
[11] Beriah Gwynfe Evans, *Glyndŵr: Tywysog Cymru – The Welsh Historical Investiture Play* (Caernarfon, 1911), pp. 5–6.

Henry Tudor was a Welsh King of Great Britain.¹² 'It should not be forgotten by us', wrote Owen Rhoscomyl, 'that the lad will be Prince of Wales, even as his father will be King of England, by virtue of descent from Harry Tudor, born and bred a Welshman, of ancient kin and descent, and King of England by right of victory, won against the last King of the stranger-race of the Normans on the swamped ringed slope of Bosworth Field'.¹³ The Tudor connection was a central motif in the décor of the ceremony itself. The thrones upon which the King and Queen sat were of 'Tudor style', and the interior of the castle was decorated in the 'Tudor colours' of green and white.¹⁴ The King took his cue from popular Welsh histories when addressing the crowds in front of Caernarfon Castle: 'I do not need to remind you that by his descent through the House of Tudor, my dear son derives a natural and intimate claim upon your allegiance.'¹⁵

Throughout the 1911 Investiture, Wales was presented as a Celtic nation. Journalists used the terms 'Welsh' and 'Celtic' interchangeably. The press drew parallels between the music and art of the Welsh and their Celtic cousins. In conjunction with the investiture, the town of Caernarfon held a series of 'Celtic concerts' featuring a mixture of traditional Welsh, Irish, Scottish and Breton music.¹⁶ Everything ranging from investiture souvenirs and medals to official invitations displayed a generalized Celtic style of art that borrowed heavily from Irish and Scottish as well as Welsh antiquities.¹⁷ One souvenir, a decorative envelope sold by the Welsh Housing Association, included a leaflet explaining the artwork as a depiction of Celtic designs copied from historic Welsh and Irish specimens,

12 Owen Rhoscomyl, *Flame-Bearers of Welsh History* (Merthyr Tydfil, 1905), pp. 232–55.
13 *Western Mail*, 24 May 1910.
14 *Manchester Dispatch*, 12 July 1911; *The Times*, 12 July 1911.
15 *Daily Telegraph*, 14 July 1911.
16 Anon, *The Investiture of H. R. H. The Prince of Wales at Caernarfon: Handbook and Official Programme of Festivities* (Liverpool, 1911), pp. 46–7, 51.
17 Official Invitation to the Investiture of the Prince of Wales, printed invitation, Gwynedd Record Office, Caernarfon; *Investiture of H. R. H. The Prince of Wales: Medals and Souvenirs Designed and Manufactured by Fattorini & Sons* (Bradford, 1911).

including the Tara Brooch and the Shrine of St Patrick's Will.[18]

The 1911 Investiture, then, signified the reconciliation not only of the Welsh and English but of the Saxon and Celtic races as well. This rapprochement held deep implications for that 'other great community of British Celts', the Irish. The *Birmingham Post* drew specific parallels between the suffering of the two nations:

> If Ireland remembers Cromwell and the Boyne, Wales, too, has its mementos of desperate and savage antagonisms. Carnarvon Castle itself is one of them. If Ireland resents the incursion of the Protestant community of Ulster, Wales had as much or more to hate in the Wardens of the Marches, who set up their strongholds of Usk, Raglan and a score more places and so dominated the south and centre of the Principality that they were hardly recognized as Wales at all. In spite of them all, Wales has preserved her nationality.[19]

The investiture itself was part of a larger tour of the Celtic fringe that sought to demonstrate that King George V did not 'regard himself as the King of any one special area singled out by accident for peculiar favour but as bound by a mutual bond to the people of each land over which he reigns'.[20] Before arriving in Wales for the investiture, the Royal Family paid an official visit to Dublin. After the investiture, they retired to the more familiar grounds of Scotland. The *Morning Post* wrote: 'It will not be very long before the King and every section of his subjects understand one another as well, and are as sure of one another, as the King and Londoners already are.'[21]

The Royal Family's 1911 trip to Ireland was filled with the same message of national recognition and reconciliation that characterized the investiture. The nationalist *Cork Examiner* recognized the King's decision to start his coronation tour in Dublin as a mark of special favour and high regard for the Irish nation.[22] A commentator from the unionist *Irish Times* wrote:

[18] Welsh Housing Association, 'Souvenir of the Investiture of His Royal Highness the Prince of Wales, K.G., at Carnarvon Castle on the 13th of July, 1911' (1911).
[19] *Birmingham Post*, 14 July 1911.
[20] *Morning Post*, 13 July 1911.
[21] *Morning Post*, 13 July 1911.
[22] *Cork Examiner*, 8 July 1911.

'It is not expected that the memories of an unwise and cruel past can be wiped out in a moment, but the signs all point to a renewed confidence in the friendship of the King and his subjects in Great Britain.'[23]

Like the symbols of Welsh nationality at the investiture, the royal visit to Dublin was submerged in an emerald sea of Irishness. Decoration committees posted the Gaelic greeting 'Céad Míle Fáilte' (a hundred thousand welcomes) on signs and banners all along the route of the royal procession.[24] Buildings were brilliantly illuminated with royal crowns and monograms arranged amongst Irish shamrocks and green harps.[25] During the procession, the Queen wore a green gown of Irish poplin and lace and later received an address from the 'Women of Ireland' elaborately decorated with Celtic ornament in the style of the Book of Kells.[26] The republican newspaper *Irish Freedom* was aghast at a suggestion made in the nationalist *Freeman's Journal* that the King, in imitation of the high kings of ancient Ireland, should gather about him an Irish court drawn from the scholars of the Gaelic League, the literary worthies of the Celtic Revival and a piper selected by the Feis Ceoil.[27] Such a desire to embrace the contemporary cultural awakening in Ireland was indicative of the atmosphere of Celticism in which the royal visit was conducted. Like the investiture's recognition of Welsh nonconformity, Irish religious sentiment was specifically indulged through a royal visit to Maynooth Seminary. Cardinal Logue, Archbishop Walsh and Archbishop Healy received the King and Queen and presented them with a loyalty address on behalf of the Irish Catholic hierarchy. As the King and Queen inspected the college chapel, the royal and papal standards symbolically flew side by side before the seminary gates.[28]

Although Irish republicans would make their opposition known and their protest heard, the Dublin crowds, buoyed up by the Liberal promise of home rule, enthusiastically greeted

[23] *Irish Times*, 10 July 1911.
[24] *Manchester Guardian*, 10 July 1911.
[25] *Irish Times*, 10 July 1911.
[26] *Irish Times*, 10 July 1911.
[27] As quoted in *Irish Freedom*, July 1911.
[28] *Irish Times*, 10 July 1911.

the monarch. The Liberal *Manchester Guardian* wrote of the welcome: 'No one had imagined that it would be other than friendly, but its warmth came as a surprise even to those who knew the Irish well.'[29] According to the nationalist *Cork Examiner*, by noon the streets were filled with a crowd the likes of which Dublin had seldom seen before. It argued that 'the whole proceedings showed how general was the feeling of welcome, and the visit will be remembered as a remarkable testimony to the better sentiment of mutual understanding which now happily prevails amongst the people of both sides of the Channel'.[30] In newspaper accounts, the cheering of the Dublin crowds was synonymous with enthusiasm and sincerity. One commentator wrote that the: 'English visitors here who saw the coronation procession declare that the cheers of the London crowd were as politeness is to enthusiasm compared with the cheers that were heard in the streets of Dublin today.'[31] Fostering a feeling of friendly rivalry between the two Celtic nations, Welsh commentators observed the Irish reception of the King and vowed to match it. An editorial cartoon by J. M. Staniforth that appeared in the *Western Mail* depicted the figure of Dame Wales spying on the Irish welcome and declaring, in her best stage-Welsh: 'Well done Ireland! Indeed, now, that is a grand reception; but I will beat it, look you!'[32]

Rejecting the construction of Britain as an English nation-state, the 1911 Investiture and the royal visit to Dublin presented the monarchy as a symbol of an explicitly multinational Britishness. This sense of British identity encompassed but was greater than the more intimate national identities of England, Ireland, Scotland and Wales. To the *Morning Advertiser*, the investiture was part of a 'wise policy of allowing and even cultivating diversity of race and character within one Imperial bond'.[33] The Conservative *Birmingham Post* felt compelled to recognize the positive value of the 'spirit of nationalism' and described the investiture and the tour of the Celtic fringe as a demonstration that George V was not:

[29] *Manchester Guardian*, 10 July 1911.
[30] *Cork Examiner*, 9 July 1911.
[31] *Manchester Guardian*, 10 July 1911.
[32] *Western Mail*, 11 July 1911.
[33] *Morning Advertiser*, 13 July 1911.

an alien Sovereign of England ... holding sway over races who fell centuries ago before the military forces of his ancestors, but ... the gladly-accepted overlord of men of diverse origins, who symbolize their unity of interest by their unity of devotion to a single Monarch, equally the property of them all.[34]

The *Morning Post* described the vision of the British state reflected in the ceremony as one of unity through diversity rather than through absorption:

> The idea of uniformity, which may have been appropriate to the age of Henry VIII, when nations were being consolidated by the growth of monarchical power, has lost its importance in an age when monarchy is the stronger for the development of the representative system. Accordingly, the Welsh are free to develop their national characteristics without anyone thinking that thereby the unity which is the purport of British history will be in any way prejudiced. As they cry 'God Bless the Prince of Wales' they will cry with equal sincerity 'Long Live the King'.[35]

The commentary and symbolism of the investiture defined the British state as a collection of distinct and diverse nations bound together through their loyalty to the monarch and their service to the empire. Each nation had its own talents, its own characteristics to contribute to the organic whole. The *Manchester Dispatch* wrote that the investiture demonstrated that the small nations with their distinctive characteristics were valuable to the 'work of the world' and that their merging into one vast and uniform agglomeration would be as harmful as it would be sad.[36] The *Daily Chronicle* stated:

> There are those who distrust national sentiment and whose ideal is not so much diversity in union as unity by subordination of local patriotism. But they are wrong. The loyalty of the whole burns the brighter the more it is fed by satisfaction of the national sentiment of the parts; the life of the nation flows in a broader and a richer stream in proportion as the several confluents contribute distinctive elements to its genius. That is one moral, we think, of the national festival in Wales.[37]

[34] *Birmingham Post*, 13 July 1911.
[35] *Morning Post*, 13 July 1911.
[36] *Manchester Dispatch*, 14 July 1911.
[37] *Daily Chronicle*, 14 July 1911.

By 1911, Conservatives and Liberals agreed on the multinational function of the monarchy and this consensus extended to some degree to recognition of the multinational nature of the British state. Where they disagreed, however, was on the form which that recognition should take. For the Liberals, national recognition came in the form of repealing imposed 'English' institutions. In the immediate sense, this translated into disestablishment for Wales and home rule for Ireland. In the fullness of time, it would include a general policy of devolution that would establish a federal system of national parliaments for England, Ireland, Scotland and Wales. Such a scheme was aired at the Constitutional Conference of 1910 and was the subject of vigorous campaigning by a small number of Welsh and Scottish Liberals in the summer of 1911.[38] Significantly, when the third Irish Home Rule Bill was produced in the House of Commons in 1912, Prime Minister Asquith introduced it as but the first step in a broader policy of home rule all around.[39]

The Conservatives were willing to recognize and even celebrate Celtic distinctiveness, but only to a point. In contrast to the national chauvinism of late Victorian Conservatism, many Conservative newspapers and politicians gave lip service to the basic premise of 'unity in diversity' during the investiture. The *Daily Telegraph* agreed with the Liberal press that the ceremony of the investiture was 'essentially a festival symbolizing the combination of the spirit of racial patriotism with that of a larger union'.[40] In a surprising if somewhat improbable confession made at an investiture banquet, party leader Arthur Balfour even claimed a long-held desire to speak the Welsh language.[41] From the vantage point of the summer of 1911, the days of English denigration of Welsh culture seemed to recede into the distant past. Linguistic, cultural even religious differences could be acknowledged and even celebrated but the institutional basis of the British state had to be maintained.

[38] K. O. Morgan, *Wales in British Politics 1868–1922* (Cardiff, 1963), pp. 255–9.
[39] *Hansard's Parliamentary Debates*, 5th ser., vol. 36 (April 1912), col. 1403.
[40] *Daily Telegraph*, 8 July 1911.
[41] *Manchester Guardian*, 15 July 1911.

Above all, the integrity of Parliament, Church and the British constitution had to be preserved.[42]

The limitation of the compromise between Liberal and Conservative views of the British state are evident in the way commentary on the investiture treated the issue of Irish home rule. However, this issue also illustrates the flexibility of consensus in that both pro- and anti-home rulers could adapt the symbolism of the ceremony and the rhetoric of 'unity in diversity' to support their arguments. The Liberal *Manchester Guardian* argued for Irish home rule in stating that a loyal and contented Wales, so evident in the investiture ceremony, was the result of a successful policy of conciliation and respect for national self-consciousness. This policy had also formed the basis on which Scotland had entered the union. By withholding home rule, Ireland had been denied this policy with evident results of dissension and bitterness. With the lessons of the investiture at hand, the *Manchester Guardian* asked: 'How soon shall we begin to set the mischief right?'[43] The Conservative *Birmingham Post*, however, used the example of the 1911 Investiture to argue that the experience of Wales disproved the Irish case for home rule:

> All that she [Wales] has cared to preserve – her language, her literature, her song, her liberty of thought and conscience – are hers still. As a constituent unit of the United Kingdom, cooperating with other units towards a common end, she rests secure in the enjoyment of all the intangible spiritual blessings, which Ireland seeks to attain by violent separation. One sympathizes with the Irish aspiration after the full and free development of her own national identity; but clearly the method by which it is proposed to hasten the coming of the Irish ideal is not the only one applicable to the special circumstances of the case.[44]

---

[42] Alan O'Day, 'Irish Home Rule and Liberalism', in Alan O'Day (ed.), *The Edwardian Age: Conflict and Stability* (London, 1979), p. 121; Hugh Cunningham, 'The Conservative Party and Patriotism', in Robert Colls and Philip Dodd (eds), *Englishness: Politics and Culture 1880–1922* (New York, 1986).
[43] *Manchester Guardian*, 14 July 1911.
[44] *Birmingham Post*, 14 July 1911.

Gazing at Ireland with the sound of loyal Welsh cheers ringing in its ears, *The Times* could only ask; 'Quis separabit?' (Who will separate us?)[45]

What Liberals and Conservatives could agree upon, however, was that each of the nations of the United Kingdom contributed 'distinctive elements' and had a special role to play in Britain's destiny. But what 'distinctive elements' did the Welsh, and by extension the Celts, supposedly contribute to the genius of the British state? Commentary on the investiture suggests an answer. The investiture's construction of the Celt largely followed the lead of Victorian cultural theorist Matthew Arnold and other Celticists.[46] According to investiture commentary, the Welsh were full of fervour and 'Celtic ardour', responding quickly to encouragement but chafing under neglect.[47] At the root of Welsh character was a dogged sense of pride and tenacity that manifested itself in a strong patriotism for their native land.[48] They were excitable, anything and everything stirring them to enthusiasm. We are told by the *Morning Post* that: 'intoxication makes the Saxon sing, but it is singing that intoxicates the Celt.'[49] Above all, the Welsh were a spiritual people, resilient against the materialism of the age. Newspapers and programmes described the Welsh as traditional and romantic, reverent of the past and susceptible to the dramatic.[50] The *Evening Standard* informed its readers 'the Welsh are more intimate with romance than most others in times largely given over to realism'.[51] The 1911 Investiture was described as an event which appealed to the 'strong vein of romance and imagination that is part and parcel

[45] *The Times*, 14 July 1911.
[46] Matthew Arnold, *On the Study of Celtic Literature* (London, 1891); John S. Ellis, 'Celt versus Teuton: Race, Character and British National Identity, 1850–1918', *Irish German Studies* (2001/2002), 13–27; Gerry Smyth, 'The Natural Course of Things: Matthew Arnold, Celticism and the English poetic tradition', *Victorian Studies*, 1 (fall, 1996); Malcolm Chapman, *The Celts: The Construction of a Myth* (New York, 1992); Frederic E. Faverty, *Matthew Arnold: The Ethnologist* (Evanston, 1951).
[47] *Daily Telegraph*, 14 July 1911.
[48] *Evening Standard*, 13 July 1911.
[49] *Morning Post*, 13 July 1911.
[50] *Glasgow Herald*, 14 July 1911.
[51] *Evening Standard*, 13 July 1911.

of the Celtic blood' and stirred Welsh people in a fashion unknown to the 'more phlegmatic Saxon'.[52] The Welsh were the singy, dreamy Celts characterized by the power of their imaginations, emotions and spirituality.

Commentators did not discuss the character of the English in as much detail, but English character was always present by inference. If the Celt was romantic and imaginative, the Saxon was practical and down to earth. If the Celt was enthusiastic and excitable, the Saxon was moderate and restrained. If the Celt was spiritual, the Saxon was worldly minded.[53] Alone, the Saxon and the Celt were incomplete; together they formed a whole, each functioning in its own capacity to the benefit of the British state.

Such images of Celt and Saxon help to explain why the largely rural town of Caernarfon was selected as the site for the investiture over the bustling metropolis of Cardiff, the self-proclaimed capital of Wales. Certainly in terms of facilities, population and transport, Cardiff was in a far superior position to host a royal event than remote Caernarfon. Yet, despite Cardiff's considerable claims to the honour, most commentators thought Caernarfon the only appropriate site for the ceremony. In fact, it was the very character of Cardiff as a vibrant, modern, commercially successful city which made it an unacceptable site for the ceremony. Celts who made fortunes and a metropolis out of the 'despotism of fact' instead of romantically rebelling against it just did not fit into the scheme. London, which was only just beginning to come into its own as the grand centre of British ceremonial life, wanted no provincial competition. By placing the event in the sleepy town of Caernarfon, no comparisons with London could be made and the dreamy, singing Celt could be found in abundance. According to *The Times*, English opinion was overwhelmingly united with north Wales in claiming Caernarfon to be the only natural setting for the ceremony.[54]

To a remarkable degree, the investiture's characterizations of Celts and Saxons correspond to Victorian and Edwardian gender roles. Although already under serious challenge by the

[52] *Daily Telegraph*, 12 July 1911.
[53] Chapman, pp. 201–64.
[54] *The Times* as quoted in the *Carnarvon & Denbigh Herald*, 7 July 1911.

'New Woman' and suffragette movement, the dominant gender ideology of the age held that men and women had distinct and natural traits that inclined them toward separate spheres of life. Operating in the public sphere of business and competition, men were worldly, practical and unemotional. Operating in the private sphere of home and family, women were spiritual, romantic and excitable. The two spheres functioned in tandem: men and women dependent upon each other to utilize the special qualities that they possessed for the welfare of the family.[55] The British family provided the model for the British state, a unified whole composed of mutually supporting but distinctive parts organized in a benevolent hierarchy. By the end of the century, such familial analogies were becoming commonplace in political rhetoric that tried to define the role of a new and expanding electorate.[56]

It is no surprise that commentary and symbols of the 1911 Investiture teemed with gendered characterizations of the Welsh people. Investiture commentary often depicted the Welsh nation in feminine language and imagery. In the editorial cartoons of J. M. Staniforth, the *Western Mail* had long used a rather rotund and matronly 'Dame Wales' as a symbol of the nation, but investiture posters, advertisements and souvenirs were more likely to depict Wales as a young, comely maiden dressed in the quaint top hat and shawl of traditional Welsh costume.[57] Reporters made much of the 'particular beauty and freshness' of the young women of north Wales. The ladies of the choir appeared in traditional costume and presented such a spectacle that, according to one witness, the men of the choir 'dwindled into insignificance'.[58]

This feminine characterization of Wales was consistent with the image of the investiture ceremony as a wedding between

[55] See Leonore Davidoff and Catherine Hall, *Family Fortunes: Men and Women of the English Middle Class 1780–1850* (London, 1987); Sonya O. Rose, *Limited Livelihoods: Gender and Class in Nineteenth Century England* (Berkeley and Los Angeles, 1992).
[56] Bill Schwarz, 'Politics and Rhetoric in the Age of Mass Culture', *History Workshop Journal*, 46 (1998), 129–59.
[57] *North Wales Chronicle*, 2 June 1911; *The Investiture of H. R. H. The Prince of Wales at Carnarvon: Handbook and Official Programme of Festivities* (Liverpool, 1911).
[58] *Pall Mall Gazette*, 13 July 1911.

the Welsh nation and her young prince. Part of the ritual of investiture involved the placing of a ring, composed of two interlaced Welsh dragons, upon the prince's hand to signify 'that he must be a husband to his country'.[59] Commentators likened the *Loyalty Address of the Welsh People* and the prince's reply to wedding vows. The *South Wales Daily News* wrote: 'It will be the name of one whom we recognize as "Our Prince" who has made his vows to us and we to him, who in a more intimate sense than ever before is pledged to labour for the Welfare of Wales, and to serve and inspire her in realizing her national destiny.'[60] Commemorative poetry was littered with wedding imagery:

> The nuptial morning! Our nation the bride
> Is come to Carnarvon her tryst to abide;
> A gallant young suitor is offering his hand
> The Prince of her old fatherland[61]

The investiture was a symbolic marriage between the Welsh nation and the British monarchy, which in turn personified the British state. Like the role of the wife and mother in the ideal of the British family, Wales played an important but ultimately subordinate role in the British state. Such gendered imagery helped to legitimize and naturalize an ethnic hierarchy in which the English were imbued with a fatherly authority at the apex of power.[62]

While the feminine image of Wales was a pronounced part of the ceremony, certain elements of the investiture also associated the Welsh with a youthful masculinity. Within the confines of the Royal Family itself, the prince served as the embodiment of the Welsh nation. This masculine ideal, however, was also a fundamentally subordinate image. Within the investiture ceremony and reflected in commentary, the prince was presented not as a man in his own right but as his father's young and obedient son. Journalists focused a great amount of attention upon the prince's youth.[63] Similarly, in his reply to the *Loyalty*

[59] *The Lady's Realm*, June 1911; *New York Evening Post*, 13 July 1911.
[60] *South Wales Daily News*, 13 July 1911.
[61] *The Lady's Realm*, June 1911.
[62] Tom Nairn, *The Enchanted Glass* (London, 1988), p. 228; Smyth, 12.
[63] *Morning Advertiser*, 13 July 1911.

Address of the Welsh People, the prince told the nation that he hoped the day would be marked as one that brought Wales a new friend. 'He is, it is true, a young friend', said the prince: 'I am very young, but I have a great example before me. I have my dear father and my dear mother, and good friends to help me.'[64] If the prince was young, then by analogy so were the Celtic Welsh. One writer reflected on the prince's reply, opining that the Welsh too, 'like all races that have Celtic blood in their veins, are very young and very enthusiastic and they dream dreams and sometimes the dreams come true'.[65] King George V, in contrast, was represented as the epitome of English fatherhood and mature masculinity. The *Carnarvon and Denbigh Herald* described the King's personal character as 'distinctly and ideally English', marked by simplicity, directness, concentration, firmness, determination, stability, and strength. The King found his chief happiness, we are told, in the domestic circle, always preferring a quiet evening at home surrounded by his many healthy and happy children.[66] Significantly, the prince held his father's hand as he was led around the castle and presented to the people of Wales.

As a young son, the prince's role in the family revolved around duty and loyalty to his father. The prince's act of homage combined feudal and familial bonds of loyalty.[67] Commentary depicted the investiture itself as a kind of ordeal or rite of passage, a duty to one's father, and a ceremony particularly appropriate for someone of the prince's tender years. Owen Rhoscomyl described the event in emotional terms as a ceremony between 'a young lad and his father'. He asked: 'what father in all the crowd but felt his heart go out at once to the boy as if to one of his own! How many of us whispered unconsciously, "good, good boy; you're doing well, that's it, you'll pull through all right".'[68] Such themes of filial duty even surfaced in advertisements of the day. The Tango

[64] *Daily Telegraph*, 14 July 1911.
[65] *Lloyd's News*, 16 July 1911.
[66] *Carnarvon and Denbigh Herald*, 14 July 1911.
[67] *Ceremonial to be observed at the Investiture of His Royal Highness The Prince of Wales, K.G., at Carnarvon Castle, July 11 1911* (London, 1911), p. 13.
[68] *Western Mail*, 14 July 1911.

Iron Wine Company equated the King's command that the prince learn some Welsh for the ceremony to the wise father's instruction that his son take daily doses of their medicine for creating strong blood and nerves – the analogy presumably being that both tasks were rather unpleasant but were ultimately for the betterment of the dutiful child.[69]

The filial duty and loyalty of the prince was paralleled by that of the Welsh soldiers and boy scouts that adorned the crowded streets of Caernarfon during the ceremony. Like the prince, these young warriors were committed through bonds of duty and obedience to the King and empire. The prince's words of homage, 'I will bear unto you to live and die against all manner of folks', held obvious martial and imperial connotations. The organizers of the event directly associated the prince with the Welsh martial presence at the ceremony. Representatives of the three Welsh regiments marched in positions of honour directly behind the prince in his procession.[70] After the ceremony, the prince's carriage halted before an assembly of 2,000 boy scouts drawn up in front of the castle as the future defenders of the empire. A boy scout approached the prince and handed him a staff in recognition of the prince's new position as the 'Chief of the Welsh Boy Scouts'.[71] The investiture's connecting of the prince, the Welsh soldiers and boy scouts suggests that the Celt was allowed his youthful form of masculinity primarily through his association with imperial endeavour.

This concern to present the Welsh nation as a dutiful son of empire was intensified by a nagging sense that the Welsh may have neglected their imperial duty in the past. The supposed traditional antipathy of the Welsh for the military was well known and thought to be deeply rooted in the innate pacifism of their national character and nonconformist religion.[72] The

---

[69] *Illustrated Programme of the Investiture of the Prince of Wales* (Caernarfon, 1911).
[70] *Ceremonial to be Observed*, 4.
[71] *Morning Advertiser*, 13 July 1911.
[72] John S. Ellis, 'A Pacific People – A Martial Race: Pacifism, Militarism and Welsh National Identity', in Matthew Cragoe and Chris Williams (eds), *Wales and War: Society, Politics and Religion in the Nineteenth and Twentieth Centuries* (Cardiff, 2007), pp. 15–37; Kenneth O. Morgan, 'Peace Movements in Wales, 1899–1945', *Welsh History*

chairman of the National Investiture Committee was only too aware of such sentiments. Like Owen Rhoscomyl, Lord Plymouth was personally committed to overcoming the supposedly traditional Welsh distaste for military service, serving as president of the Glamorgan Territorial Association and an officer in the Glamorgan Rifle Association.[73] Addressing his territorials in July 1910, he admitted that there was an extraordinarily strong feeling in Wales against what 'the ignorant called "militarism"' and he prophetically called for a military spectacle that would arouse the strong interest of the Welsh in military matters.[74] Consequently, the 1911 Investiture would be aptly described by one commentator as a piece of brilliant military pageantry such as the principality had seldom seen before.[75]

A breathtaking 12,000 troops converged on Caernarfon to participate in the 1911 Investiture. Shoulder to shoulder, they lined the route of the royal progress from Griffith's Crossing to Castle Square. Every battalion in the Western Command was represented but pride of place was given to the three Welsh regiments who turned out in force for the event.[76] The spectators greeted the arrival of the troops with lively interest, the arrival of the Welsh regiments being received with special enthusiasm. The mass military encampments in the hills outside of town were just as much objects of curiosity as the setting of the ceremony itself. During the ceremony, detachments of the Royal Welch Fusiliers, the South Wales Borders and Welsh-speaking sailors and marines from *HMS Carnarvon* occupied a place of honour in Castle Square. The band of the Second Battalion Welsh Regiment played Welsh martial airs such as 'The March of the Men of Harlech' for the spectators

Review (1982), 234–56; Goronwy J. Jones, *Wales and the Quest for Peace* (Cardiff, 1969), pp. 78–96.

[73] During the First World War, Owen Rhoscomyl was the chief figure in the raising of the Welsh Regiment of Horse and Lord Plymouth was instrumental in raising the 38th Welsh Division. Both units sought to attract Welsh recruits by reconciling Welsh nationality with military service: Bryn Owen, *Owen Rhoscomyl and the Welsh Horse* (Caernarfon, 1990); *Western Mail*, 8 March 1923.

[74] *Western Mail*, 1 July 1910.

[75] *Birmingham Post*, 14 July 1911.

[76] *Daily Telegraph*, 12 July 1911.

within the castle walls.⁷⁷ The twenty-one-gun salutes of artillery units on the surrounding hills and the big guns of the Home Fleet fully assembled in the harbour punctuated the royal procession and ceremony. The smallness of the quaint town of Caernarfon contrasted with the vast and magnificent presence of the soldiers of the King.

The *Loyalty Address of the Welsh People* celebrated the martial achievements of the Welsh past and the Welsh nation's commitment to defending the Empire in the future. As read by Sir John Rhys, the great Celtic scholar and principal of Jesus College, Oxford, the address stated:

> We are bound to the Throne of your forefathers by six centuries of a common past, by the memory of imperishable deeds in peace and war, and by our hopes of greater things to come. The bowmen and the pikemen of Wales followed the Black Prince to Cressy and Henry of Monmouth to Agincourt. Her sons have stood side by side with Englishmen on many a stricken field, facing equal danger; with no unequal courage.⁷⁸

At the investiture, Wales not only wore the traditional tall hats and druid robes of the Welsh *gwerin*. It also donned the bright scarlet tunics of British imperialism.

Investiture commentary depicted the Welsh as an imperial people spread across the globe. In his romantic style, Owen Rhoscomyl called the Welsh back to Wales to witness the investiture of its prince:

> The race is gathering. Like a trumpet call across the world the cry to the Investiture has gone through all the echoes, and from lone lands and grey wreathed seas, from tropic marts and equatorial forests, back now come the Cymry. . . From ranch and back-block station, from the mines that make the wealth of colony on colony, from ports whose very names breathe romance, back, back, they gather.⁷⁹

Writers presented the land of Wales as the oldest territorial possession to be added to the 'glory of the Imperial heritage'. Alternatively, Welsh roots were sought for the Empire. They proudly asserted that the empire was founded by the scion of

---

77 *South Wales Daily News*, 14 July 1911.
78 *Daily Telegraph*, 14 July 1911.
79 *Western Mail*, 13 July 1911.

Henry Tudor, the great Welsh King of Britain.[80] In discussing the investiture, Rhoscomyl defined Welsh nationalism in distinctly imperial terms:

> Welsh nationalism is the determination to bring Wales to the front in the Empire in every way that offers. Welsh nationalism is the spirit which recognizes all that Wales has still to make up, in spite of the progress of the last generation, and then stubbornly sets itself to help in bringing Wales at least abreast of the rest, ready to think of helping her to outstrip them, if that be possible. Nationalism believes that Wales has a distinct and definite value to bring to the Empire and to the world, in all things where mere numbers do not count, if once we can but organize and set that value going.[81]

Through the investiture, the state recognized Wales as a full member of the British imperial enterprise. The *Western Mail* thought of the ceremony as an opportunity to pledge the devotion of the Welsh to the common interests of Empire: 'With Englishmen, Scotsmen and Irishmen, we are joint heirs of Empire, joint servitors in the great task of maintaining and developing that heritage.'[82]

While buttressing the imperial enthusiasm of the Celt, the investiture's stress on the empire served a broader function. The ceremony's underlying theme of 'unity in diversity' was not confined to Wales, or even to the nations of the United Kingdom, but rather encompassed the imperial dominions. The investiture's message of ethnic and national diversity set within a familial hierarchy of power was particularly well suited to imperial conditions. Its emphasis on the initial conquest and ultimate reconciliation and recognition of ethnically distinct nationalities reflected current imperial realities. The Boer War, the grant of self-government to the Boer states, and the subsequent union of South Africa under the British Crown in 1910 were all important backdrops to the 1911 Investiture. In fact, the prominence of accounts of bloody battles and the subsequent peace and goodwill between conquerors and conquered in investiture commentary held a greater sense of immediacy to the recent history of South Africa than it did for

---

[80] *Daily Telegraph*, 14 July 1911; *Western Mail*, 14 July 1911.
[81] *Western Mail*, 15 August 1910.
[82] *Western Mail*, 13 July 1911.

Wales. Writers often drew analogies between the two nations. The *Manchester Guardian* compared their histories, struggles, and the ultimate recognition of South African and Welsh nationality by the British state:

> The institution of the Prince of Wales may be said – conditions of time and civilization accounted for – to be an exact analogy of the grant of self-government to the Transvaal in our own days. Like the Transvaal, Wales was subdued by force; like the Transvaal, its geographical conditions were such that, though force could subdue its armies and rulers, it could never subdue its people if they had chose to hold out. And as in the case of the Transvaal, the wisdom and foresight of the English Parliament found the one way out to contentment and peace, so the political genius of the greatest of the Plantangenets found it in Wales.[83]

South Africa, however, was not just a backdrop to the investiture, it was an actual participant. Once a general in the field fighting against the British, South African Prime Minister Louis Botha was the only colonial premier to be invited to the event. In addition to witnessing the investiture, Botha made his own grand gesture of reconciliation during the ceremony by accompanying his old foe, General R. S. S. Baden-Powell, in a review of the assembly of Welsh boy scouts drawn up before the castle walls.[84]

The investiture served to communicate a message of national reconciliation and recognition within a multinational empire. In fact, all the celebrations in connection with the Coronation of George V were designed to spread across the empire the message of 'unity in diversity'. The *Manchester Guardian* correctly observed that King George V's reign was the first to recognize the separate identity of each part of the United Kingdom and the British Empire.[85] The actual coronation coincided with the 1911 Imperial Conference that declared the King did not rule over the colonial commonwealths as the King of England but as the King of Canada, Australia and South Africa in their own rights.[86] Prime Minister Asquith opened the conference by declaring the

83 *Manchester Guardian*, 14 July 1911.
84 *Carnarvon & Denbigh Herald*, 26 May 1911.
85 *Manchester Guardian*, 14 July 1911.
86 *Manchester Guardian*, 24 May 1911.

crown to be the centre and symbol of imperial unity. After describing the diversity of climate, soil, people, religion, race and language within the empire, he asked:

> What is it that we have in common which amidst every diversity of external and material conditions makes us and keeps us one? . . . the combination of local autonomy – absolute, unfettered, complete – with loyalty to a common head . . . In the Victorian era there were two rough and ready solutions for what was regarded with some impatience by the British statesmen of that day as the 'Colonial problem'. The one was centralisation . . . the other was disintegration . . . After seventy years experience of Imperial evolution it may be said with confidence that neither of these theories commands the faintest support today either at home or in any part of our self governing Empire . . . Whether in this United Kingdom or in any one of the great communities which you represent, we each of us are and we each of us intend to remain master in our own household. This is here at home and throughout the dominions the life blood of our policy. It is the *articulus stantis aut cadentis imperi*. It is none the less true that we are and intend to remain units but units in a greater unity.[87]

At a luncheon for the colonial premiers, David Lloyd George commented on the growing attachment of the colonies for the Mother Country under the conditions of self-government and observed: 'The greatest mistake statesmanship could commit was to imagine that the narrower patriotism excluded the wider one.'[88] The 1911 Investiture of the Prince of Wales and the royal tour through the Celtic fringe applied the message of 'unity in diversity' to the nations of the United Kingdom itself. A few months later, George V moved on to India, where the concept of 'unity in diversity' was celebrated in yet another invented tradition, the Imperial Durbar. At the ceremony, the King outlined a series of reforms designed to reconcile Indian national sentiments with British imperial belonging, including the reunification of Bengal and the moving of the colonial capital from Bengal to Delhi.[89] The *Morning Advertiser* declared shortly before the Investiture:

> We are now as far removed from the ideals of a centralized Empire which seemed to dominate our politics ten years ago, and the revival

[87] *Manchester Guardian*, 9 June 1911.
[88] *Freeman's Journal*, 29 May 1911.
[89] *Morning Advertiser*, 13 July 1911.

of Liberalism has definitely substituted for those ideals the conception of nationalisms and a great commonwealth of free peoples. The visits to Ireland, Wales and Scotland show the same idea at work nearer home. More and more is the Crown becoming the symbol of unity in diversity.[90]

An analysis of the 1911 Investiture of the Prince of Wales reveals a pluralist construction of British national identity. The investiture's vision of the British nation and state was based on Liberal ideals of national recognition, reconciliation and 'unity in diversity'. Arguing against an Anglo-Saxonist conception of Britain as being synonymous with England, the investiture defined British nationality in multinational and multicultural terms. The monarchy provided the focus and the bond between this family of essentially different nations. Investiture commentary described the distinctive character of Saxon and Celt as mutually reinforcing, their differences contributing to the efficiency of the British state and empire. National diversity, however, was set within a familial hierarchy of power in which the Celt was delegated a subordinate position as the embodiment of a feminine or immature masculine character. This sense of Britishness was beyond ethnic definitions and was peculiarly suited to imperial conditions. Although implying a subordinate role to England, Britishness was defined as open-ended and capable of accommodating the diverse population of a vast empire. As Tom Nairn has observed, the monarchy symbolized a Britain that was not just England but: 'a supernal realm to which Welsh, Scots, Irish and even Hindus and Xhosas in good conscience could belong.'[91] Such a vision of Britishness established a consensus between Liberals and Conservatives because it left issues such as Irish home rule and Welsh disestablishment open to debate and focused on ideals of national and imperial unity. From a unitary, uniform and Anglocentric conception of a British nation-state, Britishness had been transformed into an essentially supra-territorial and multinational identity for which the monarchy provided the focus and the bond.

---

[90] *Morning Advertiser*, 13 July 1911.
[91] Nairn, 228.

6
The red dragon and the red flag

For the most part, outright opposition to the 1911 Investiture of the Prince of Wales was muted. There can be no doubt that the more Liberal elements of the investiture's message frustrated many Conservatives, but public criticism of the monarchy was simply unthinkable to them. In contrast to the protests of the republican fringe of the Irish nationalist movement against the royal visit to Dublin, there was no concerted dissent from any section of Welsh Liberal nationalism. In fact, Welsh nationalists overwhelmingly lent their active support to the Liberal project of the investiture. This support was particularly notable in north and Welsh-speaking Wales. Those aspects of the ceremony that could reasonably draw objections from Welsh nationalists were largely overlooked in the light of the investiture's celebration of Welsh nationhood and its explicit depiction of a multinational Britain. The only significant organized opposition to the investiture came from the socialists of south Wales led by James Keir Hardie, the Labour MP for Merthyr Tydfil. With the exception of explicitly socialist organs, the British press responded to this opposition largely by ignoring it. When opposition was mentioned in print at all, commentary on it merely underscored the scarcity of support that such views enjoyed. As for James Keir Hardie, he was portrayed by the British press as a mere socialist crackpot. At best, socialist opposition to the ceremony was localized and ultimately only a marginal factor in the shaping of the wider public perception of the event. The true significance of this opposition lay in its impact on socialist ideology and the political culture of the Labour Party in Wales. The investiture's evocation of Welsh nationhood spawned a debate amongst socialists on the relationship between Welsh nationalism and socialist internationalism. This was a formative debate that would profoundly define socialist attitudes to the question of Welsh nationalism in the future.

Regarding the coronation and the investiture as means of placating and deceiving the Welsh working class, Welsh socialists attempted to counter the royal events by holding a massive alternative ceremony the month before the coronation took place. Since an 1889 declaration of the International Working Men's Association in Paris, British socialists had adopted the red flag and observed the first of May as a holiday for the workers of the world.[1] When May Day was celebrated for the first time in Merthyr Tydfil in 1911, however, the ceremony was distinct in its direct relationship to the growing popular anticipation for the coronation and investiture in Wales. James Keir Hardie went to great lengths to organize the celebration as an antidote to the royal show. The event was hailed as 'the largest demonstration ever held in the Borough'. Numerous local bodies contributed funds and Labour dominated local councils closed schools for the holiday. The entire Aberdare valley halted work and between 12,000 and 15,000 workers participated in the marches and rallies. Led by Keir Hardie, a massive procession made its way through the town to a park, where demonstrators assembled around four platforms for an afternoon of speeches.

The effort, size and intensity of Merthyr's May Day celebration were directly related to the flood of royalist propaganda descending upon the Welsh valleys at that time. Keir Hardie's speech defiantly declared that: 'We recognise no better save the God that gave us being. To neither lord nor master shall we bend the knee in the future as we have in the past.'[2] Keir Hardie was concerned with the royal attempt to manipulate the children of the Welsh working class and was determined to beat the royal show at its own game. In this regard, he considered the closing of the schools to be a particular victory as it would ensure that:

> These lads and lasses will associate Labour Day with a holiday, with sport, with the sunshine, with the green fields, with the singing birds,

[1] Eric Hobsbawm, 'Mass-Producing Traditions: Europe, 1870–1914', in Hobsbawm and Ranger, *Invented Traditions*, pp. 283–6.
[2] *Merthyr Pioneer*, 6 May 1911.

with the flowers – and they will think of the Labour movement as a thing of joy and of beauty, and will work for it in the future when you and I have gone to our rest.³

As an alternative to the multinational British patriotism evoked by the investiture, the May Day ceremony celebrated the internationalism of the worker. David Bowman, the leader of the Labour Party in Australia, presided over the festivities in Merthyr as the guest of honour. The afternoon of speeches was punctuated with cries for international solidarity and the focal point of the demonstration was a resolution sending 'fraternal greetings to our comrades of the Labour Movement in Great Britain and Ireland, and in all lands without regard to creed or colour'.⁴ Keir Hardie proclaimed that:

> When you go to Germany, or to France, or to Russia or to Spain, or away down to Australia, or to India or to China or Japan, you meet the Socialist there, meet the Labour Party man there, and he takes you to his heart as a friend and comrade.⁵

At a special luncheon that day, Keir Hardie told his constituents: 'We declare ourselves one with them; their object, our object, is the same; our difficulties, their difficulties, are the same; we are comrades not merely in name; we are comrades in suffering and comrades in sacrifice, and comrades in reality.'⁶ In contrast to the 'saturnalia of militarism' characterizing the royal ceremonies, the internationalism of May Day was expressed in terms of pacifism. The demonstration passed a resolution in favour of the 'Abolition of War' and Keir Hardie declared to the mass meeting that the Labour movement was 'a movement that believed in peace'.⁷

Although strongly couched in terms of socialist republicanism and internationalism, Welsh socialist opposition to the investiture was also markedly nationalist in tone. With the investiture's paeans to Welsh nationhood and glowing accounts of May Day's internationalism thick in the air, an article by R. T. Evans appeared in the *Merthyr Guardian* posing the question: 'Is Nationalism with its insistence on national individuality

3   Ibid.
4   Ibid.
5   Ibid.
6   Ibid.
7   Ibid.

compatible with Socialism and its Universal Brotherhood?' To this, he replied: 'True national sentiment does not involve hatred of a neighbouring nation, more than the love for a brother involves a hatred of a person who is not ... It is my contention that the present awakening among the nations of the earth is the first step in the direction of International Socialism.'[8] This pronouncement was certainly consistent with the views of James Keir Hardie, who often professed his identity as a Scot and his belief in the ideal of nationality. Moreover, as the MP for a Welsh constituency, Keir Hardie identified strongly with Welsh nationalist sentiment and supported Welsh language, culture and traditions. A stalwart advocate of traditional Welsh demands in education, temperance and disestablishment, his nationalism was more advanced than that of many Liberals. As a candidate for Merthyr, Keir Hardie included Welsh home rule on all of his election platforms. He closed political meetings by singing 'Hen Wlad fy Nhadau' and chose the red, green and white of the Welsh flag as his campaign colours. Influenced by Mathew Arnold and contemporary Celticism, Keir Hardie explained the Welshman's supposed inclination for socialism as a part of his essential racial character. 'The Celts can never drive out of their blood', he wrote, 'that element of communism placed there by their wild, free, wandering forefathers who loved song and poetry during the thousands of years they lived with everything in common'.[9] Believing that the Welsh 'like all Celts ... are socialist by instinct', Hardie saw traditional Welsh cultural institutions in socialist terms, hailing the eisteddfod as an ancient form of union to protect the bards from literary blacklegs.[10]

James Keir Hardie considered the nationalism of subject nations like that of the Welsh to be essentially compatible with the wider international solidarity of the worker. Like the worker's exploitation by the capitalist, the subject nations of

---

[8] *Merthyr Pioneer*, 6 May 1911.
[9] J. Keir Hardie, 'Sosialaeth a'r Celt', in T. Stephens (ed.), *Cymru: Heddyw ac Yforu* (Cardiff, 1908), p. 91; as quoted in D. Hywel Davies, *The Welsh Nationalist Party 1925–1945: A Call to Nationhood* (Cardiff, 1983), p. 17.
[10] Kenneth O. Morgan, *Keir Hardie: Radical and Socialist* (London, 1975), pp. 113, 118.

the world were exploited through the system of imperial capitalism. Indeed, Keir Hardie's support of Welsh, Irish and Indian nationalism was part and parcel of his international socialism and a product of his belief that socialism could only take root by identifying with the genius of the nation within which it worked.[11] Blending his socialist principles with nationalist sympathies, Keir Hardie espoused a form of Welsh nationalism that drew not only from the traditional Welsh religious, educational and cultural aspirations but also voiced the demand for the nationalization of the land, mines, furnaces and railways within the borders of Wales. 'That is the kind of Nationalism that I want to see brought about', he told an audience of striking molders in Dowlais shortly after the investiture. 'And when that day comes the red dragon of Wales will be emblazoned on the red flag of Socialism, the international emblem of the working class movement of the world!'[12]

Holding forth this definition of 'True Nationalism', Keir Hardie claimed that the Labour Party was the only faithful advocate of Welsh nationhood. He had nothing but contempt for the Welsh Liberals and their 'spurious imitation' of Welsh nationalism. Following the death of two young men at the hands of British troops during the railway strike of 1911, Keir Hardie attacked the Liberals who travelled across the country 'making noise about Welsh nationalism.' He asked:

> . . . had they heard one of them offer one single word of sympathy or compassion to the old mother and father who were crying their hearts out in the lonely home in Llanelly for the Welsh lad who was shot through the heart? Not one. They talked of Welsh Nationalism when they wanted votes, but when it came to doing anything for the workers they were not nationalists, they were not even Welshmen, they were simply party politicians intent upon keeping the workers in their rightful places.[13]

It was in this light that Keir Hardie and his newspaper, the *Merthyr Pioneer*, interpreted the investiture. By emphasizing the active oppression at the heart of the relationship between

[11] Morgan, *Keir Hardie*, p. 184.
[12] *Merthyr Pioneer*, 14 October 1911.
[13] Ibid.

England and her colonial subjects, Hardie's rhetoric reversed the investiture's message of reconciliation:

> Wales is to have an 'Investiture' as a reminder that an English King and his robber barons strove for ages to destroy the Welsh people, and finally succeeded in robbing them of their lands and driving them into the mountain fastness of their native land like hunted beasts, and then had the insolence to have his son 'invested' in their midst. The King is to make a Coronation tour in Ireland to view the miles of lonely waste from which the persecution of his royal forbearers has driven the Irish people into exile in other lands. And, crowning infamy, one million pounds is to be spent on a Coronation Durbar at Delhi, in the district round which 20,000 PEOPLE ARE DYING EVERY WEEK of plague and hunger.[14]

The investiture was nothing more than a ceremony designed to celebrate the English conquest and domination of Wales. Claiming that he could find no one to take his tickets to the event, Hardie sighed:

> I don't wonder at self-respecting Welshmen staying away from a ceremony which reminds them of the fact that Wales was robbed of all the outward trappings of a nation by the rapacious kings and barons of England . . . The person to be invested is a foreign prince, and the reason for his investiture is to show the people of Wales that they are merely a 'province of England' . . . Surely, then, the 'patriotic Welshmen' . . . will be showing their patriotism best when they stay away from the investiture.[15]

Although drawing upon long established anti-monarchical rhetoric, Keir Hardie's attack on the Germanic associations of the Royal Family took on a special meaning and character in Celtic Wales. He effectively melded the traditional Welsh antagonism toward the Saxon invader with current anxiety over Prussian militarism.[16] Cynically lampooning the investiture's insistence on the Welsh roots of the Royal Family, Keir Hardie needled the king by emphasizing his Teutonic background and referred to him as 'the titled German who now

[14] *Merthyr Pioneer*, 17 June 1911.
[15] *Merthyr Pioneer*, 1 July 1911.
[16] For anti-German attacks on the monarchy, see Antony Taylor, '*Down with the Crown*': *British Anti-monarchism and Debates about Royalty since 1790* (London, 1999), pp. 122–5.

'rules' Britain'.[17] Under the title of the 'The Investiture of our German Conquerors', the *Merthyr Pioneer* ran a copy of Thomas Gray's 'The Bard'. This famous eighteenth-century poem depicted a medieval Welsh bard calling down curses upon the conqueror, Edward I, before throwing himself off a precipice in despair and defiance. Contrasting the patriotic anguish of Gray's bard with the enthusiasm of the Welsh Liberals for the investiture, the poem was preceded by the cutting comment, 'The following was not recited by Mr. Lloyd George on Thursday last'.[18] The Revd T. E. Nicholas was an ardent socialist, nonconformist minister, eisteddfod bard and the Welsh-language editor of the *Merthyr Pioneer*. He did not mix words in his attitude towards the investiture and those 'nationalists' who revelled in it:

> Pwy yw'r Cymro aiff i Arfon
>
> I Arwisgo Y Tywysog?
>
> Bradwr fydd i achos Cymru!
>
> Bradwr fydd i achos gwerin!
>
> A gonestrwydd gwerin Cymru
>
> Ymhen canrif a'i melldithia!
>
> Ac a boera ar ei enw
>
> Fel arch-fradwr cenedl gyfan.
>
> Y mae dagrau yn fy nallu;
>
> Mae chwyldroad yn fy ysbryd;
>
> Mae fy llaw ar garn y cleddyf!
>
> Y mae ysbryd beiddgar Glyndŵr,
>
> Y mae taran-floedd Llywelyn
>
> Heddyw'n sibrwd wrthyf:-
>
> 'TARO'.[19]

---

17 *Merthyr Pioneer*, 24 June 1911.
18 *Merthyr Pioneer*, 22 July 1911.
19 *Merthyr Pioneer*, 17 July 1911.

INVESTITURE

Who is the Welshman who will go to Caernarfon
To the Investiture of the Prince?
A traitor he'll be to the Welsh cause!
A traitor he'll be to the people's cause!
And the honesty of the people of Wales
Throughout the century will curse him
And will spit on his name
As an arch-traitor of the whole nation.
Tears are blinding me;
Anger is choking me;
Revolution is in my spirit;
My hand is on the hilt of the sword!
The daring spirit of Glyndŵr,
The thunderous-shout of Llywelyn –
Today whispers to me:–
'STRIKE'.

Thus, Welsh socialists attempted to reverse the meaning of the investiture, attack the nationalist credentials of the Welsh nation's dominant political party and lay claim to the Welsh nationalist tradition for themselves.

Not all socialists in Wales, however, agreed with the nationalist flavour of the particular brand of socialism inspired by the opposition to the investiture. Directly provoked by the ceremony, a debate occurred in the pages of the *Merthyr Pioneer* when the issue of Welsh nationality was a pressing matter in the minds of Welsh socialists. Launched the day after the investiture, a body of prominent Welsh socialists including T. E. Nicholas, R. Silyn Roberts, David Thomas, Idris Davies and T. Gwyn Jones called for the joining of the 'twin movements of nationalism and nationalisation' through the formal reorganization of the Labour Party in Wales on a distinctly national basis. In effect, they were calling for the foundation of an independent Welsh labour party.[20] Although enjoying the hearty support of Nicholas and the more ambiguous support of Keir Hardie, the movement was broadsided by George Thomas, the English language editor of the *Merthyr Pioneer*:

> It is about 50 years too late to talk of a national movement in Wales. Real nationalism, as distinguished from the spurious Liberal kind, is confined today in Wales to the realm of art, and much of this, unfortunately, is degenerate. The problem to which the workers of Wales, in common with the workers of everywhere else, have to be awakened is the economic problem. There is nothing Welsh about this, and to pretend that there is, and to attempt to graft a Welsh aspect of economics on to a national history which no longer influences the majority of the people of Wales, and on to a nation which in reality does not exist, is bound to be a waste of time. Besides, it is dishonest. It is quite as dishonest as if we were to start a propaganda to make Lloyd George the king of Wales in order to win the sympathies of the people for Socialism. The plain fact that we have to realise and then to preach is, that the people of Wales are workers like the people of any other area; and they have to be taught that they are being oppressed in common with their fellows throughout the world, and that they have to fight shoulder to shoulder with those fellow workers for the destruction of the Capitalist system.[21]

Unlike Keir Hardie, Thomas equated all forms of Welsh nationalism to the bourgeois variety espoused by Lloyd George and the Welsh Liberals. His variety of working class internationalism denied the legitimacy of any form of Welsh nationalism. Despite such opposition, efforts to form a separate Welsh Labour Party would continue through 1912. Although this attempt failed, the debate that it provoked effectively articulated the division over the issue of nationality within the ranks of Welsh socialism during the Edwardian period, a division that would prove to be enduring within the Labour Party in Wales.[22]

The important role of the investiture in the formation of socialist attitudes to Welsh national identity has not been fully

[20] Ibid., 15 July 1911, 22 July 1911, 29 July 1911, 19 August 1911, 14 October 1911.
[21] Ibid., 5 August 1911.
[22] See R. Merfyn Jones and Ioan Rhys Jones, 'Labour and the Nation', in Duncan Tanner, Chris Williams and Deian Hopkins (eds), *The Labour Party in Wales 1900–2000* (Cardiff, 2000).

appreciated by historians of the Labour Party. The investiture launched a public discussion on Welsh and British nationhood, a discussion with which Welsh socialists felt compelled to engage. In the atmosphere created by the royal ceremony, Welsh socialists debated the relationship between socialist internationalism and Welsh nationhood. The attempt to create an independent Welsh labour party was a direct byproduct of the investiture's political culture. Of more lasting significance, opposition to the investiture was a crucial factor in the formation of what would become 'centralist' and 'devolutionist' wings of the Labour Party in Wales.

7
Recessional

In the years immediately following 1911, the national vision projected by the investiture seemed to come to full and glorious fruition. The official state recognition of Welsh nationhood inherent in the symbolism of the investiture subsequently found substantial legislative and constitutional form. Having passed the Parliament Act that abolished the House of Lords veto, the Liberal government introduced the Welsh Disestablishment Bill in the House of Commons in 1912. At approximately the same time, the Liberals introduced the Irish Home Rule Bill. Having passed through the Commons twice, these controversial measures of constitutional reform received the Royal Assent and were placed on the statute book in 1914. However, the implementation of this momentous constitutional reform was fatefully postponed by the outbreak of the First World War.

In many respects, the military spectacle of the 1911 Investiture proved to be a dress rehearsal for Welsh involvement in the Great War. Inspired by the fight for the rights of small nations, the Welsh widely regarded the war as an opportunity for a revitalized Welsh nation to prove its worth in defence of a reformed, multinational British state and empire. The 38th Welsh division was envisioned as a nation-at-arms, replete with dragon insignia, Welsh-speaking officers, and pocket hymnals for the Cymry on the march. With their prince later serving as colonel, the elite Welsh Guards was created by George V in 1915 to satisfy Welsh national sentiments. Superficially, at least, divisions of class appeared to have been engulfed by the wave of patriotism that surged across the coal field. James Keir Hardie opposed the war with characteristic passion but died embittered and broken in 1915, his dream of the international solidarity of the worker shattered by the spectacle of the rush to enlist. Having been the leanest of recruiting grounds before the war, Wales would contribute a larger percentage of its population to the armed forces than any of the other constituent nations of the United Kingdom. To many, the elevation of David Lloyd George to the Premiership in December 1916 provided symbolic confirmation of Welsh equality with her sister nations of the empire, a coming of age foreshadowed in Caernarfon some five years earlier.

Welsh triumphalism, however, would fail in the horrors of war and the changing circumstances of postwar Britain. Lloyd George's coalition government did disestablish the Anglican Church in Wales in 1920, but under far more lenient terms than those traditionally demanded by nonconformist nationalism. Having responded enthusiastically to the opportunity to reassert their role as national leaders by serving in battle, the Welsh gentry that had marched in tandem with the Prince at Caernarfon were devastated by the mortality of the war. Landed fortunes were further wrecked by the postwar agricultural depression. As the gentry faded from the scene, the Welsh tenantry realized its ambitions for the ownership of the land. The Liberal programme in Wales had thus been achieved in a state of postwar trauma and melancholy anti-climax. Lloyd George's formation of a coalition government in 1916 led to the Liberal Party itself splitting into hostile 'National' and 'Independent' Liberals. Moreover, the eruption of armed conflict in Ireland in the 1920s presented the spectacle of David Lloyd George, the hitherto champion of small nations, leading an attempt to suppress the rights of another small nation through brute force. As a consequence, the Irish Home Rule Act was made irrelevant and the promise of 'home rule all around' moot. Although the bulk of Welsh nationalists continued to support Lloyd George, former nationalist allies like W. Llewelyn Williams became embittered, vocal critics who attacked Lloyd George for turning his back on Wales and betraying the ideals of the Welsh nation.[1] Industrial depression, class conflict, ethical scandals and the continuing bloodshed in Ireland increasingly tarnished Lloyd George's reputation. As the great Welsh war hero fell from grace, so did the predominant faction of the Welsh nationalist movement that had hailed

[1] Morgan, *Wales in British Politics*, pp. 286–97; Morgan, *Rebirth of a Nation: Wales, 1880–1980*, pp. 180–90.

him as the epitome of Welsh democracy back in 1911. Although marginal during the war itself, traditional Welsh pacifism found its voice in an increasingly disoriented and disillusioned Wales. In the end, Welsh liberal nationalism declined into political insignificance, with only eight of Lloyd George's National Liberals and two Independent Liberals being returned for the thirty-five Welsh parliamentary seats in the 1922 general election.

Recognizing the extent to which traditional Welsh nationalism had collapsed following the First World War, a group of Welsh intellectuals led by the poet and litterateur Saunders Lewis attempted to redefine the nature of Welsh nationalism by creating anew its aims, methods and ideology. Shunning affiliation with any British based party, they formed Plaid Genedlaethol Cymru (the National Party of Wales) in 1925. Politically, Plaid Cymru demanded self-government in the form of Dominion status under the Crown but its rhetoric was markedly separatist in tone. Its principal message was one of protest against the decline of the Welsh language. Although its electoral appeal remained negligible, Plaid Cymru achieved a great deal of popular interest and notoriety among the Welsh-speaking population. Much of this support was inspired by the direct action tactics of the party's leadership. In a 1936 protest against the locating of an RAF bombing school in the Welsh-speaking heartland at Penyberth, Saunders Lewis, D. J. Williams and Lewis Valentine burned down a builder's shed on the base's construction site. Although their original trial in Caernarfon resulted in a hung jury, they were subsequently sentenced to prison by a court in London. Upon their release, the 'Three' were greeted by an enthusiastic crowd of over 15,000 supporters assembled in Caernarfon. In the shadow of Edward's keep, the cheers of a new form of Welsh nationalism smothered the echoes of 1911.

In the same year that the leaders of the new nationalism burned down the bombing school, King Edward VIII paid an official visit to Wales. Thirty-five years after the jubilation of his investiture in north Wales, the newly installed king toured the poverty-stricken valleys of south Wales. The coal field was in the midst of the economic dislocation and unemployment of the Depression. Surveying the plight of the mining villages, he memorably exclaimed: 'Something must be done.' With its seeming promise of state intervention, those words became the symbolic agenda of an emerging political force in Wales.[2] The time of liberal nationalist hegemony in Wales was clearly at an end and a new political ascendancy was on the rise.

In contrast to the dismal performance of the Liberals in the 1922 general election, the Labour Party won nineteen of thirty-five Welsh seats. Labour steadily built upon its success in Wales in the following decades, its initial rise to power taking place in an atmosphere of industrial decline, unemployment and growing class conflict. Although it continued to support Welsh home rule in the years immediately following the First World War, the conflict and misery of the Depression led the party away from specifically Welsh issues to an almost exclusive concern for broader, British-based social and economic affairs. Being concerned with the realities of power and struggling on behalf of the British working class as a whole, Labour focused on winning and using the fulcrum of centralized government at Westminster to achieve its socialist aims. Welsh political concerns increasingly focused on issues related to class and material welfare rather than nationality and culture. Informed by the misery of the Depression, many Welsh members of the Labour party resisted any attempt to remove Wales from the mainstream of British political life and were critical of Welsh national aspirations. Rather than quibble over national distinctions like the Liberals or engage in the cultural fantasies of Plaid Cymru, Labour leaders such as Aneurin Bevan argued that the Welsh working class should recognize that their interests were the same as the working class elsewhere in Britain and that progress towards a welfare state would come through centralized state power. For Wales, the benefits of such a policy was dramatically demonstrated with the nationalization of the coal mines in 1947 and the establishment of Aneurin Bevan's sainted National Health Service in 1948. Within the centralized structure of the welfare state, Wales was rarely used as an administrative unit and had a negligible official existence as a

---

[2] For a full discussion of the political and economic context of the visit of Edward VIII to south Wales, see Ted Rowlands, *Something Must be Done: South Wales vs Whitehall 1921–1951* (Merthyr Tydfil, 2000).

unified or corporal entity. For the most part, Wales returned to being a mere geographic expression.

However, the alternative devolutionist tradition within Welsh Labour continued to argue for the melding of socialism and nationalism. Following in the footsteps of Keir Hardie, they identified Labour as the heir to a specifically Welsh radical tradition wrested from the moribund Liberals. While recognizing the benefits of centralization to social progress, this branch of Labour was concerned that the state should recognize and effectively respond to the regional needs, special concerns and even national aspirations of the Welsh people. There was also the sense that the Welsh should be allowed to address more of their own problems. They believed that the machinery of government would be more efficient at the regional level by devolving some measure of power from the central government to Wales itself. While the larger demand for an elected Welsh assembly existed vaguely on the horizon for some Labour politicians, the most immediate demand for Labour's devolutionist wing was for the establishment of a Welsh Office led by a cabinet level Secretary of State for Wales. By the 1950s, the party's failure to give Wales a distinctive political voice aroused fears among Labour devolutionists that Welsh national sentiment might be captured and exploited by others. The new nationalism of Plaid Cymru may have been highly marginal in electoral terms, but it provided a clear alternative focus for national loyalty and represented a palpable threat to Labour's claims as the 'Party of Wales'.

The 1969 Investiture would reveal how much Wales, Britain and the monarchy had changed since 1911. The drama in 1969 would involve new actors and take place in very different historical circumstances, but the investiture would continue to revolve around the central issue of Welsh national identity. What was Welsh? Who was Welsh? Who spoke for the Welsh nation? What was the relationship between Wales and the British state? These were the questions upon which the rite would once again be staged.

Part 3

*Pomp, perspex and protest:
The 1969 Investiture*

8
'Let's Go!' Labour and Wales

The Labour governments of 1964–70 have not fared well in the estimation of many commentators. The period is often characterized as one of economic mismanagement, political indecision and popular disillusion in which the Labour Party under the ineffectual leadership of Harold Wilson lost its sense of ideological direction and squandered its opportunities. First elected in 1964 by a narrow margin, the Wilson government's initial popularity was underscored by Labour's comfortable victory in the British general election of 1966. Attitudes, however, began to sour soon afterwards. Rather than vigorous and purposeful promotion of economic growth, the public was confronted with the spectacle of an impotent government struggling vainly to halt an ever deepening crisis. Turned out of office in 1970 with a dismal record of low economic growth, the trauma of devaluation and high unemployment, the Wilson government was soon afterwards eulogized in grim tones of disillusion and failure, the shadow of its shattered reputation all the darker for the bright light of earlier enthusiasm.[1]

While acknowledging the obvious shortcomings of the Wilson government, more recent work has questioned the credibility of this indictment and offered a less harsh reassessment of Wilson's preimership.[2] There is a new awareness that, despite their own admittedly extravagant ambitions and claims, the

[1] David McKie and Chris Cook, *The Decade of Disillusionment: British Politics in the Sixties* (London and Basingstoke, 1972). For a detailed historiography, see the introduction of Richard Coopey, Steven Fielding and Nick Tiratsoo (eds), *The Wilson Governments 1964–1970* (London and New York, 1993), pp. 1–9.

[2] For a recent and comprehensive re-evaluation of the Wilson years, see Stephen Fielding and John W. Young (eds), *The Labour Governments 1964–70*, vols 1–3 (Manchester and New York, 2003). See also Coopey, Fielding and Tiratsoo, *The Wilson Governments*.

Labour governments of the latter 1960s should not be condemned for failing to solve what were really intractable structural problems of relative economic decline and reorganization in post-imperial Britain. A more balanced evaluation of the Wilson governments also recognizes the fact that Labour's term of office took place in the midst of the cultural revolution of the 1960s. A host of forces profoundly impacted every aspect of life and shook the foundation of traditional hierarchies, loyalties and world view.[3] Political, cultural and social identities were in a whirlwind state of flux, driven by a newly affluent working class, a rebellious youth culture, and feminist movement. Liberal legislation reflected a relaxation of social mores and a transformation of attitudes. The rising tide of Commonwealth immigration and racial hostility, the outbreak of the 'Troubles' in Northern Ireland, growing ethno-nationalist movements in Scotland and Wales and the continued withdrawal from empire abroad represented further fundamental challenges to received notions of British identity. One contemporary assessment described the period in terms of violent, unstoppable and cataclysmic change.[4]

Given the troubled context of their times, the Wilson governments' navigation of the 1960s was perhaps better than its bleak reputation would imply. While its efforts to stabilize and modernize the economy were largely in vain, it must be remembered that the people of Britain enjoyed affluence at unprecedented levels during the period. Rather than the poverty or austerity of the not too distant past, theirs was largely a relative deprivation, borne of anxiety over a stagnating economy in the face of the rising fortunes of their competitors in Germany, France and the United States. In the face of cultural revolution, Labour responded positively to the centrifugal forces of the 1960s. In the estimation of a recent study of postwar national

---

[3] Arthur Marwick, *The Sixties: Cultural Revolution in Britain, France, Italy, and the United States, c.1958–1974* (Oxford, 1998); Steven Fielding, *Labour and Cultural Change*, vol. 1 of Fielding and Young, *The Labour Governments 1964–70*; David Alan Mellor and Laurent Gervereau Dorléac, *The Sixties: Britain and France, 1962–1973: The Utopian Years* (London, 1997); Bernard Levin, *The Pendulum Years: Britain and the Sixties* (London, 1979).

[4] Bernard Levin, *Run it Down the Flagpole: Britain in the Sixties* (New York, 1970), p. 9.

identity, the Wilson government offered a clear vision of Britain's potential as a world leader and constructed 'a cohesive and highly patriotic definition of what it meant to be British' in a time of intense change and controversy.[5]

In many respects, the reputation of the Labour governments of the 1960s has suffered in relation to the exceptionally high expectations that inaugurated their return to office. After some thirteen years of Conservative rule, a narrow electoral victory in 1964 returned Labour to power for the first time since the Atlee government. Inspiring comparisons to the recently assassinated American president John F. Kennedy, Labour leader Harold Wilson promised resolute leadership, strong government and a distinctly modern, professional and innovative response to the country's ailments. Labour campaigned on a message of creating economic growth and returning Britain to a position of global prominence through modernization, professionalism and planning. Shedding class-bound limitations on talent, Labour's meritocratic 'New Britain' would draw on and develop the untapped national potential of a professional, technocratic elite and a trained, modernized workforce. The traditional British working class, Labour's former bedrock of support, was in decline and Wilson moved to embrace a more complicated social structure characterized by working class affluence and a progressive middle class. The party's jaunty 'Let's Go!' election slogan reflected a new national mood of confidence, optimism and exhilaration.[6]

A modernist spirit pervaded the rhetoric and policies of the party. Believing that their defeat in 1959 was the result of being out of touch with contemporary life, the Labour Party of the 1960s carefully cultivated an image of a 'modern forward looking Party, clean, efficient and belonging to the space age'.[7] Often cited as a pivotal moment in defining a new direction and identity for Labour, Harold Wilson delivered a famous speech in 1963 tying Labour's social democracy to 'the white heat of technological change'. In Wilson's estimation, 'planned, purposive use of scientific progress' provided the

---

[5] Richard Weight, *Patriots: National Identity in Britain, 1940–2000* (London, 2002), p. 360.
[6] Fielding, pp. 72–6; McKie, pp. 3–5.
[7] Fielding, p. 74.

means for reorganizing the British economy and society.[8] He conjured with an image of a future where government intervention in research and development coupled with professional management and planning would place Britain at the cutting edge of production and restore her to a position of world leadership.

Youth, modernism and ambitions for a post-imperial global prestige were neatly entwined in Labour's embrace of the contemporary culture of 'Swinging Britain'. At a time when the 'British invasion' swept the pop music scene and the world reeled from Beatlemania, Britain believed itself to be on the cusp of a creative resurgence that would establish it as the cultural centre of the world. As Richard Weight has commented, post-imperial Britain had reinvented itself in the 1960s as 'a peculiarly creative nation; no longer the workshop of the world, perhaps, but its recording studio and catwalk instead'.[9] Given the apparent positive impact of such cultural activity on patriotic pride and economic vitality, the Wilson government did much to cultivate this image of Britain and to wed it to the national vision of its party. Best epitomized in his controversial decision to award the Beatles with the MBE, this somewhat incongruous association between the avuncular Harold Wilson and the hip icons of pop culture perfectly reflected the youthful and modern image of old Labour's new Britain.

A tempestuous period in general, the 1960s presented Labour with particularly acute challenges in Wales. Like Britain, Wales as a whole was far better off economically in the sixties than it had been within recent memory. Periodic waves of government investment following the Second World War helped introduce diversified industry and service employment. Particularly in the area of Wales' southern coastal strip along the M4 motorway, economic diversification spurred growth in cities like Cardiff and Swansea and brought iron production and prosperity to towns like Port Talbot and Llanelli. Yet, affluence and economic development did not occur smoothly or evenly. The Welsh were painfully aware that Wales was

[8] Victor Keegan, 'Industry and Technology', in McKie, *Decade of Disillusion*, pp. 137–42; Jim Tomlinson, *Economic Policy*, vol. 3 of Fielding and Young, pp. 101–12.
[9] Weight, pp. 394–8.

relatively much poorer than England, the average Welsh income by the end of the 1960s being well below and the rate of unemployment twice as high as that of Britain as a whole. Nowhere was the impact of economic restructuring greater than in the industry which had formed the historical basis of the Welsh economy. In what Kenneth Morgan has called 'the deliberate and consistent rundown of the Welsh coal industry', the National Coal Board in the 1960s pursued an accelerated policy of contraction. The coal industry in Wales shed nearly 40 per cent of its workforce of approximately 100,000, averaging ten pit closures per year.[10] During the course of the decade, the number of coal mines in the Rhondda fell from twelve to one. The Aberfan disaster in 1966 dramatized apparent government insensitivity to the painful disappearance of communities and a way of life that had become closely associated with Welsh identity. Claiming the lives of 114 children and 30 adults, the collapse of the coal tip above the village of Aberfan shocked the world. The British state's National Coal Board was clearly implicated in the tragedy. To make matters worse, the Labour government met the demand to remove the remains of the killer tip with intransigence, forcing the villagers to contribute to the expense through its own private relief fund. The irony and bitterness of the situation was magnified by the fact that it was a Labour government that had provided such a niggardly response to this industrial disaster in a traditional working class community.

This was also a period of sharp contraction and painful transformation for rural Wales. A fragile prosperity for the narrowing few in the agricultural sector came at the price of massive capital investment in mechanization, the virtual extinction of employment in agricultural labour and a spiralling drop in the rural population. Railway lines became unprofitable and were closed, leaving many of those left in the countryside feeling isolated and abandoned. In the late 1950s and 1960s, the sense of rural powerlessness was elevated and confirmed by the demolishment of Welsh rural communities like Capel Celyn in the Tryweryn valley. In order to construct

[10] Kenneth O. Morgan, *Rebirth of a Nation: Wales, 1880–1980* (Oxford: Oxford University Press, 1981), p. 317.

water reservoirs for the growing English cities of Liverpool and Birmingham, a community of about seventy Welsh-speaking farmers and villagers was evicted and relocated by the state. First approved under a Conservative government in 1957, the opening of the dam and the flooding of the Tryweryn valley occurred under Labour auspices in 1965. Frustratingly, this took place against Welsh popular opinion and the universal opposition of the political representatives of Wales.[11] Like the disaster at Aberfan, the destruction of Tryweryn seemed to illustrate the powerlessness of the Welsh nation at the hands of a callous, distant and imperious British government. Thus, despite general affluence, the economic and political trends of the postwar years threatened precisely those areas of industrial and rural society that were most strongly associated with Welsh identity and heritage.

This sense of crisis was particularly acute in relation to the Welsh language.[12] The decade started ominously with news from the 1961 census that those speaking the Welsh language had fallen to 26 per cent of the population, a dramatic decline from its position of relative strength of over 50 per cent at the turn of the century. Moreover, the Welsh language was found to be concentrated in the rural areas of the north and west where unemployment and population decline were most marked. Use of the language was also crucially low among the nation's youth. By the early 1960s, the very survival of the language was clearly in jeopardy. Alarmed by the statistics and agitated by the fact that English was the sole, official language of public life, activists increasingly demanded greater Welsh

---

[11] For the Welsh economy in the 1960s, see John Davies, 'Wales in the Nineteen-sixties', *Llafur*, 4 (1987), pp. 78–82; Morgan, *Rebirth of a Nation*, pp. 307–39. For Tryweryn and Capel Celyn, see Einion Thomas, *Capel Celyn: Deng Mlynedd o Chwalu: 1955–1965* (Abertawe, 1997); Gwyn Erfyl, 'Tryweryn: The Drowning of a Valley', *Planet*, 73 (1989), 49–53.

[12] For the Welsh language and language activism in the 1960s, see Dylan Phillips, 'The History of the Welsh Language Society, 1962–1998', in Geraint H. Jenkins and Mari A. Williams (eds), *'Let's Do Our Best for the Ancient Tongue': The Welsh Language in the Twentieth Century* (Cardiff, 2000), pp. 463–74; John Davies, *History of Wales*, pp. 644–50; Mogan, *Rebirth of a Nation*, pp. 359–62, 382–5.

language provisions in government, education, radio and television. Anxiety over the language crystallized in 1962 in the form of Saunders Lewis's seminal BBC radio address, *Tynged yr Iaith* (The Fate of the Language). Breaking a long public silence, Lewis predicted the extinction of the Welsh language by the end of the century unless the people of Wales rallied to its defence through militant, even revolutionary methods.

Answering Lewis's call to action, Cymdeithas yr Iaith Gymraeg (the Welsh Language Society) was formed in 1963. Founded as an offshoot of Plaid Cymru but soon gathering its own momentum, the society successfully attracted and mobilized the support of Welsh-speaking youth. In contrast to the persuasive tactics of older Welsh-language organizations like Undeb Cymru Fydd or the linguistic youth movement Urdd Gobaith Cymru, Cymdeithas yr Iaith aggressively defended the language through protest and confrontation. Targeting government, courts, broadcasting and academia, this Welsh version of the youthful protest movements of the 1960s set out to disrupt public business unless it afforded equal status to the Welsh language. As the decade progressed, the anger, volume and combativeness of these protests only intensified. In the year of the 1969 Investiture, their campaign would take its most dramatic and controversial form with the defacing and painting out of English language traffic signs all over Wales.

Like the Liberal Party in 1911, the Labour Party plausibly claimed to represent the national voice of Wales in the 1960s. Fighting for social equity and the establishment of an active and progressive relationship between government and society, the Labour Party had come to inherit the hegemonic position in Wales once enjoyed by Welsh Liberals. In the estimation of John Davies, Labour dominance at the local level was such that it took on the appearance of a 'system of one partyism' designed to 'perpetuate the power of dour apparatchniks'.[13] Having taken twenty-eight out of thirty-six Welsh parliamentary seats in the general election of 1964, Wilson's government reached the zenith of Labour's ascendancy in Wales in the general election of 1966 by winning all but four Welsh seats. The more divided nature of England's electorate ensured that,

[13] Davies, 'Wales in the Nineteen-Sixties', p. 84.

like the Edwardian Liberals, the Labour Party would be indebted to the support of the Celtic fringe. This informed Labour's consciousness of the multinational nature of the United Kingdom. Like the Liberals before them, Labour asserted with confidence that it was the political voice of the Welsh nation, the veritable 'Party of Wales'.

Despite pride in this self-proclaimed status, Labour had a rather ambiguous relationship to Welsh national aspirations.[14] Although heated at times, the debate over devolution within the Labour Party ultimately resulted in gradual administrative devolution, the party groping for mechanisms whereby centralized government policy could be shaped for specific Welsh circumstances. After a long series of half measures instituted by both Conservative and Labour governments, Labour's 1964 electoral victory resulted in the establishment of the much-anticipated Secretary of State for Wales replete with his own Welsh Office.[15] According to Wilson, the Secretary of State for Wales was created as a cabinet position in order to 'express the voice of Wales and put pressure on the Government and other Welsh Departments to see that Wales gets a fair crack of the whip'.[16] Further devolution, however, continued to be hotly contested within the party. Devolutionists favoured the establishment of an elected Welsh assembly while centralists

[14] For the Labour Party and Welsh nationalism, see R. Merfyn Jones and Ioan Rhys Jones, 'Labour and the Nation', in Tanner, Williams and Hopkin (eds), *The Labour Party in Wales* (Cardiff, 2000), pp. 241–63; Kenneth O. Morgan, *The Red Dragon and the Red Flag: The Cases of James Griffiths and Aneurin Bevan* (Aberystwyth, 1989); Peter Stead, 'The Labour Party and the Claims of Wales', in John Osmond (ed.), *The National Question Again: Welsh Political Identity in the 1980s* (Llandysul, 1985), pp. 99–123.

[15] Labour first established a special 'Welsh Day' of discussion in Parliament in 1944, then created an appointed advisory Council for Wales and Monmouthshire in 1947. Trumping the Conservative's creation of a Minister for Welsh Affairs in 1951, Labour finally adopted as part of their official 1959 election manifesto the demand for the creation of a Welsh Office administered by a Secretary of State for Wales. The Conservatives won that election and, in answer to Labour's electoral pledge, created in 1960 a Welsh Grand Committee in the House of Commons.

[16] E. Rowlands, 'The Politics of Regional Administration: The Establishment of the Welsh Office', *Public Administration*, 50 (autumn 1972), 339.

opposed the measure, fearing the isolation of Wales, the fragmentation of Labour's electoral power at Westminster, and the ultimate loosening of the bonds of the United Kingdom. In 1966, an aborted attempt by Secretary of State Cledwyn Hughes to include an elected council for Wales as part of local government reform aroused strong opposition within the cabinet and from Labour centralists in Wales. The plan was scuttled, although an inquiry on the constitution known as the Kilbrandon Commission was later appointed to further investigate the matter. Labour thus limited its commitment to devolution in the 1960s within an overall centralist political framework. However, the nature, form and extent of devolution were left unresolved and devolution would remain a topic of political debate within Wales and the Labour Party for decades to come.

The birth of the Welsh Office in the mid-1960s was not an easy one.[17] The Secretary of State was first granted only limited executive responsibility and marginal powers of oversight. The new Welsh Office was regarded with hostility by jealous civil servants in Whitehall and by some influential members of the cabinet, who deemed it 'an idiotic creation . . . all the result of a silly election pledge'.[18] Many in government hoped for the Welsh Office's early demise.[19] At the same time, the newly formed institution was under increasing pressure from the Welsh people to deliver on the promises of its creation. In the context of industrial stagnation, rising unemployment, the continued decline in the Welsh language, controversy over the construction of water reservoirs, and the disaster at Aberfan, the Labour government and its ethos of centralized socialism became increasingly vulnerable to allegations of being distant and imperious, blind or unresponsive to the needs and concerns of Wales. These were the very kind of allegations that the existence of the Welsh Office was designed to refute.

It was under these circumstances that Plaid Cymru came out of the political wilderness, promising specifically Welsh solu-

[17] Russell Martin Deacon, *The Governance of Wales: The Welsh Office and the Policy Process 1964–99* (Cardiff, 2002), pp. 1–25.
[18] Richard Crossman, *The Diaries of a Cabinet Minister: vol. 1, Minister of Housing 1964–1966* (1967), p. 317.
[19] Deacon, p. 24

tions to Welsh problems and pressing for greater forms of Welsh self-government. Under the leadership of Gwynfor Evans, Plaid Cymru refined its ideology, merging nationalist aspirations and the desire to preserve a distinct national culture with the socio-economic needs of a populace increasingly frustrated with the inability of a succession of Labour governments to soften the ravages of industrial decline. Startlingly, a series of by-elections cracked the crust of Labour hegemony in Wales. In 1966, Gwynfor Evans's successful campaign against Labour in Carmarthen gave Plaid Cymru its first Member of Parliament. This was followed by closely-run contests in the former Labour strongholds of Caerphilly and Rhondda-West in 1968. Such a challenge to the hegemonic power of Labour within the very bedrock of its support prompted anxious navel-gazing within the party. 'In the Midlands, the slump in the Labour vote looked like the collapse of a habit', reported the *Guardian*; 'in South Wales it looks like the death of a religion'.[20] At the same time, the civil disobedience campaigns of Cymdeithas yr Iaith were taking a decidedly aggressive and accelerated tone. Moreover, a series of bombings targeting water reservoir pipelines demonstrated that some militants were prepared to go to extreme lengths in pursuit of nationalist objectives. Taken together, these developments represented a serious and worrisome nationalist challenge to Labour's reputation as the 'Party of Wales'.

Evidently, the infant Welsh Office would have to learn to run before it could crawl. During the Labour governments of 1964 to 1970, the terms of the first three Secretaries of State were defined by the daunting task of securing and justifying the existence of the Welsh Office. They were compelled to wrest powers away from a jealous Whitehall, demonstrate the value and effectiveness of the Welsh Office to an often sceptical government, respond to the increasing demands of the Welsh population, and bolster Labour's special claim to the loyalties of the Welsh people.[21] In the process, the Welsh Office would

---

[20] *The Guardian* quoted in Dafydd Gwynn, 'Arwisgiad 1969: Yr Ymateb Gwleidyddol', *Cof Cenedl XV*, p. 163.

[21] Deacon, pp. 1–26; J. B. Jones, 'The Development of Welsh Territorial Institutions: Modernization Theory', *Contemporary Wales*, 2 (1988), 47–61; Ian Thomas, *The Creation of the Welsh Office: Conflicting*

assert itself not only as a means of implementing the central government's policy in Wales but would take its first small steps as a generator of a distinct Welsh policy agenda in its own right.[22]

In recounting the origins of the Welsh Office, primary focus is often given to James Griffiths, the founding Secretary of State (1964–6), but more attention needs to be paid to the development of the Welsh Office under his successors, Cledwyn Hughes and George Thomas. Cledwyn Hughes was Secretary of State from 1966 to 1968. He was a nationally minded, Welsh-speaking north Walian who served as a Labour MP for the northern, semi-rural constituency of Anglesey. As Secretary of State, Cledwyn Hughes set the Welsh Office on a distinctly expansionary course by securing additional powers and areas of responsibility for the fledgling institution.[23] A devoted Labour devolutionist, Hughes was later accused of having 'nationalist aspirations' by his Minister of State and successor, George Thomas.[24] This perception of Hughes as being soft on nationalism no doubt contributed to Wilson's decision to move Hughes from the Welsh Office to the Ministry of Agriculture in 1968 in the wake of Plaid Cymru's by-election success. Clearly signalling a more hard-line approach to nationalism, the prime minister appointed George Thomas as Hughes's successor from 1968 through 1970. A man later described as a 'chirpy South Wales sparrow in Mr Wilson's palm', George Thomas was the opposite of Cledwyn Hughes in nearly every respect.[25] A product of the southern mining valleys, an MP for Cardiff Central and ideologically a Labour

Purposes in Institutional Change (Glasgow, 1981); E. Rowlands, 'The Politics of Regional Administration: The Establishment of the Welsh Office', *Public Administration*, 50 (autumn 1972), 333–51; P. J. Randall, 'Wales in the Structure of Central Government', *Public Administration*, 50 (autumn 1972), 353–69.

[22] Deacon, pp. 1–5.
[23] Emyr Price, *Lord Cledwyn of Penrhos* (Pen-y-groes, 1990), pp. 47–62; Meic Stephens, 'Lord Cledwyn of Penrhos (1916–2001)', *Planet* 146 (2001), 95; Owen Gwilym, 'Un o'r Cymry da', *Barn*, 459 (Ebrill 2001), 40–1.
[24] E. H. Robertson, *George: A Biography of Viscount Tonypandy* (London, 1993), p. 170.
[25] *Manchester Evening News*, 19 November 1974, as quoted in Price, p. 62.

centralist, Thomas was largely unsympathetic to the Welsh-language movement and regarded Welsh nationalist sentiments with great suspicion. Nevertheless, Thomas was proud of his 'Welsh heritage' and his political orientation was firmly fixed on the economic and social problems of Wales. Although a vocal opponent of parliamentary devolution, Thomas largely followed the expansionist development policy of his predecessor and continued to pursue and accumulate additional powers for the Welsh Office.[26] Collectively, this ministerial 'odd couple' was responsible for the institutional security and dynamic growth of the Welsh Office in its critical early years.[27] Significantly, it was this combination of Hughes and Thomas that would construct Labour's most ambitious and visible Welsh project – the 1969 Investiture of the Prince of Wales.

---

[26] E. H. Robertson, *George: A Biography of Viscount Tonypandy* (London, 1993); Hunston Ramon, *Order! Order! : A Biography of the Right Honourable George Thomas* (Basingstoke, 1981); George Thomas, *George Thomas, Mr. Speaker: The Memoirs of Viscount Tonypandy* (London, 1985).

[27] Deacon, pp. 24–5.

9
Reinventing the investiture

It is often supposed that the 1969 Investiture was conceived by the Labour government specifically to thwart the resurgence of nationalism in Wales. However, the idea of holding another grand investiture was not Labour's innovation but was in fact inherited from the previous Conservative government. The earliest appearance of the investiture in people's thinking was in 1952 when Caernarfon Borough Council petitioned the soon to be crowned Queen to invest her son at Caernarfon Castle as in 1911.[1] In 1955, the issue was raised again when Cardiff was at last granted the official title of 'capital city' of Wales by Queen Elizabeth II. Fearing to reopen the 1911 battle of the sites, an arrangement behind the scenes reassured the town of Caernarfon that it would remain the site of a future investiture despite Cardiff's new status.[2] The matter rested there for a few years, until the Conservatives had cause to publicly raise the issue again. Having opposed recommendations for the creation of a Welsh Office and having approved the building of a dam by the Liverpool Corporation to flood the Tryweryn Valley in 1957, the Harold Macmillan government orchestrated the 1958 Festival of Wales as a way of salving bruised Welsh national feeling. Accompanied by a full schedule of Welsh cultural events, the highlight of the festival occurred with the hosting of the Commonwealth Games in the newly recognized Welsh capital.[3] Suggested by Macmillan in a private audience only the month before, the Queen was 'not unattracted to the idea' of using the occasion to publicly announce that her seven-year-old son would be granted the title 'Prince of Wales', a calculated climax to the festival's

[1] *Wrexham Leader*, 11 April 1969.
[2] *Western Mail*, 25 June 1969.
[3] Richard Weight, *Patriots: National Identity in Britain, 1940–2000* (London, 2002), 277–83.

consolation of Welsh national sentiment.⁴ In the opinion of Henry Brooke, Macmillan's Minister for Welsh Affairs, the creation of a new Prince of Wales was bound to be tremendously popular, especially given the fact that the title had been vacant for some twenty-five years. In his estimation, in a nation with precious few historical national institutions, the title could be seen as the royal embodiment and guarantor of national existence. 'To possess a Prince of Wales', opined Brooke 'has a meaning and a value for Welshmen which is easy for us in England to underestimate'.⁵ Consequently, at the closing ceremony of the games in Cardiff Arms Park, Prince Phillip played a tape recorded message from an absent and ailing Queen:

> I want to take the opportunity of speaking to all Welsh people, not only in this arena, but wherever they may be. The British Empire and Commonwealth Games in the capital, together with all the festivities of the Festival of Wales, have made this a memorable year for the principality. I have therefore decided to mark it further by an act which will, I hope, give as much pleasure to all Welshmen as it does to me. I intend to create my son Charles Prince of Wales today. When he is grown up, I will present him to you at Caernarfon.⁶

The announcement was dramatic and unexpected. Even an embarrassed nine-year-old Prince Charles was caught by surprise as he watched the event on television with his school chums.⁷ By all accounts, the response in the stadium was ecstatic, the crowd of 36,000 spontaneously taking up verses of 'God Save the Prince of Wales'. The creation of Charles as Prince of Wales was a royal act of national recognition designed to spark enthusiasm in the present, in the context of the Festival of Wales. It was boosted in its appeal by the promise of an investiture in Caernarfon sometime in the future.⁸

4   Memorandum, Harold MacMillan to T. A. Critchley, Home Office, 6 June 1958, BD 67/2, PRO.
5   Memorandum, Henry Brooke to Harold Macmillan, 16 June 1958, Welsh Office, BD 67/2, PRO.
6   Anthony Holden, *Charles: A Biography* (London, 1998), pp. 48–9.
7   Ibid.; Sarah Bradford, *Elizabeth: A Biography of Her Majesty the Queen* (London, 1996), p. 282.
8   In the years immediately following the Festival of Wales, this message

The question for Labour, then, was what to do with an inherited opportunity. After 1964, the newly created Welsh Office anticipated the promised investiture with apparent relish. The Crown was less eager. Responding to the prompting of the Welsh Office in 1965, the Queen informed Harold Wilson that the ceremony would be put off until Charles had at least completed his education.[9] In the spring of 1966, the Welsh Office reinitiated the discussion with Buckingham Palace on when and in what manner the investiture would take place.[10] As the discussion developed over the ensuing months, Cledwyn Hughes envisioned a preparatory period for Prince Charles prior to the investiture where the prince would receive regular briefings on current affairs in Wales directly from the Welsh Office. More dramatically, he suggested that Prince Charles actually attend a term at a university college in Wales to study 'the history, traditions and problems of Wales'.[11] It was only at the insistent cajoling of Hughes that the Queen, with some misgivings, finally agreed in February 1967 to hold the investiture before the prince's graduation from Cambridge in the summer of 1969.[12] As regards the proposed term at a Welsh university and other suggestions, the Queen's secretary informed the prime minister that the Palace had met

of recognition was reinforced by further acts of royal attention, with visits by the Royal Family to Cardiff, the National Eisteddfod and the Crown's recognition of the 'Red Dragon' banner as the official flag of Wales.

[9] Michael Hall to Harold Wilson, 3 August 1965, Prime Minister's Papers 13/2359, PRO.
[10] G. H. Daniel to Michael Adeane, 1 April 1966, 1.0.I 1969 Investiture, CA.
[11] Secretary of State's brief for meeting with Adeane, 29 November 1966, BD 25/296, PRO; Memorandum, Meeting between the Secretary of State for Wales and Sir Michael Adeane, 29 November 1966, BD 25/296, PRO.
[12] See series of correspondence between G. H. Daniel, Michael Adeane and Cledwyn Hughes, 1 April–26 July 1966, 1.0.I 1969 Investiture, CA; Secretary of State's brief for meeting with Michael Adeane, 29 November 1969, BD 25/269, PRO; Memorandum, Meeting between Cledwyn Hughes and Michael Adeane, 29 November 1969, BD 25/296, PRO; G. H. Daniel to Michael Adeane, 14 December 1966, PREM 13/2359, PRO; Michael Hall to Harold Wilson, 18 December 1966, PREM 13/2359, PRO; Michael Adeane to Cledwyn Hughes, 10 February 1967, PREM 13/2359, PRO.

'Mr Cledwyn Hughes satisfactorily on all points'.[13] The Prince would begin an eight-week intensive course of study at the University College of Wales, Aberystwyth in May 1969. For the time being, however, the plans for the investiture were kept strictly confidential, the date of the ceremony not being publicly announced until May and the Prince's attendance at the University College of Wales kept secret until November 1967.

Nominally, arrangements for the investiture were in the hands of the royal establishment. Since 1483, the Dukes of Norfolk held the position of Earl Marshal in the Royal Household, with hereditary responsibility for organizing royal ceremonial and presiding over the College of Arms, a royally sponsored body of genealogists and antiquarians charged with keeping records of the heraldry, genealogy and ceremony of the British nobility. Having been ignored in the eighteenth and nineteenth centuries, the rights of the Earl Marshal over royal ceremony were reasserted in the early twentieth century by the fifteenth Duke of Norfolk. The Earl Marshal gradually reclaimed his role in royal ceremonial, albeit in a diminished capacity as the chair of a series of ad hoc committees made up largely of government officials.[14] Bernard Marmaduke Fitzalan Howard, the sixteenth Duke of Norfolk, had thus served as apprentice to his father at the funeral of George V and the Coronation of George VI in 1936 and successfully chaired in his own right the organization of George VI's funeral in 1952, Elizabeth II's Coronation in 1953 and the state funeral of Winston Churchill in 1965. At sixty, the badger like Duke was described as 'a simple and uncomplicated man who has spent his lifetime making simple, uncomplicated decisions with a minimum of fuss' and as someone who 'would stand no nonsense from anybody in ensuring the precise and punctual performance of majestic ceremonial'.[15] Once the Crown had set a date for the ceremony with the Welsh Office, it was thus to the Duke that the Queen turned to chair a committee to plan

---

[13] Michael Adeane to Michael Halls, 3 February 1967, PREM 13/2359, PRO.
[14] William Kuhn, *Democratic Royalism: The Transformation of the British Monarchy, 1861–1914* (New York, 1996), pp. 112–39.
[15] *Daily Mirror*, 1 July 1969

the arrangements of the investiture.¹⁶ Norfolk's colleagues at the College of Arms had begun preparing for this summons for quite some time. As early as 1963, the Queen had appointed Welsh antiquarian and genealogist Major Francis Jones as an adjunct to the college with the investiture explicitly in mind.¹⁷

The Royal Family itself took a more active role in the planning of the 1969 Investiture than it had in 1911. Its participation would be profoundly shaped by the marriage of Princess Margaret to Antony Armstrong-Jones in 1960. Up to that time, the love life of Princess Margaret had a tragic and public reputation. In 1955, the Palace's refusal to allow Princess Margaret to marry divorcee Peter Townsend had made the Crown seem aloof, hidebound and out of touch. By traditional standards, Armstrong-Jones would have been considered as inappropriate for a royal marriage as Townsend had been. Armstrong-Jones was a professional photographer, hired by the palace for official portraits. Unlike Margaret's former aristocratic suitor, Armstrong-Jones was technically a mere commoner, engaged in trade. Yet Antony Armstrong-Jones was the quintessential modern man, valued for his professional and creative skill rather than for the station of his birth. The product of an Eton education and at home in aristocratic circles, he was a handsome and charming suitor with an artistic flair and a cultured and professional interest in theatre and design. Amidst a welcome burst of public enthusiasm, the marriage thus provided an opportunity for the monarchy to set the bitter memories of Margaret's forlorn love affair to rest. The Royal Family's genuine acceptance and chummy relationship with Armstrong-Jones helped reconcile the image of the Royal Family with the modern times in which it reigned.¹⁸ As stated in the wedding's official souvenir programme: 'The alliance of an artist with the Royal Family is something new in

---

[16] Michael Adeane to Cledwyn Hughes, 10 February 1967, PREM 13/2359, PRO.
[17] *Western Mail*, 25 June 1969.
[18] Pimlott, 299–300; *The Wedding of Her Royal Highness the Princess Margaret and Mr. Antony Armstrong-Jones, Westminster Abbey 6 May 1960* (London, 1960), pp. 18–19.

its modern history, and an enrichment of its capacity to represent every facet of the life of the Commonwealth.'[19]

Capitalizing on this association, the Royal Family turned to Armstrong-Jones's expertise in design, theatre and the arts when they first began to consider Prince Charles's investiture. Loosely connected to Wales through his father's estate in Caernarfonshire and having been bestowed the suitably Welsh title of Lord Snowdon in 1961, Armstrong-Jones was assured a prominent role in the investiture when the Queen appointed him as the Constable of Caernarfon Castle in 1963. This was, of course, Lloyd's George's title in 1911. Of Snowdon's role in the ceremony, the *Sheffield Star* would later note:

> The Earl of Snowdon ... is beginning to play a major part in the arrangements – acting almost like a deputy to the Earl Marshal, the Duke of Norfolk, who is master of ceremonies. No one is sure that the Constable has the official authority to be quite so involved, but of course, people tell you, the Earl, whose own family roots are not far from here, has such a flair for these things.[20]

From the first, the Palace ensured that the investiture would be associated with a royal whose image was as youthful, hip and creative as that of the 1960s themselves. Personally associated with professional expertise and contemporary style, Lord Snowdon proved to be a good match for the technocratic tenor of Wilson's swinging New Britain.[21]

The active involvement of the Crown would be greatly facilitated by the revolution that occurred within the Palace itself upon the retirement of the Queen's press secretary in 1968. Traditionally regarded as a duty to protect the Royal Family from the prying eyes of the press and public, the role of the Palace press secretary was dramatically reversed under William Hesseltine, an Australian public relations expert. Rather than keeping them at bay, Hesseltine energetically engaged the public and press, actively seeking to promote the

---

[19] *The Wedding of Her Royal Highness the Princess Margaret and Mr. Antony Armstrong-Jones*, p. 19.
[20] *Sheffield Star*, 27 July 1968 as recorded in Press Clipping, BD/67/7, PRO.
[21] Brian Hoey, *Snowdon: Public Figure, Private Man* (Thrupp, 2005).

monarchy through the media. Hesseltine orchestrated coverage that promulgated a less mysterious and more modern, human and open image of the Royal Family.[22] Aided by Prince Phillip and David Checketts, Prince Charles's equerry, the Queen was encouraged to court the world's press by lifting the veil from the mystical monarchy. The investiture would be the first test case of this new relationship between the media and the monarchy. To Hesseltine, it presented a grand opportunity, not only to launch the heir to the throne in his public life but to relaunch and reconstruct the image of the Royal Family itself. He envisioned the period leading up to the investiture in terms of a gradually expanding programme of royal publicity for newspapers, radio and, most importantly, television, a campaign reaching its crescendo with the investiture ceremony itself.[23] Indeed, the oft commented upon blending of celebrity and ordinariness in the media's coverage of the Royal Family actually originated with the Crown's public relations strategy on the investiture. This development has continued to alternately benefit and plague the Royal Family ever since.

Unlike Prince Edward in 1911, Prince Charles would be intimately familiar with the planning of the investiture and would help shape the ceremony. At a restless twenty years of age, the prince was not content to merely play his theatrical part but energetically sought to engage with the substance of the investiture and the issues surrounding it. It is evident that young Prince Charles regarded the ceremony as his first assignment in the role of heir apparent to the throne. He was determined to make a good show of it. The prince was clearly absorbed by what was going on and what was being said around him and he tried to respond in a positive and proactive way. In the year before the ceremony, he showed a genuine interest in Wales and Welsh culture. He insisted on writing his own speeches and, although formulaic in part, his utterances were often thoughtful and sincere efforts to grapple with the issues of the day. On occasion those speeches would go further in their recognition of Welsh national aspirations than the

---

[22] Pimlott, 376–9; Douglas Keay, *Elizabeth II: Portrait of a Monarch* (London, 1991), pp. 217–20.
[23] *Observer*, 29 June 1969.

Welsh Office would have liked, but for the most part Prince Charles helpfully followed the Labour line in regards to the investiture.

The royal establishment was thus clearly active in the investiture project, but its influence on the ceremony was ultimately second to that of the Welsh Office and Labour Party. The central role of the Secretary of State for Wales was evident from the earliest planning. Having already agreed to Hughes' suggestions for the timing of the investiture, the Queen's first instruction to the Earl Marshal was to establish an Investiture Committee composed of himself, the Secretary of State and Lord Snowdon.[24] Noting that 'the Secretary of State will probably have an early opportunity of discussing the investiture with the Queen and the Duke and of advising on a form of ceremony which will readily commend itself to the people of Wales', the Welsh Office produced by the end of March 1967 the first plan outlining the investiture, its related events and the organization of the work involved. It stated that the:

> Welsh Office will be involved in every part of the programme outlined above. Whatever other persons may do in the various parts of the Royal programme and of Welsh celebrations for that year, the Secretary of State is likely to be held responsible for ensuring the success of the programme as a whole. His personal reputation and that of the Welsh Office will therefore be involved. The Permanent Secretary will need to ensure that an adequate team of officers and supporting staff is appointed to look after Welsh Office involvement in this work exclusively.[25]

Armed with this brief, Cledwyn Hughes met with the Duke of Norfolk on 11 April 1967. Hughes suggested to the Duke the appointment of a full-time investiture officer at the Welsh Office and the appointment of a small steering committee that would use the Welsh Office's draft plan as the basis for its deliberations.[26] On 2 May 1967, the first meeting of this steering committee took place.[27] Shortly thereafter, a meeting

---

[24] Michael Adeane to Cledwyn Hughes, 10 February 1967, PREM 13/2359, PRO.
[25] Idris Evans to GH Daniel, 30 March 1967, BD 67/132, PRO.
[26] G. H. Daniel to Diamond, 31 March 1967, BD 67/132, PRO.
[27] First Meeting of Investiture Committee, 2 May 1967, PREM 13/2359, PRO; These minutes were removed and destroyed in 1998 before the

between G. H. Daniel, Permanent Secretary to the Welsh Office, and officers of various other government departments produced further Welsh Office recommendations, outlining a formal committee structure and suggesting appointments.[28] On 17 May 1967, it was announced publicly for the first time that the investiture would be held in the summer of 1969 and that the Earl Marshal, Secretary of State and Lord Snowdon were involved in its planning.[29] This steering committee continued to meet during the summer of 1967, but the Earl Marshal adopted the suggestions of the Welsh Office nearly in their entirety from the first. The basic outline of investiture events, the organization of the work, and the composition of the committees all bore the imprint of the Welsh Office.

After these early but substantive meetings, the official planning infrastructure for the investiture was put in place. In May 1967, civil servant R. H. Jones was appointed to the Welsh Office to take charge of the administrative details from an Investiture Office based in London.[30] On 26 October 1967, a large 'Investiture Committee' was formally charged by the Earl Marshal with planning the ceremony. Chaired by the Duke, its membership read like a 'Who's Who' in Welsh social, political and cultural circles. It included the Secretary of State, Permanent Secretary and Minister for Wales; the Constable of Caernarfon Castle, members of the College of Heralds, the Queen's Private Secretary, Prince Charles's equerry and other members of the royal household; Welsh peers and members of parliament; Welsh mayors, lord lieutenants and clerks of local authorities; representatives of Welsh churches and chapels; representatives from Welsh education; chairs of the Wales Tourist Board, Welsh Sports Council and Welsh Arts Council; commanding officers of the western and London commands; and representatives of the Welsh press. Noted Welsh luminaries included politicians James Griffith and Goronwy Roberts;

> documents were made public. The dates, however, correspond with other documents that would indicate that this was the meeting of the steering committee.

[28] G. H. Daniel to Sir Burke Trend, et. al, Investiture of Prince Charles as the Prince of Wales, 20 April 1967, BD 67/132 PRO.
[29] *Western Mail*, 18 May 1967.
[30] Welsh Office Notice 33/67, BD 67/132, PRO.

INVESTITURE

cultural leaders A. E. Jones (Cynan, the archdruid) and Sir Ifan ab Owen Edwards (president of the Welsh youth organization, Urdd Gobaith Cymru); and Professors Gwyn Jones and Glanmor Williams.[31] A second 'Officials Committee' of civil servants, government and military officers coordinated the 'nuts and bolts' work of the various government departments under the chairmanship of G. H. Daniel, the Permanent Secretary to the Welsh Office.[32]

---

[31] Ibid.; 'Minutes of the First Meeting of the Investiture Committee held in St. James Palace, Thursday 26 October 1967, PREM 13/2359, PRO; The full list of members includes: Duke of Norfolk; Cledwyn Hughes MP; Earl of Snowdon; Lord Cobbold, GCVO; Mrs Eirene White MP; Marquess of Anglesey; Lord Dynevor; Lord Ogmore; Lord Morris TD JP; Lord Morris of Borth-y-Gest CBE MC; Lord Champion; Lord Maelor; Lt Col Sir Michael Adeane GCVO KCB; James Griffiths CH JP MP; Robert Mellish MP; Brigadier Sir Michael Venables-Llewellyn BT MVO; Sir Michael Duff Bt; Sir Anthony Wagner KCVO Dlitt FSA; Commander sir Richard Colville KCVO CB DSC; Lt Gen. Sir Antony Read KCB CBE DSO MC; Sir Ifan ab Owen Edwards JP LID; Col Sir Cennydd Traherene TD LIK: Sir Alick Jeans; Sir Alfred Nicholas CBE; Sir Eric St Johnston CBE; G. H. Daniel, Esq. CB; Vice Admiral IL Hogg CB DSC; Major General BOP Eugster; Rev AE Jones (Cynan); Alderman Hr Thomas; Professor Gwyn Jones; Squadron leader David Checketts; Lt Col W Jones Williams; I Bowen Griffith; Emrys Roberts; Air Vice Marshal AHC Boxer; Dr Coleman; DJ Davies; Ednyfed Hudson Davies MP; Revd WJ Pennar Davies; Alderman E. C. Dolman; Revd E. Gwyndaf Evans; Alderman Sylvia E. Harris; Major Francis Jones; W. G. Morgan MP; Revd Alfred Edwin Morris; Alderman Alwyn Morris; Revd John A Murphy; Goronwy O. Roberts MP; Alderman Philip Square; David W. Thomas; Alderman Tudor E. Watkins; Alderman Clifford Williams; Professor Glanmor Williams.'

[32] Minutes of the Seventh Meeting of the Officials Committee, 12 December 1967, PREM 13/2359, PRO; Members of the Officials Committee included G. H. Daniel (Welsh Office, chair); L. F. Barclay (Board of Trade), Alexander Cairncross (Home Office) and Standish (Cabinet Office); Lt Col R. O. Dennys (College of Arms); Mr A. S. Coombs, Idris Davey, Idris Evans, Hosegood, and H. N. Jerman (Welsh Office); C. F. Fox (Ministry of Public Building and Works); Captain R. G. Lewis Jones RN (Ministry of Defence), Major R. Dixon (HQ Western Command), and Commander J. P. Fisher (HM Royal Yacht Britannia); Lt Col W. Jones Williams (Chief Constable of Gwynedd), J. E. Owen-Jones (Caernarfonshire County Council Clerk), J. O. Smith (Royal Borough of Caernarfon clerk), T. Lloyd Roberts (Caernarfonshire county surveyor) and T. Gwynne Davies (Caernarfon

Despite the establishment of these formidable organizing bodies, the investiture was still largely in the hands of the original steering group of the Earl Marshal, the Constable of Caernarfon Castle and the Secretary of State for Wales. They were ably and actively assisted by the Permanent Secretary to the Welsh Office, G. H. Daniel. Although formally charged with organizing the investiture ceremony and coordinating with other events, the grand Investiture Committee was described in a memo to the prime minister as merely 'a "front" committee which will meet only a few times and will be designed mainly to satisfy Welsh opinion that it is being given an adequate part to play in the preparations'.[33] This was perhaps an overstatement, but substantive parts of the planning had already in fact been established well before these larger official planning committees were put in place. The Welsh Office supervised most of the general administration, planning and publicity for the event while the Earl Marshal, his heralds and Lord Snowdon focused on the narrower matters of protocol, ceremonial detail, historical precedent, staging and decoration of the ceremony.

Following his traditionalist instincts and reinforced by the College of Arms, the Duke of Norfolk had intended for the ceremony to closely imitate that of 1911 but these plans soon began to unravel. When the Earl Marshal publicly announced that the ceremony would largely follow the form of the 1911 Investiture, the *Western Mail* complained: 'The adherence to a pattern over laid with the tones of a different period of British history will be criticized as unimaginative and unsuited to modern times.'[34] The Welsh Office expressed anxiety over the 'basic inconsistency between the 1911 type ceremony and what would be appropriate in 1969' and began to push for 'an almost entirely new concept for 1969'.[35] The Minister of State for Wales, Eirene White, even made the startlingly suggestion

 Borough surveyor); F. Southgate (British Rail); R. H. Jones and R. E. Davies (Investiture Office).
[33] Sir Burke Trend to Michael Hall, 21 June 1967, PREM 13/2359, PRO.
[34] *Western Mail*, 7 July 1968.
[35] J. S. Orme to G. H. Daniel, 23 August 1968, 1.0.I 1969 Investiture, CA; R. H. Jones to G. H. Daniel, 9 April 1968, 1.0.I. 1969 Investiture, CA.

that, rather than the medieval robes worn by the Prince in 1911, Prince Charles should appear at his investiture in a leisure suit.³⁶ Although such a suggestion no doubt made the flesh of the heralds crawl, it attracted considerable support in the Investiture Committees. These sentiments were reinforced by Lord Snowdon who pushed for the ceremony to be in keeping with the age, particularly in the area of design and décor. The press soon picked up on what they reported as a subterranean rift between the 'Trads' and the 'Mods' on the investiture planning committee:

> The traditionalists feel that there are certain rules from the past about dress and ceremonial which have to be obeyed if they are going to be true to the historic occasion. Modernists, less interested in precedent and the past, would like to use the occasion for a display of modern design. The sort of area where secret battle could be joined is over whether the Prince of Wales should wear for his investiture glorious robes redolent of the Middle Ages, or a twentieth century lounge suit.³⁷

Indeed, the Earl Marshal and heralds baulked at attempts to modernize the ceremony. A suitably minimalist and innovative focal point for the ceremony in the eyes of Snowdon, the investiture's simple slate dais was regarded by the Heralds as an expensive boondoggle that squandered limited funds. In their opinion, the money could have been better applied to increasing the traditional splendour of heraldic arms in the castle's decoration.³⁸ A similar conflict broke out over the traditional heraldic devices provided by the College of Arms for use on investiture invitations and the official programme cover. Lord Snowdon threatened publicly to divorce himself from those aspects of the investiture's design if they were not suitably improved.³⁹ The Duke of Norfolk initially attempted to defend the 'traditional and correct' design of heraldic devices against the general desire for 'modern interpretations' of Lord Snowdon's design steering group. He also tried to

[36] *Sunday Times*, 22 September 1968.
[37] *The Times*, 12 November 1968.
[38] Sir Anthony Wagner to Goronwy Daniel, 13 September 1968, 1.0.II. 1969 Investiture, CA.
[39] Somerset to Sir Anthony Wagner, 30 April 1969, 1.0.II. 1969 Investiture, CA.

stand his ground against the Welsh Office's intention to create a contemporary concept for the ceremony. The Duke of Norfolk proclaimed: 'There will be no monkeying about in the name of modernization.'[40] Yet, in the end, it was the Mods who emerged victorious from the fray. While the Duke held the line at maintaining the actual ritual of investing the Prince in its traditional form and successfully insisted on the participation of the military, the nature and composition of everything else associated with the ceremony proved malleable and open to negotiation.

Following the announcement of the investiture in May 1967, speculation was rife over the expense the ceremony would entail. The 1953 Coronation having cost £2 million, the figure of £2½ million was soon being bandied about in the press as the figure for the investiture.[41] Alarmed, Cledwyn Hughes tried to correct this misinformation in a speech on 17 November 1967, claiming that this figure was much too high and that the cost had yet to be established. This did little to curtail speculation or the circulation of the £2½ million figure. In response, Hughes reported to Parliament that he expected the total Exchequer cost 'to be well below ½ million', excluding expenses for road improvements.[42]

The figure of £500,000 did not pacify the anxious Chancellor of the Exchequer, Roy Jenkins. Despite his own Welsh background, Jenkins was singularly unimpressed with the idea of government expenditure on the royal show in Caernarfon. He was also keenly aware of criticism emanating from the left of his party that such extravagance at a time of reductions in public spending was contrary to socialist principles. From the first, the Treasury's discussions with the Welsh Office emphasized the need for expenditure 'to be kept under close scrutiny'.[43] The Treasury found the Officials Committee's original estimate of £230,000 to be 'grossly excessive' and demanded that it be reduced to £125,000. The Investiture Committees agreed to cut back on various items, reduce the numbers of troops, and find ways to increase revenue to offset

[40] *Observer Magazine*, 15 June 1969.
[41] Cledwyn Hughes to G. H. Daniel, November 1967, BD 67/26, PRO.
[42] *Hansard's Parliamentary Debates*, 5th ser., vol. 755 (1967), col. 28.
[43] Note for the Record, W. B. Jones, 24 May 1967, BD 67/132, PRO.

costs through souvenirs, ticket sales and significant financial contributions from the television authorities. The committee baulked, however, at the Treasury's suggestion of eliminating the royal carriage procession or putting the cost for accommodating the throng of spectators on the local rates. Such action, they maintained, would reduce the event to a mere local celebration rather than the dignity and splendour of a ceremony of state. It would also arouse the ire of local ratepayers in north Wales, the exact opposite reaction the investiture was intended to provoke. In the end, the Investiture Committees insisted that expenses could not be reduced beyond £200,000 unless 'there was a drastic reappraisal of the whole event'.[44] In reply, Jenkins told Thomas: 'an elaborate pageant at public expense does not seem to me in keeping with the times, and I am strongly opposed to the idea of spending £200,000 or more on this.'[45] A heated debate ensued. Presenting himself as a man 'anxious to secure the maximum economy', George Thomas in the end took up the side of the Investiture Committees.[46] Threatening to refer the impasse directly to the person of the prime minister during a meeting of the Cabinet, the Welsh Office prepared a brief that claimed the committees had 'sought to reduce the cost to the minimum consistent with the occasion being treated as a state ceremony', that the total was 'low in relation to the cost of previous important state occasions', and that a minimum figure of £200,000 was needed from the Exchequer 'if the investiture is to be suitably organised as a state ceremony in Caernarvon'.[47] Unexpectedly strong-armed by the infant Welsh Office, Jenkins grudgingly agreed to £200,000 as the maximum contribution from the

---

[44] Minutes, Tenth Meeting of the Officials Committee, 24 April 1968, PREM 13/2360, PRO.

[45] G. H. Daniel to J. F. Hewit, 8 May 1968, PREM 13/2360, PRO.

[46] Minutes, Tenth Meeting of the Officials Committee, 24 April 1968, PREM 13/2360, PRO; P. Cousins to G. H. Daniel, 1 April 1968, BD 67/26, PRO; Minutes, Ninth Meeting of the Officials Committee, 20 March 1968, PREM 13/2360, PRO; D. E. J. Dowler to P. Cousins, 7 March 1968, TRES 227/2925, PRO.

[47] G. H. Daniel to Roy Jenkins, 3 May 1968, PREM 13/2360, PRO; GH Daniel to J. F. Hewit, 8 May 1968, PREM 13/2360, PRO.

Exchequer.⁴⁸ Significantly, these funds were to be channelled through the Welsh Office. Fully satisfied, George Thomas became a stalwart defender of the government's spending limit and held the Investiture Committees firmly to it. When the news was released, the press was quick to describe the ceremony as a 'Cut-Price Pageant' appropriate to a period of economic pressure. Questions and criticism regarding the expense of the ceremony, however, would continue to plague the planners.⁴⁹

The Welsh Office was assuming an important role in mediating and directing the relationship between the Labour government and the royal ceremony, a role further revealed in a dispute between the Treasury and the College of Arms. The aristocratic College of Arms, no doubt offended the egalitarian sensibilities of Roy Jenkins and his colleagues at the Treasury, who believed somewhat unfairly that 'it would not be difficult for anyone, armed with a few books on ceremonial and reports of the 1911 Investiture, to give the sort of advice which Garter would be providing at such heavy cost'.⁵⁰ From the earliest discussions with the Welsh Office, the Treasury had advocated very much lower fees for the services of Sir Anthony Wagner, the Garter Herald of Arms, and his colleagues than they felt they were entitled. In demanding that the estimates for the ceremony be slashed, the Treasury singled out the College for particularly heavy cuts, suggesting they reduce their fees from £15,000 to £5,000 and that they be required to justify every item of expense.⁵¹ The fee of the college was reduced to £8,000 in the final budget. This satisfied George Thomas but angered the Earl Marshal and his heralds. 'It is incredible to me', Norfolk spluttered to Thomas, 'that one is cut by virtually

[48] Reference to a letter from Roy Jenkins to Harold Wilson, 29 May 1968 in D. E. J. Dowler to G. B. Diamond, 2 July 1968, PREM 13/2360, PRO; Memorandum, Investiture of the Prince of Wales, George Thomas to Harold Wilson, 4 June 1968. According to the Welsh Office, actual expenditure on the investiture ended up at $131,000 when costs were offset by the sale of seats, programmes and medals. But this did not include the cost of police expenditure or road improvement. See 8 January 1970, HC 102/69/70, BD67/133, PRO.
[49] *Guardian*, 4 April 1968; *Daily Mail*, 7 April 1968.
[50] D. E. J. Dowler to P Cousins, 7 March 1967, TRES 227/2925, PRO.
[51] P. Cousins to G. H. Daniel, 1 April 1968, BD 67/26, PRO.

50% without any explanation. I think you should know that it is probably impossible for the College of Arms to carry out its work under these conditions.'[52] What made matters worse was that the funding was also heavily reduced for decorating the castle, a matter of principal interest not only to the Earl Marshal and College of Arms but to Lord Snowdon, and therefore presumably to the Royal Family itself.

Arousing the ire of the Earl Marshal risked the embarrassment of involving the prime minister or even the Queen in the dispute. Replying to a letter in which Norfolk refused to accept the reduction, Roy Jenkins took a conciliatory but firm tone, explaining: 'this is a time when the most rigorous constraints have been placed on public expenditure.' He rationally justified the cut by stating that 'very strict limits have to be imposed on all sorts of projects, however desirable they may be . . .'[53] It did little to mollify the Duke, who continued to grouse in committee and even to voice his complaints in public and press. Managing the blustery Duke very quickly became the responsibility of the Welsh Office.[54] In February 1969, George Thomas tried to clear the air of the issue in an originally private meeting scheduled between the Duke and the prime minister. Supplying Wilson with a thorough brief and arranging for his own attendance, Thomas suggested that the prime minister should confront the Earl Marshal's 'continued public expression of dissatisfaction', adding that:

> The Earl Marshal is still critical of the limit set, for example for expenditure by the Ministry of Public Buildings and Works and the College of Arms. He again expressed his dissatisfaction in his press and television interviews today. As the Secretary of State indicated, there is no reason so far to think that it will not be possible to do justice to the occasion within the set budget. The Prime Minister may wish to suggest to His Grace that a public disagreement on this matter will not be advantageous to anyone.[55]

[52] Norfolk to George Thomas, 6 June 1968, BD 67/26, PRO.
[53] Norfolk to Roy Jenkins, 28 June 1969, BD 67/26, PRO; Roy Jenkins to Norfolk, 28 June 1968, BD 67/26, PRO.
[54] See the exchange between Norfolk and Thomas in Minutes, Third Meeting of the Investiture Committee, 9 October 1968, PREM 13/2360, PRO.
[55] Brief for the prime minister for his meeting with the Earl Marshal, 17 February 1969, PREM 2901, PRO.

Expressing surprise at Thomas's presence at the meeting, Norfolk cannily failed to take the bait. While referring to the problems experienced by the heralds, he declined to voice any dissatisfaction with the financial constraints.[56] Instead, some weeks later, he dryly informed the prime minister that the organizers would 'overspend slightly', citing an increase of 10 per cent in general and an increase of £1,000 for the College of Arms in particular.[57] Wilson responded by covertly kicking the issue back to the Welsh Office, requesting text that he could include in his reply to the Duke.[58] Citing criticism of the cost of the investiture, the answer from the prime minister was Welsh Office boiler plate:

> I well realise how much you would like to be able to spend more on the Investiture. I am afraid, however, that we are publicly committed to our firm expenditure limits and we must, therefore, do the best we can within the budget.[59]

With the exception of the occasional grumble, the Duke was effectively silenced. The Welsh Office had been given the whip hand.

Although initiated by the previous Conservative government, the Labour Party loomed large in every aspect of planning the investiture. The Earl Marshal, the College of Arms, Lord Snowdon, the new palace press secretary William Hesseltine, and Prince Charles himself all had parts to play in the planning and shaping of this royal ceremony, but their contributions were largely overshadowed by that of Labour's newly created Welsh Office. The Secretary of State for Wales initiated the discussions with the Crown that led to the fixing of a date and the implementation of planning. Establishing the early arrangements for the investiture and supplying detailed briefs outlining the ceremony and its affiliated events, the Welsh Office steered discussions that defined the nature of the event, the process of its creation and its administrative structure. Although under the nominal authority of the Earl

[56] Confidential minutes of meeting with Earl Marshal, 17 February 1969, PREM 2901, PRO.
[57] Norfolk to Prime Minister, 25 April 1969, PREM 2901, PRO.
[58] Roger Dawe to J. King, 16 May 1969, PREM 2901, PRO.
[59] Prime minister to Earl Marshal, 27 May 1969, PREM 2901, PRO.

Marshal, the centre of gravity in the investiture's planning committees was clearly the Secretary of State for Wales and his ministers. The Welsh Office's hold on the planning process was reinforced by notable victories on behalf of the investiture's budget at the level of the Cabinet, and in defence of the government's financial limits from the vocal and public disapproval of the Earl Marshal. While the Duke, the gentlemen of the College of Arms and Lord Snowdon were left to their own devices in determining the proper number of curls in the tail of the dragon, the Welsh Office got down to the serious political work of shaping the public perception of the ceremony and its affiliated events.

10
The investiture and 'The Way Ahead'

A few months after the date of the investiture was announced, Cledwyn Hughes released the 1967 White Paper, *Wales: The Way Ahead*. This pioneering if often neglected document applied the Wilson government's prescriptive passion for planning to the matter of Wales. In its introduction, Hughes wrote: 'This White Paper is, indeed, the first occasion when Her Majesty's Government have brought together all the issues which affect the economic, social and cultural background of Wales.'[1] Foreshadowed by Labour's 1966 Welsh election manifesto, it was nothing less than the first comprehensive and integrated government plan for the future development of Wales. Although it contains some policy initiatives, most of the White Paper is concerned with policies developed at Westminster but adapted by Cledwyn Hughes and his advisors for the particular problems, culture and environment of Wales. Significantly, it also implied the need for the continued expansion of administrative devolution and the accumulation of Welsh Office responsibilities and powers.

The timing of the Welsh Office's involvement in the investiture and the release of *Wales: The Way Ahead* should not be regarded as mere coincidence but as twin manifestations of the same effort – the White Paper spelling out Labour's programme and identity in Wales through government policy, the investiture physically embodying that programme and identity through royal ceremony. The 1969 Investiture was to be far more than a mere afternoon of pageantry. Both Hughes and Thomas envisioned and employed the investiture as a means of demonstrating the value of the Welsh Office, of projecting and even implementing Labour's Welsh policy, and of re-establishing Labour's credentials as the 'Party of Wales'.

[1] *Wales: The Way Ahead* (Cardiff, 1967).

Actively seeking to align themselves with the forces of progress and modernity, the Crown proved a willing accomplice in the creation of this politically useful royal ceremony. Fully aware of the changing times around them and the fragility of their own popularity and position, the Palace recognized that the monarchy was in danger of obsolescence and decline. As the culture of the 1960s became increasingly fixated upon youth, informality and social equality, the middle-aged royal couple and the hierarchy implicit in monarchy became distinctly out of style.[2] While formally eschewing any political partisanship, the Crown was certainly amenable to royal association with the progressive, contemporary and egalitarian tone espoused by Wilson's Labour Party.

The Welsh Office was eager to use the investiture to publicize the economic policies of the Labour government. To heal the economic woes of Wales, the 1967 White Paper prescribed a mixed dosage of diversifying industry, retraining the labour force, easing off the traditional heavy industry of coal while buttressing the newer but troubled heavy industry of steel. Centralized government would aid the economic recovery of defined 'Development Areas', 'Special Development Areas' and 'New Towns' through various incentives to promote new industries and urban development. As proclaimed in *Wales: The Way Ahead*, nearly the whole of Wales was defined as a single 'Development Area' containing no fewer than three projected 'New Towns' and a 'Special Development Area' in the struggling coal field.

Capitalizing on the excitement generated in the countdown to the investiture, the prince was initially brought to the principality in the summer of 1968 to highlight Labour's Welsh economic policies and programmes. In his much-touted first official engagement in public life, Prince Charles accompanied the Duke of Edinburgh and the Welsh Secretary of State on a visit to government retraining and employment centres in Llanelli, Swansea and Cardiff. In these new installations, unemployed Welsh miners and steel workers were taught skills in the use of new technologies and manufacturing techniques. Reporting on the prince's visit and his interest in 'the trainees at

---

[2] Ben Pimlott, *The Queen: A Biography of Elizabeth II* (London, 1996), p. 376; Douglas Keay, *Elizabeth II: Portrait of a Monarch* (London, 1991), pp. 218–19.

work and the crafts they are learning', the *Llanelli Star* observed that: 'While coal is being gradually run down and steel is undergoing a massive revamp, a traumatic change is being shaped in the pattern of South Wales industry. Retraining is the only hope for the present generation of many of those in heavy industry.' The government retraining centre provided graduates who are 'going out into a swiftly changing world having exchanged new skills for old'.[3] The tour ended at the Welsh Office in Cardiff, where the prince and the Duke of Edinburgh passed through noisy demonstrators to join a monthly conference of department heads discussing Labour's plans for road improvement, education and the economy in Wales. The *Western Mail* described the Prince's visit as a 'discreet and informal introduction to the country's grass root problems of employment and administration'.[4] A few weeks later, the prince returned in the company of the Queen and the rest of the Royal Family to open the new Gulf Oil Corporation refinery in Pembrokeshire, a particularly celebrated example of successful foreign investment and diversification of industry in Wales.[5]

Before the end of 1968, the prince returned with the Queen to open yet another new industry in Llantrisant, then being considered for 'New Town' status. The location of the new royal mint in Llantrisant promised to provide a significant number of jobs to the depressed coal town. This highly coveted, large government installation owed its relocation from London to Wales as much to the direct, persistent and well-publicized advocacy of the Secretary of State for Wales in the Cabinet as it did to the Labour government's 'Development Areas'. Pejoratively referred to as the 'hole with the mint', Llantrisant exemplified not only the benefits of Labour's centralized policies for Wales, but the role and value of the Welsh Office itself. The royal visit to Llantrisant thus focused attention in equal measures on both Labour's economic planning for Wales and on the achievement and worth of Labour's Welsh Office.

[3] *Llanelli Star*, 29 June 1968.
[4] *Western Mail*, 29 June 1968.
[5] *Western Mail*, 12 August 1968.

After the investiture ceremony in July 1969, the prince's tour of Wales included reassuring visits to the coal fields and steel works. Instead of coal tips and abandoned pit head wheels, the prince was presented with the 'New Town' of Cwmbran. Aberdare was colourfully described as a 'former coal town which turned to other industries and showed South Wales the secret of survival'.[6] Instead of despondent unemployed miners, Prince Charles was greeted by the jubilant Rhondda in all its bunting-draped splendour. The temptation to compare Prince Charles's progress through the coal field with that of his great uncle in 1936 was too enticing for the media to resist. In the estimation of Trevor Fishlock:

> Today it was the turn of the valleys. The Prince of Wales was in the land of song, socialism and coal, where black ugliness and green beauty are shoulder to shoulder, where many towns are storehouses of hard memories. It is almost 40 years since the last Prince of Wales was here. Then the depression was biting deep and South Wales was paying for its dependence on coal. The Prince's murmured phrase 'Something must be done' was passed from mouth to mouth, a sad echo down the valleys. Today coal is still a vital industry, but South Wales has diversified and so in the main heads for prosperity. The children who were out in their thousands to greet the prince on the third day of his triumphant journey enjoy conditions that the prewar children who waved to the former prince never dreamed of.[7]

The gloom of the interwar past effectively highlighted Labour's 'way forward'. 'The tour of the new Prince', commented *The Times* 'brought him in close contact with a revitalized Wales in which the grime of the pits has given way to a variety of new industries. The valleys are cleaner and people, released from the dread of unemployment, are happy and forward looking.'[8] While the emphasis in the coal field was on diversifying industry, the message in the steel towns was one of encouragement. At the steel works in Ebbw Vale, the works manager was even moved to declare to the prince that the works would 'never, never, never' be closed.[9]

[6] *The Times*, 5 July 1969.
[7] *The Times*, 5 July 1969.
[8] *The Times*, 7 July 1969.
[9] *Western Mail*, 5 July 1969. For the Ebbw Vale works, 'never' took place on 5 July 2001.

Although the heavy industries were featured in investiture-related events, much attention was focused on new, light industry. The 1967 White Paper had argued that promotion of light industry was an effective alternative to the declining old industries and a major means of diversifying and strengthening the Welsh economy. Correspondingly, the Welsh Office highlighted the manufacture within the principality of souvenirs and products specifically associated with the investiture as an example of the 'way forward'. Encouraging county councils to shunt the expected large orders for commemorative investiture mugs to Welsh ceramic manufacturers, the Welsh Office fanned a general discussion in Wales on the benefits of light industry and the souvenir trade. In the opinion of the *Cambrian News*:

> Those seeking new ideas for the setting up of profitable light industries in Wales, particularly in the tourist areas, may find a partial answer to their quest in the scarcity of quality souvenirs of Wales available to holiday makers in the shops. Compared with continental resorts which abound in colourful souvenir shops offering a wide range of choice, and price of articles made in their own country, Wales is very backward. The visitor has to search for such shops and when found the range is often very limited indeed . . . It must also be puzzling to the tourist to find that some of the Welsh souvenirs are marked 'Made in Italy' or Japan or some other country than Wales. There is surely a challenge here to private enterprise in Wales to fill this gap by making the production of good class souvenirs a local industry in each area. There is an assured market, money to be made, tourists to be satisfied and, what is also important, jobs would be provided for local people in their own areas in making the souvenirs. The prospects are there. But has Wales the will and know how to help itself and cash in on the tourist boom?[10]

Decrying the fact that the souvenir trade was largely in the hands of foreign manufacturers, Lyn Howell, secretary of the Wales Tourist Board, declared: 'There is no point in having a souvenir from Wales if it's made in Hong Kong.'[11] In the heady environment cultivated by this discussion, the Caernarfonshire Trades Council asked for government sponsorship of a souvenir factory in Pwllheli to combat seasonal unemployment. A local Caernarfon 'rock' candy manufacturer went so far as to

[10] *Cambrian News*, 11 October 1968.
[11] *Western Mail*, 27 October 1967.

lobby the Secretary of State to copyright the national Welsh costume, harp and dragon for the exclusive use of Welsh manufacturers.[12]

In Wilson's 'New Britain', creativity and technology were to breathe life into industry. In line with the current economic thinking of the government and the chattering classes, much attention was focused on the importance of creative design, quality and the use of new materials and techniques in manufacture. In a speech delivered in Cardiff at the end of his investiture tour, Prince Charles set out Labour's prescription for a revitalized economy through national creativity:

> All over Wales there seems to be a resurgence in the cultural as well as the political side of life. People will want to produce more and more the sort of things that are typically Welsh. But they will never sell very well or be of much value unless they are imaginatively designed and manufactured. It is only too easy to make cheap and short lived articles and souvenirs but I am sure there is already a market for things of longer lasting quality, even though they may be more expensive . . . I cannot help feeling that Cardiff, with its colleges of further education and capital status, can be of immense assistance in training young designers and craftsmen, who in turn can influence standards throughout Wales and so ensure the appearance of imaginative and irresistible products. The same, I do not doubt, can be said for other artistic standards – for instance in music and painting and possibly hand made pottery.[13]

To promote the quality of Welsh manufacturers, the Welsh Office orchestrated prominent 'investiture' displays of Welsh goods in the heart of the London shopping district. It also collaborated with the export magazine *Ambassador* on a special 'investiture' issue focusing on traditional and contemporary Welsh industries and products.[14]

Particular measures were taken to 'maintain a high standard of design' in products related to the ceremony. The Investiture Committee established a souvenirs subcommittee under the chairmanship of Lord Snowdon to provide quality-approved designs free to manufacturers. Snowdon believed that the measure would 'prevent the markets being flooded with cheap

[12] *Western Mail*, 23 October 1967.
[13] *Sunday Telegraph*, 6 July 1969.
[14] U. Staples Smith to Idris Evans, 28 January 1969, BD 67/101, PRO.

and nasty souvenirs'.[15] Innovation and creativity were encouraged and channelled through a design competition for souvenir manufacturers organized by the Welsh Office, the Council of Industrial Design and the Wales Tourist Board. Judged by Lord Snowdon and other design doyens, entries were evaluated in terms of 'imagination in design combined with high standards of workmanship in relation to cost, interesting uses of materials and techniques and an appropriate awareness of the historical significance of the occasion'.[16] Of the 450 designs submitted, 144 were awarded with a certificate of approval, public exhibition, and status as an official investiture souvenir to be sold at the ceremony by the Ministry of Public Buildings and Works.[17]

Even when not wholly of native Welsh origin, the production of investiture artefacts and products could be used by branches of the central government to instruct and inspire industrialists and entrepreneurs in the use of new materials, modern manufacturing processes and contemporary design. The much-celebrated investiture chairs in use in the stands inside and around the castle during the ceremony were constructed to be purchased, folded up and taken away as souvenirs by spectators and invited guests. An exemplar of contemporary design, the scarlet seat emblazoned with a modern stylization of the Prince of Wales feathers was designed by the Ministry of Public Building and Works and manufactured by a Remploy firm in Wales.[18]

Under the personal attention of Lord Snowdon, the design ethos heavily penetrated the ceremony itself. As the leader of a 'design steering group' charged with the general decoration of the ceremony's castle setting, Snowdon hand-picked top designers to produce contemporary decorative treatments of castle gates, walls and towers as well as the various heraldic and traditional emblems to be displayed.[19] When the budget

[15] *Western Mail*, 31 December 1968.
[16] The Investiture 1969 Souvenirs Competition, 1.0.IX 1969 Investiture, CA.
[17] *The Times*, 2 January 1968.
[18] Investiture chair order form, BD 67/77, PRO.
[19] Note of a meeting to discuss the preparation of Caernarfon Castle for the Investiture of the Prince of Wales, 2 February 1968, 1.0.VII 1969

reduction mandated décor on a more modest scale, Lord Snowdon dictated that the design would be marked by 'stark realism', that the emphasis would be on 'dignity and simplicity' but that the scheme would be 'extremely impressive and extremely modern' and the setting one 'that reflects the style of 1969'.[20] Rejecting the red carpet and gilding of 1911, Snowdon envisioned the ceremony in terms of contemporary interest in 'theatre in the round'. Surrounded by the largely unadorned grey walls of the castle and the greensward of the courtyard, the dramatic action of the investiture took place on a circular dais made of black Welsh slate, outfitted with matching slate thrones of stark, contemporary style. This stage was surmounted by an enormous, transparent and aerodynamic perspex canopy, etched with the ostrich feathers of the Prince of Wales. A gift from Imperial Chemical Industries and constructed and wind-tunnel tested by the British Aircraft Corporation, the much commented-upon canopy was the largest structure of the time to be entirely composed of cemented acrylic. Its construction attracted the attention of newspapers and trade magazines alike.[21] The gold coronet placed upon the prince's head during the ceremony was equally inventive and modern. It was manufactured according to a new technique of gold electroforming, developed specifically for it but with future industrial applications in mind.[22] The design elements in the decoration of the castle and investiture regalia were a significant focus of commentary in television coverage of the event.[23] The investiture ceremony thus served as an object

---

Investiture, CA; Designer Desmond Healey produced the first sketches for the castle decoration but later withdrew from the project because of other commitments. Designer Carl Toms was then appointed to carry out the work, incorporating some of Healey's original designs.

[20] *Western Mail*, 17 May 1968, 1 April 1969.
[21] Memorandum, Office of Public Building and Works, no date, BD 67/51, PRO; *Plastics and Rubber Weekly*, 4 July 1969; *Western Mail*, 1 April 1969.
[22] Interestingly, the process produced a crack in the original crown and a duplicate had to be constructed at great expense; *Daily Express*, 27 June 1969; *The Times*, 25 June 1969; Press Release, 28 February 1969, BD 67/75, PRO.
[23] Suggested coverage of Investiture on BBC 1, BD 67/12, PRO.

lesson to industry on the value of taste in design and innovation in manufacturing.

Perhaps the most startling application of contemporary design in the ceremony was the figure of Lord Snowdon himself. As Constable of Caernarfon Castle, Snowdon took the part once played by David Lloyd George, being personally charged with ceremonially presenting the keys and unlocking the castle to allow the entrance of the monarch. Knowing his prominent role in the ceremony, Snowdon prepared himself to be a suitable object of attention with an outfit of his own design. Discarding the fancy court dress uniform worn by Lloyd George on the last occasion, Snowdon appeared in an outfit 'so self effacing it shrieked for attention', a 'figure hugging, zip up tunic in hunting green barathea, with tails and a black silk sash' complete with Nehru collar.[24] 'Great, cool, sweet, adventurous, very clever, were some of the accolades bestowed by the fastidious high priests of mod male fashion on the bottle green high-necked tail-coat that Lord Snowdon designed for himself' declared the *Sun*.[25] Staking his claim from the earliest days of planning, Snowdon was closely associated with every aspect of design in the ceremony. In his stylish Nehru tunic, however, Snowdon literally came to embody the investiture's ethos of design and modernity.

The investiture publicized and instructed the public on Labour's economic programme, but the Welsh Office was determined that the ceremony should bring direct and tangible benefits for Wales as well. The Welsh Office was eager for the investiture to help jump start the expansive and much needed road improvement programme detailed in *Wales: The Way Ahead*. The Secretary of State made the poor and inadequate infrastructure in Wales a major subject of discussion in early communications with the Queen and the Duke of Norfolk, prompting a series of letters from the Earl Marshal to the prime minister suggesting that several projects in Wales be allowed to jump the queue in Britain's scheduled road work in anticipation of the ceremony.[26] Towns and villages across Wales were

[24] *Daily Mail*, 2 July 1969.
[25] *Sun*, 3 July 1969.
[26] Memo, Meeting between the Secretary of State for Wales and Sir Michael Adeane, 29 November 1966, BD 25/296, PRO. See series of

encouraged to spruce themselves up, especially around Caernarfon, where an organized campaign, supported by the National Trust, produced a glossy brochure laying out a street improvement scheme detailing voluntary services, free materials and even a palate of 'Carnarvon Colours' for repainting. In a bilingual foreword designed to mobilize an anxious army of tidy Welsh mams, Lord Snowdon reminded residents that millions 'will be allowed through television to scan your streets, to see your shop, to pause for a moment before your house'.[27] Another tangible benefit for the principality came in the form of the Ministry of Public Building and Works shepherding to Welsh firms the lion's share of the nearly £160,000 of construction work related to the ceremony.[28] In the opinion of the *Holyhead & Anglesey Mail*: 'The crash programme of improving roads, lights and the general appearances of the town itself creates employment and should lead to lasting benefits.'[29]

The Welsh Office felt the most significant and widespread benefit of the investiture would be in the area of tourism. A central part of the economic strategy outlined in *Wales: The Way Ahead* concerned the development of tourism. Although domestic tourism of the 'sea side and mountain' variety had long been established in Wales, the prominence of the tourist trade as a major plank in economic policy was something new and remarkable. The international tourist trade was really a fresh phenomenon at this time, born of low jet fares and affluent 'ugly Americans' abroad. For the Labour Party in Wales, this potential 'tourist boom' offered a near panacea for many of the nation's economic woes and the investiture was seen as the one, great opportunity for Wales to develop this trade.

The development of tourism seemed particularly promising in the regeneration of a rural economy suffering from declining agricultural employment. Attracted by the natural beauty of

    correspondence between Norfolk and Harold Wilson, July 1967, PREM 13/2359, PRO.
[27] *Guardian*, 28 October 1968.
[28] Clipping, House of Commons, 4 February 1969, BD67/16, PRO; House of Commons, 8 January 1970, 102/69/70, BD 67/133, PRO.
[29] *Holyhead & Anglesey Mail*, 5 July 1969.

the Welsh hills and valleys, tourists could increase the flow of money to the countryside, providing jobs through the hospitality business and markets for rural crafts and products. Eirene White, the Welsh Office's Minister of State, placed Labour's rural economic programme firmly in the context of the investiture and tourism:

> During this Investiture year the spotlight will be truly on Wales – and not just the Wales of the industrial valleys or the picturesque castles, but the Wales of the small villages and rural workshops . . . The fostering of rural industry, the encouragement of tourism, allied to the legislation embodied in the Countryside Act, the slow but steady investment in light industry in Mid Wales especially are all helping to arrest the drain and to provide alternative outlets for those who under improved techniques in agriculture are no longer needed to work on the land. The natural beauty and traditions of rural Wales are more than a precious heritage. They are also an asset which with proper management can strengthen and enrich the whole of our economy.[30]

Designed to protect the natural beauty and improve the public's access and enjoyment of the countryside, the 1968 Countryside Act was an important part of Labour's economic strategy for rural Britain. By protecting its natural assets, the countryside would enhance its value as a tourist and recreational resource. Under Welsh Office pressure, the Countryside Commission established to carry out the Act devolved its powers in Wales to the Welsh Committee for the Countryside under the auspices of the Secretary of State. To publicize the potential benefits of this Act to Wales, Prince Charles was named the honorary chairperson and presided over the first meeting of this committee at the Welsh Office as part of the general run-up to the investiture ceremony. Opening the meeting, Prince Charles spoke of conserving the Welsh countryside and developing rural life and economic resources.[31]

Rather than a convenient by-product, the development of tourism was a major feature of the investiture from its inception. In the earliest of Cledwyn Hughes's correspondence with Buckingham Palace, the Welsh Office was in close consultation with the Wales Tourist Board. Indeed, it appears that the needs

---

[30] *Western Mail*, 16 January 1969.
[31] *Western Mail*, 11 December 1969.

of the Wales Tourist Board were a major motive for the Welsh Office's pressuring of the Palace to provide a date.[32] In a memo drafted as early as October 1966, the Welsh Office declared that the investiture should be employed to 'build up the largest possible number of visitors to Wales for the occasion, many of them from overseas', 'to strengthen the resources of the tourist industry in Wales', and to provide better facilities for staff training and the expansion, modernization and construction of guest accommodations.[33] So closely was the ceremony associated with the development of tourism in Wales that the Wales Tourist Board itself expressed concerns that investiture planners avoid the impression that the investiture was merely a tourism campaign:

> In embarking upon this undertaking, care must however be taken to ensure that the Investiture itself is not presented as a tourist attraction. It would be prostituting the historical and national significance of the event if too great an emphasis were placed upon its tourist potential and clearly any tendency in this direction might well find disfavour in the highest quarters. The approach should rather be that, since Wales is to be honoured in this unique way, the least Wales can do in appreciation of the honour is to present herself to the world as it were 'in her best clothes'.[34]

Taking their cue from a similar calendar of events established for the 1958 Festival of Wales, the Welsh Office envisioned a full year of activities and events all across the principality to entice and welcome the visitor.[35] The Wales Tourist Board (WTB) was quick to respond to the suggestion that it should lead the effort to encourage and coordinate the holding of this collection of special events. The WTB called for a grand, national conference under the chairmanship of the Secretary of State to launch the project and invited all the local authorities,

---

[32] See correspondence between G. H. Daniel, Michael Adeane, Cledwyn Hughes and DJ Davies, 1 April to 29 November 1966, 1.0.I 1969 Investiture, CA.
[33] T. S. Orme to GH Daniel, 10 October 1966, 1.0.I 1969 Investiture, CA.
[34] Memorandum for consideration by the Steering Committee at its meeting at Llandrindod Wells on 20 September 1967, Wales Tourist Board, PREM 13/2359, PRO.
[35] Idris Evans to G. H. Daniel, 30 March 1967, BD 67/132, PRO.

cultural and civic organizations in Wales to attend. This broad gathering inspired Cymdeithas yr Iaith to cynically quip:

> Leaders of every colour and form, fat and thin, long and short, urban and rural, an incredible mixture of committee men, historians, furniture makers, foresters, haulers, cadets, fusiliers, scouts, organists, boys in the band, motorists, cricketers and footballers, actors, ambulance and the BBC; representatives of the Hotels Committee, Rivers Authority, the British Freemasons Inner Wheel, Salvation Army, Male Voice Choirs, Motoring Club and Electrical Society for Women . . . there is one thing in this old world that is enough to bring these birds of every colour together – Croeso 69 and the 'divestiture' in Caernarfon.[36]

'The whole object of the scheme', explained the WTB, 'is to display Wales as attractively as possible to the thousands of visitors who will be coming to the Principality for the Investiture and during the Investiture summer and to arrange as varied and interesting a programme of activities as can be devised for their entertainment'.[37] A national committee, largely under the auspices of the WTB, would establish the national programme of events while a host of regional conferences would carry the scheme across Wales to independent organizers and patrons of events at the local level. Collectively, the events would be coordinated and publicized under the banner of 'Croeso 69' (Welcome 69). At the national 'Croeso' conference held on 17 November 1967, WTB chairman D. J. Davies proclaimed to the delegates: 'this enterprise will stand or fall by local interest and effort. You must be determined to carry the spirit of enthusiasm into your towns and counties.'[38] Publicly unveiled in Cardiff with the release of hundreds of doves, a parade of thirty floats and the Treorchy Male Voice Choir's rendition of 'God Bless the Prince of Wales', the final 'Croeso' programme contained over 1,000 exhibitions, singing festivals, carnivals, plays, pageants, rallies, sports meetings and other events.[39]

[36] *Tafod y Ddraig*, February 1968.
[37] Memorandum for consideration by the Steering Committee at its meeting at Llandrindod Wells on 20 September 1967, Wales Tourist Board, PREM 13/2359, PRO.
[38] *Western Mail*, 18 November 1967.
[39] *Western Mail*, 26 May 1967.

The Welsh Office in league with the Wales Tourist Board, the British Travel Association and the Central Office of Information orchestrated a massive international publicity campaign for Croeso 69. The British Travel Association reported: 'all our publicity has been directed not towards publicizing the Investiture as a single event, in isolation, but towards using the ceremony as a means of drawing attention to the tourist attractions of Wales in general, and to the special programme of attractions for next summer gathered together under the title Croeso 69 in particular.'[40] Tours were organized for visiting journalists, a slew of press releases on various aspects of Wales and Welsh life were prepared for the consumption of the foreign press, radio programmes and promotional films were produced and distributed widely across North America and Australia, and advertisements touting Wales were taken out in leading American magazines. The Wales Tourist Board produced over 50 tons of tourist literature and doubled the usual run of their accommodation guide while the British Tourist Association printed 200,000 copies of a 36-page colour booklet on Wales for free distribution overseas. Expensive models of Caernarfon Castle, the 1911 investiture robes and the prince's shiny new coronet were employed in a blitz on the American airwaves.[41] A comely young 'Croeso' Hostess journeyed 10,000 miles across North America in the company of the Wales Tourist Board chairman for a series of television appearances, radio interviews, travel agent receptions and meetings with Welsh ethnic societies. In the climax of her tour, she even appeared on the widely watched Johnny Carson television programme dressed in tall hat and shawl to emphasize the romance of the investiture and the wonders of Wales. The efforts to secure overseas interest resulted in the holding of the Welsh National Gymanfa Ganu in Cardiff in honour of the investiture celebration, the first time this large gathering of Welsh Americans and Canadians was held outside of North America since its inception in 1929. The Wales Tourist Board estimated that the cymanfa alone would bring in

[40] Report on Publicity, December 1968, BD 67/73, PRO.
[41] Report on Publicity, December 1968, BD 67/73, PRO; *Liverpool Daily Post*, 15 January 1969; *Evening Post*, 14 January 1969.

THE INVESTITURE AND 'THE WAY AHEAD'

$250,000.[42] Another notable achievement of these efforts was the 18-page, full colour feature on Wales in *National Geographic*, an American magazine whose advertising rates of £27,000 per page was duly noted by one member of Parliament.[43]

By far, the greatest exposure for the principality would be through the television coverage of the investiture itself. As a professional photographer, Lord Snowdon was preoccupied with designing the investiture as a television spectacular from the beginning. The transparency of the perspex canopy and the open 'theatre in the round' design of the dais were formulated with unobstructed views for the television cameras in mind.[44] Generally a stickler for adhering to the traditional form of the ceremony and an opponent of televising the coronation in 1953, the Duke of Norfolk was convinced of the need to make modifications to accommodate television in 1969.[45] While plans were made to feed television coverage to large 'repeater' screens for the spectators assembled in stands outside the castle, the number of spectators within the castle walls was sharply reduced from 1911's 9,000 guests to 4,000, so as not to obscure the romance of the battlements or mar the grandeur of the visual spectacle with crowded spaces.[46] Lord Snowdon expressed concerns that microphones be carefully hidden around the Watergate and dais so that the drama of the Queen's entrance and the investiture ceremony could be captured without the use of unsightly microphone stands.[47] Even the turf within the castle was painstakingly re-laid with an exactly uniform hue of green for the benefit of colour television.[48] A special television compound to house vehicles and equipment was constructed and 'suitably camouflaged' against

---

[42] *Evening Post*, 14 January 1969.
[43] House of Commons, no 102/69/70, 8 January 1969, BD 67/133, PRO.
[44] Minutes, Third Meeting of the Investiture Committee, 9 October 1968, PREM 13/2360, PRO; *Evening Standard*, 1 July 1969.
[45] Minutes, Fourth Meeting of the Investiture Committee, 17 February 1969, PREM 2901, PRO.
[46] Minutes, Second Meeting of the Investiture Committee, 15 May 1968, PREM 13/2360, PRO.
[47] Office for the Investiture of the Prince of Wales to Idris Evans, 28 May 1968, BD 67/19, PRO.
[48] *Evening Standard*, 1 July 1969.

the southern castle wall near the Slate Quay.[49] Nearly forty television and film cameras were strategically fixed within the castle walls alone, prompting the *Daily Mail* to jest of a siege of the medieval fortress where: 'Ye Olde ITV have stormed the Postern Gate; the BBC have taken up attacking positions over the southwest wall, and the proud men of Harlech ... are strategically over the Queen's Tower.'[50]

Nearly six hours in length, the ceremony was broadcast in its entirety by BBC 1 in colour, by BBC 2 and ITV in black and white, and by the BBC on radio. In what was reported as the 'longest, most involved and probably most expensive colour TV transmission ever made', BBC coverage was broadcast live via satellite to the United States, Canada, Mexico, Australia, Europe and Japan.[51] Notably, all the major American broadcasters televised the event. In addition, the Pathe and Movietone newsreel firms and three documentary companies recorded the ceremony, a film called *A Prince for Wales* was released for theatrical showings in cinemas in Britain and the Commonwealth, a commercial LP recording of the ceremony was cut, thirty-six press photographers covered the event and 200 seats were provided to journalists from Britain, the Commonwealth, Europe and America.[52] Reportedly the largest television audience for any programme to that date, the ceremony attracted some 500 million viewers worldwide, some 19 million within the United Kingdom itself.[53]

Despite their own words of caution against giving the impression that the investiture was merely a tourism campaign, the Welsh Office and Wales Tourist Board constantly and loudly assured the public that the unprecedented international publicity given to the principality would result in copious financial returns in the form of tourist dollars and foreign investment. Cledwyn Hughes asserted that 'the Investiture would arouse tremendous interest for the tourist trade in

[49] Report of Subcommittee on Preparation of Castle, 9 October 1968, PREM 13/2360, PRO.
[50] *Daily Mirror*, 2 July 1969.
[51] *Sun*, 2 July 1969.
[52] Coverage of the Investiture, BD 67/18 PRO; *The Times*, 5 July 1969.
[53] Report by the Director of Information for the Investiture 25 June 1969, BD 67/127, PRO; *Daily Telegraph*, 5 July 1969.

Wales', while George Thomas later predicted that the ceremony would result in £30 million in 'invisible' benefits.[54] Thomas explained:

> Never before has interest in our country been so great . . . This is the right time to be telling the world what Wales has to offer and of its growing importance industrially and economically. Many small nations would give their ears to have a prince, and would only be too happy to cash in on an investiture. Wales is a country recovering from the economic shocks caused by over reliance on one or two basic industries and now broadening its skills and extending its influence over the whole range of modern industry. Wales needs friends abroad . . . The Investiture is advertising with a capital A, the kind that creates wealth; its pomp and ceremony is the attractive packaging we need to boost Wales. The more we put into it, the better results we will get.[55]

These sentiments were frequently repeated in the press, the *Western Mail* proclaiming that: 'The occasion gave Wales a splendid opportunity to project itself to the world' and the *South Wales Echo* declaring that the exposure 'could mean a great deal in terms of income, expansion and work.'[56] The *Liverpool Daily Post* projected that north Wales alone would realize £5 to £10 million from tourism in 1969 while the *Guardian* reported the sentiment that the investiture was 'the elevator to a new plateau of prosperity'.[57] Recognition of the public relations potential of the investiture even entered the ceremony itself, the *Loyalty Address of the Welsh People* triumphantly proclaiming that the investiture would 'enhance its image in the eyes of the world'.[58]

The idea of the investiture as a financial venture was a prominent theme in answering critics of its expense. Cledwyn Hughes characterized the investiture as 'a very good investment for the people of Wales' and George Thomas claimed that the Welsh people would 'see a thousandfold return on the

---

[54] House of Commons No 41/68/69, 28 November 1968, BD 67/132, PRO; *Western Mail*, 14 February 1969.
[55] *Western Mail*, 27 October 1968.
[56] *Western Mail*, 4 July 1968; *South Wales Echo*, 18 December 1968.
[57] *Liverpool Daily Post*, 12 October 1968; *Guardian*, 28 October 1968.
[58] *Western Mail*, 2 July 1969.

money to be spent on the investiture'.[59] No doubt, the volume of such pronouncements was partially in response to criticism of the public expense of the investiture. 'This project is not going to be a burden on the economy of Wales, but a boost to the Welsh economy if properly organized', argued the Secretary of the WTB: 'The dividends that can be reaped on this will more than repay any capital outlay involved.'[60] Claiming that 'the investiture must be used in the fullest possible way to strengthen the momentum of the progress of tourism in Wales', another member of the Wales Tourist Board tried to put the cost of the investiture in perspective, pointing out that the £200,000 budgeted for the ceremony was less than 1/24 of what was spent on tourism each year in Ireland.[61] No wonder that in response to the question 'Is the investiture a solemn and historic State ritual, symbolizing the loyalty of Wales to the crown and its special relation to it as a Principality, or is it a super publicity enterprise for Wales?', the *South Wales Evening Post* answered: 'Well, of course, it's both.'[62]

However, the investiture did more than just project Wales abroad and develop the principality's tourism potential. The ceremony's connection to tourism concretely led to the development of greater administrative devolution and the further use of Wales as a single administrative unit by government. When the date of the investiture was announced in 1967, tourism fell outside of the Welsh Office's remit and the WTB was strictly a voluntary organization funded by donations from local authorities. Merely supplementing the work of the British Travel Authority (BTA), the WTB was concerned almost entirely with specialized publicity and had no role in tourism policy or development. Surviving on a meagre budget and having run up a deficit of £14,228 by 1966, the WTB was not fully recognized by Westminster as an official body and its small government grant was routed through the official BTA.[63]

[59] *Liverpool Daily Post*, 28 December 1968.
[60] *Western Mail*, 18 January 1968.
[61] *Liverpool Daily Post*, 21 January 1969.
[62] *South Wales Evening Post*, 8 January 1968.
[63] *South Wales Argus*, 14 November 1968; *Welsh Nationalist*, 4 July 1967; Lyn Howell, *The Wales Tourist Board: The Early Years* (Cardiff, 1988).

In this J. M. Staniforth cartoon, Dame Wales anticipates the 1911 Investiture and the competition with Ireland for the warmest royal welcome. By permission of Llyfrgell Genedlaethol Cymru/The National Library of Wales.

Tegwyn Jones's 1969 cartoon ridicules Welsh servility and echoes the verse of Gerallt Lloyd Owen: 'Weep, weep, Llywelyn . . .' By permission of Tegwyn Jones and Llyfrgell Genedlaethol Cymru/The National Library of Wales.

David Lloyd George stands sentry as Constable of Caernarfon Castle during the 1911 Investiture. By permission of Llyfrgell Genedlaethol Cymru/The National Library of Wales.

Dressed in his self-designed tunic, Lord Snowdon makes a stylish appearance as Constable before the 1969 Investiture. Courtesy of Popperfoto.

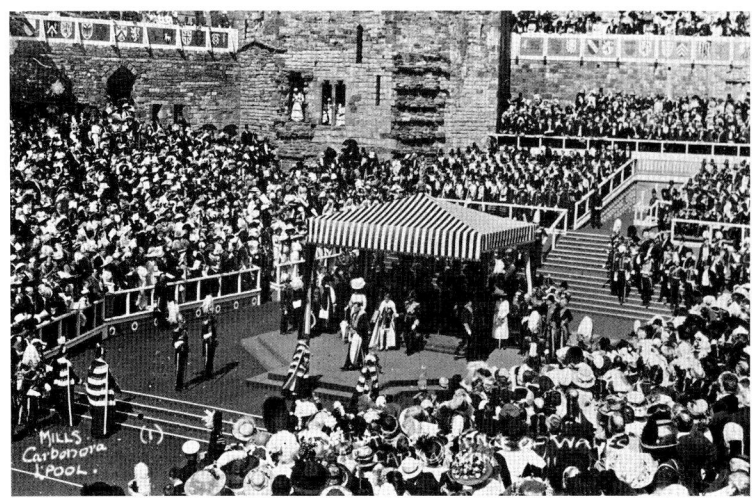

The 1911 ceremony plays to a packed house beneath a Tudor-style canopy surmounted by the gilded image of St David. By permission of Llyfrgell Genedlaethol Cymru/The National Library of Wales.

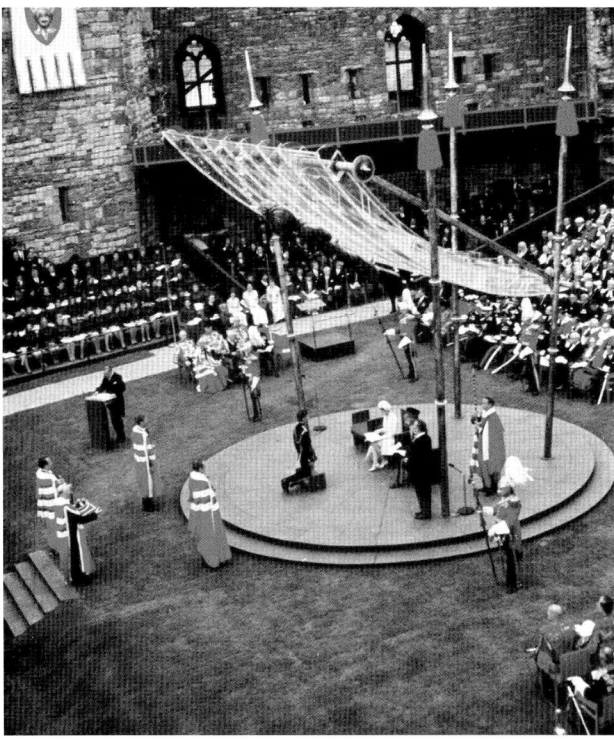

A sleeker stage 'in the round' for the 1969 ceremony features a perspex canopy, minimalist thrones, slate dais and a less cluttered seating arrangement for the benefit of television cameras. Courtesy of Empics.

As the crowd sings 'Hen Wlad fy Nhadau', Prince Edward is presented by George V to the people of Wales from the Queen's Gate. By permission of Llyfrgell Genedlaethol Cymru/The National Library of Wales.

After being invested by the Queen, Prince Charles kneels in homage and vows to 'bear unto you to live and die against all manner of folks'. Courtesy of Empics.

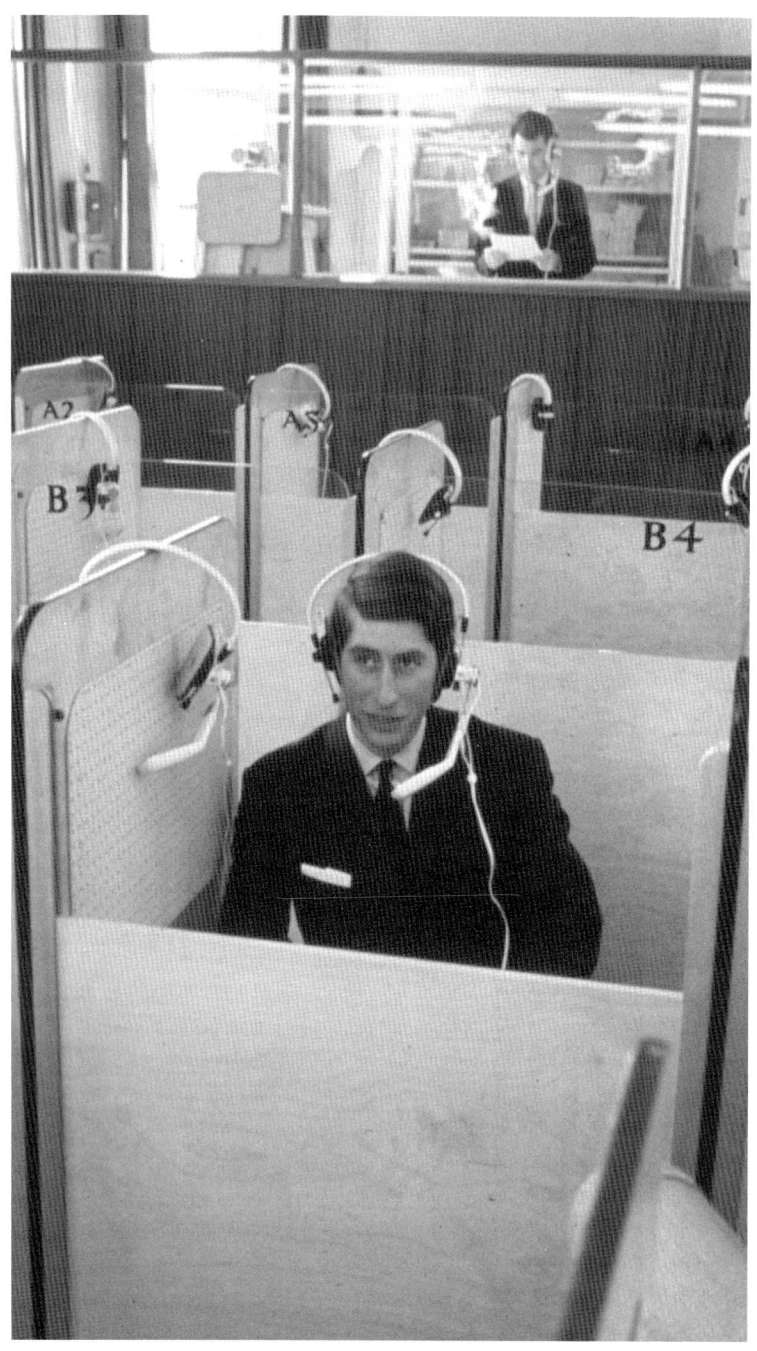
Prince Charles practises his Welsh as a student at the University College of Wales, Aberystwyth. Courtesy of Empics.

Groomed and dressed in suitable attire, the youth of Wales wait outside the castle for their cue to march with the prince. By permission of Llyfrgell Genedlaethol Cymru/The National Library of Wales.

Bearing the slogans 'Brad 1282' and 'Carlo', the youth of Wales march in protest against the investiture in Caernarfon earlier that spring. By permission of Llyfrgell Genedlaethol Cymru/The National Library of Wales.

Members of the Free Wales Army relax during a training camp. In the centre, Denis Coslett and Julian Cayo-Evans pose with uniform and weapons. By permission of Llyfrgell Genedlaethol Cymru/The National Library of Wales.

'Riding when bomb went off during royal salute.' Found amongst the papers of George Thomas, this notation was attached to this photograph of Prince Charles, the Secretary of State and the prince's equerry travelling in procession towards Caernarfon Castle. Courtesy of Empics.

THE INVESTITURE AND 'THE WAY AHEAD'

The Welsh Office seized the opportunity of the investiture to reorganize, invigorate and devolve the organization of the tourist industry in Wales. As early as 1966, it was using the impending ceremony to air schemes for strengthening the WTB organizationally and financially, decouple it from the BTA and house tourism directly under the responsibilities of the Secretary of State for Wales.[64] In 1968, the government grant to the WTB was substantially increased from £8,000 to £24,000, while the Welsh Office directly gave the WTB an additional £40,000 specifically for the investiture.[65] The WTB assumed the primary duties of organizing and promoting tourism in Wales during the 'Croeso' year, leaving the BTA a marginal supporting role. In March 1969, the WTB published a comprehensive survey on Welsh tourism advocating that it be given statutory authority in the development of tourism policy and development. The Welsh press agreed, claiming:

> It is inevitable that tourism will, in the future, have to be coordinated to a much greater extent than in the past. Old patterns of advertising used by individual towns will have to be replaced by the projection of Wales as a whole. The Wales Tourist Board as a statutory authority will be in a better position than ever before to achieve this . . . The survey should cause every local authority in Wales to reconsider the level of help it now offers the board. The Welsh Office, too, must give the board substantial financial backing.[66]

By the end of 1969, responsibility for tourism had shifted to the Welsh Office and through the 1969 Tourism Act the WTB became a statutory body, independent of the BTA and under the direct authority of the Secretary of State for Wales. Flexing its developing muscle and further strengthening the devolution of tourism, the Welsh Office successfully lobbied for the establishment of a generous government grant and loan programme to be administered by the WTB for the improvement of tourism facilities in Wales, a boon not granted to other parts of the

[64] Memorandum, G. H. Daniel to Clement, Informal Meeting with Mr Lickorish, General Manager of the British Travel Association, 16 November 1966, Historical Background 1969 Investiture, CA.
[65] *Hansard's Parliamentary Debates*, 5th ser., vol. 756 (1967), col. 542; *The Times*, 28 March 1968.
[66] *Western Mail*, 11 March 1969.

UK.[67] It should be noted too that for the 'Croeso' year of 1969 the Welsh Office itself experienced a jump of nearly £750,000, a gain of approximately 10 per cent, in its vote from the Chancellor of the Exchequer and an increase of almost 5 per cent in its staffing.[68]

The investiture clearly articulated and in some cases brought into operation the Welsh economic strategy of the Labour Party, but like the 1967 White Paper on Wales it was not only devoted to economics. Indeed, the most distinctive example of a policy initiative arising from the Welsh Office was in the area of Welsh culture. *Wales: The Way Ahead* declared that 'A large part of the cultural heritage and history of Wales is embodied in the language' and that 'the Government and local authorities have increasingly recognised that they can do much to create conditions in which the language can flourish'.[69] It then went on to describe the Welsh Language Bill, soon to become the Welsh Language Act 1967, and its provisions to enable Welsh to be used in an official capacity in courts and on select government documents. Although a significant achievement in the history of the language, the 1967 Welsh Language Act did not bring tranquility to language politics. Admittedly, much of Labour's progress in the area of the language was in response to the protests of Cymdeithas yr Iaith, which was unhappy with the limited nature of the Act and continued to demand complete linguistic equality and full official status for the Welsh language. Following the Act, the society actually stepped up its activities and in October 1968 instituted its controversial traffic sign painting campaign. Surprised by the broad demand for Welsh-language forms, the Welsh Office experienced logistical delays in providing translated government documents, prompting further frustration and criticism from many Welsh-language speakers. In the face of such censure, the investiture provided an opportunity to emphasize and dramatize the Labour Party's professed commitment to the language and the new, semi-official status of 'yr hen iaith'.

While Welsh tax forms, licence applications and other government documents were slowly made available on a piecemeal

[67] Deacon, p. 7.
[68] *The Times*, 28 March 1968; *Western Mail*, 28 March 1968.
[69] *Wales: The Way Ahead*, p. 96.

THE INVESTITURE AND 'THE WAY AHEAD'

basis, the 1969 Investiture was bilingual at its inception. Like its 1911 predecessor, this ceremony of state was conducted in both English and Welsh. However, equality of language was far more serious and real in 1969 than the somewhat token and symbolic usage evident in 1911. From the official programme booklet to the instructions for folding up the souvenir investiture chairs, nearly all official documents related to the investiture were published bilingually.[70] Even the parking and traffic guidelines of the Gwynedd police were in Welsh and English.[71] Like the official investiture medal designed by the Ministry of Public Building and Works, articles of a more symbolic nature were often in Welsh only. In the shadow of the processing Archdruid, the Welsh language was widely used in the ceremony itself through Welsh anthems and bilingual religious services. As in 1911, the Home Secretary read the letters patent bestowing the regalia and robes of the prince's title. He was then followed by the Secretary of State for Wales, who read the letters patent in Welsh at the climax of the ceremony. In the opinion of Frances Jones, Wales Herald Extraordinary:

> ... the use of the Welsh language when reading the Letters Patent is very important, and it will have a long-term result. The feeling for the language is particularly strong, and you will have noticed from the press that this is the root of the extremism of the Welsh Language Society. Acknowledgement of the language by its use in the Investiture will have a most favourable effect on public opinion in Wales, and will go a long way to answering those critics who assert (wrongly of course) that the Investiture is an 'English' occasion. It is always wise to disarm, rather than invite criticism. The use of the language at the Investiture will be a help to the Prince in his Welsh relations in the years following for it must be borne in mind that the Investiture is really the beginning of the Principality and of the Prince's further associations with Wales.[72]

For the honour of reading the Letters Patent in Welsh, George Thomas had to be tutored by one of his junior ministers, a task

[70] Clipping, House of Commons, 30 January 1969, 100/68/69, BD 67/133, PRO.
[71] Investiture 1969 Caernarfon Handbook, BD 67/102, PRO.
[72] Extract from notes, Frances Jones, February 1968, 1.0.II 1969 Investiture, CA.

for which Thomas showed little enthusiasm.[73] Understandably, given the language of many of the participants, English was the primary language used within the chambers of the investiture planning committees. However, during Cledwyn Hughes's tenure, members of the committee could use Welsh with the expectation that their remarks would be translated by the Secretary of State. George Thomas put an end to this practice, stating that comments could be made in Welsh but no provisions for translation would be provided – thus effectively isolating the Welsh speaker in committee.[74] This private failure to observe the principle of 'equal validity' in language use demonstrated that beneath the uniform public façade of bilingualism, tensions and divisions over the languages of Wales still brewed behind the scenes of both the investiture and the Labour Party in Wales.

Of even greater significance than bilingual documentation was the personal use of the language by the enthusiastic prince. Having begun instruction with a phonograph course some months before, Prince Charles's eight-week summer term at Aberystwyth focused on the Welsh language. When the course of study was publicly announced in November 1967, college principal Dr Thomas Parry explained that the prince's stay 'would not result in Welsh fluency but he would know something about the language and understand the feelings in Wales'.[75] Apparently, the results surpassed expectations. Instructed in the new, cutting edge language laboratories at Aberystwyth and genuinely engaged in the subject, the prince was soon giving speeches in what the press claimed was 'impeccable Welsh'. In a televised appearance in June 1969, Prince Charles delivered his first speech in Welsh in front of an audience of approximately 6,000 at the Eisteddfod of Urdd Gobaith Cymru, the Welsh-language youth organization. Despite some members of the audience walking out in protest and a nervous hesitation at the beginning of his speech, the prince performed admirably in what was a dreadful trial of fire

[73] Sir Anthony Wagner to R. H. Jones, 9 June 1969, 1.0.II 1969 Investiture, CA; R. H. Jones to G. H. Daniel, 7 March 1969, 1.0.II 1969 Investiture, CA.
[74] Robertson, p. 199.
[75] *Western Mail*, 2 November 1967.

by anyone's standard. His accomplishment delighted many in the Welsh press, causing the *Cambrian News* to bubble:

> His enunciation was remarkable and most successful with the more difficult words. His 'diwylliant' was perfectly delivered, could not have been bettered by any Welshman. Every R was rolled in Scottish style, while the LL gave him no trouble at all; delivery was smooth and unhesitating, and pleased an appreciative audience.[76]

'Apart from being a considerable intellectual application', judged the *Western Mail*, 'his speech proved the sincerity of his concern for the continued vigour of the Welsh culture and language'.[77] Consequently, lengthy sections in Welsh were a regular component of the prince's many subsequent speeches in the principality during the investiture year. Of course, all of this linguistic activity led to the prince's speaking role in the ceremony of investiture itself. Rather than reciting a mere slogan in Welsh as in 1911, Prince Charles replied to the *Loyal Address from the People of Wales* in a bilingual speech of his own crafting. According to the *Daily Telegraph and Morning Post*: 'The finely delivered Welsh speech of Prince Charles and the sincerity behind it has helped to bury the past and preserve only its inspiration.'[78] The Welsh language royally vocalized in an official ceremony of state became the physical embodiment of the long overdue official status now ostensibly provided by the 1967 Welsh Language Act. 'If learning Welsh is the occupational hazard of a Prince of Wales', opined the *Daily Mail* 'so be it.'[79]

In the general enthusiasm of the investiture year, politicians and newspapers began to claim that the fortunes of the Welsh language itself had been materially changed by those royal utterances. Ednyfed Davies, Labour MP for Conwy, claimed that the efforts of Prince Charles had 'given real prestige to the language and made it respectable to learn Welsh'.[80] The press reported how the people of Wales, inspired by the prince's example, took to the language laboratories and their cassette

[76] *Cambrian News*, 6 June 1969.
[77] *Western Mail*, 2 June 1969.
[78] *Daily Telegraph and Morning Post*, 2 July 1969.
[79] *Daily Mail*, 2 July 1969.
[80] *Western Mail*, 23 June 1969.

players to learn the ancient tongue once more. Writing in the *Guardian*, Anne Clwyd noted:

> Since publicity for investiture year went into full swing, the popularity of the Welsh language has steadily increased. This year about 15,000 people have sent for the pamphlets which go with the BBC radio lessons; an increase of 5,000 over last year. In the town of Aberystwyth alone, the numbers of people learning Welsh at evening classes have more than trebled in a year to 150 and the classes have increased from four to 11.[81]

In answer to the demand, Harlech Television re-ran its Welsh lesson series and E. G. Millward, the prince's tutor launched a new correspondence course using 'the same basic techniques of teaching Welsh as a second language as the ones Mr Millward had used for Prince Charles'.[82] Indeed, the investiture may have had a positive impact on the development and popularity of 'Living Welsh', a style of Welsh instruction focusing on informal, conversational Welsh favoured by Millward and other language teachers at the time. In the opinion of the *Western Mail*: 'Prince Charles's pledge of support for the language and his admirable attempts to master it may well have contributed towards enabling it to survive.'[83] Even Gwynfor Evans, president of Plaid Cymru, agreed that the Welsh language would get a boost from the prince's interest.[84]

In the late 1960s, the Wilson government was under increasing pressure to demonstrate the value and effectiveness of its policies in Wales. Guided by the newly minted Welsh Office, assisted by the royal establishment and dutifully reported by the press, the 1969 investiture and its affiliated events illustrated and in some instances implemented Labour's programme for Wales. Through the ceremony, the prince travelled not only through the principality but through the chapters and proposals found in Cledwyn Hughes's 1967 White Paper, *Wales: The Way Ahead*. Through royal visits, princely utterances and press commentary, the glare of publicity following the prince was focused on Labour's efforts at economic planning for

---

[81] *Guardian*, 25 June 1969.
[82] *South Wales Evening Post*, 5 July 1969; *Guardian*, 25 June 1969.
[83] *Western Mail*, 1 July 1969.
[84] Gwynn, p. 171.

a Wales in the throes of transformation. In a nation dominated by failing heavy industry, the prince helped to demonstrate that economic recovery and growth would be achieved through the government's policies for aid, retraining and the promotion of light industry. Like the investiture, the 'way forward' was marked by Wilson's much vaunted confidence in professional expertise, innovative methods and creative design. Moreover, the royal ceremony itself was seen as a rare opportunity upon which the principality could gain international notoriety, build a tourism industry and realize significant financial returns. On the cultural front, the investiture provided the occasion for Labour to demonstrate its commitment to the Welsh language and to promote the benefits of the 1967 Welsh Language Act. All the activity generated by the investiture was an excellent stimulus for further administrative devolution, a fact fully appreciated by the struggling Welsh Office. The responsibilities and perceived worth of the fledgling institution were directly enhanced by its involvement in the ceremony. Collectively, the investiture's series of events reasserted Labour's claim to be the 'Party of Wales'.

11
We'll keep a welcome?

Upon taking up power in 1964, the Labour government looked forward to the investiture that they had inherited as a popular and uncontroversial opportunity to project the party's voice and vision for Wales. The Welsh Office was confident that objections to the anachronistic nature of the investiture could be addressed by a concerted effort to provide meaning and contemporary relevance to the royal ceremony. They recognized that the expense of the royal ceremony would no doubt raise objections from the far left, but they believed that such resistance could be contained through loyalty to a Labour government. The government, however, had not counted on the degree of opposition that the ceremony would encounter in some sections of Welsh opinion or the potential the investiture had for fanning the flames of youth protest culture and paramilitary activity in Wales. As Cledwyn Hughes enthusiastically encouraged the Queen to set a date, he did not foresee that the ceremony would become the focus of controversy, protest and violence. Neither could he predict the development of the massive security operation that would give Wales the appearance of an occupied nation, a nation at war with itself as well as with its English neighbour.

As a party of government, Labour had long since dropped the republicanism of its formative years but the subject of the monarchy still caused disagreement within its ranks.[1] For his part, Prime Minister Harold Wilson was an enthusiastic supporter of the monarchy and had great respect for its traditions, ceremony and pageantry. As the Rhodesian crisis of 1964 illustrated, Wilson was more than willing to employ the mon-

[1] For a historical account of English republicanism, see Antony Taylor, *'Down with the Crown': British Anti-monarchism and Debates about Royalty Since 1790* (London, 1999).

archy as an effective political tool and ally when the opportunity presented itself.[2] Accordingly, he took a personal and sympathetic interest in the investiture from its earliest stages and remained highly concerned in its arrangements throughout.[3] However, the monarchy fitted uneasily into the socialist consciousness of many Labour supporters. Although rarely adopting the republican position, many simply dismissed the monarchy as an unfortunate and atavistic extravagance, to be either ignored or curtailed. As the Chancellor of the Exchequer's parsimonious attitude towards the investiture suggests, several ministers in Wilson's cabinet were not enamoured of monarchy, still less of expensive, hierarchical and atavistic royal ceremony. Expenditure on a royal ceremony at a time of apparent economic crisis and reduction in public spending left Labour vulnerable to accusations of hypocrisy. The proximity and contrast between the government's support of the investiture ceremony and the state's poor response to the Aberfan disaster was painfully glaring. Malcontents within the cabinet were not prepared, however, to break ranks with their government over the issue of the investiture. Others of like opinion within the party and among its supporters no doubt followed suit. Eight out of thirty-two Welsh Labour MPs declined to attend the investiture, but they disavowed any political significance to their absence.[4]

However, the temptation to attack the Wilson government systematically over the investiture proved to be irresistible to Labour's most vocal dissident. Emrys Hughes, the MP for the Scottish constituency of South Ayrshire, was the voice of dissent within the Labour Party on a host of issues but the investiture seemed divinely designed for his opposition. A prolific writer in his own right and the editor of the radical Glasgow periodical *Forward*, Hughes was a Welshman hailing from Tonypandy and the son-in-law of Keir Hardie. Like

[2] Ben Pimlott, *The Queen: A Biography of Elizabeth II* (London 1996), pp. 343–54.
[3] See correspondence and papers in PREM 13/2359, 13/2360, 13/2901, 13/2903, 13/2907, 13/2505, PRO. For a particular example of Wilson's interest in being directly informed of developments in the arrangements, see Sir Burke Trend to Michael Hall, 21 June 1967, PREM 13/2359, PRO.
[4] *Western Mail*, 24 May 1969.

Hardie, Hughes was a combative advocate of the working class in the old style, a thorough socialist and republican. Like Hardie, he also sympathized with certain elements of Scottish and Welsh nationalist aspirations. Primarily focused on issues of expense, misplaced priorities, general antipathy to monarchy and the supposed lack of public support for the ceremony, his acerbic criticism of the investiture appeared frequently in the House of Commons and was published in a booklet entitled *The Prince, the Crown and the Cash*.[5] In typical style, Hughes explained in the House of Commons that '35,000 people in Wales are without water closets, including 2,000 to 3,000 in Caernarfonshire' and suggested that 'this ridiculous, absurd, mini-Coronation be postponed and priority be given to people who have no sanitary accommodation'.[6] He often laced his remarks on the investiture in the House of Commons with stinging personal attacks on George Thomas. 'Why is the Secretary of State determined to be the prodigal son of the Labour Government and to insist on this expensive spending spree at a time when the nation is in such financial difficulties?', he demanded.[7] Mocking the expenses associated with the ceremony's use of the Welsh language, he informed Thomas of his 'capacity for telling him in forcible language – in Welsh – what I think of him'.[8] Frequently put on the back foot in such exchanges, the Secretary of State was in the rather awkward position of having a member of the Conservative opposition routinely rally to his defence. David Gibson-Watt, Conservative MP for Hereford, answered invective for invective, once warning Hughes 'that if he bangs on much longer', he would be 'in grave danger of being shut up in a dust bin'.[9]

Although never a serious threat to the government's command of its party, Emrys Hughes embarrassed the Wilson government and helped define the terms of engagement for those few within Labour's ranks willing to raise critical questions regarding the ceremony and its expense. The criticism of some Labour county councillors in Wales and the action of the

[5] Emrys Hughes, *The Prince, The Crown and the Cash* (London, 1969).
[6] Clipping, House of Commons, 4 February 1969, BD 67/16, PRO.
[7] 28 November 1968 HC no 41/68/69, BD 67/133, PRO.
[8] 30 January 1969 HC 107/68/69, BD 67/133, PRO.
[9] 6 March 1969 HC 145/68/69, BD 67/133, PRO.

15,000-strong Port Talbot Trade Council certainly reflected Hughes's influence. The trade union declared that an 'investiture in a modern industrial society is ridiculous and a drain on our national resources' and voted to boycott the local celebrations of the Labour controlled borough council.[10] However, such incidents of Labour dissent within Wales were rarely successful. While anti-investiture resolutions at the annual meeting of the Welsh Young Socialists failed to even get a hearing, an 'All-Wales Labour Rally' applauded George Thomas for his efforts on behalf of the ceremony.[11] Over all, at a time of popular protest and anti-establishment politics, the left in Britain was remarkably silent in its attitude to the investiture.

As in 1911, Labour's use of the monarchy and royal ceremony effectively short circuited the opposition of their traditional rival, the Conservative Party. The fact that the idea of holding the investiture originated with a Conservative government left little ground for direct criticism. Instead, Conservative opposition was expressed by proxy and largely focused on allegations of Labour's political exploitation of the young prince. The harshest comments were reserved for Labour's plans to send him to the University College of Wales, Aberystwyth. Admitting that the university at Aberystwyth was an institution regarded by the political right 'with much the same enthusiasm as the Rev Ian Paisley reserves for Rome', Sir David Llewelyn, a former government minister and Conservative MP for Cardiff North, described Labour's plans for Prince Charles's summer term as 'the wrong place for the wrong course for the wrong pupil for the wrong reason at the wrong time'. For Llewelyn, the investiture was 'a means of diverting public opinion from the Government's failure to get to grips with the real problems of Wales'.[12] Like some anonymous Cambridge dons, historian A. J. P. Taylor was incensed over 'the sordid plot to exploit Prince Charles'. By snatching him away from Cambridge and inflicting the trauma of Aberystwyth on him, 'just when his mind is maturing', Labour

[10] *Western Mail*, 11 December 1968.
[11] *Western Mail*, 28 April 1968, 30 June 1969.
[12] *Sunday Observer*, 30 March 1969.

was causing irreparable harm to the prince's psyche and intellect. 'I can think of many universities where a year's residence might benefit the history student', conceded the Oxford professor '. . . Aberystwyth is not among them'. Citing Labour's electoral difficulty with nationalists in Scotland and Wales, Taylor attributed the prince's ordeal solely to 'reasons of party', a political abuse of an apolitical institution that could ultimately threaten the prestige of the monarchy itself.[13] Despite these barbed comments, the response of the political right to the investiture itself was not unlike that of the left. On the investiture and its affiliated ceremonies, a polite silence was largely observed.

Plaid Cymru was equally flummoxed in its response to the investiture, but the stakes for the small party were much higher. The ceremony, after all, put it in a very difficult position. The party leadership generally agreed that the ceremony amounted to a scheme to bolster unionism and to shore up Welsh support for Labour in the face of the growing electoral threat of their party. However, nothing in Plaid Cymru's programme or ideology placed them in opposition to the monarchy or to the existence of a Prince of Wales. Seeking a more moderate course than that of Irish republicanism, Plaid rejected the goal of complete independence from Britain in favour of home rule and Dominion status under the Crown. Their policy thus implied at least a passive acceptance of the monarchy. Furthermore, in an effort to appeal more broadly to electors and to garner support in south Wales, Plaid was heavily engaged in refocusing its programme on inclusive and progressive policies concerned with pragmatic matters of economics and national development rather than on more divisive cultural and symbolic politics. In the wake of Gwynfor Evans's 1966 breakthrough victory in Carmarthen, the party concentrated their efforts on expanding their success in elections, not on staging protests over matters of airy principle or abstract republicanism. Moreover, the party leadership understood that outright opposition to the investiture would most likely alienate voters among the general population of Wales, whose royalist sympathies were assumed to be traditional and

[13] *Sunday Express*, 12 May 1968.

marked. This lesson had been clearly demonstrated in the decline of public support for the party following its opposition to the coronation of George VI in 1936.[14]

However, there was passionate interest in opposing the ceremony among young nationalists, a group rapidly expanding in size and importance among the party's supporters and workers. In the midst of the investiture controversy, the closely fought 1968 by-elections demonstrated the critical role of young activists in Plaid's success. The Conservative candidate for Caerphilly was goaded into describing Plaid Cymru's campaign as a 'kid's crusade' without 'a bona fide tax payer or rate payer' among the party's supporters.[15] Noting that the majority of those working for Plaid Cymru were under the age of 30, Gwynfor Evans stated in the summer of 1969 that: 'The national struggle in Wales is a battle of the generations.'[16] Yet, the Plaid Cymru leadership found it increasingly difficult to control a group that had been mobilized and fundamentally transformed by the cultural revolution of the 1960s. Nowhere was this more marked than among the Welsh-language community from which Plaid Cymru support was primarily drawn. Turning away from the chapel and toward the pub, Welsh-language youth culture was contemporary, cocky, and irreverent. It was as scathing of the old, Victorian standards of Welsh culture as it was hostile to the English. The new interests and identity of an affluent Welsh-speaking youth generated commerce and a thriving material culture, creating an independent cultural space setting them apart from their elders. Symptomatic of this development, Robert Griffiths founded a small Welsh-language publishing venture called Y Lolfa a few years before the investiture. It cut its teeth on the production of Cymdiethas yr Iaith propaganda, a book of bawdy pub songs and a satirical magazine called *Lol* (Nonsense) sold at the National Eisteddfod. With its photographs of semi-nude Cymraesau, the comic magazine scandalized older eisteddfodwyr. A vibrant Welsh-language pop and folk music scene elevated singer Dafydd Iwan to iconic status on Welsh-language

[14] Rhys Evans, *Gwynfor: Rhag Pob Brad* (Tal-y-bont, 2006), pp. 46–7, 299–300.
[15] *Western Mail*, 6 July 1968.
[16] *Welsh Nationalist*, June 1969.

television, radio and phonograph singles. Significantly, he was the scion of a line of celebrated Cardiganshire preachers, the Welsh cultural personalities of a previous generation. In the Croeso year of 1969, Iwan founded the successful and influential Welsh-language pop label, *Sain*. 'Nationalism among the youth has turned its back on the chapel', explained the young poet Meic Stephens in an article on the investiture: 'If they have any mores now, it's more likely to be beer, the guitar and hitchhiking.'[17] In keeping with the rebellious tone of this youth culture, many young nationalists rejected the reverence for the monarchy of their parents' generation. Accordingly, they regarded the investiture as an historic insult to the nation and a symbol of English oppression. In an age where anti-establishment protest was the height of fashion, the ceremony became the perfect focus for Welsh hippies looking for a popular target on which to vent their spleen. The investiture thus put Plaid Cymru in a dangerous dilemma, forcing on it a decision they feared would either offend the general Welsh electorate or alienate their active youthful base.

Faced with such cross-currents and political pitfalls, Plaid Cymru groped for a response that would avoid the extremes of either open support or outright opposition. Party activist Harri Webb, a celebrated Anglo-Welsh poet and former member of a defunct Welsh republican movement, drafted a long memorandum on the subject of the monarchy for the party's leadership. While admitting that 'the Investiture, the Principate, and the Principality must be categorized as fundamentally obnoxious' and symbolized 'an alien conquest and centuries of subjugation', Webb argued that a stance 'of calculated coolness verging on contempt' was 'unquestionably the most effective attitude to adopt on our platforms'. Rather than outright, active opposition, a message of 'Prosperity not Pageantry, Jobs before Jamborees' was the right tone for an age where symbolism, ceremony and myth were supposedly losing their potency.[18] This complemented the reasoning of the party's president and sole MP, Gwynfor Evans, who recommended that Plaid should remain 'as quiet as possible' on the subject of the investiture while efforts were made behind the scenes to try to turn the

[17] *Observer Magazine*, 22 June 1969.
[18] Harri Webb, 'The Prince Question', Tŷ Cenedl 1 AI/5, NLW.

event to their advantage.¹⁹ Plaid Cymru's official line was thus publicly to ignore the event as an essentially meaningless and irrelevant diversion to the problems of Wales. Consequently, there was minimal coverage of the investiture in most of the party's publications.²⁰ 'Plaid Cymru regards the awakening of the Welsh people to their rights as a nation as more important than worrying about the investiture', summarized E. G. Millward, Plaid's Vice President.²¹

Despite this official party line, Plaid Cymru's response seemed muddled and confused. This was furthered by the actions of various members and representatives of the party, not least by its President and Vice President. Gwynfor Evans's public response to the investiture appeared incoherent.²² In one breath, he described the ceremony in positive terms as a 'tremendous honour' for Prince Charles and then negatively as 'a way of integrating the Welsh nation in the English state'.²³ On another occasion, Evans stated that the ceremony should express a real concern for Wales and demanded that the prince fully identify himself with the life of the nation. Despite Prince Charles's apparent fulfilment of these terms, Evans would later dismiss the ceremony as merely a 'tourist gimmick'.²⁴ In Parliament, he avoided outright criticism of the principle of the investiture but launched a series of attacks narrowly aimed at its expense, particularly in relation to the military presence at Caernarfon. Confusingly, Gwynfor Evans pointedly turned down the invitation given to all Welsh MPs to attend the investiture, yet he and his wife would personally greet and meet the prince on the second day of his investiture tour in his capacity as a local MP.²⁵ Unenthusiastic when the ceremony was announced, Gwynfor Evans was voicing the opinion that the investiture would do more good than bad for Plaid Cymru

[19] Rhys Evans, pp. 299–300.
[20] Dafydd Gwynn, 'Arwisgiad 1969: Yr Ymateb Gwleidyddol', *Cof Cenedl*, XV (2000), 8–9.
[21] *Western Mail*, 8 January 1968.
[22] For a detailed account of Gwynfor Evans's thought and actions during the period of the investiture, see Rhys Evans, pp. 295–320.
[23] *Western Mail*, 18 May 1968.
[24] Harri Webb, 'The Prince Question', Tŷ Cenedl 1 AI/5, NLW; *Western Mail*, 29 October 1967.
[25] *Western Mail*, 3 July 1969.

by the time the ceremony was actually held.²⁶ Despite his resignation as Vice President before taking up the task, Edward Millward's acceptance of the post as Prince Charles's principal tutor at Aberystwyth confused things further. As expressed in private correspondence, Evans and Millward believed that the direct access to the prince that Millward's position entailed gave Plaid an unprecedented opportunity to influence the thinking of Prince Charles and to turn the ceremony to the party's advantage.²⁷ Millward's decision to accept the post, however, became the focus of much press commentary that gave the party activist the appearance of being firmly in the pro-investiture camp.

Conversely, the party found it embarrassingly difficult to disown opposition to the investiture emanating from its own subsidiaries. County councillors affiliated with Plaid Cymru called for boycotts of investiture activities while local branches of the party demanded that the ceremony be called off and, in one instance, for the funds to be used for relief in Biafra instead.²⁸ Vigorously led by a young Dafydd Elis Thomas, Plaid Cymru's official youth organization took an openly hostile line to the investiture. In the columns of Plaid's youth magazine, Dafydd Elis Thomas sharply declared to Prince Charles: 'If you don't want to make a fool of yourself in the greatest farce of modern Welsh history, don't come to Caernarfon in 1969 – but go back to Cambridge, Charlie boy, Wales has her own leaders and her own destiny now.'²⁹ To the chagrin of the party leadership, the party's youth branch launched a 'Senedd Nid Tywysog' (Parliament Not Prince) bumper sticker campaign and devoted much of the 1968 issue of the Plaid Cymru youth magazine, *I'r Gad*, to anti-investiture polemic and satire.³⁰ Plaid's Executive Committee attempted to silence such activity, but Dafydd Elis Thomas and the Plaid Cymru youth branch would remain defiantly and openly

---

[26] Rhys Evans, pp. 295, 319–20.
[27] Rhys Evans, p. 315.
[28] *Welsh Nationalist*, December 1967; *Rhyl & Prestatyn Gazette*, 14 July 1968.
[29] *Sunday Express*, 7 January 1968.
[30] *I'r Gad*, spring 1968; *Sunday Express*, 7 January 1969.

involved in anti-investiture activities.³¹ Yet, despite such transgressions, Dafydd Elis Thomas was selected and warmly endorsed by Gwynfor Evans as the party's parliamentary candidate for Conwy in the month before the investiture.³² As Harri Webb recognized, the issue of the prince was a difficult one to resolve for Plaid Cymru and it would be regularly raised and debated at the party's meetings throughout the period.³³

Division over the investiture within the party came to a head at the annual Plaid Cymru conference in September 1968, coincidentally yet poignantly held in Aberystwyth. Outside the conference hall, pamphleteering, demonstrations and placards demanding that the party adopt an anti-investiture policy were complemented by a midnight attempt to saw off the head of a university statue of the former Prince of Wales. Inside the conference, a motion was placed on the agenda by the Bridgend branch calling upon Plaid Cymru to disassociate itself from all activities concerning the investiture and to denounce the ceremony 'as a continuation of the historic insult to our Nation'. A complementary motion by the Swansea East Branch demanded that the Executive Committee 'stop sitting on the fence' and definitively declare either its support for or opposition to the investiture.³⁴ In calling for the Bridgend motion to be tabled, a delegate warned the party not to 'play into the hands of English politicians' who would be watching their actions. 'This is a bait to catch Plaid Cymru and nothing else', he declared: 'Our first priority is to attack King Harold, not Prince Charles.' He concluded with the suggestion that the constitutional question of Prince Charles's relationship to the nation be deferred until they had achieved a 'Free Wales'.³⁵ Another delegate dismissed the issue of the investiture as irrelevant, described it as 'a trap set up by the Government for Plaid Cymru' and warned that a division on the question would destroy their chances at the next general election.³⁶

[31] *Welsh Nationalist*, May 1968.
[32] *Welsh Nationalist*, June 1969.
[33] Harri Webb, 'The Prince Question', Tŷ Cenedl 1 AI/5, NLW.
[34] 1968 Plaid Cymru Conference Programme, Aberystwyth, September 1968, ex 1669 NLW.
[35] *The Observer*, 22 September 1968.
[36] *Western Mail*, 23 September 1968.

Behind the scenes, Gwynfor Evans was taking steps to resist the demands of the anti-investiture wing of the party.[37] Taken up early in the conference before all the delegates had arrived, both measures were tabled by a large majority of those delegates present in preference to the party's established, if not consistently observed, position. No official action would be taken and the party would try to ignore the ceremony. The leadership could breathe a sigh of relief over what deceptively appeared to be the safe option, but the party's passive response to the investiture embittered young supporters. At the same time, the party's decision did little to disarm critics from the Labour Party who continued publicly to associate Plaid with anti-investiture protest and violence.

With Plaid effectively abdicating the nationalist response, opposition to the investiture was largely left to the activist youth. In fact, a distinct Welsh variant of youth protest culture was liberated, invigorated and emboldened as a result of Plaid Cymru's decision to opt out. Freed from the guidance of their parents' generation, opposition to the investiture would crystallize and define the Welsh counter-culture of the 1960s. Above all, pop singer Dafydd Iwan gave voice to that culture with 'Carlo', a satirical anthem lampooning the prince. Deriving its title from the juxtaposition of an informal Welsh form of 'Charles' and a popular Welsh name for a dog, the record sold over 10,000 copies. This was an impressive achievement in the Welsh-language market of the time and Iwan's most successful record up to that date.[38] *Y Cymro* went so far as to prophesy that Iwan and 'Carlo' would stand by the likes of the BBC lecture of Saunders Lewis, the establishment of Cymdeithas yr Iaith Gymraeg, and the victory of Gwynfor Evans in Carmarthen as one of the defining historical moments of the 1960s.[39] The publishing house of Y Lolfa and a new Welsh-language bookshop in Aberystwyth, Siop y Pethe, became notable centres of anti-investiture activity and distribution points of propaganda and paraphernalia. Epitomized in the cartoons of Tegwyn Jones in *Lol* and the Cymdeithas yr Iaith periodical *Tafod y Ddraig*, satire and humour were often

[37] Rhys Evans, p. 310.
[38] *Sunday Telegraph*, 6 July 1969.
[39] *Y Cymro*, 25 June 1969.

main ingredients in such material. Trevor Fishlock described the environment of Aberystwyth, the 'cultural centre of Wales', in which Prince Charles would be studying:

> He may see, hear and sense the opposition to his stay: a few students wearing tin lapel badges inscribed 'Dim Sais am Tywysog Cymru', a satirical poster of himself . . . and a few bars of a lighthearted satirical record called 'Carlo'. . . . All these can be seen and heard in Aberystwyth now. Fun poking at the investiture has generated a miniature industry. A 2s 6d book of Welsh public house songs in which the investiture gets a ribald roasting is selling like hot cakes here and elsewhere.[40]

In a more literary vein, popular young Welsh-language poets like Bobi Jones, Alan Llwyd and Gerallt Lloyd Owen attacked the investiture in verse. Anti-investiture poetry became a staple of several Welsh-language periodicals.[41] Resolutions from students in Aberystwyth, the Welsh regional committee of the National Students Union and the Central Students Representative Council condemned the 'political use of the Prince'. Small groups of students initiated a series of demonstrations, sit-ins and hunger strikes at the universities in Aberystwyth, Bangor, and Cardiff.[42] Even school children were caught up in the enthusiasm when a group of boys went on hunger strike against the involvement of their school in investiture celebrations.[43] Prefiguring the road sign campaign of Cymdeithas yr Iaith, vandalism provided a vehicle for anti-investiture protest through the painting of slogans, the painting out of investiture related signs and the destruction of investiture displays, bunting and flags.[44] Still recovering from the attempt to saw off its head, Aberystwyth's much abused statue of the former Prince of Wales received its coat of green paint in due

[40] *The Times*, 28 January 1969.
[41] Gwynn, p. 27.
[42] *Western Mail*, 6 November 1967; *Western Mail*, 15 February 1969; Transcript of interview by David Allen of hunger strikers at Aberystwyth, BD 67/52, PRO; *Western Mail*, 21 January 1969, 8 March 1969, 11 March 1969.
[43] *Western Mail*, 19 March 1969.
[44] *Cardigan & Tivy Side Advertiser*, 9 August 1968; *Western Mail*, 27 June, 28 June, 2 July 1969.

course.[45] The effect went beyond active nationalists. More generally, among Welsh-speaking and even among some sections of non-Welsh-speaking youth in Wales, an almost carnival like atmosphere of protest cultivated a distinct negative response to the investiture. Signs of ambivalence, if not hostility, were reflected in an apparent lack of enthusiasm to the hype of the ceremony. Ostentatiously recruited from singers across Wales under the age of thirty, the investiture choir ran into difficulties when it experienced a lower than expected volume of auditions. Similarly, the deadline for the televised Croeso 69 hostess pageant had to be postponed because of the lack of entries. In the end, only half the number of expected contestants would compete for the honour.[46]

Perhaps the most visible indication of youthful opposition to the investiture came in the dramatic series of events surrounding the Urdd Gobaith Cymru (Welsh League of Youth). Founded in 1922 by Sir Ifan ab Owen Edwards, son of the famous educator and writer Owen Morgan Edwards, the Urdd promoted the social and cultural use of the Welsh language among the nation's youth. Similar in some ways to the scouting movement, the Urdd was pacifist, non-political and enjoyed broad public support. Given the respectable and non-controversial character of the Urdd, investiture planners regarded the 43,000-member organization as a natural ally and had envisioned it playing a major role in the investiture ceremony and its related events. The ailing 73-year-old Sir Ifan ab Owen Edwards was named a member of the official Investiture Committee and both he and senior Urdd organizer R. E. Griffith served on the national committee of Croeso 69.

However, the elderly founder and president of the Urdd could not deliver the support of the Welsh youth as expected. In October 1968, the Urdd's National Council voiced serious dissatisfaction with the form and nature of the investiture but, at the urging of Sir Ifan and Urdd officials, voted to send representatives to the ceremony if invited.[47] The council's decision erupted in controversy almost immediately, with

[45] *Western Mail*, 28 June 1969.
[46] *Western Mail*, 25 June, 20 August 1968.
[47] *Western Mail*, 21 October 1968; *Liverpool Daily Post*, 21 October 1968.

many members and staff objecting and demanding that the Urdd reconsider.[48] A Tegwyn Jones cartoon in *Lol* ridiculed the Urdd, depicting Welsh youth slavishly worshipping Sir Ifan and playing musical chairs beneath a portrait of the prince.[49] In early December 1968, two prominent Urdd leaders resigned their positions in protest of the league's support of the investiture, arguing that it did not conform to the Urdd's promise of being 'faithful to Wales, fellowman and Christ' and violated the non-political character of the organization. They claimed that everyone in the movement was 'against the pantomime in Caernarfon' and warned of a major split.[50] About a week later, the National Council caved into the pressure, reversing its position by voting to boycott the ceremony by a three to one margin. At the insistence of Sir Ifan and Urdd officials, however, the prince was invited to visit the Urdd summer camp and Eisteddfod in consolation.[51] Sir Ifan was alarmed over the prospect of his movement collapsing. Although subsequent correspondence with the Welsh Office reveals that he continued to support the investiture privately, Sir Ifan performed a dramatic public about-face, explaining to the press that the investiture had split both Wales and the Urdd:

> We are a youth movement, a loyal youth movement, but we don't want to get into politics. We will help the Prince, but we are not going to help a political stunt invented by Lloyd George in 1911. That is what the investiture is. It has no tradition behind it, it does not belong to Wales . . . We are not going to boycott the investiture. It is simply that we do not feel like going because it has got into the political arena. On the other hand, we are very anxious to welcome the Prince to any of our activities.[52]

Of his continued membership on the Investiture Committee, Sir Ifan told the press: 'That is one of the matters causing me to think pretty hard these days . . . I am not a politician. I am simply a youth leader.'[53] Clearly stunned by the turnaround,

[48] *Western Mail*, 28 October 1968.
[49] *Lol*, Haf 1968.
[50] *Western Mail*, 5 December 1968.
[51] *Western Mail*, 16 December 1968.
[52] *Western Mail*, 17 December 1968; Ifan ab Owen Edwards to Idris Evans, 3 November 1969, BD 67/9, PRO.
[53] *Western Mail*, 17 December 1968.

Secretary of State Thomas issued a statement citing his respect for the elderly dignitary but denying that the investiture was 'a political stunt': 'I had thought that his active participation in the work of the Investiture Committee properly reflected the place that the Urdd has established for itself in Wales as a non-political youth organization, as well as the non-political position of the Royal Family itself.'[54]

Against this background of public controversy, Prince Charles did in fact accept the invitation to attend the Urdd Youth Eisteddfod, where he gave a much publicized and televised speech in Welsh in front of an audience of approximately 6,000. Despite the dissent of the Eisteddfod committee, the invitation was extended at the direct behest of older Urdd officials rather than through the more representative and youthful National Council.[55] Although certainly not universal, discontent within the gathering was readily apparent in the marquee. The representatives from Merioneth refused to take part in an Eisteddfod ceremony, periodic cat-calls of 'Carlo' could be heard from the audience and scuffles broke out between police and protesters. Under the watchful eye of the television camera, about 100 demonstrators silently stood and filed towards the exit as Prince Charles mounted the platform. One protester tried to jump the barrier in front of the stage in an unsuccessful attempt to cut the microphone wires.[56] Perhaps most tellingly, the chair for poetry was awarded to 25-year-old Gerallt Lloyd Owen for a series of poems on the theme 'Wales Today'. The collection included a harsh condemnation of the investiture in the form of 'Fy Ngwlad', a poem that would go on to garner critical literary acclaim and enduring popularity.[57] Reflecting on the event a few months after the investiture, Sir Ifan wrote apologetically to the Welsh Office regretting that he 'did not by a long way pull my weight' as a member of the Investiture Committee and citing in explanation

---

[54] Secretary of State on reported statement by Sir Ifan ab Owen Edwards, 1.0.XI 1969 Investiture, CA.
[55] See letters to the editor in *Western Mail*, 4 June, 6 June 1969.
[56] *Western Mail*, 2 June 1969.
[57] *Cerddi'r Gadair* (Urdd Genedlaethol Cymru, 1969), p. 4; For Gerallt Lloyd Owen's poetry, see Jerry Hunter's series in *Barn*, 406–10 (1996–7).

his failure to realize the extent of the opposition that the investiture would generate among Welsh youth.[58]

Although its purpose was narrowly concerned with pressing for linguistic rights rather than with broader issues of political and symbolic nationalism, Cymdeithas yr Iaith got caught up in the anti-investiture movement and became the principal organization to oppose the ceremony. In the early 1960s, the youthful energies of the protest culture in Welsh-speaking Wales had been effectively channelled into the activities of the society. That protest culture had now embraced the investiture as an issue and was demanding leadership. It was a demand that the society was disinclined to ignore. As early as October 1967, the members of Cymdeithas yr Iaith passed a resolution claiming that 'the investiture is an insult to our people and history' and called on their fellow countrymen to take part in a national campaign to oppose it. Thirty members were appointed to an investiture protest committee and plans were announced to demonstrate outside the Temple of Peace in Cardiff, where the Croeso 69 conference was to be held that November.[59] As will be discussed later, this meeting also attracted the attention of paramilitaries who set off a bomb in the building's entry hall the night before it was convened. About 250 members of Cymdeithas staged a sit down on the steps of the damaged building. Carrying placards reading 'Republic not Royalty', singing Welsh folk songs and chanting 'No Prince', they booed the appearance at the hall of Lord Snowdon and Cledwyn Hughes.[60] The society's magazine, *Tafod y Ddraig*, became a major vehicle of anti-investiture propaganda and members were encouraged to disrupt the Croeso 69 campaign by proposing 'mickey-taking' events to its national and local committees. Amongst what they characterized as the 'nose-picking championships' and 'biggest arse contests' of the Croeso celebrations, Cymdeithas offered such dubious contributions as a 'Crowning our Prince' pageant, a meeting 'in memory of Llywelyn, our last prince', and the

[58] Sir Ifan ab Owen Edwards to Idris Evans, 3 November 1969, BD 67/9, PRO.
[59] *Western Mail*, 23 October 1967.
[60] *Western Mail*, 18 November 1967.

publication of a 'Tribute to Carlo'.[61] Amazingly, these events were initially accepted by the unsuspecting Croeso authorities as serious proposals. 'Their faces are going to be red when they realize what we are doing ...', laughed society chairman Gareth Miles: 'We shall stage a few very special events to show what we think about having an Englishman as Prince of Wales.'[62] The annual general meeting of the society in October 1968 was momentous, signalling the society's escalating radicalism with the launch of its campaign to paint out English language traffic signs and the renewal of its opposition to the investiture. Then riding the popularity of his hit single 'Carlo', Dafydd Iwan was elected chairman of Cymdeithas yr Iaith and issued a statement outlining the society's anti-investiture campaign:

> We oppose the investiture of Charles Windsor as Prince of Wales on moral grounds. Further because he has no right to this title and therefore all further considerations are irrelevant. Despite its frenzied efforts, the Wales Tourist Board has failed to whip up enthusiasm for this organized insult to Welsh nationhood. Our members have been urged to oppose and obstruct the few local efforts organized as part of Croeso 69. Leaflets and posters will be published by the society and an anti-investiture rally will be held in Caernarfon on St David's Day 1969.[63]

Cymdeithas yr Iaith would organize the two chief rallies in opposition to the investiture. The 1969 St David's Day demonstration proved to be the largest. In what Dafydd Iwan felt was 'an indication of the widespread feeling throughout Wales against the investiture', some 5,000 supporters converged on Caernarfon.[64] In a procession mirroring that which would conduct the prince to his investiture, two motorcades composed of hundreds of cars and coaches wound its way through the town to the castle, following a car equipped with a loud speaker blaring 'Carlo'. The convoys were coming directly from large rallies held that morning in Machynlleth and Dolbadarn Castle. Many of the cars displayed caricatures of Prince Charles and a coach from Aberystwyth bore the slogan

[61] *Tafod y Ddraig*, February 1968.
[62] *Western Mail*, 12 February 1968.
[63] *South Wales Evening Post*, 21 October 1968.
[64] *Liverpool Daily Post*, 3 March 1969.

'Charles – No Welcome'. The protestors met in the slate quay in the shadow of Caernarfon Castle for the rally, where they listened to a series of speeches, waved placards and planted a Welsh flag atop the scaffolding on the castle walls. The crowd then dispersed, some of them no doubt equipped with cans of green paint for excursions along the way home.

On 29 August 1969, some three days before the investiture, the second major Cymdeithas yr Iaith anti-investiture rally was held at Cilmery, the site of the death of Prince Llywelyn in 1282. In a 'public expression of the opposition felt throughout Wales to the investiture and as a symbol of the respect felt for Llywelyn and other historical heroes', about 2,000 supporters assembled at the memorial to Llywelyn the Last. A wreath was laid at the memorial by two elderly dignitaries – the respected poet Waldo Williams and D. J. Williams, one of the 'Three' who had burned the Penyberth bombing school in the early days of Plaid Cymru. With Dafydd Iwan presiding, a letter of support from Saunders Lewis was read to the rally. The crowd was subsequently entertained and edified with recitations of patriotic poetry, musical performances and rousing speeches.[65] From the platform, it was prophesied that this would be the last investiture to be held in Wales. Before the crowd descended upon an affiliated Welsh pop concert held nearby, supporters were encouraged to paint out all the English signs in the principality as an anti-investiture protest.[66] Desiring, no doubt, to avoid confrontations with an escalating and nervous security campaign, no official activity was planned and Cymdeithas members were left to their own devices on the day of the investiture itself.

Given that the society's purpose was narrowly defined in support of linguistic rights, Cymdeithas yr Iaith's active opposition was bound to alienate some supporters and to leave it vulnerable to allegations that it was confusing its message and squandering its energies. The society's position was further complicated by the apparent interest of the prince in learning

---

[65] Dafydd Iwan and Huw Jones performed and lectures were delivered by Emyr Llewelyn Jones and Dr Tudor Jones.
[66] *Y Cymro*, 2 July 1969; *Baner ac Amserau Cymru*, 3 July 1969; *Western Mail*, 30 June 1969.

the Welsh language and his outspoken support for the language's preservation. In January 1968, an essay in *Barn* warned that by abandoning their focus on the language issue and trespassing into the territory of politics, Cymdeithas yr Iaith was in danger of deteriorating into a band of 'professional protesters' looking for reasons to make trouble. If the society fell into the trap of 'protesting everything' it would discredit its central cause of linguistic rights for the Welsh language.[67] These sentiments were publicly shared by Edward Millward, then the Vice President of Plaid Cymru and a former leader of Cymdeithas yr Iaith himself. Millward warned: 'It would be a mistake for the Welsh Language Society which has achieved so much to go into a political field.'[68] The Revd E. Gwyndaf Evans, the Archdruid of Wales, regretted the association between Cymdeithas and the anti-investiture movement, noting that: 'The hard core of Welsh-speaking Wales and many ardent supporters of equal validity for the Welsh language cannot be termed anti-Royalist. For this reason, the movement could lose considerable goodwill among the rank and file in Wales.'[69] The danger which anti-investiture protest posed to the language struggle was evident to many within the society, some of whom vocally opposed its commitment to the anti-investiture campaign during the 1968 annual meeting.[70] Even Dafydd Iwan expressed some concern that the anti-investiture campaign not detract from the society's efforts on behalf of the language.[71] The dilemma facing Cymdeithas yr Iaith was similar to and bound up with that of Plaid Cymru. With Plaid Cymru declining to take up the issue, the pressure from the youthful supporters of Cymdeithas to actively oppose the investiture became irresistible, whatever the consequences for the language campaign. To the question 'Why are you opposing the investiture and what is a language movement doing leading an opposition of this sort?' *Tafod y Ddraig* gave the somewhat unsatisfactory answer: 'Because nobody else offered to do it.' The journal expressly looked forward to the day when

[67] *Barn*, January 1968.
[68] *Western Mail*, 8 January 1968.
[69] *Western Mail*, 30 June 1969.
[70] *Sunday Telegraph*, 13 October 1968.
[71] Dafydd Iwan, *Dafydd Iwan* (Caernarfon, 1981), p. 43.

the investiture was over and the society could refocus its efforts on the language alone.[72] This apologetic tone was echoed by Dafydd Iwan, stating in an interview with *Y Cymro*:

> Someone must oppose the investiture; to anyone who sees it with clear eyes it is a symbol of that which makes our nation subservient, subordinate. Because there was nobody else to lead the opposition, it was necessary for the Cymdeithas to do that. But I would not count this campaign amongst the most important campaigns of the Cymdeithas.[73]

Contrary to these assertions, however, there were others competing with the society for the leading role in the anti-investiture movement. The orderly if irreverent protests of Cymdeithas yr Iaith took place against a backdrop of a more militant and potentially dangerous opposition to the ceremony.

Rather than a secondary issue, paramilitary organizations on the margins of the nationalist movement seized on the anti-investiture issue as their central focus. In the form of the Mudiad Amddiffyn Cymru (MAC – the Movement for the Defence of Wales), the Free Wales Army and the Patriotic Front, militants sought to enflame the sense of alienation and resentment among Welsh youth and mobilize it in the form of a violent confrontation with the British state. Pre-dating the investiture controversy, these groups shared similar origins arising from the frustration over the weakness of constitutional methods in opposing the flooding of the Tryweryn Valley. As a consequence, they advocated direct, violent action in seeking Welsh freedom and independence. Apart from a vague anti-socialism, they had no coherent ideology other than a militant demand for action and a hyper form of patriotism. Never having many active members and often identified with only a few individuals, the paramilitary groups relied upon shadowy claims to a secret substratum of public support and to a reservoir of hidden but as yet inactive resources. Organization was slight and coordination between paramilitary groups negligible but public distinction between the groups was intentionally vague and porous. In truth, the paramilitaries were more interested in conducting a propaganda war than in waging an

---

[72] Translated from the original Welsh: *Tafod y Ddraig*, June 1969.
[73] Translated from the original Welsh: *Y Cymro*, 25 June 1969.

active terrorist or guerrilla campaign. Aimed at destroying property and symbolic targets rather than the taking of life, their activities were meant to influence public opinion and alarm the authorities. They hoped that provoking an oppressive response from British security forces would in turn radicalize a resentful Welsh population. In many respects, their activities resembled the vandalism campaigns of Cymdeithas yr Iaith writ large – but gelignite is not spray paint and death threats are not the equivalent of placard slogans. The use of bombs, military manoeuvres, uniformed marches, and violent rhetoric was a form of political intimidation that ultimately depended on the potential infliction of mayhem, injury and death.

A secret organization consisting of only a handful of active agents and their supporters, the MAC was formed by Emyr Llewelyn Jones, an Aberystwyth university student and the son of a celebrated poet, and Owain Williams, a Pwllehli café owner who had picked up knowledge in the use of gelignite from Quebecois nationalists during a stint in a Canadian logging camp. In 1963, Jones and Williams were arrested and served short prison sentences for blowing up a power transformer at the Tryweryn dam construction site. Inactive as MAC operatives following their release, Emyr Llewelyn Jones became closely associated with Cymdeithas yr Iaith while Owain Williams became loosely attached to other paramilitary groups like the Free Wales Army and the Patriotic Front.[74] Largely moribund following the arrests of its founders, the MAC was revitalized with the recruitment and elevation to leadership of John Jenkins. An unlikely Welsh militant, Jenkins was an English-speaking soldier from south Wales. Trained in explosives, he was actively serving in the Royal Welch Fusiliers as a non-commissioned officer, dental technician and drummer. The MAC carried out three additional operations aimed at water installations in Wales – an explosion at the Clywedog reservoir in March 1966, a failed attempt in March 1967 to bomb the Elan Valley water pipeline to Birmingham, and the

[74] For details on the origins of the MAC, see Roy Clews, *To Dream of Freedom: The Struggle of the M. A. C. and the Free Wales Army* (Tal-y-bont, 1980) pp. 17–29.

Lake Vyrnwy pipeline explosion in September 1967 – before its attention was clearly refocused on opposing the investiture.

Orchestrated by its drummer commandant, the MAC conducted a campaign to accompany investiture related events with a rhythmic beat of explosions and flying debris. Having been identified as a site of protest by Cymdeithas yr Iaith, the MAC targeted the Croeso 69 national conference. On 17 November 1967, an explosion ripped through the entrance hall of the Temple of Peace in Cardiff only seven hours before the much ballyhooed conference was scheduled to begin. With chunks of masonry dislodged, metalwork twisted, windows smashed and displays destroyed, the bomb caused £20,000 in damage. While workers raced to clean up the mess, Lord Snowdon, Cledwyn Hughes, and local dignitaries and representatives from across Wales were forced to enter the hall through a side door.[75] The MAC's unrelated bombing of the Inland Revenue Office in Cardiff on 24 March 1968 was followed by a series of incidents anticipating the prince's week long series of engagements marking his first official visit to Wales in June 1968. Jenkins gave a rare and clandestine interview to the *Daily Mail* in early May, publicly identifying the MAC as an organization and claiming responsibility for the previous bombings. Panicking the authorities who promptly suppressed much of the interview from publication, Jenkins grimly warned that the MAC could not guarantee the safety of the prince when he set foot in Wales. Although they bore him no personal ill-will, he would be 'in grave danger' if the investiture took place.[76] On 25 May, an explosion rocked the administration block of the Welsh Office. Two pipeline attacks occurred on the eve of the prince's arrival in the principality, temporarily cutting the water supply of Liverpool by half. 'There is no doubt that this is a very serious incident coinciding as it does with the Prince's visit to the Principality', said George Thomas: 'Like everyone else, I draw my own conclusions about it.'[77] Later that December, yet another MAC pipeline explosion announced the prince's return to the principality, this

---

[75] *Western Mail*, 18 November 1969.
[76] Clews, pp. 153–7; *Daily Mirror*, 31 July 1968.
[77] *Western Mail*, 29 June 1968.

time to chair the first meeting of the Countryside Committee for Wales.

The month of April 1969 witnessed the commencement of the prince's term at the University College of Wales and a slew of bombing attacks. An explosion ripped through an Inland Revenue office in Chester. The attack was timed to coincide with a visit to the town by the Duke of Norfolk. Ironically, Norfolk was scheduled to speak on the armed services' role in the investiture at an engagement at the army headquarters located there. On the day of the prince's arrival in Aberystwyth, an explosion occurred at the new police headquarters in Cardiff. Elsewhere in Cardiff, a bomb was discovered in a locker at the Queen's Street railway station and an explosion damaged the Central Electricity Generation Board. All of this was, of course, to be but a prelude to the plans being laid by the MAC for Caernarfon in July.

In the beginning, the Free Wales Army (FWA) was as insubstantial as the mists of Snowdon from which it seemingly sprang. In the wake of the MAC bombing of the Tryweryn dam in 1963, a variety of painted slogans and graffiti spontaneously spread across north and mid Wales. Along with 'Cofiwch Dryweryn' (Remember Tryweryn), the words 'Free Wales Army' and 'FWA' began to appear scrawled on stone walls, bridges and rocks. In its first form, then, the FWA was merely a daub of paint, more the expression of a frustrated wish than an actual corporal body of men. However, as the graffiti spread and grew in popularity, a few individuals became determined to emulate and reify the myth. One who was inspired by the slogans was 27-year-old Julian Cayo-Evans, an army veteran and horse breeder from Cardiganshire and the son of a former Lord Lieutenant. In October 1965, he and two of his cousins attracted considerable attention from photographers and reporters by appearing in makeshift uniforms carrying red dragon banners at a large rally to protest the opening of the Tryweryn dam. Stones were thrown, a Union Jack was burned and the Free Wales Army was born.[78]

In donning uniforms, titles and pretence, they were soon joined by several other young men in their teens and early

[78] Clews, pp. 30–43.

INVESTITURE

twenties, primarily from mid and south Wales. Of the organization of the Free Wales Army, Gethin ap Iestyn would later explain:

> It's a mistake, fostered by both the press and the FWA itself, to think of the FWA as a cohesive unit. Basically, the FWA was anyone who said they were the FWA . . . The FWA was organized in autonomous groups and individuals which sprang up all over Wales in the late 60s. There was no central organization of any kind, other members were met through personal friendship or locally organized meetings, and only later through nationally organized meetings, rallies and training sessions. Any FWA group or individual could decide on any action or policy they wanted quite independently of any other FWA members.[79]

Founder Julian Cayo-Evans was soon joined by self-proclaimed commandant Denis Coslett, an eccentric character from Llanelli who had served stints in the army, the merchant marines and coal mines. The FWA was ostensibly devoted to the holding of military operations, but it developed little in the way of military strategy and was armed only with a motley collection of shotguns, antique firearms and the occasional stick of gelignite secured from a local quarry. Their primary activity was to appear in uniform at rallies, conduct pirate radio broadcasts and paint graffiti and slogans. Collectively, these activities could misleadingly suggest that a large underground army may in fact exist. Unlike the secret MAC, Cayo-Evans and Coslett were public figures who openly courted the increasing media attention that was given to them as a result of the resumption of the MAC bombing campaign. With his eye patch, Alsatian dog and ever present commandant's uniform, Coslett in particular was a glutton for the media spotlight. The MAC was only too glad to have attention focused elsewhere and did little to stop the public association between the bombs and the FWA. Indeed, laying claim to the bombings and posturing in uniform for reporters and cameras seems to have been the FWA's primary modus operandi. Interviews, training camps, armed manoeuvres and parades were conducted largely for the benefit of the press. Looking back at them after the

[79] Clipping, 'Seize the Time', Penderyn, Tŷ Cenedl 1 AI/4, NLW.

revelations of their trial, *The Daily Telegraph and Morning Post* summed up the organization in the following terms:

> They gave interviews to newspapers and magazines, they appeared on television – and the brighter the limelight, the bolder became their words. The Free Wales Army, some claimed, could mobilize 7,000 men, armed and skilled in guerrilla warfare; they were backed by millionaire patriots; somewhere at a secret hideout they had an aeroplane; they swore each other to secrecy by an oath which offered 'death as a traitor' to anyone who broke his vows. They hailed explosions which damaged pipelines and public buildings as blows against the English oppressors. They wore Castro-style uniforms; they posed for photographs with weapons and they insulted Prince Charles – soon to become Prince of Wales. But, in truth, the Free Wales Army was largely fantasy, the day dream of young men who still wanted to play at soldiers. It probably never numbered more than 14. There were no millionaire backers, there was no aeroplane and its armoury was a meagre collection of wartime souvenirs, some of which did not even work. In the pubs where they drank and boasted, the locals laughed at the soldiers of the Free Wales Army.[80]

If fact, many nationalists regarded the FWA as either a farce or a mere gang of boyos 'raising a two fingered salute to authority'.[81] The FWA was often ridiculed in the journal of Cymdeithas yr Iaith and the leaders of Plaid Cymru were suspicious that they and the bombers were in fact agent-provocateurs designed to discredit the nationalist movement.

But not everyone dismissed them so flippantly. Although many among the police and press rightfully doubted the FWA's claims of responsibility, the bombs were a disturbing and dangerous reality that could not be ignored. However marginal the organization, the words and actions of FWA leaders demanded serious consideration from the press and authorities. Furthermore, the FWA claimed that it had external links and cooperative relationships with other paramilitary groups in Scotland, France, Spain, Quebec and Ireland.[82] Displaying its international paramilitary credentials, Cayo-Evans and Coslett even marched with a contingent of FWA volunteers in a

[80] *Daily Telegraph and Morning Post*, 1 July 1969.
[81] *Daily Mirror*, 11 September 1968.
[82] *Daily Telegraph Magazine*, 6 September 1968.

Dublin parade marking the IRA's 1966 commemoration of the Easter Rising. While claiming that they intended to 'blow up places when there is no one around' and did not plan to hurt anyone, the leaders of the FWA engaged in increasingly violent rhetoric and issued dire warnings. 'If I must kill, I'll kill', explained Coslett to a reporter: 'If a politician comes to Wales prepared to kill Wales as a nation, I'm prepared to kill that politician. I'll assassinate him.'[83] The Free Wales Army may have been a bit of a joke in its chrysalis form, but it was a palpable threat in potential. When and in what form that danger might emerge was unpredictable, even by the commandants of the Free Wales Army themselves. All that might be needed was a triggering event for the Free Wales Army to blossom and, to paraphrase Yeats, for a terrible beauty to be born.

The same 1965 demonstration at the Tryweryn dam that created the FWA also gave rise to the Patriotic Front, a uniformed nationalist organization based in Cwmbran and originally catering to English-speaking nationalists in south Wales. Its founders were Anthony Lewis, a 28-year-old veteran of the air force and a bus driver from Cwmbran, and Gethin ap Iestyn, a 19-year-old labourer from Bridgend originally named Keith Griffiths. Although their group of militants arrived on site too late to join the demonstration at Tryweryn, Lewis and ap Iestyn met with Cayo-Evans and formed the Patriotic Front shortly thereafter. Envisioned as the political wing of the paramilitary struggle, the Patriotic Front advocated direct action for the nationalist cause through the production of propaganda, the holding of rallies and the orchestration of confrontations with the police. The Front served as an umbrella organization, instigating the creation of a plethora of small, rather insubstantial groups devoted to various nationalist causes and largely composed of a close circle of the front's supporters, filled out by young, radical members of Cymdeithas yr Iaith and Plaid Cymru.[84] Among others, these subordinate organizations included the Patriots Aid Committee, Young Patriots League, Confederation of

[83] Ibid.
[84] Court statement by Keith Griffiths, Tŷ Cenedl 1 AI/4, NLW; Clews, pp. 91–95.

Welsh Workers, Llywelyn Society, Cymdeithas Glyndŵr, Owain Glyndŵr Memorial Committee, Patriotic Press, Patriotic Enterprises, Eagle Publishing, Cymru ein Gwlad, the Welsh Monarchy Society and the Independent Welsh Labour Party.[85] Unlike that of Cymdeithas yr Iaith, their activities and propaganda were largely conducted in the English language.

The Patriotic Front and the FWA were inevitably associated with one another. The leaders of the Patriotic Front regarded themselves as covert commandants of FWA columns and participated in training sessions as such. Conversely, Cayo-Evans and Coslett were a near constant presence at Patriotic Front rallies and events. However, divergent leadership, personality clashes, missteps and frustration over the antics of Coslett in the press frayed the relationship. An incident where Cayo-Evans avoided arrest by surrendering a cache of arms to police finally led the Patriotic Front to publicly split with the FWA in November 1968.[86] The activities and destinies of the two organizations, however, were inescapably linked.

The leaders of the Free Wales Army and the Patriotic Front regarded the 1969 Investiture as the best chance to trigger the Welsh fight for national liberation. Consequently, the ceremony became the principal focus of their activities after the announcement of the ceremony in May 1967. The distinction for producing the earliest organized anti-investiture campaign falls to the Patriotic Front, who in September 1967 formed the Llywelyn Society to oppose the ceremony as 'an insult to our nation' and to propagate the memory of Prince Llywelyn as the last true Prince of Wales.[87] It began a 'Charles Windsor Shall Not Pass' petition drive, produced leaflets, posters and buttons. Although much of its propaganda was amateurish, even juvenile in appearance, the themes and slogans it developed became very influential in the anti-investiture movement in general. In October, members of the Llywelyn Society lobbied

---

[85] Statement of the people of Wales to the English government and the press, television and radio, Anti-Investiture Campaign Committee, 12 October 1968, Tŷ Cenedl, 1 AI/5, NLW; *Western Mail*, 8 January 1968.

[86] On the Patriotic Front-FWA split, see Central Committee of Patriotic Front to J Cayo-Evans, 2 November 1968, Tŷ Cenedl 1 AI/4, NLW; Cayo-Evans to Tony Rees, Tŷ Cenedl AI/4, NLW.

[87] Court statement by Keith Griffiths, Tŷ Cenedl 1 AI/4, NLW.

for anti-investiture policies at the 1967 annual meeting of Cymdeithas yr Iaith, and demonstrably influenced the society's decision to oppose the investiture. In making the case against the investiture, the Llywelyn Society was notably and ably assisted by MAC founder Emyr Llewelyn Jones.[88] At the September 1968 Annual Meeting of Plaid Cymru, the Patriotic Front orchestrated the protests and resolutions against the party's neutral stance on the investiture.

Providing opportunities to appear in uniform, issue threats and clash with the police, the Patriotic Front held a series of anti-investiture protests and rallies at which the FWA habitually appeared. In contrast to the large protests held by Cymdeithas yr Iaith, these were minor affairs attracting fewer than 100 demonstrators. Yet, they produced some of the more memorable episodes of the anti-investiture campaign and successfully attracted the attention of the press. Under the auspices of the Front's Llywelyn Society, the first organized anti-investiture rally was held in conjunction with a commemoration of Llywelyn the Last at Cilmery on 11 December 1967.[89] It began with a meeting at the Llywelyn Inn and continued with a torchlight procession to the standing stone monument to the slain prince. A wreath was laid, incendiary speeches made and a Union Jack burned. In June 1968, a remarkable incident occurred during a Patriotic Front protest against the prince's visit to the Welsh Office. His attention drawn by booing from the crowd, Prince Charles surprised everyone by approaching the security barriers to speak directly with the protestors. An unpleasant confrontation then ensued, in which the prince was verbally insulted and smoke bombs hurled. With scuffles breaking out in the crowd, the startled police abruptly ended the encounter and arrested four members of the Front, including Gethin ap Iestyn and Gwenllian Wynne-Jeffries, the teenage daughter of Robert Wynne, a blue blooded paramilitary sympathizer.[90] The incident received a tremendous amount of

[88] *Western Mail*, 23 October 1967, 8 January 1968.
[89] The Cilmery commemoration of Llywelyn began in 1966 under the auspices of the Patriotic Front. It became an explicitly anti-investiture rally in 1967.
[90] *Western Mail*, 29 June 1968; *The Times*, 29 June 1968; *Guardian*, 29 June 1968. A member of the north Wales gentry, Robert Wynne was

press coverage and commentary, the *Observer Magazine* even publishing a large photograph of the comely Cymraes under banner headlines that incredulously asked 'What made Gwenllian Wynne-Jeffries throw a smoke bomb at Prince Charles?'[91]

The paramilitaries were clearly attempting to compete with Cymdeithas yr Iaith as the voice of nationalist protest. Timed to coincide with the annual general meeting of Cymdeithas yr Iaith in October 1968, the Patriotic Front organized a meeting of the so-called Anti-Investiture Campaign Committee at the Owain Glyndŵr Institute in Machynlleth. Directly confronting Cymdeithas yr Iaith's claim to the honour, the delegates resolved to recognize the Patriotic Front as the 'official anti-investiture movement' and a collection of its own subsidiaries pledged support for the leadership of the Front in the upcoming campaign.[92] With an eye to the activities of Cymdeithas, the Patriotic Front subsequently began to refer to itself in its propaganda as 'The Only United Anti-Investiture Movement'.[93] This was followed by a much-vaunted protest march on the Croeso 69 office in Caernarfon on 16 November 1968, described by the press as a 'flop' because it attracted only about 70 demonstrators.[94] The subsequent rally held at Cilmery on 14 December 1968 proved to be the most notorious of the Patriotic Front/FWA demonstrations. It began with dissension and arguments between members of the FWA and the Patriotic Front and later escalated into a heated clash between protestors and local police.[95]

<blockquote>
a rather unusual ally of the Patriotic Front who had maintained a claim to the crown of Llywelyn the Last and was at the centre of the Patriotic Front's Welsh Monarchy Society. Roy Clews reports that he occasionally bailed members of the Free Wales Army out of jail following confrontations with police.
</blockquote>

[91] *Observer Magazine*, 22 June 1969.
[92] Statement of the people of Wales to the English government and the press, television and radio, Anti-Investiture Campaign Committee, 12 October 1968, Tŷ Cenedl 1 AI/5, NLW.
[93] 'Charles Windsor Shall Not Pass Petition', Tŷ Cenedl, 1 AI/5, NLW.
[94] *The Times*, 18 November 1968.
[95] Court statement by David John Underhill, Tŷ Cenedl 1 AI/4, NLW; Western Mail, 16 December 1968; *Observer Magazine*, 15 December 1968; Clews, pp. 180–1.

INVESTITURE

The FWA and Patriotic Front were actively plotting some form of action to obstruct the investiture itself. 'Oh, we've got plans for next year's Caernarfon Investiture ceremony', Coslett darkly promised the *Daily Telegraph Magazine* in the autumn of 1968: 'We've got plans for something that will make the whole world hold its breath.'[96] At the 1968 Cilmery rally, Gethin ap Iestyn threatened 'Anyone who gets an honour or an award for organizing the investiture will automatically receive the death penalty. They are traitors to Wales and should be wiped out'.[97] George Thomas would later claim that he received almost weekly threats to his life during the period leading up to the investiture and that his mother was threatened constantly.[98] Evidence and testimony later produced in court would reveal details of the paramilitary intentions for the ceremony. Reminiscent of the 1916 Easter Rising, an armed revolt was being planned by the FWA with the intention of occupying Caernarfon Castle shortly before the investiture. A proposed raid on the army barracks at Chester would provide weapons for the uprising and a marksman would take a shot at the Secretary of State to frighten him into resigning.[99] An open letter called on militants to occupy as much of Caernarfon as possible by force on investiture day:

> We call upon Welshmen to organize, train and equip, to arm themselves with guns, bombs, Molotov cocktails, grenades, pikes, bows and arrows, swords, bayonets, clubs . . . eggs filled with sand, flour and smoke bombs, nuts and bolts, sharpened pennies . . . Stock them up and bring them to Caernarfon.[100]

'It's up to the FWA and the Patriotic Front to take the lead', wrote Cayo-Evans, 'and if stopped on the way to Caernarfon, we smash our way through or infiltrate into the town . . .'[101]

[96] *Daily Telegraph Magazine*, 6 September 1968.
[97] *Western Mail*, 16 December 1968.
[98] George Thomas, *George Thomas, Mr. Speaker: The Memoirs of Viscount Tonypandy* (London, 1985), p. 118.
[99] *Daily Mail*, 14 September 1968. These details were produced in evidence at the September 1968 trial of Owain Williams.
[100] As quoted in Meic Stephens (ed.), *A Most Peculiar People: Quotations about Wales and the Welsh* (Cardiff, 1992), p. 141. See also *Western Mail*, 9 May 1969.
[101] *Western Mail*, 9 May 1969

Found in the home of Gethin ap Iestyn, a document meant to be issued to FWA volunteers in June 1969 called for 'a more violent campaign than ever before to weaken the English grip on Wales':

> Members of the underground resistance will be active throughout Wales. Most groups of Celts will be on active service throughout the duration of the investiture and its celebrations and will be responsible for sabotage. They will also bring traitors and Quislings to justice and punish them. An active service guerrilla column will be operating in the interior and will wage a full time campaign against occupation forces and enemy installations. A special service section, with teams operating in English towns and cities will attack installations in England itself. It will be a campaign to take the war into the home of the enemy.[102]

Coslett would later claim that it was his own intention to take advantage of the preoccupation with Caernarfon by seizing and occupying the Welsh Office in Cardiff.[103] In August 1968, Cayo-Evans and ap Iestyn organized an FWA encampment specifically to train for the investiture campaign. Infiltrated by the police and under surveillance, it was aborted.[104] Given the nature of paramilitary activities in the past, there was no doubt an element of wishful thinking and posturing in all this. But the extent to which such plans may have been actually carried out cannot be gauged because the leaders of the FWA and the Patriotic Front were arrested and imprisoned early in 1969. Julian Cayo-Evans, at least, anticipated such a turn of events and hinted at a more pragmatic if more limited strategy in connection to the investiture. Predicting in November 1968 that he and other FWA leaders would be in prison by the time of the investiture, Cayo Evans said:

> But there are so many Welshmen either in or outside nationalist organisations who would be willing to demonstrate, that Whitehall can do only one thing – ring Caernarfon with 20,000 troops. Everyone living or working in the town will have to have a pass six weeks before the ceremony. It will be an investiture at gun point.[105]

[102] *Western Mail*, 19 May 1969.
[103] Clews, p. 190.
[104] Clews, pp. 167–70.
[105] *Daily Mirror*, 9 November 1968.

In cultivating an environment of fear and violence and in provoking a seemingly disproportionate response from the state, the paramilitaries of the MAC, FWA and Patriotic Front could claim considerable success. Although miniscule in terms of active members, the paramilitary groups voiced a radical discontent that the British press believed to be shared more broadly in Wales. In the estimation of the *Daily Mirror*:

> One of the biggest problems facing the police is that Wales is riddled with nationalist organisations. And however peace loving the average Welshman may consider himself, he is usually fanatically proud of his country. So the authorities are faced with a nation of potential suspects.[106]

Elements in Welsh counter culture did suggest a sinister trend towards political violence, particularly among a youth watching the spectacle of riots in Paris and the United States. In Aberystwyth in the summer of 1969, the sale of popular wax 'bomb' candles was suppressed by police and the first prize for a Welsh-language pop song in an intercollegiate Eisteddfod was awarded to a ditty entitled 'Prince Charles, Look Out!'[107] An environment of violence was palpable and the prospect of what it could inspire was disturbing. Even Home Secretary James Callaghan conceded that 'the most elaborate precautions will not prevent a determined extremist from doing some mischief'.[108]

There was certainly an atmosphere of anxiety surrounding the 1969 Investiture, particularly in regards to the safety of Prince Charles. In the eyes of the press, the 1969 Investiture would be the first British ceremony of state 'to be held against the grim new background of bomb threats', unique in being 'preceded by so much apprehension and attended by such heavy security precautions'.[109] With tongue only slightly in cheek, the *Sun* wondered how literal the prince's fealty oath, 'I will bear unto you to live and die against all manner of folks', might become when faced with 'bands of wild men in the hills,

---

[106] *Daily Mirror*, 11 September, 1968.
[107] *Western Mail*, 24 February 1969.
[108] Home Secretary to prime minister, 12 February 1969, PREM 13/2903, PRO.
[109] *Western Mail*, 2 July 1969; *Scotsman*, 2 July 1969.

some of whom understand dynamite'.[110] A cartoon in the *Evening Standard* portrayed the prince with sword in hand ascending the castle tower, atop of which perched a smouldering dragon labelled 'Taffy'. Spurring the prince onwards, a worried Archdruid proclaims: 'And now we come to the trickiest part of the ceremony!'[111] 'It takes a brave non-Taffy who would presume to speak for Wales while imported English coppers look for gelignite . . .' opined the *Daily Mail*.[112] Reflecting the general mood a few months before the ceremony, British army regiments assigned to the investiture were engaged in training manoeuvres in Cyprus to find 'Barrabas the Bomb', a fictitious guerrilla said to have been trained in Wales.[113] The tense situation in Wales even attracted the attention of the Russian KGB, which briefly considered conducting a covert operation to frame the MI5 as agent provocateurs for the planting and detonating of a bomb on the route of the prince's procession.[114] Apprehension was certainly evident in Welsh churches and chapels where ministers read special prayers for peace during the investiture week.[115]

Such anxiety was clearly shared by the Wilson government. Even before the bombing of the Temple of Peace declared open season on the investiture, Welsh extremists were among the 'subversive threats' examined by the Home Office's formidable sounding Working Group on Countermeasures to Communism (more accurately renamed the Official Committee on Subversion at Home in January 1969).[116] With the Temple of Peace bombing in November 1967, the Welsh Office warned the prime minister that the threat posed by the paramilitaries had become 'very serious indeed'.[117] Wilson was notably anxious over the safety of the prince and the adequacy of the security

[110] *Sun*, 1 July 1969.
[111] *Evening Standard*, 1 July 1969.
[112] *Daily Mirror*, 2 July 1969.
[113] *Western Mail*, 1 May 1969.
[114] *The Times*, 13 September 1999.
[115] *Observer*, 29 June 1969.
[116] Three paragraphs of their 1967 report, 'Subversion in the United Kingdom', were devoted to Welsh paramilitaries. The actual contents of the report have been censored from the public record. See Burke Trend to G. H. Daniel, 10 November 1967, CAB 164/386, PRO.
[117] G. H. Daniel to Burke Trend, 20 November 1967, CAB 164/386, PRO.

INVESTITURE

measures being taken, persistently questioning and at one point having to be warned by his staff not to step on the toes of Jim Callaghan, the Home Secretary.[118] With statements of concern regarding the safety of Prince Charles being made in the House of Commons, the prime minister was almost frantic in his communication with the Home Secretary by August 1968:

> I am troubled by the persistence of the more extreme forms of Welsh nationalism; and, with one eye on the Investiture of the Prince of Wales which is now less than a year away, I am concerned that we should do all we can both to identify the terrorists, their supporters, their sources of finance, etc. and to ensure that the intelligence and security organization in Wales is tightened up to the point of maximum efficiency. I should be glad if you could let me have a note on both these points; and perhaps we might then discuss the matter in September with the Secretary of State for Wales (whom you will no doubt consult in the preparation of the note in so far as you think it necessary).[119]

Despite assurances from the Home Office, Wilson remained 'uneasy' about the plans for the investiture and in February 1969 asked for additional assurances and details so that he could advise the Queen 'with confidence' to go forward with the plans.[120] Insisting that security arrangements were adequate and that the prince was in more danger of being embarrassed than harmed by an incident, Callaghan argued that the schedule of events connected to the ceremony should go forward as planned.[121] Momentarily reassured, the prime minister was again alarmed by the flurry of paramilitary activity and bombings in April 1969. This was compounded by the arrival of a letter from the principal of the university in Aberystwyth expressing grave fears about the current atmosphere among the students and refusing to accept responsibility for the safety of the prince.[122] Unsettled, Wilson challenged

[118] Cubbon to prime minister, 1 March 1968, PREM 13/2903, PRO. See correspondence generally in PREM 13/2903, PRO.
[119] Prime minister to Home Secretary, 1 August 1968, PREM 13/2903, PRO.
[120] Prime minister to Home Secretary, 4 February 1969, PREM 13/2903, PRO.
[121] Home Secretary to prime minister, 12 February 1969, PREM 13/2903, PRO.
[122] Thomas, p. 119.

Callaghan's commitment to the events going ahead as planned, asking: 'Would the Home Secretary please reconsider in the light of the latest outrage actually in the Police Headquarters in Cardiff. Might we not be wiser to cancel Aberystwyth?'[123] Both Callaghan and George Thomas were adamant that cancelling the plans for the prince at Aberystwyth and Caernarfon 'would be wrong'.[124] On the eve of the Troubles in Northern Ireland, Thomas advised Wilson: 'We cannot have a part of the United Kingdom where a member of the Royal Family dare not go for safety reasons. We must proceed.'[125]

Prompted by these deepening concerns, the Home Office orchestrated what was called 'the biggest security network ever established in Wales', designed not only as the 'most prolonged personal protection job ever undertaken in Britain' but as an operation whose overwhelming size would actually 'discourage extremists from planning attacks'.[126] In January 1968, the Home Office and the Secretary of State for Wales organized a special meeting of police and security forces to discuss the activities of Welsh extremists and to assess the risk of outrages connected to the investiture. A special 'prince protection squad' composed of one detective from each of the forces in Wales was created to collect and collate intelligence related to Welsh paramilitaries and extremists. Although MI5 and the Special Branch were kept in close consultation, initially this was an effort primarily of Welsh authorities and personnel.[127] By August 1968, increasing concerns resulted in the reorganization of the security effort, reassigning the responsibility to protect the prince and to weed out paramilitaries to a unit of handpicked agents from the Special Branch and MI5. Headquartered in Shrewsbury, this unit was led by Detective Chief Superintendent Jock Wilson, one of Scotland Yard's most experienced

[123] Harold Wilson to BC Cubbon, 16 April 1969, PREM 13/2903, PRO.
[124] Home Secretary to Harold Wilson, 16 April 1969, PREM 13/2903, PRO.
[125] 'Everyone Held Their Breath', BBC 1, Airdate 1 July 1994, AM 1099/03, Television and Film Archive, NLW; Thomas, p. 119.
[126] *Daily Mirror*, 31 July 1968; *Observer*, 6 July 1969.
[127] Phillip Allen to Burke Trend, 26 February 1968, CAB 164/389, PRO; Burke Trend to prime minister, 28 February 1968, PREM 13/2903, PRO.

Special Branch officers.[128] Of the new arrangements, Jim Callaghan would assure the prime minister:

> The Shrewsbury Unit is undoubtedly of value. What was lacking before was a central intelligence organization which could bring together and assess the value of information from a number of sources. Penetration of Welsh nationalist organizations is very difficult but at least there is now effective machinery for exploiting any break.[129]

Responsible for general security arrangements in connection to the prince's appearances, the Chief Constables of Aberystwyth, Caernarfon and the various towns of the prince's tour could rely upon the close cooperation of the United Kingdom's security and intelligence services and the aid of a legion of borrowed police officers gathered from across Wales and England.

A massive campaign of surveillance was associated with the special police operation to protect the prince. In the year before the investiture, members of the Free Wales Army were reportedly being hunted day and night by watchful inspectors. Julian Cayo-Evans claimed that Scotland Yard was tapping his telephone and reading his mail while Denis Coslett complained to the television cameras of constant police harassment.[130] Robert Wynne, the nationalist aristocrat, was singled out for special attention and interviewed repeatedly.[131] By September 1968, with Jock Wilson's new team in place, the net expanded more broadly to include surveillance and interviews of outspoken nationalists as well as known paramilitaries and their sympathizers. Plaid Cymru was moved to protest against police 'persecution' of its members.[132] Things continued to escalate. Gethin ap Iestyn would later claim:

> From the early spring onwards over 100 prominent nationalists were watched full time, day and night, by teams of up to 6 policemen on each individual. Members of their families were also kept under

[128] *Herald of Wales*, 7 September 1968; *Daily Telegraph*, 26 August 1968; *Western Mail*, 26 August 1968; *Daily Mirror*, 31 July 1968.
[129] Home Secretary to Harold Wilson, 12 February 1969, CAB 164/386, PRO.
[130] *Daily Telegraph Magazine*, 6 September 1968; *Daily Mirror*, 11 September 1968.
[131] *Observer Magazine*, 21 June 1969.
[132] *Observer*, 22 September 1968.

surveillance. This made it almost impossible for meetings and effective communication to continue.[133]

Emyr Llewelyn and Owain Williams, the founders and former members of the MAC, were watched by relays of detectives.[134] In the days before the investiture itself, round the clock surveillance of 'gentlemen who might disrupt the ceremony' came to a crescendo. Seemingly, anyone associated with anti-investiture protest was kept under careful watch by teams of undercover police. A journalist for the *Scotsman* interviewed Euryn ap Rhobart, a 22-year-old student from Llanberis who had gone on a five-day hunger strike at the university in Bangor earlier that year. He reported:

> They started last night when we went over to Caernarfon to see the Stanley Baker film 'Zulu' about British imperialism again. We had a chaperone throughout at the cinema. Since then they have been following us all the time. Sometimes two, sometimes more.
>
> As we spoke, two of the detectives . . . stood about 20 yards away staring at us . . . The detectives turned out to be Regional Crime Squad people from Manchester. They had been in the village for a week – part of the massive police reinforcements drafted into the area from all parts of Britain.[135]

This campaign of surveillance, interrogation and investigation led to a series of police actions with rather mixed results. Following the explosion of a small bomb in a country club in Gwynedd in January 1968, the prime minister was told that the new security team had procured the arrest of three men who 'had in their possession guns and explosives, and were evidently members of the Free Wales Army'.[136] Among them was MAC veteran Owain Williams. While the other two were given one-year suspended sentences for the unlawful possession of gelignite, Owain Williams fled to Ireland and was later arrested while attempting to re-enter the country in September 1968. He was found not guilty in a Caernarfonshire courtroom packed with cheering FWA and Patriotic Front supporters.[137]

[133] Press clipping, 'Seize the Times', Penderyn, Tŷ Cenedl, 1 AI/4, NLW.
[134] *Sunday Telegraph*, 6 July 1969.
[135] *Scotsman*, 2 July 1969.
[136] Phillip Allen to Burke Trend, 26 February 1968, CAB 164/389, PRO.
[137] Clews, pp. 131–5, 171–4; *Daily Mail*, 14 September 1968.

INVESTITURE

In August 1968, the police so thoroughly penetrated a 'secret' FWA rendezvous and training camp at Abergweswyn that the FWA men had to pull up stakes and flee across the hills. In September, a mail bomb severely injured an officer at the RAF base in Pembrey. Although the press widely credited the FWA with the attack and condemned the paramilitaries for its first shedding of blood, the incident was inconsistent with the profile of previous bombings and was publicly disowned by the FWA and later by the MAC. That night, the prince's protection squad immediately rounded up known FWA men for interrogation. Most likely, the police became convinced that the men had nothing to do with the Pembrey bomb but decided to play the seriousness of the crime to their advantage. DCS Jock Wilson personally interviewed Julian Cayo-Evans and reputedly secured with him a deal whereby FWA armaments would be surrendered in exchange for the release of those arrested. As per the agreement, Cayo-Evans covertly dumped the arms in a lake near Tregaron and phoned the police of their whereabouts. To the flash of press photographers, police frogmen pulled the weapons from the lake the following day. The existence of the pact between Jock Wilson and Julian Cayo-Evans was later denied by police but the nature of the alleged agreement was soon in public circulation, prompting condemnation by the Patriotic Front and its public split from the FWA in November 1968.[138] The extensive security network had certainly disrupted the activities of the FWA and the Patriotic Front, but the MAC was still frustratingly beyond their reach and the bombings continued apace.

The most spectacular action of DCS Jock Wilson's special squad was the series of arrests leading to the dramatic 'FWA trial' in the spring of 1969. In February 1969, the Home Secretary wrote to the prime minister that although the 'Shrewsbury Unit' had failed to collect enough evidence for a prosecution of a bombing, the Attorney General had decided that a number of Welsh nationalists should be prosecuted for

[138] Clews, pp. 167–70, 175–79; *Daily Telegraph and Mirror*, 1 July 1969; *The Times* 7 March 1969; Central Committee of the Patriotic Front to J. Cayo-Evans, 2 November 1968, Tŷ Cenedl 1 AI/4, NLW; Transcript of a soundtrack of a film on Welsh nationalism, Tŷ Cenedl 1 AI/4, NLW.

other offences: 'The proceedings should at least establish that Welsh extremists who contravene the Public Order cannot expect to go scot-free and the police hope that a good deal of information may emerge in questioning and in the search of premises belonging to suspects. I expect arrests in a few days.'[139] Requiring the direct sanction of the Attorney General, the men would be charged with various counts under the Public Order Act of 1936, a law prohibiting the wearing of uniforms and the promotion of violence for political objectives. It carried a maximum sentence of two years in prison and a £500 fine. Late in the evening of 25 February, squad cars and minibuses with police carrying portable searchlights set out to different parts of Wales for a series of simultaneous raids.[140] At dawn, the police swept down on the homes of nine men: Julian Cayo-Evans, Denis Coslett, William Vernon Griffiths, Vivian George Davies, and David Bonar Thomas of the FWA; Gethin ap Iestyn, Anthony Lewis and Dafydd Glyn Rowlands of the Patriotic Front; and David Underhill, an anti-investiture activist associated with the Bridgend branch of Plaid Cymru and the Llywelyn Society. With the exception of Underhill who was quickly acquitted and released, the accused were kept in solitary confinement, visits by relatives were prohibited and bail denied. This continued during the four months between their arrest and the end of their trial.[141] Although they had anticipated arrest, ap Iestyn would later state that the FWA and Patriotic Front were unprepared for the sheer size and force of the operation against them and that the organizations were literally crushed by the arrests, the confiscation of equipment and the continual harassment of members and their families that followed.[142]

Conducted against the continued bombing campaign of the MAC, the 'FWA trial' began in the Swansea Assizes in May and lasted fifty-three days. At the time, it was the second longest trial in the criminal history of Wales.[143] Considering its context

[139] Home Secretary to prime minister, 12 February, CAB 164/386, PRO.
[140] *Daily Telegraph*, 27 February 1969.
[141] Home Secretary to Harold Wilson, 14 April 1969, PREM 13/2903, PRO; *The Times*, 11 March 1969; Clews, pp. 192–6.
[142] Press clipping, 'Seize the Times', Penderyn, Tŷ Cenedl, 1 AI/4, NLW.
[143] *Daily Telegraph and Morning Post*, 1 July 1969.

within the overall campaign to secure the ceremony and given the nature of the charges and the inordinate length of the trial, it is hard to dismiss the defence barrister's allegation that the prosecution was purely political and designed to get the men out of the way of the investiture.[144] Indeed, as the trial wore on and the investiture approached, Justice Thompson picked up the pace of the trial so that the accused would stand in the dock to receive their sentences in Swansea only a few hours before the prince took his oath of fealty in Caernarfon.[145] The prosecution was based almost entirely on newspaper cuttings, photographs and transcripts of interviews and television programmes featuring the defendants. Their case was predicated on the assumption that the FWA was in fact a serious revolutionary group – in other words, on taking the FWA at their word. In surprising contrast, the defence tried to prove that the claims of the paramilitaries were nothing more than wild and foolish fantasies. Shattering the credibility of the FWA and Patriotic Front, the politically disastrous nature of this defence was recognized by Gethin ap Iestyn, whose change of plea to guilty came too late to mitigate the damage.[146] The jury took only twenty minutes to deliver their verdict. Only Julian Cayo-Evans and Denis Coslett were found guilty of substantive charges, joining Gethin ap Iestyn in prison sentences ranging from nine to fifteen months. Either acquitted or convicted of lesser offences, the others were given suspended sentences. In the revolutionary tradition of speeches made from the dock, Denis Coslet delivered a defiant oration in Welsh defending his use of violence in defence of his country and favourably comparing his actions with those of the British state, army and security forces. This inspired an eruption from supporters and provoked the judge to clear the court. Despite such rebelliousness, the trial ended with a whimper. Dafydd Glyn Rowlands, Dai Bonar Thomas and David Underhill all pledged to help authorities 'calm the hotheads' and Julian Cayo-Evans and Denis Coslett publicly denounced the use of political violence and signed statements that they would never again illegally

[144] Ibid.
[145] *Western Mail*, 24 June 1969; *Daily Mirror*, 2 July 1969.
[146] Press clipping, 'Seize the Times', Penderyn, Tŷ Cenedl, 1 AI/4, NLW.

hold weapons or explosives.¹⁴⁷ In passing sentence, Judge Thompson stated that he felt he could be more lenient because 'however misguided' the accused were 'lovers of Wales'. Yet, they had caused anxiety and alarm among their fellow countrymen and had 'served Wales ill'. Noting that there was no evidence connecting the accused to the bombing incidents, the judge said:

> What is not known is what encouragement your boastings, public displays and private propaganda have given to others ... [The accused] are not the only people with violent ideas in this land of Wales. Maybe a judge has got to give discouragement to those who have not yet come before the court.[148]

The FWA and Patriotic Front were destroyed as organizations, but the trial had done nothing to stem the bombings. The special police operation had yet to infiltrate the elusive MAC or track down John Jenkins. As the *Daily Telegraph and Morning Post* recognized: 'Somewhere in Wales, the silent, English hating saboteurs are still at large.'[149] Of equal risk, there was still the prospect of an outrage committed by an individual or small group unaffiliated but inspired by the FWA and the MAC. These facts were certainly not lost on DCS Jock Wilson and his Shrewsbury unit.

Security precautions in Wales before the investiture were extensive and elaborate, growing in intensity as the ceremony approached.[150] MI5 and Special Branch took extensive measures against attempts to assassinate or kidnap the leading personalities associated with the ceremony.[151] Army helicopters monitored the pipelines, patrols around water reservoirs were stepped up, and the Birmingham Corporation actually hired its own private force to guard the water facilities.[152] Security was increased around the Severn Bridge, Severn Tunnel and the Royal Mint in Llantrisant. Access to explosives

[147] *Western Mail*, 2 July 1969.
[148] *Daily Telegraph and Morning Post*, 2 July 1969.
[149] Ibid.
[150] *Observer*, 6 July 1969.
[151] Home Secretary to Harold Wilson, 14 April 1969, PREM 13/2903, PRO; Thomas, p. 119.
[152] *Western Mail*, 3 March 1969, 24 June 1969; *Guardian*, 25 June 1969.

in north Wales quarries was tightened and lockers in Cardiff and Swansea railway stations were closed.[153]

In coming to Aberystwyth, Prince Charles was entering the lion's den of Welsh nationalist sentiment and precautions to prevent some kind of violent or embarrassing incident were marked during the prince's term of study. In addition to a Special Branch officer living in the prince's suite of rooms and a Welsh-speaking policeman being posted at Pantycelyn Hall, a Special Branch unit set up shop and an army bomb disposal expert took up residence in the town below.[154] Reinforcements of detectives and uniformed police descended upon the town, filling most of the accommodation in the hotels along the seaside promenade and taking over a dance hall as a makeshift barracks.[155] In February 1969, the Home Secretary reported to the prime minister that, with the aid of university authorities, MI5 had established 'a number of sources within the College who are already proving productive'.[156] Rumours soon began to circulate within the student body of the presence of undercover agents amongst them. Prompting a resolution of protest from the Aberystwyth Student Union and disingenuous denials from university authorities, student Tegid Jones complained:

> During this year, it can be seen that there are mature students looking amazingly like agents from the Special Branch. There are far more students here on police and services scholarships this year ... These dubious characters are wandering about town asking questions and are always at pubs and parties. They have a wondrous aptitude for making friends, particularly among the greener members of our union. Such action must be abhorred, for if they are not detectives they are students planted to obtain information and paid by the Special Branch.[157]

Because the police 'appeared to be taking an interest in their activities', members of the student Welsh society Y Geltaidd

[153] *Daily Telegraph*, 26 March 1969; *Western Mail*, 26 June 1969.
[154] Home Secretary to Harold Wilson, 12 February 1969, CAB 164/386, PRO; *Western Mail*, 24 February 1969.
[155] *Observer*, 26 January 1969; *The Times*, 28 January 1969; *Western Mail*, 22 February 1969.
[156] Home Secretary to Harold Wilson, 12 February 1969, CAB 164/386, PRO.
[157] *Western Mail*, 10 February 1969.

cheekily invited Jock Wilson and all the officers specially drafted into the town to a special tea party where they could all 'get to know one another better'.[158]

Of course, the most extensive security arrangements were made for the site of the ceremony itself in Caernarfon. The defences of Caernarfon Castle were reputed to be 'as impregnable as they have ever been since the 13th century'.[159] From November 1968, police began a nightly patrol of the ancient fortress with Alsatian dogs. High-powered RAF spotlights were mounted to illuminate the castle walls and shine down on anyone approaching. One resident of the town likened it to living near Wormwood Scrubs prison.[160] The castle was guarded around the clock, police conducted nightly six-hour searches of the castle grounds and close-circuit television cameras were installed to monitor the surrounding area.[161] 'You can stand and look at the magnificent castle', reported the *South Wales Evening Post*, 'But move too close and you come under immediate suspicion'.[162] With the castle perched on a harbour commanding the southern end of the Menai Strait, security extended out to sea. With two minesweepers stationed nearby, high-speed police boats patrolled a boom stretched across the harbour to prevent small craft from nearing the castle. Meanwhile, frogmen policed the strait from beneath the waves.[163] Guests entering the castle were searched and even the cases and instruments of the investiture musicians examined. To the delight of the press, Princess Margaret was duly searched as she entered the castle for a private tour.[164] During the ceremony, undercover detectives mingled in the stands, prompting the correspondent for *National Geographic* to report: 'Plains clothesmen seemed as numerous as guests inside the castle.'[165]

[158] *Western Mail*, 25 April 1969.
[159] *Sun*, 1 July 1969.
[160] *Western Mail*, 13 November 1968.
[161] Brian Cubbon to Michael Halls, 26 June 1969, PREM 13/2903, PRO; *Western Mail*, 30 June 1969, 2 July 1969.
[162] *South Wales Evening Post*, 30 June 1969.
[163] *Sun*, 1 July 1969.
[164] Ibid.; *Evening Standard*, 1 July 1969.
[165] *National Geographic*, November 1969.

In the town outside the castle walls, Caernarfon reputedly felt 'like a goldfish bowl in a Scotland Yard office'.[166] For some time before the ceremony, Special Branch and army bomb experts extensively searched the maze of streets around the castle. Manhole covers were sealed with adhesive to prevent the entry of saboteurs.[167] Teams of detectives conducted surveillance and searches of houses and businesses along the processional route, asking occupants for lists of names, addresses, and the personal details of those in the buildings.[168] An unknown quantity of plainclothes detectives were thickly placed among the spectators, prompting the *Evening Standard* to invite attendees to a game of 'Spot the Special Branch Man'.[169] Spaced every 3 to 10 yards, 1,186 uniformed police officers were stationed along the processional route. With the 2,230 servicemen posted along the ceremonial way, the overall spacing was one man per 2.3 yards on each side of the road. Although the servicemen were there for ceremonial purposes alone, their presence was expected 'to greatly assist the police'. A further 716 uniformed police officers patrolled the streets in the investiture area, 500 were on duty elsewhere in the town and other officers were held in reserve.[170] In the skies, three army helicopters surveyed the town and the surrounding environs from above.[171] 'In Caernarfon yesterday', reported the *Sun*, 'there were an awful lot of people watching other people.'[172] Getting into the spirit of the occasion, a *Daily Mail* cartoon portrayed the Special Branch Male Voice Choir, suitably dressed in macs and low-brimmed hats, singing 'All Through the Night'.[173]

[166] Extract from 24 Hours, Recorded from transmission BBC 1 2220, 28 February 1969, PREM 13/2505.
[167] *Western Mail*, 30 June 1969.
[168] Brian Cubbon to Michael Halls, 26 June 1969, PREM 13/2903, PRO; Memo, Police Arrangements by Chief Constable of Gwynedd, 12 February, 1969, PREM 13/2903, PRO; *Western Mail*, 27 June 1969.
[169] *Evening Standard*, 1 July 1969.
[170] Memo, Police Arrangements by Chief Constable of Gwynedd, 12 February 1969, PREM 13/2903, PRO.
[171] J. F. Mayne to A. N. Halls, 27 June 1969, PREM 13/2903, PRO; *Sun*, 1 July 1969.
[172] *Sun*, 1 July 1969.
[173] *Daily Mail*, 3 July 1969.

In the environs outside of town, authorities were particularly concerned about preventing attacks on the transport routes leading to Caernarfon. While the prince would arrive by yacht moored off of Holyhead, the Queen and Royal Family were to travel by express train. With the Royal Family due to arrive on the morning of the investiture itself, sabotage on the railway and road network could effectively derail the ceremony. Its exact route kept in strict secrecy, the royal train would travel to Wales the day before the ceremony and stop overnight under armed guard at a secret destination near Abergele before proceeding on to Caernarfon. The royal train and a VIP train transporting the prime minister along the route that morning would be preceded by pilot trains. MI5 drew up a survey of vulnerable points along the route in England and Wales and preventive measures were put in place under the supervision of HM Inspector of the Constabulary. Police watched or frequently visited the strategic points along the railway in the month before the ceremony. The line leading from the layover to Caernarfon was guarded through the night, every inch of track, cuttings and embankments inspected. County surveyors were to be ready with road clearing equipment and arrangements were made for the Royal Engineers to be on hand to repair or replace any bridges which might be blown up. If necessary, the army helicopters being used for surveillance in the area were also available for emergency tasks, such as repairing bridges or even providing an airlift for stranded royals.[174] Soldiers on duty were instructed to be on guard against attempts to subvert personnel, steal armaments or bomb the army camps.[175]

Despite the FWA arrests, massive surveillance, extensive precautions and an overwhelming police presence, intelligence and security forces could not prevent a series of attacks and hostile incidents from occurring. Conveniently, John Jenkins spent the day of the investiture unsuspected in the army camp

[174] Home Secretary to Harold Wilson, 14 April 1969, PREM 13/2903, PRO; Brian Cubbon to Michael Halls, 26 June 1969, PREM 13/2903, PRO; J. F. Mayne to A. N. Halls, 27 June 1969, PREM 13/2903, PRO; *Sun*, 1 July 1969.
[175] Report on the Services Participation, Standing Orders for Llandwrog Camp, BD 67/135, PRO.

INVESTITURE

stationed just a few miles from Caernarfon. He was there as part of a medical backup team supporting the troops participating in the ceremony. From this location, Jenkins had plenty of opportunity to direct and engage in hostilities.[176] However, one of the strengths of the MAC was that its activities fostered emulation and it is hard to distinguish between the organized paramilitaries and those acting on their own accord. Jenkins claimed, credibly, that the MAC was engaged in only three of the many incidents that occurred in the days immediately surrounding the investiture.[177] Rather than a centrally organized and led uprising, what occurred appears to have been the spontaneous opposition of unconnected but commonly inspired small groups and individuals. Throughout the period, the police were inundated with hoax bomb warnings in Caernarfon, Cardiff, Swansea and the towns along the route of the prince's post investiture tour. In north Wales outside Caernarfon, the painting of slogans and vandalism against investiture decorations was rife.[178] Five days before the prince was scheduled to arrive aboard the royal yacht, a bomb was discovered under the MacKenzie Pier in Holyhead. A mail bomb exploded in a post office in Cardiff on the morning before the investiture. Elsewhere that day, dummy bombs and sabotage on the railway had delayed the progress of the Queen's arrival in Wales. In Caernarfon that evening, the police had to clear the town square outside of the castle of about 100 resisting protestors.[179] The day that began with an explosion in Cardiff ended late that night with a blast that claimed the lives of two young men in Abergele. Later eulogized as the 'Abergele Martyrs', Alwyn Jones and George Taylor were killed by their own bomb, apparently while transporting it to the railway line the Queen was due to arrive upon the following day.[180]

[176] Clews, p. 215.
[177] Ibid. The official MAC actions were the bomb in the railway siding in Caernarfon, the bomb in a Caernarfon back garden along the procession route that severely injured a boy on 5 July, and a bomb removed from Llandudno Pier unreported by the press.
[178] *South Wales Evening Post*, 1 July 1969.
[179] Ibid.
[180] Although reputedly members of a MAC cell, the bomb planted by Jones and Taylor was not among the three actions recognized by John Jenkins as official MAC operations during the investiture.

WE'LL KEEP A WELCOME?

With the news of the deaths in Abergele the night before, investiture day dawned uneasily. That morning, a bomb was discovered on the A5, the prince's route from Holyhead to Caernarfon. It was removed thirty minutes before the prince's entourage passed. As the prince processed through the streets of Caernarfon towards the castle, a MAC bomb exploded in a wood near the railway sidings where the prime minister's train was parked and where the emptied royal train was due shortly to arrive. No one was hurt and no property was damaged, but the blast was dramatic enough to rattle the windows along the processional route in the town. Two men were spotted fleeing the scene and apprehended, but were later released. Detonating precisely one minute after the royal carriage had reached the procession's starting point, Jenkins claimed that the bomb was meant to add an extra beat to the twenty-one-gun salute fired in honour of the Queen's arrival. George Thomas, who accompanied the prince in the open carriage, later recalled the moment:

> About five minutes after we had left the station, a shattering roar came from an adjoining field. An extremist had exploded a bomb. People watching television saw the police run after and capture a suspect, but neither Prince Charles nor I knew what was happening. He turned to me: 'What is it, Mr. Thomas?' I improvised 'It's a royal salute, Prince Charles'. When he said it was a peculiar royal salute, I could only reply, 'There are peculiar people up here, Prince Charles'.[181]

Although the public assembled along the processional route received the prince and Queen with enthusiasm, there were traces of dissent within the crowd. One observer detected some booing as the prince's carriage approached the castle. As the Queen's carriage passed, the police pounced on three demonstrators in Castle Square for making rude gestures and two youths were arrested near the King's Gate for throwing an apple. Two others were arrested for carrying offensive weapons – a sheath knife and a lead cosh. Somewhat surprisingly,

---

Interestingly, Jones bore 'FWA' tattoos on his arm and chest. However, it appears likely that Jones and Taylor were operating on their own accord with little if any supervision from the MAC or FWA; Clews, pp. 211–12, 215; *Sun*, 1–2 July 1969; *Daily Telegraph and Morning Post*, 1 July 1969.

[181] Thomas, p. 120.

that was the extent of the public disorder among the spectators. The investiture passed without further incident. However, just when the authorities in Caernarfon began to feel they could relax, disaster struck. Late that evening, a military police van parked outside of the castle gate was blasted by an explosion, throwing it three feet into the air and engulfing the vehicle and its driver in flames. Understandably, there was immediate suspicion that the unnerving death of this serviceman was the work of the bombers. It was never claimed as an MAC operation by Jenkins and the conclusion of the investigation to establish its cause is unclear.[182]

Hostile incidents continued to plague the prince's progress as he toured the principality between 2 and 6 July. On the morning of 2 July, frogmen searched Llandudno Pier where the prince's yacht was due to arrive. Although police reported that they found no explosives, John Jenkins maintained that an MAC bomb was in fact planted there. Later that day, a biscuit tin packed with explosives was discovered near Betws-y-Coed under a bridge only ten minutes before the prince was scheduled to pass over. Hoax bomb warnings continued apace and more fake bombs were discovered in Blaneau Ffestiniog, Swansea and Hirwaun. Then, on 5 July, the bombing campaign ended with bloodshed and tragedy. A bomb had been set by the MAC in a back garden along the route of the prince's procession in Caernarfon and timed to go off early on the morning of the investiture. Jenkins claimed that the MAC had contacted the authorities to warn them about the bomb when it failed to explode but that the thinly stretched police had disregarded it because of the flood of hoax calls received that day.[183] Consequently, the bomb had lain abandoned until discovered by Ian Cox, a youngster from Surrey, vacationing with his family in Caernarfon. The bomb detonated when the boy disturbed it, the explosion causing severe injuries to his legs and subsequent disability.

[182] The author has been unable to locate any report on the conclusions of this investigation. Clews states 'Despite the immediate suspicions of a planted bomb no evidence was ever discovered to confirm this'; Clews, p. 214; *Daily Telegraph and Morning Post*, 2 July 1969; *Daily Mail*, 2 July 1969.
[183] Clews, p. 215.

When the tour ended with the prince's departure from his principality on 6 July, the security forces, government and Royal Family no doubt breathed a sigh of relief. While some blood had been spilled, they had avoided a confrontation, disaster or embarrassment of major proportions. According to the *Daily Telegraph*:

> There were surely many fingers crossed yesterday for the Prince of Wales. Few people expressed openly the fears which nearly all felt: to have done so could only have cast a blight over an event which could no longer be cancelled and which might turn out a resounding success. Now that it has done so, the fears themselves seem unreal and unworthy. Yet there was always the possibility of disaster – the police clearly took it seriously enough. Nor was horror actually missing on the day.[184]

The FWA and the Patriotic Front were defunct, their leaders serving time. Yet danger remained. The far more serious threat of the MAC still lingered. Police were no closer to identifying and apprehending its leader on the day of the investiture than they were at the beginning of the investigation. At the end of the prince's tour, the *Sunday Telegraph* reported that the MAC was planning fresh attacks.[185] The bombers would actually carry out two more operations before they were identified by an informant. This information led to the November 1969 arrest of John Jenkins and fellow soldier Frederick Alders. They were subsequently sentenced on explosive charges for ten and six years' imprisonment respectively. As recounted by Roy Clews, the last explosion conducted by the MAC was on Guy Fawkes Night. Having gathered the remaining stocks of the organization's gelignite on a piece of waste land, an operative disposed of the MAC arsenal by setting it off.[186] With that spectacular boom, the insurrection in Wales was over.

Propaganda, rallies, protests, trials, vandalism and bombs established that there was considerable and determined opposition in Wales to the investiture. There were even indications that the breadth of opposition extended beyond youthful radicals. While only two local authorities officially withheld

---

[184] *Daily Telegraph and Morning Post*, 2 July 1969.
[185] *Sunday Telegraph*, 6 July 1969.
[186] Clews, pp. 218–21.

their support of the investiture, objections to local participation in investiture festivities were frequently made at the meetings of local authorities and many of those who lodged them did not fit the profile of the young extremist.[187] Hardly a vehicle of counter culture, the 4,000-member West Carmarthen Congregational Church Association denounced the investiture.[188] Although sceptical of the FWA and suspicious of the MAC, the Welsh-language intelligentsia and media were highly ambivalent towards the investiture. *Baner* and *Y Cymro* refused to place the investiture story on the front page but devoted copious inner column space and photographs to the protest rally of Cymdeithas yr Iaith at Cilmery. Groups like the Union of London Welsh Literary Societies boycotted the investiture. The Welsh Office had to wrestle with the potential embarrassment of several pointed refusals emanating from the Welsh Art Council's list of literary dignitaries to be invited to the ceremony.[189] *The Daily Sketch* reported that only 59 of 1,000 Caernarfonshire teachers were willing to take students to welcome the prince, reputedly resulting in only 2,000 of the 20,000 school children of the county participating in the celebrations.[190]

However, the virulence and prominence of anti-investiture activity was hardly an accurate reflection of public opinion in Wales. Initially, at least, investiture planners were concerned that the ceremony would lack popular support. If the bulk of the Welsh population was not actively opposed to the ceremony, much commentary in the press suggested they were apathetic and indifferent. But opinion seemed to polarize as the investiture approached and events unfolded. Commentators were particularly convinced of the positive effect on public opinion of the prince's study at Aberystwyth and his speech at the Urdd. The *South Wales Evening Post* asserted that after the prince's speech 'appreciation and recognition already evident

[187] Minutes, Third meeting of the Investiture Committee, 9 October 1968, PREM 13/2360, PRO. For example of verbal exchanges in meetings of local authorities, see general newspaper coverage September through November 1968.
[188] *Carmarthen Times*, 26 July 1968.
[189] *Western Mail*, 19 February 1969; G. H. Daniel to Diamond, 3 January 1969, BD 67/54, PRO.
[190] *Daily Sketch*, 1 November 1968.

reached flood peak'.[191] DCS Jock Wilson noted that 'Since Prince Charles made his speech in Wales at Aberystwyth there has been a dramatic change in attitude of Welsh people towards him and they were now more friendly', while George Thomas felt that the prince's speech 'broke through' to the Welsh people. While the Welsh supported the investiture before, he exclaimed: 'Now it is a landslide.'[192]

Polls of popular opinion reveal the relative strength of the investiture's support and opposition. The earliest poll was a canvas of a 'representative audience' of a BBC television show conducted in July 1968. It found the principality roughly divided in its attitude towards the investiture.[193] The Opinion Research Centre conducted the most comprehensive survey for the *Western Mail* in September 1968. On the pivotal issue of the monarch's eldest son bearing the title of Prince of Wales, 74 per cent of the Welsh population felt it was a good tradition compared to 15 per cent who thought it was a bad one. There was slightly more support for the tradition among non-Welsh speakers than Welsh speakers, but this only amounted to a 2 per cent difference. Comprising the great majority of the Welsh population, Labour supporters were the most solidly behind the investiture, with 86 per cent supporting the tradition compared to 8 per cent opposed. On the other hand, the much smaller body of Plaid Cymru supporters were nearly equally divided with 46 per cent opposing the tradition compared to 42 per cent in support. Opposition to the tradition grew as the age of the respondents fell. The majority in support of the investiture shrank to 61 per cent among those aged 21–34, while nearly a quarter of them actively opposed the tradition. On the related question of the ceremony's expense, attitudes were less supportive. 50 per cent of the general population of Wales felt the ceremony was money well spent, compared to 44 per cent who thought it was wasted. Labour supporters were more diffident on this aspect of the investiture, with 54 per cent in favour and 40 per cent objecting to the expense. However, a 72 per cent majority among Plaid Cymru supporters and 53 per cent among those aged 21–4 were critical of the

---

[191] *South Wales Evening Post*, 1 July 1969.
[192] *Western Mail*, 27, 30 June 1969.
[193] *Western Mail*, 4 July 1969.

expense. There was little support for republicanism among any party's supporters, although 28 per cent of Plaid Cymru supporters favoured abolishment of the monarchy compared to 6 per cent of Labour and 5 per cent of Conservatives.[194] In March 1969, the British Market Research Bureau reinforced the findings of September with 76 per cent of those in Wales supporting the investiture, with support falling to 60 per cent for those under the age of 45.[195]

Collectively, this data suggests that support for the investiture among the general population in Wales was clear but not universal. A visible and vocal yet small minority opposed the investiture in the most strident terms, their voice amplified by explosions, protest rallies and media attention. The most unified opinion was amongst supporters of Labour, the nation's largest political party. The most divided opinions were found among nationalists and the nation's youth, with approximately half of them opposing the investiture on some grounds. Active hostility to the investiture seems to have represented the opinion of about a quarter of Welsh youth. The excitement of the investiture itself combined with the negative publicity regarding the deaths of the men at Abergele and the crippling of the Sussex boy in Caernarfon probably contributed to a rise in public support for the investiture in the immediate aftermath of the ceremony. A National Opinion Poll conducted shortly after the investiture found that 92 per cent of the population in Wales favoured the ceremony.[196] By September, opinion seems to have stabilized, with 75 per cent in support of Prince Charles as Prince of Wales, while 18 per cent insisted that his investiture should never have taken place.[197]

Signs of Welsh popular support for the investiture were clearly evident. In the end, the much maligned Croeso 69 campaign was largely successful in arousing local participation in investiture celebrations. 'For those who doubted the grass roots enthusiasm of the investiture, the programme of over

[194] *Western Mail*, 27 September 1968.
[195] *South Wales Evening Post*, 23 April 1969.
[196] *National Opinion Polls Monthly Bulletin*, July 1969, Harold Wilson MS C.1084, Bodleian, Oxford.
[197] *National Opinion Polls Monthly Bulletin*, no date, Harold Wilson MS C.1085, Bodleian, Oxford.

1,000 events published by the National Organizing Committee of Croeso 69 will have come as something of a shock', reported the *Western Mail*.[198] Dramatically, angry supporters confronted anti-investiture protestors on a number of occasions. The protest at the Welsh Office in June 1968 involved about twenty-five vocal protesters, but approximately 200 supporters of the prince were also gathered on the pavement. After throwing smoke bombs in the direction of the prince, the heavily outnumbered protestors were set upon by the crowd.[199] Pro-investiture students in Bangor attempted to break up a sit-down. When protesters descended upon the prince's residence hall on the eve of his arrival in Aberystwyth, about twenty residents manned the rooftops of Pantycelyn armed with pro-prince banners and dustbins filled with water.[200] During the St David's Day demonstration, school children greeted the Cymdeithas yr Iaith motorcade in Llanberis with banners reading 'Leave Our Prince Alone!' and 'God Bless the Prince of Wales' while a gang of housewives swept down from a housing estate in Caernarfon to boo the demonstrators.[201] While calls of 'Carlo' could be heard in the marquee of the Urdd eisteddfod, other youths booed the 100 demonstrators who walked out during the prince's address. Noting the 6,000 still assembled in the tent, the Urdd's Eisteddfod secretary observed from the stage, 'I see there are many more of us left than went out'. Earlier during a pop music session at the event, Dafydd Iwan was hissed by a section of the crowd.[202] Indeed, as one of the most visible faces and voices of the anti-investiture movement, Dafydd Iwan drew the ire of many Welsh supporters of the prince.[203] 'Carlo' was as controversial as it was successful. The *Herald of Wales* called for a boycott of the song, pubs excluded it on their juke box, and some of Iwan's concerts were cancelled in reprisal. 'God help us if this is the kind of stuff that pleases our youth', wrote 'Cymraes' in a letter to *Y Cymro*, 'And to think that

[198] *Western Mail*, 26 May 1969.
[199] *Western Mail*, 29 June, 4 July 1968; *The Times*, 29 June 1968; *Guardian*, 29 June 1968.
[200] *Western Mail*, 12–13 March 1969.
[201] *News of the World*, 2 March 1969; *Sunday Observer*, 2 March 1969.
[202] *Western Mail*, 2 June 1969.
[203] *Sunday Telegraph*, 6 July 1969.

Dafydd Iwan is a son of the Manse and from the lineage of the Bois y Colie. Shame on him, I say'.[204] Inundated with a flood of derogatory letters and phone calls, Iwan would later claim that the response to the society's anti-investiture activities was much more hostile than that to its controversial sign painting campaign.[205] Perhaps in a case of wishful thinking, erroneous rumours circulated on investiture day that Dafydd Iwan had been assaulted and put into a hospital.

Certainly, investiture supporters were not shy of physical confrontations or violent rhetoric. In the streets of Caernarfon, police claimed to have arrested the small number of protestors at the investiture primarily for their own protection. The lad who threw the apple at the Queen's carriage was led away by police with the spectators calling, 'Don't take him away, hang him', 'Let's kill him now', and 'Lynch him'.[206] Upon receiving the news that two men had been killed in Abergele, one woman commented to the press: 'It is better for them to do away with themselves rather than kill decent, innocent people. I feel ashamed to be Welsh when I hear about things like this.'[207] Clearly, passions were running as hot on the side of those who supported the investiture as they were among those who opposed it.

Enthusiasm for the investiture seems to have been particularly marked in the south. Press coverage of the tour emphasized the size and volume of the prince's welcome in the valleys. This was often done in comparison to the reception in Caernarfon, where only 90,000 of the anticipated 250,000 had turned out along the thinly lined route of the royal procession.[208] The 14-mile route between Llanelli and Swansea, however, was lined with a reported 250,000 well wishers while in the city of Cardiff spectators stood along the streets ten deep to catch a glimpse of the prince's motorcade.[209] 'Wild enthusiasm along the route slowed the procession down and

[204] *Y Cymro*, 13 March 1969.
[205] Iwan, *Dafydd Iwan*, pp. 42–7.
[206] *Sun*, 2 July 1969; *Evening Standard*, 1 July 1969.
[207] *South Wales Evening Post*, 1 July 1969.
[208] *Western Mail*, 2 July 1969.
[209] *Western Mail*, 4 July 1969; *Sunday Express*, 6 July 1969.

schedules went to the winds', exclaimed the *Daily Express*.[210] Even in locations through which the tour did not pass, south Wales was jubilant. Nowhere was this more true than in the Rhondda:

> If you had made a tour of the Rhondda yesterday you would have been overwhelmed by the sights. Practically every house displayed a flag and every street had created a ceiling of colour and sparkle in the variety of bunting. Lamp posts were brightened by colour and greenery; window displays showed great ingenuity in the portrayal of the Prince in every mood. Strips of paper matt and shining Welsh dragons, Welsh flags, Welsh slogans, pictures of the Queen and Prince Phillip adorn the windows of shops and private houses. Months ago every street seemed to have a committee planning for investiture day. Collectors were appointed to go from door to door for contributions. Competitions and jumble sales were organized to swell the funds. On the day, out came the tables in the streets, the chairs, the linen and crockery. Women cheerfully prepared the food. Games were organized and children received mementos of the occasion. So the Rhondda is transformed into fairyland – for this week at least. I doubt if you would find anywhere else in the Principality such whole hearted cooperation to make a memorable day.[211]

'History books may record that the investiture took place in Caernarfon', observed the *Sun*, 'but as far as the children of Gelli in the Rhondda are concerned the most important ceremony was in their town.'[212]

In the end, Labour was correct in thinking the investiture would be popularly received. They were wrong, however, in thinking that the ceremony would be uncontroversial. While political parties avoided any direct resistance to the investiture, the cause of opposing the ceremony was embraced by politically active Welsh youth and language activists. Although the numbers involved in opposing the investiture were minimal, their protest and actions effectively projected an image of the investiture as a source of division and polarization in Wales. The potential danger of paramilitary actions against the ceremony prompted an overwhelming security response that

---

[210] *Daily Express*, 5 July 1969.
[211] *Western Mail*, 2 July 1969.
[212] *Sun*, 2 July 1969.

exacerbated and lent credence to that image. Despite overwhelming popular support for the ceremony in Wales, such developments threatened to derail the ceremony and divert its meaning.

12
Bradwyr *and extremists*

The commentary, press releases and symbolism of the investiture ceremony were meant to establish Labour's image of the Welsh people and nation. The Welsh Office took an active approach to the construction of the ceremony's meaning, originally fearing that the investiture would be regarded by the Welsh as a meaningless anachronism. It need not have worried. Rather than regarded as meaningless, the ceremony would be loaded with contradictory and conflicting meanings. Conducted through the language of the press and the slogans of the street, the dispute over the meaning of the investiture was really a contest between different visions of the nature of the Welsh nation and its relationship to the British state. In struggling to define the investiture publicly, supporters and opponents of the ceremony attempted to align themselves and their political opponents in relation to their own antagonistic constructions of Wales. While building an image of their own inherent Welshness, they sought to deny the Welshness of their opponents through contrasting images of '*bradwyr*' and 'extremists'.

Early in the process, planners were greatly concerned that the investiture would be regarded by the Welsh as an atavistic ceremony that had very little to do with Wales. The Welsh character of the 1911 Investiture did nothing to reassure the population of the inherent Welshness of the event in 1969. Memories of 1911 had largely faded and the Liberal image of the Welsh nation that it projected had long since been discredited. What was left was a void that some critics regarded as anachronistic and meaningless. Opponents frequently referred to the investiture as a mere 'pantomime' or as 'Circus 69'. According to a motion of the Vaynor and Penderyn Rural District Council, the ceremony was 'archaic, reactionary and a complete negation of progressive thinking', while a member of the Aberaeron Urban Council said that investing a Prince of Wales was 'smacking of a hundred years ago'.[1] Initially, the young prince himself did little to inspire confidence. In contrast to his familiarity and identification with the Scottish Highlands, Prince Charles had rarely visited the principality before and was largely an 'unknown figure' in Wales. Even the *Western Mail* itself, a strong advocate for the investiture, admitted that Prince Charles seemed more at home in Scotland.[2] 'What exactly is a "Prince of Wales"?', asked a columnist: 'A mere title, leading him to the throne? Then let it be that. But why crown him at Caernarfon?'[3]

Determined that the ceremony should have meaning in a specifically Welsh context, the organizers of the investiture fostered a special, personal relationship between the prince and the people of Wales. Anticipating criticism, the Investiture Committee felt it 'very important to avoid the impression that the Prince was making an isolated visit to Wales for the conferment of a title'. Instead, the investiture should 'have the theme of his taking up a Principality whose people he already knew and to whom he would be available, not just for a week but frequently thereafter'.[4] To accomplish this, several committee members felt 'it was of the utmost importance that the Prince should be seen to show interest in Wales and its affairs before the year of the investiture' and that Prince Charles 'should acquaint himself as far as possible with the history and culture of Wales'.[5] Taking up the same refrain immediately following the announcement of the investiture in May 1967, the *Western Mail* recommended that the investiture 'ought to dwell less on external pomp and circumstance and concentrate on the real significance of the occasion – the Prince's introduction to his people'.[6] The Duke of Norfolk would promise that

[1] *Cambrian News*, 11 October 1968; *Western Mail*, 12 October 1967.
[2] *Western Mail*, 19 September 1967.
[3] *Western Mail*, 15 July 1968.
[4] Minutes of the First Meeting of the Investiture Committee, 26 October 1967, PREM 13/2359, PRO.
[5] R. H. Jones to G. H. Daniel, 17 January 1968, BD 25/296, PRO; G. H. Daniel to Glanmor Williams, 28 October 1967, BD 25/296, PRO.
[6] *Western Mail*, 18 May 1967.

the prince would eventually 'become thoroughly acquainted with every part of Wales'.⁷

Of course, this was all anticipated by the Welsh Office. In its earliest letters to the Palace, the Welsh Office had outlined the need for a period of preparation for the prince before the investiture took place. Following Cledwyn Hughes's personal meeting with Prince Charles in April 1967, the Welsh Office tutored the prince by sending him monthly bulletins and confidential notes on current affairs in the principality.⁸ In November 1967, Cledwyn Hughes publicly announced that the prince would attend the university at Aberystwyth to study the culture and contemporary problems of Wales. Commenting on the investiture, Hughes explained: 'We do not want it thought of as an empty, meaningless ritual . . . It will be a happy occasion – one in which the Prince and the people will walk together.'⁹ The *Western Mail* at least was satisfied, stating that the prince's summer term would:

> ensure that he will not be a complete stranger to Wales when he is invested at Caernarfon in the summer of 1969. The ceremony is no longer in danger of appearing meaningless or of becoming merely a tourist exercise; it will be what most Welsh people would like it to be – a symbol of the special interest which the heir to the throne has in Wales.¹⁰

Seeking to bridge the gap between the anarchic character of the 1960s and the anachronistic character of the monarchy, the 1969 Investiture accorded a special place for the Labour ideals of social democracy and egalitarianism. At the first meeting of the official Investiture Committee, delegates were instructed to reflect on the example of 1911 and to consider 'what modifications are desirable in view of the political, social and economic changes of the last fifty years'.¹¹ Ceremonial details were refitted to match the democratic and egalitarian tenor of the times. Contrary to traditional protocol and the druthers of the heralds, the Welsh Office insisted that the democratically

---

⁷ *Western Mail*, 4 July 1968.
⁸ Memorandum, G. H. Daniel, 25 April 1967, BD 25/296, PRO.
⁹ *Western Mail*, 18 November 1967.
¹⁰ *Western Mail*, 2 November 1967.
¹¹ The Investiture Ceremony – Note by the Chairman, PREM 13/2359, PRO.

elected County Councils be given precedence over the royally established Lord Mayors, that local authorities march in alphabetic order rather than by the rules of hierarchical precedence and that royally bestowed privileges on towns be set aside for a proportional and democratic system of representation based on the size of population.[12] Seeking better to align the *Loyalty Address of the People of Wales* with the priorities of the Labour government, G. H. Daniel suggested that references to social democracy be cited alongside commitments to Welsh language and traditions.[13] The final version of the loyalty address recognized the impact of the 'force of change' on social conditions in Wales and anticipated the prince's continued association with the principality, 'its aspirations and problems' and 'the welfare of its people'.[14] Press commentary helped establish an egalitarian atmosphere for a ceremony founded upon the principle of monarchical hierarchy. 'Caernarvon's castle does not perch snobbishly on a lofty rock', observed the *Daily Mail*: 'It is right down there with the people in Castle Square, rubbing granite shoulders with the tap room of the Castle Vaults, Owens the merchant and the People's Café.'[15] According to the press, the castle's trimmed-down décor revealed Lord Snowdon 'to be a genuine democrat in that he was determined not to be a party to the tradition of red plush and all that'.[16] As for the investiture tour, it was not 'a royal progress in the old stately style' but an opportunity for the prince to meet with the people and 'experience the essential life of the gwerin'.[17]

Projections of social democracy and egalitarianism were perhaps best reflected in the prince's summer term at Aberystwyth. Although the 1911 Investiture displayed the democratic credentials of the monarchy by emphasizing royal support of the Welsh university movement, the actual matriculation of a member of the Royal Family at the 'People's College' in

[12] G. H. Daniel to R. O. Dennys, 10 October 1968, 1.0.II 1969 Investiture, CA.
[13] G. H. Daniel to King, 19 February 1969, 1.0.II. 1969 Investiture, CA.
[14] *Western Mail*, 2 July 1969.
[15] *Daily Mail*, 1 July 1969.
[16] *Western Mail*, 1 April 1969.
[17] *South Wales Evening Post*, 4 July 1968.

Aberystwyth would have been inconceivable. In 1969, however, the prince's term at this 'chip university with a pub culture' was celebrated for bringing the heir to the throne down to the level of the common man:

> The educational progress of the Prince of Wales has been making Royal history for the past ten years but nowhere will the break with tradition have been more apparent than when he walks into the college at Aberystwyth in the summer of 1969. The university college has none of the expensive aristocratic traditions of these other establishments, but draws many of its students from the working classes of Wales – the people who established the college . . . It was due to the efforts of the 100,000 people who subscribed sums of less than 2s. 6d. that the college survived its early years.[18]

Prince Charles was housed with 250 other students in Pantycelyn Hall where he was supposedly 'to follow the routine of the average student', including queuing for meals, scrambling for a seat in the cafeteria, paying tuition and Student Union fees, and even taking his turn on the hall's jobs rota.[19] If driving his sporty MG to class distinguished the prince from his fellow students, the press reported that he would be granted no special parking privileges by the university and would have to search for a spot near the college like everyone else.[20] Flashy sports car aside, the student prince at Aberystwyth was the very image of a royal social democrat.

In media coverage leading up to the investiture, the ordinariness of Prince Charles and the Royal Family was carefully cultivated by the Palace. This image helped obscure the presence of class and privilege while reinforcing the social democratic ethos of the modern monarchy. Seeking to cultivate a more familiar and informal relationship between the monarchy and the British public, Palace press secretary Michael Hesseltine orchestrated a series of personal interviews in print, radio and television designed to familiarize the population with Prince Charles as a normal and conscientious young man. Unusual at the time, lines of questioning were candid and

---

[18] *Western Mail*, 2 November 1967.
[19] *Western Mail*, 13 March 1969.
[20] *Western Mail*, 21 April 1969.

ranged from queries on his opinion of Welsh nationalism to his love life. Of the prince's first interview, the *Western Mail* exclaimed:

> ... until recently the Monarchy was in danger of appearing remote from the lives and problems of ordinary people. Now a heavy curtain has been dramatically tugged aside. Almost overnight, Prince Charles has succeeded in identifying himself and indeed the Royal Family with the anxieties, hopes and fears of the nation. He has done it, quite simply, by showing that he too is an ordinary person.[21]

What followed was a programme of royal publicity and exposure of unprecedented scale, climaxing with the remarkable film, *Royal Family*. This documentary was broadcast on television to record-breaking audiences the month before the investiture and then rebroadcast on the eve of the ceremony itself. A behind the scenes exposé of life in the Palace, the film portrayed the Royal Family at work and leisure, most notably in 'an ordinary family scene' at a backyard barbecue.[22] In watching the investiture in the light of these revelations, one commentator asked whether:

> ... the nation is mildly celebrating the discovery that the Royal Family are human, and is pleased that there is a group 'at the top' who are, extraordinarily enough, easier to identify with than the politicians? In Caernarfon Castle on Tuesday, one did have a peculiar sensation that the politicians were less familiar than the Royal Family. There was the Queen; on her throne, true, but because of the film, we could still hear her voice telling the story about the man who looked like a gorilla; and there was the Duke, last seen wielding the barbecue fork; and there was Charles, and we knew what he thought about the girl he would marry. What did we know about Mr. Heath's thoughts about the girl he would marry? When had we seen Mrs. Wilson buying bulls eyes?[23]

Other commentary and ceremonial details reinforced the theme of the ordinary domesticity of the royals. The Queen did not appear at the investiture in ceremonial robes or military uniform but in fashionable contemporary attire. In investing

---

[21] *Western Mail*, 3 March 1969.
[22] *Western Mail*, 21 June 1969.
[23] *Observer*, 6 July 1969.

the prince, she tugged at the gold clasps of the prince's ermine trimmed mantle 'like any other mother dressing a child'.[24] 'The divinity that hedged the Throne', concluded the *Observer*, 'has been discarded for life in the modern world'.[25]

Informed by the experience of the Depression but looking towards a more prosperous future, the investiture defined the Labour party's vision of the mutually beneficial relationship between Wales and the United Kingdom. Investiture commentary placed the union squarely upon ideas of quality governance and economic success. 'There is plenty of room for all of us to live here in happiness, prosperity and unity', wrote the *Daily Telegraph and Morning Post*, 'if only we can succeed in governing ourselves better.'[26] At a time when George Thomas was reminding people through television interviews that Wales was being subsidized by Westminster to the tune of millions of pounds a year, the union symbolized by the prince promised to correct the problems of most immediate concern to the Welsh population – economic dislocation. Like so many transfer payments from the central Treasury to a depressed region, the investiture involved the use of British cultural resources and royal personnel to bolster the Welsh economy and focus global attention on the often overlooked Welsh nation. To some extent, this engagement involved Labour's recognition that 'Wales has had a raw economic deal in the past'. The investiture signified the party's expressed willingness to consider new arrangements in government to ensure that the needs of the principality were being addressed.[27] Regional economic planning and the Welsh Office itself were brightly highlighted by the investiture and seemed to promise a new relationship between the British state and the Welsh nation. By the time of the investiture, even the prospect of further devolution in the form of a devolved Welsh parliament was back on the table. Although expressing his personal opinion that 'the Welsh people are against separating from the rest of the United Kingdom', George Thomas conceded that: 'if the country

[24] *Daily Mail*, 2 July 1969.
[25] *Observer*, 29 June 1969.
[26] *Daily Telegraph and Morning Post*, 2 July 1969.
[27] *Observer*, 22 June 1969.

wants change, well change must come, because we are a democracy and the will of the people must prevail.'²⁸

Whatever the state of devolution, the 1969 Investiture echoed the 1911 Investiture in projecting an image of the inherent integration of the United Kingdom through the diversity of its parts. Somewhat pointedly given its source, the *Belfast Telegraph* declared: 'The investiture of the Prince on Welsh territory marks the essential unity of the United Kingdom which transcends local boundaries and national loyalties.'²⁹ The investiture 'is a symbolic expression of the loyalty and continuity which binds together two of the parts of the United Kingdom', opined the *Glasgow Herald*.³⁰ Closer to home, the *Western Mail* regarded the title Prince of Wales as both 'testimony to the nationhood of Wales' and 'a link connecting Wales through 800 years of history with the rest of the UK'.³¹ Framing the narrative of Welsh history in the context of the 1969 Investiture, a film documentary reflected on the climactic scene of Prince Charles receiving his regalia and greeting his people:

> And now of course, here we are. We are as independent, probably, as Llewelyn ap Grufydd [*sic*] ever hoped to be. We have the Welsh University that Owain Glyndŵr dreamed of. We have the biggest nuclear power station in Europe, which no one dreamed of . . . Edward's castles ceased to be the most expensive installations in Wales a long time ago (brief cut to oil installations in Pembroke). We are still overrun by foreigners. Only nowadays, they pay to come in. A very tame dragon, you might say . . . Somewhere in the back of our minds on an occasion like this, there are I think really – all those people – Helen Luyddog, the saints of Bardsea, Llywelyn, Glyndŵr (cut back to new prince as he stands before his nation). What is happening here is nothing to do any more with political power. What we are doing, as two races is to assure each other that our great ghosts are still sleeping in peace. That the lion and the dragon still lie down together.³²

---

²⁸ Transcript of a film on Welsh nationalism, Tŷ Cenedl 1 AI/4, NLW.
²⁹ *Belfast Telegraph*, 1 July 1969.
³⁰ *Glasgow Herald*, 2 July 1969.
³¹ *Western Mail*, 1 July 1969.
³² Outline Script, The Proud Dragon by Shirley Cobham, BD 67/60, PRO.

As expressed by the *Loyalty Address from the Welsh People*, the royal connection to Wales fostered by the investiture would serve not only to 'strengthen its own life' but to 'enrich its contribution to the UK'.[33] In a feature on the investiture in the *Sunday Express*, one Welshman surveyed the Westminster government and concluded: 'We are not doing so badly either if you think of Aubrey Jones, Prices and Incomes; Roy Jenkins, Chancellor; Ray Gunter, Minister of Labour; Jim Callaghan, Home Secretary.'[34] As Sir James Lyon, a director of the WTB and the former Lord Mayor of Cardiff, explained: 'I love Cardiff and I love Wales, but I want it to be part of Great Britain and the world.'[35]

If the Welsh nation was more British for the ceremony, it is equally true that the British state had become far more Welsh. Like Prince Charles, the United Kingdom had enrolled on an intensive course in Welshness during the summer of 1969 and the investiture marked its graduation towards a renewed multinational self-awareness. Redolent of 1911, the *Sunday Times* felt that the Prince: 'is in a unique position to draw together the claims of both of unity and diversity. His new office can form a bridge between the level plains of national uniformity and the wilder shores of nationalism: much of it is symbolic; but symbolism can be a political force.'[36]

Although set within the context of union, the social democracy evoked by the investiture was a specifically Welsh one. As in 1911, the 1969 Investiture was a celebration of a distinct Welsh nationhood. Rather than a 'major state occasion of the United Kingdom', the Welsh Office conceptualized the investiture as 'an essentially Welsh occasion, but one which involves the future head of the Commonwealth'. Accordingly, invitations to witness the event within the castle walls would be extended primarily to 'representatives of Welsh life' with a small number of invitations reserved for the chief government dignitaries and ambassadors.[37] People actually selected to play

[33] *Western Mail*, 2 July 1969.
[34] *Sunday Express*, 7 January 1968.
[35] *Observer*, 22 June 1969.
[36] *Sunday Times*, 29 June 1969.
[37] Hall to Richard, 20 October 1967, PREM 13/2359, PRO; R. H. Jones to G. H. Daniel, 8 November 1967, BD 67/3, PRO.

a role in the ceremony would, 'above everything have made a distinct contribution to contemporary Welsh life'.[38] To the great anxiety of the prime minister, no invitation would be extended to the Archbishop of Canterbury, as he had nothing to do with a disestablished Wales.[39] Conversely, to the great annoyance of ultra-Protestant opinion, the Revd John Murphy, the Catholic Archbishop of Cardiff, played a leading role in the planning and performance of the investiture's religious services.[40]

The prince's own tenuous links with the principality were corrected by conferring upon him a bona fide Welsh pedigree. This was the job for which Francis Jones, the recently created Wales Herald Extraordinary, earned his keep. On the front page of the Welsh-language newspaper *Y Cymro* and then in English through the *Western Mail*, Francis Jones traced Prince Charles's 'proven descent from all the main dynasties that formerly ruled Wales'.[41] Jones included in his 'roll call of forebears' such illustrious figures from Welsh history as Cunedda, Rhodri Mawr, Hywel Dda, Llywelyn the Great, the Tudors, Bleddyn ap Cynfyn, Owain Glyndŵr and Lord Rhys:

> Genealogically, Prince Charles is as good a Welshman as any of us. He is a link between us and our storied past. When he comes to Wales, he comes to the 'Land of his Fathers' in a very special sense, among friends and kindred, his own people.[42]

The story of the prince's Welsh genealogy was widely and enthusiastically covered by the media. In the prince's first radio interview, Jack DeManio declared, 'We've been hearing a lot about you being more Welsh than any other Prince of Wales', to which Prince Charles replied: 'I'm told that I'm descended three times over from the original Welsh princes . . . So I seem

[38] R. H. Jones to Sir Anthony Wagner, 14 March 1968, 1.0.II Ceremony, 1969 Investiture, CA.
[39] Harold Wilson to Michael Halls, 24 July 1968, PREM 13/2360, PRO; Series of correspondence between Michael Hall and G. B. Diamond, July–August 1968, PREM 13/2360, PRO.
[40] Press statement by the Secretary of State for Wales on the role of Roman Catholics in the Investiture Ceremony, BD 67/28, PRO; *Western Mail*, 17 June 1969.
[41] *Y Cymro*, 27 February 1969; *Western Mail*, 5 March 1969.
[42] *Western Mail*, 5 March 1969.

to have a bit of Welsh blood in me.'⁴³ Much was made of the inclusion of Llywelyn the Great's heraldic badge of four lions on the personal banner Prince Charles used in Wales. Other genealogical explorations emphasized the prince's close family connections to Llywelyn the Last himself. A group of local county councillors even went so far as to suggest that the prince pay a formal visit to Llywelyn's memorial at Cilmery while a proposed Croeso event envisioned Prince Charles riding by horseback through Wales on a pilgrimage to the site.⁴⁴ Although never realized, such ideas reflected an ambition to aggressively contest and appropriate the symbolic space of Cilmery itself, the centre of anti-investiture protest.

As in 1911, the investiture signified, celebrated and publicized the continuing life and vitality of the Welsh nation and set the ceremony within a context of a new national awakening. In a Croeso 69 bulletin, the Wales Tourist Board recited the origin myth of the ceremony, claiming that in co-opting the title of the Prince of Wales, Edward I had: 'acknowledged Wales as a separate entity – different in history, language, culture and outlook from his own Realm of England.' 'As long as the title remains', it explained, 'the Royal holder makes this fact plain to the rest of the world.'⁴⁵ Generally ambivalent to the ceremony, the Welsh-language journal *Barn* admitted that the investiture was a form of ceremonial recognition that established Wales's existence as an entity in spite of its negligible legal and governmental status.⁴⁶ 'The ceremony itself will be both a pageant and an expression of Welsh national life', explained the *South Wales Evening Post*.⁴⁷ On a BBC television programme, the Lord Mayor of Caernarfon spoke of the town's castle in familiar terms:

> . . . the glory of the castle is that it is empty. People keep on saying it is a sign of oppression. It isn't; it is a sign of the toughness of the Welsh people because we've seen the Romans coming and going, the Normans coming and going, the English coming and going. The English built the castle, now they pay two bob to come and see their

[43] *Western Mail*, 3 March 1969.
[44] *Western Mail*, 16 July 1968, 18 January 1969.
[45] Croeso 69 Bulletin, No. 1, BD 67/54, PRO.
[46] *Barn*, Mawrth 1969.
[47] *South Wales Evening Post*, 4 July 1968.

own castle. It's fine. But it is empty – that is the point. And the houses outside are full.[48]

The *Sunday Times* explained that the investiture recognized the proud distinctness of Wales, valued all the more for having been preserved 'so long in the face of the probabilities'.[49] Claiming that 'the ceremony today is in honour of local loyalties and the love of small places', the *Daily Mail* was moved to declare that the investiture was proof that the twentieth century had failed to 'crush the rich life and language of Wales'.[50] Closer to home, the *Western Mail* routinely spoke of the ceremony as an impressive demonstration of nationhood in the eyes of the world and claimed that the 'new consciousness of, and pride in being Welsh which has developed in the sixties has been given a stimulus by the investiture and the presence in Wales of Prince Charles'.[51] The *Rhyl & Prestatyn Gazette* followed suit, recognizing that: 'Welshmen in general are discovering in themselves a new pride. The Prince of Wales has by his interest in things Welsh, his obvious desire to identify himself with us, brought to us a new sense of nationhood.'[52] The global attention attracted by the investiture not only publicized the principality in an economic sense but assured Wales of its own national existence. As Tom Nairn has recognized, the British state reified the Welsh nation through the investiture, crystallizing the Welsh essence and broadcasting it across the world.[53] With apologies to Descartes, the motto of Wales during the investiture could have been 'I am on Johnny Carson, therefore I am'.

By its very nature, the ceremony was enveloped with historical romanticism but an emphasis on modern and modernizing elements of the investiture helped to establish an image of a progressive Wales. In his reply to the people's loyal address, Prince Charles noted the dynamic and ongoing change in Wales since the last investiture and stated: 'Wales needs to look

[48] Extract from 24 Hours, Recorded from transmission BBC 1 2220, 28 February 1969, PREM 13/2505, PRO.
[49] *Sunday Times*, 29 June 1969.
[50] *Daily Mail*, 1 July 1969.
[51] *Western Mail*, 1 July 1969, 14 February 1969, 27 September 1968.
[52] *Rhyl & Prestatyn Gazette*, 9 July 1969.
[53] Nairn, p. 227.

forward without forsaking the traditional and essential aspects of her past.'[54] Following suit, ancient and modern were blended in the investiture regalia. While the last investiture provided Goscombe John's ring, rod and sword to the ceremony, a sleek 'mod Coronet' was minted as something new to specifically represent the modern age.[55] The Ministry of Public Buildings and Work promised that the décor for the ceremony would be 'extremely impressive and extremely modern'.[56] Decorating the medieval castle in strikingly contemporary style, Lord Snowdon's design group produced abstract brass star bursts, Carnaby Street renditions of the Prince's feathers, minimalist slate thrones and dais, and dragons with bell-bottom like claws. The ultra-modern design of the enormous transparent canopy suspended over the investiture's slate dais was inspired by the medieval canopies used at the battle of Agincourt, prompting Lord Snowdon to later reflect that it was nothing more than 'what Henry V would have done if he had Perspex'.[57] According to the press, this was 'a medieval pageant staged in the month of the moon walk' where a 'space age' prince was bestowed with a 'sputnik coronet'.[58] In their own fashion, even the heralds contributed to the theme, pairing holders of ancient and modern peerages in the ceremony as a way for the investiture to assume 'a contemporary as well as a traditional complexion'.[59] Outside the ceremony itself, the National Museum of Wales staged two special investiture exhibitions – one being a conventional exhibit on the historical background of the investiture and the Princes of Wales, the other a grand exhibition on 'Cymru Yfory – Wales of the Future'. Encased in a giant, inflatable plastic bubble, the exhibit featured displays of modern design furnished by a member of the investiture's design steering group.[60] As an emblem for 'Croeso 69', the Wales Tourist Board produced an angular and

[54] *Western Mail*, 2 July 1969.
[55] *Belfast Telegraph*, 1 July 1969; *Sun*, 1 July 1969.
[56] *Western Mail*, 19 June 1969.
[57] *Everyone Held their Breath*, Air Date: BBC 1, 1 July 1994, AM 1099/03, National Screen and Sound Archive, NLW; Hoey, p. 137.
[58] *Daily Mail*, 1 July 1969; *The Times*, 25 June 1969.
[59] Frances Jones to Sir Anthony Wagner, 19 February 1968, 1.0.II 1969 Investiture, CA.
[60] *Western Mail*, 16 June 1969.

edgy Welsh 'dragon passant' supposedly more in keeping with a 'progressive monarchy' and 'brought up to date and streamlined to keep pace with our helter-skelter age'.[61]

Although tall hats, leeks and dragons would be plenty evident, the image of the Welsh that the planners of the 1969 investiture sought to promote differed significantly from that of either the traditional *gwerin* or the imperial revision of Welsh national identity projected by the 1911 Investiture. In the vision and pronouncements of the planners, there was an implicit rejection of the kind of Celticism that had characterized the 1911 ceremony. Labour's vision of Welshness emphasized that, while rooted to their ancient culture and traditions, the Welsh were essentially rational, tolerant and forward-looking people. 'A sense of Welshness is unpleasant, inward looking, and self indulgent', instructed the *South Wales Echo*, 'unless it is imbued with humour, tolerance and a modern outlook.'[62] It was sentiments such as these that allowed the Catholic Archbishop of Cardiff to assume such a prominent role in the investiture against the vocal objections of some Protestant opinion. In connection to the investiture, the *Western Mail* spoke of: 'the rising and strengthening voice of a Wales eager to show its talents and abilities and to have a say in its own affairs.' It cited: 'the powerful optimism that in 1969 the Queen's son will not hold an empty title, but a name that will stand for all that is strong and forward looking in a Wales with the opportunity to establish its national identity and rightful place in the world.'[63]

The role of the military was a mere shadow of that which it played in 1911. Although equally a matter of economic necessity, this was a development with a clear ideological foundation. The nightmare of the First World War had discredited the militarism associated with Edwardian Welsh nationalism and elevated the idea of pacifism to a defining characteristic of Welsh national identity.[64] Controversy and protest over the Wilson government's support of the American policy in

[61] *Western Mail*, 30 July 1968.
[62] *South Wales Echo*, 4 January 1969.
[63] *Western Mail*, 7 December 1967.
[64] John S. Ellis, 'A pacific people – a martial race: pacifism, militarism and Welsh national identity', in Matthew Cragoe and Chris Williams (eds),

Vietnam gave the issue a pointed contemporary relevance. A pacifist himself, George Thomas was disturbed by the martial images he saw in a film of the previous investiture. To the Duke, Thomas expressed his hope that the processions could be designed so that 'they do not have the militaristic, Prussian looking appearance conveyed by the film of 1911'.[65] Given the figures of military participation for 1911, members of the Investiture Committee were leadingly asked: 'Will it be appropriate in 1969 for the Armed Services to play so prominent a role?'[66] In the end, only 150 officers and 2,600 other ranks drawn from eleven Welsh regiments participated in the investiture, a mere shadow of the 12,400 soldiers present in 1911.[67] Such a steep reduction in the ceremony's military presence represented, in a domestic context, as dramatic a retreat from Britain's imperial glory as the ceremonial lowering of the Union Jack then occurring in newly independent colonies around the globe. The representation of the military within the prince's procession was nearly eliminated and the presence of two military bands in the castle was balanced by the inclusion of a civilian brass band. Yet, this did not satisfy the Minister of State for Wales, Eirene White, who wrote to George Thomas declaring:

> We are right to resist over-militarisation. I am still unhappy at the degree to which the services will appear to predominate at Caernarfon and wish, in spite of the interesting explanation given at the last Investiture meeting, that we could have kept off 21 gun salutes and the like. It is so much out of line with Welsh ways of thought.[68]

Despite the leanings of the Welsh Office, the military presence in the 1969 Investiture could not be expunged altogether. Certainly, the Secretary of State seemed to acknowledge that

Wales and War: Society, Politics and Religion in the Nineteenth and Twentieth Centuries (Cardiff, 2007), pp. 15–37.
[65] G. H. Daniel to R. H. Jones, 20 June 1968, 1.0.I. 1969 Investiture, CA.
[66] The Investiture Ceremony Note by the Chairman, PREM 13/2359, PRO.
[67] Memorandum by GOC in C Western Command, 9 October 1968, PREM 13/2360, PRO;
[68] Eirene White to Secretary of State, 23 October 1968, 1.0.II Ceremony, 1969 Investiture, CA.

there was a limit to how far the mould of British royal ceremonial could be stretched. However sparsely spaced along the royal route, soldiers would be present and twenty-one-gun salutes would be fired. The prince himself donned a military image in the ceremony, wearing the uniform of the brand new Royal Regiment of Wales, recently amalgamated and inaugurated by the prince in his capacity as Colonel in Chief in a grand ceremony in Cardiff earlier that June. In military attire, the prince not only projected a dignified image of service but avoided the embarrassment of the 'preposterous rig' foisted on his great uncle in 1911 as well as the equally horrific leisure suit proposed by the Welsh Office.

Unlike the northern focus of the 1911 ceremony, the 1969 investiture showed the greatest affinity to the culture, community and historical experience of south Wales. Despite the traditional location of the ceremony itself, the post-investiture tour of 1969 really focused on the south and downplayed the north. In the thinking of the Welsh Office, the investiture in Caernarfon would be staged chiefly for television while the 'more authentic greeting' of the Welsh people would take place in a series of events in the south, leading to 'quite a big, and really popular event in the capital city of Cardiff'.[69] Instructed by the Welsh Office, Prince Charles spent only the first day of his four-day tour travelling in the north. In the subsequent three days, the prince's procession led him through communities across the south. After stopping in Swansea to announce the Crown's intention to bestow upon it 'city' status, the tour culminated in Cardiff with a grand day of celebration rivalling that of the investiture itself. In the climax to his visit in front of one of the largest crowds ever recorded in Cardiff's Cathays Park, Prince Charles pressed a button that set off a commemorative Investiture Fountain, spewing water twenty feet into the air in the shape of the Prince of Wales's feathers.[70] During the investiture year, the prince became closely associated with the south Walian passion for rugby, which was then entering a new 'golden age' of international glory. As Gareth Williams has

[69] J. S. Orme to G. H. Daniel, 32 August 1967, 1.0.I. 1969 Investiture, CA.
[70] *Investiture of His Royal Highness: Programme of His Visit to Cardiff, Capital of Wales*, BD 67/81, PRO.

shown, rugby provided the perfect metaphor and focus for the heterogeneous sense of Welshness found in the valleys.[71] At the 1969 Wales versus Ireland match, Prince Charles sang the Welsh national anthem for the first time, lunched with the Welsh fifteen and appeared in photographs shaking hands with the principality's sporting heroes. This association was furthered during his investiture tour when the prince stopped to greet members of the community in Llanelli, Ebbw Vale, and Pontypool, all assembled in their respective rugby grounds. 'Llanelli gave the Prince of Wales the kind of welcome it usually reserves for Springboks, All Blacks and other overseas rugby heroes', reported the *Western Mail*: 'There could be no greater tribute than this from a town steeped in rugby traditions.'[72]

Perhaps an early progenitor of the 1990s' 'Cool Cymru', the investiture projected upon Wales a rendition of Wilson's star-studded 'Swinging Britain'. Prompted by the Welsh Office, the Duke of Norfolk duly invited Welsh cinema and pop stars to the investiture. Noted celebrities like Richard Burton, Richard Baker and Emlyn Williams provided commentary for the television coverage of the ceremony. Welsh comedian, singer and 'former Goon', Harry Secombe was a guest of honour at the investiture and a frequent focus of commentary. Prince Charles's own reply to the people's loyalty address praised the Welsh contribution to the arts, citing amongst the more traditional poets, scholars and singers, 'a very memorable Goon and eminent film stars'.[73] Although including the usual fare of traditional hymns and anthems, the music for the investiture primarily consisted of works in the modern idiom composed specifically for the occasion by contemporary Welsh composers. Startlingly, the old standard, 'God Bless the Prince of Wales', was almost excluded from the ceremony as 'out of place in a programme of modern work'.[74] Perhaps even more

[71] Gareth Williams, *1905 and All That* (Llandysul, 1991), pp. 68–89.
[72] *Western Mail*, 4 July 1969.
[73] *Western Mail*, 2 July 1969.
[74] Report of the Music Subcommittee, 9 October 1968, PREM 13/2360, PRO; Minutes of the Third Meeting of the Investiture Committee, 9 October 1968, PREM 13/2360, PRO; Music for the investiture was composed by Alun Hoddinott, Arwel Hughes, Daniel Jones, Mansel Thomas and Grace Williams and conducted by Roy Bohana, Arwel Hughes, and Wyn Morris.

notably, *A Prince for Wales*, the theatrically released film on the investiture, paired the sound of Welsh choirs with the hip vocals of Tom Jones's 'Green Green Grass of Home' over the visual backdrop of the majestic Welsh hills.[75]

Allusions to modernity were matched by the investiture year's emphasis on youth. The prince's term at Aberystwyth was billed by the Welsh Office and the press as a time for the prince to meet young men and women of his own generation and for the young people of Wales to get to know their prince.[76] During his tour of retraining centres in south Wales, the Prince was said to have paid particular attention to 'teenage job hunters' and the first meeting of the Countryside Committee for Wales, over which Charles presided, featured the theme 'Youth, Leisure and the Countryside'.[77] The primary event in the climactic visit of Prince Charles's investiture tour was a grand assembly of Welsh youth organizations assembled in Cardiff Castle under the title 'Youth Welcomes the Prince – Ieuenctid yn Croesawu'r Tywysog'. No ordinary garden party, the rally featured 2,500 representatives of Welsh youth engaged in a plethora of events and demonstrations displaying 'youth achievements' in crafts, sports and culture.[78] Televised competitions were held to choose a Welsh pop music anthem for investiture year and to select a young woman as the National 'Croeso 69' Hostess.[79] The Welsh Office and the Wales Tourist Board were clearly determined that 'the investiture year shall be a young people's year'.[80]

In direct contrast to the unwashed and sullen hippies of the 1960s, the young, mild mannered and clean-cut prince was cast as the exemplar for British youth. In the eyes of the *Western Mail*, Prince Charles was 'a young man – with all the idealism of youth – not only a member of the royal household'.[81] The

[75] *The Times*, 5 July 1969.
[76] *Western Mail*, 2 November 1967.
[77] *Western Mail*, 29 June 1968, 5 June 1969.
[78] *Investiture of His Royal Highness: Programme of His Visit to Cardiff, Capital of Wales, Saturday 5th July 1969*, BD 67/81, PRO; Minutes, Fourth Meeting of Investiture Committee, 12 February 1969, PREM 2901, PRO.
[79] Memorandum, Croeso Commmittee, 24 May 1968, BD 67/22, PRO.
[80] *Western Mail*, 30 July 1968.
[81] *Western Mail*, 2 June 1969.

investiture invited contrasts between alternative models of contemporary youth. One commentator saw significance in the fact that the investiture happened to occur in the same month as a tribute concert for Brian Jones, a member of the Rolling Stones who had recently met his demise when he fell intoxicated into his swimming pool. The *Sunday Express* asked, 'Will Charles Oust the Pop Idols?' and wishfully observed that:

> He's setting a new fashion among the young. He marks the end of an era – the era of too long haired, too uncouth, too cynical, too vulgar, too opted out, too mixed up youth. For in the Prince of Wales the square virtues are revealed as not belonging exclusively to the middle aged . . . It is a strange, sad comment on the youthful scene that in the very same week two young Britons hit the public eye. The Prince who represents the new image is crowned in Wales and offers us new hope. The pop idol, only six years older, the rudderless representative of the scene that is passing, dies tragically in his own expensive swimming pool and leaves behind the shambles of his short life.[82]

In a similar vein, the *Observer* noted that Charles was 'the kind of son every mother in the crowd would like to have' and described him as the exact opposite of Dustin Hoffman in *The Graduate*, 'who when he had reached about the same stage in his career as Prince Charles, abruptly declined to meet his parents friends at all, for no good reason except that though he was laden with honours from college and they wanted to congratulate him, he simply could not see the point of doing so, and could not see the point of his honours either'.[83] In the opinion of the *Western Mail*, the Prince of Wales 'can serve most of all as an example to Welsh youth', while the *Guardian* felt that 'a young man who can talk to the British public in its present iconoclastic mood without being either pompous at one extreme or undignified at the other has qualities to be admired'.[84]

In the ceremony of investiture itself, the Welsh Office was particularly anxious that Welsh youth be given 'proper recognition'.[85] In the first meeting of the Investiture Committee, the Welsh Office expressed the desire that 'every opportunity

[82] *Sunday Express*, 6 July 1969.
[83] *Observer*, 6 July 1969.
[84] *Western Mail*, 1 July 1969; *Guardian*, 3 March 1969.
[85] *Western Mail*, 4 July 1968.

should be taken to introduce children, young people and youth organizations into the ceremony, in the processions and elsewhere' and directed the Earl Marshal to ask committee members to consider: 'Should, and if so how could a large part in the proceedings in 1969 be played by the youth of Wales?'[86] This mirrored the question put to them about the participation of the military. There was indeed a direct inverse relationship between the levels of youth and military participation, with the Welsh Office supporting 'rather greater emphasis on youth and a lesser one on the armed forces'.[87] The Welsh Office envisioned representatives of Welsh youth replacing the servicemen originally assigned positions in the ceremony by the Earl Marshal. Given the antipathy between contemporary youth culture and military service and between Welshness and militarism, they thought this a matter that needed emphasis in order to create 'a good impression' before public opinion hardened. Furthermore, the Secretary of State expressed his anxiety that 'the Prince's procession should not consist mainly of the elderly gentlemen' listed in early drafts of the ceremonial provided by the Earl Marshal. Instead, he suggested that the senior dignitaries proceed separately so that 'the Prince would then appear accompanied only by young Welsh people'.[88] In promoting these innovations, the Welsh Office had to contend with the reluctance of the heralds, who objected to the use of young people as ushers and found the idea to 'include a bunch of teenagers in the Prince's Procession' to be highly questionable. What was even worse in their eyes was the Welsh Office suggestion that the contingent of youth in the ceremony actually be located closer to the prince and in a position of ceremonial precedence over more senior dignitaries, a measure one herald felt threatened to 'add a slight touch of contemporary anarchy to the Procession!'[89] George Thomas agreed with Eirene White's statement: 'I am strongly of the view that a way

---

[86] Minutes of the First Meeting of the Investiture Committee, 26 October 1967, PREM 13/2359, PRO.
[87] G. H. Daniel to J. E. Owens-Jones, 5 October 1967, 1.0.I.1969 Investiture, CA.
[88] G. H. Daniel to R. H. Jones, 20 June 1968, 1.0.II. Ceremony, 1969 Investiture, CA.
[89] Somerset Herald to Anthony Gardner, 9 September 1968, 1.0.II. 1969 Investiture, CA.

must be found of associating young people with the Prince on this occasion . . . If the College of Heralds object, they must be asked to adjust their ideas.'[90]

In the end, the investiture ceremony fulfilled the Welsh Office's desire to portray the Prince as the young leader of a young Wales. Young people were recruited to serve as ushers and choristers. With those over 35 barred from auditioning, the investiture choir of 1969 contrasted with the choristers of 1911, where singers had to be over the age of 25 even to be considered.[91] Rather than leading representatives of the Welsh regiments as in 1911, the prince marched in his procession in front of thirty-four 'representatives of Welsh youth', well groomed and neatly attired in stylish blazers. Duly appointed by the county and county boroughs of Wales, these youthful delegates were selected no less for their tidy appearance than their achievements and service. As in the Edwardian ceremony, the Wales of the 1969 Investiture was a young Wales. However, this was not the passive youth of imperial duty and subordination found in the Edwardian ceremony. The 1969 Investiture portrayed Labour's idealization of a modern and assertive youth, characterized by equality, potential and social duty.

Service to the Welsh nation was as important as any ancestral or cultural signifier to the investiture's vision of Welshness. In this regard, much was made of the prince's motto, Ich Dien – I Serve, and the investiture itself was cast by the Queen as 'an act of dedication to a life of service in the years ahead'.[92] The object of such devotion was admittedly vague, but many expected that the 'special interest' forged between the prince and Wales would extend beyond the investiture and that the ceremony would inaugurate an ongoing, exclusive and formal relationship between prince and principality. As early as 1966, a columnist for the *Western Mail* wrote:

> The Prince of Wales should surely be given a definite job to do, and what job could be more suited to his position than to concern himself with the affairs of Wales and to live in the Principality? An investiture

[90] Eirene White to George Thomas, 23 September 1968, 1.0.II. 1969 Investiture, CA.
[91] Minutes, Fourth Meeting of Investiture Committee, 12 February 1969, PREM 2901, PRO; *Sun*, 1 July 1969.
[92] *Western Mail*, 18 December 1968.

as Prince there must be, but that should only be a beginning. After that let him be a real Prince of Wales . . . In short, the monarchy must be decentralized and a start might well be made with the Prince of Wales.⁹³

The Palace itself was unenthusiastic about such limited ambitions. Prince Charles openly stated in a radio interview that he did not entirely agree with 'being an ambassador wholly for Wales' and would rather 'be an ambassador not only for Wales, but also for the UK as a whole and from one Commonwealth country to another'.⁹⁴ Yet, the idea of Charles as Welsh ambassador continued to be implicitly encouraged by investiture organizers and proved to be a popular theme in the press. It was even reported that the Prince of Wales would become the special responsibility of the Welsh Office once the investiture was over, a development supposedly indicating that 'a close and long-term association between Prince Charles and the Principality is now firmly planted'.⁹⁵ The ceremony itself did nothing to discourage this notion. The *Loyalty Address from the People of Wales* stated that 'the Principality looks forward to a period when its Prince will associate himself personally with its aspirations and problems', to which the Prince replied: 'It is indeed my firm intention to associate myself in word and deed with as much of the life of the Principality as possible – and what a Principality!'⁹⁶ No wonder that, like the *Scotsman*, many felt the Prince had expressly dedicated himself to the future service of Wales.⁹⁷ By extension, the investiture also provided an occasion for the Welsh themselves to offer service to the Welsh nation. The *Western Mail* thought the investiture granted an opportunity to all Welshman 'of uniting in the service of their nation' and predicted a 'better Wales economically, socially and spiritually' as a result.⁹⁸ As Cledwyn Hughes put it, the investiture would not only be 'the dedicating of a Prince but the rededication of a nation'.⁹⁹

93 *Western Mail*, 14 November 1967.
94 *Western Mail*, 6 June 1969.
95 *Western Mail*, 18 September 1967.
96 *Western Mail*, 2 July 1969.
97 *Scotsman*, 2 July 1969.
98 *Western Mail*, 14 December 1969.
99 *Western Mail*, 18 May 1967.

According to the investiture's vision, Welsh ancestry and language were important to Welsh national identity but did not in and of themselves define Welshness. Instead, the 1969 Investiture offered a multicultural and bilingual vision of Welsh national identity. In a provocative speech on the eve of the ceremony, George Thomas stated:

> Today, Prince Charles's standard will fly over Caernarfon Castle. I see it as the standard of One Wales. Indeed, I see it as a good augury for our future that it is the standard of a young man whose past has been spent largely outside the Principality, for if Wales cannot welcome new comers from the outside world, and absorb them and assimilate them into her unique culture, and national personality, Wales is indeed in a sorry state. For is not Wales already an amalgam of many races and peoples? Iberians, Celts, Saxons, Normans, Danes, French Huguenots, Flemings, and more recently Poles, Germans, Czechs, Russians, Hungarians, Indians, Africans, Asians and how many other nations? We are a hybrid nation, with all the qualities of vigorous hybrid stock . . . [Prince Charles] is part of us all that we have been, and now he is a part of all that we are to be, a diverse but united people, one people, one Wales.[100]

Vowing to resist the 'bullying tactics' of Cymdeithas yr Iaith, George Thomas declared in March 1969: 'Wales does not belong to one section of the Welsh people. The test of a Welshman is not whether he speaks Welsh or whether he speaks English.'[101] Urging the people of Wales to support the prince, the Bishop of St David's proclaimed that: 'a man could be a good Welshman even though he can't speak Welsh.'[102] Shortly after the investiture, the Welsh Office's Minister of State, Eirene White, addressed a concert held in conjunction with the 1969 National Eisteddfod. Condemning the 'language idolatry' of those in Cymdeithas yr Iaith, White expressed her resentment of the self-righteousness of those 'whose command of Welsh was due almost wholly to the accident of birth'. What was important, she maintained, was not the language used but the person and the thought the language expressed.[103]

---

[100] *Western Mail*, 1 July 1969.
[101] *Western Mail*, 28 March 1969.
[102] *Western Mail*, 11 June 1969.
[103] *Daily Express*, 8 August 1969.

Indeed, the prince's own miraculous transformation in the months before the investiture became the epitome of what might be called 'aspirational' Welshness, a sense that one could become Welsh through experience, sentiment and action rather than through birth. In a business traveller's magazine, an essay on the Welsh dramatically reworked the origin story of Edward I's presentation of his son as Prince of Wales, placing the responsibility for the Welsh assimilation of the princes squarely on the Welsh themselves:

> 'This is my son!' cried Edward 'He was born not an hour ago in this very castle. I give him to you, the Welsh people, to bring up as your own prince. As I promised, he can speak not one word of English. It is now up to you to see that he learns the Welsh tongue, that he grows up as a Welshman.'[104]

'The government's long term idea is to turn him into a Welsh speaking Welshman, get him to take a serious and continuing interest in the life and future of the nation', noted the *Observer*: 'Then bingo: the restless Charles has a useful role, the monarchy is saved, and the Labour Party holds a few marginal seats in the valleys.'[105] Following the prince's speech to the Urdd, the *Western Mail* proclaimed: 'Living and working among them, speaking now their language affectionately if not yet fluently, Prince Charles has surely earned the right to be called a Welshman by adoption, whatever the debators may say about the Welshness of his ancestry. And Wales has indeed adopted him.'[106]

So overwhelming was the programme for the Cymricization of the prince, there is evidence that the impressionable youth may have taken to his instruction on becoming a Welshman only too well for the comfort of Labour centralists. During his eight weeks at Aberystwyth, Prince Charles was surrounded by faculty and students with nationalist views. The prince was clearly keen to meet with student nationalists and to understand their perspective. Edward Millward, the prince's primary language instructor, had until recently served as the Vice President of Plaid Cymru and had been a prominent figure in

---

[104] *Business Visitor to Britain*, autumn/winter 1968.
[105] *Observer*, 29 October 1967.
[106] *Western Mail*, 2 June 1969.

the early organization of Cymdeithas yr Iaith. On the prince's course of study, Millward said that it should include:

> ... discussion on what is going on in Wales, the social and political developments. There is an awakening in Wales and inevitably one would have to talk about this. The history of the language is an important facet and much of our life has been expressed through our language. It would be greatly to the Prince's benefit to hear all these things.[107]

Prince Charles's comments on Welsh history and nationality were heavily influenced by views current in Welsh academic and nationalist circles. In his first radio interview, the prince attributed the development of a unique and independent Welsh culture and national character to the historic neglect of the central government and the ruling class.[108] Ever the centralist suspicious of political nationalism, George Thomas became increasingly anxious over the prince's more emphatic pronouncements on Welsh nationality and began to fear that things had gone too far. Shortly after the investiture, the Secretary of State wrote the prime minister a confidential note:

> I am concerned by the speeches made by the Prince of Wales. I have no information about who his advisers are, but a dangerous situation is developing. On two occasions he has made public speeches which have political implications. In my presence in Cardiff he referred to the 'cultural and political awakening in Wales'. This is *most* useful for the Nationalists. If the Prince is writing his own speeches he may well be tempted to go further. The enthusiasm of youth is a marvellous spur, but it may lead to speeches that cause real difficulty. During the Prince's stay at Aberystwyth he was subjected to concentrated attention by Welsh Nationalists. His tutor, his neighbour in the next room, and the Principal were all dedicated Nationalists. It has become quite evident to me that the Aberystwyth experience has influenced the Prince to a considerable extent.[109]

Thomas went on to suggest that the prime minister have a 'discreet word' with the Queen and that the content of the prince's speeches be put more firmly under the control of the

---

[107] *The Times*, 28 January 1969.
[108] *Western Mail*, 6 June 1969.
[109] George Thomas to Harold Wilson, 22 July 1969, PREM 13/2907, PRO.

government. Despite the concerns of the Secretary of State, the prince's conduct demonstrated the remarkable degree to which he had personally absorbed Labour's programme regarding the ceremony. Charles had genuinely internalized a Welsh identity, even if only for the purposes of the summer's ceremonial.

Tying the various strands of the Welsh population together and defying the opposition of its opponents, investiture supporters asserted that the ceremony had the unique power to unify the Welsh nation. Like 1911, potted histories that inevitably accompanied commentary on the ceremony characterized the history of Wales as fractious and divided. Medieval Wales was depicted as being ruled by a number of 'war like' native chieftains living in perpetual armed strife and refusing to accept an overlord. Only the power of the princes could bring this quarrelsome people together to form a nation, and where the princes of the past had in the end failed, the modern prince of the future would succeed in uniting north and south, Welsh speaker and non-Welsh speaker, young and old, national past and future. The *Western Mail* thought that through his continuing involvement in Wales after the investiture, 'the Prince can become the unifying force, above party political divisions, which is needed in Wales, welding together efforts directed toward generally agreed aims'.[110] In a speech made in Cardiff's castle green, the prince himself took an active role in seeking to heal the rift in Wales:

> A greater interest in the language and ideals of Welsh culture is being taken by increasing numbers of people but at the same time tensions tend to build up between Welsh speakers and many non-Welsh speakers who feel themselves, quite rightly, as much a part of Wales as any Welshman. It would be more than tragic if these tensions were allowed to build up to too great a degree. Outside as well as inside Wales, tolerance and patience are what are needed – the simple effort to try to understand the other person's point of view and his idealism and not to condemn it outright.[111]

Although he may well have been directing his comments equally to the passionate partisanship of the Welsh Office as to the

[110] *Western Mail*, 1 July 1969.
[111] *Western Mail*, 12 June 1969.

investiture's opponents, the prince's statement was generally hailed as a justified rebuke of those opposing the investiture. With a barbed inference to the confrontational activities of Welsh-language campaigners, George Thomas declared in his own pre-investiture speech:

> For, in my view, our Prince has given us another chance to become one Wales, not two. As no one else could have done, Prince Charles has given Wales a new unity. I repeat, as no one else could have done. Certainly, I could not have done, nor could any other Secretary of State who has held office, nor any politician or party. That is the unique characteristic of the British Royal Family. It represents and epitomizes the aspirations and personality of us all, not just some of us. Since he has been coming to Wales, Prince Charles has made us see that whatever our differences, we, the whole population of Wales, have infinitely more to unite us than to divide us. Over the whole spectrum of political and philosophical thoughts, we have the same hopes and aspirations for Wales though we may differ on ways to achieve them. Just think what Prince Charles has done for the Welsh language . . . Prince Charles is one of thousands of young people in Wales who are making a success of learning and using Welsh. He epitomizes the effort that is being made by one language group to establish a working base in the other, and to bridge that dangerous gap which could divide Wales and prevent us ever achieving my desire – our desire, and most of all Prince Charles's desire, of one Wales.[112]

In the light of Prince Charles's commitment to serve, the *Denbighshire Free Press* asked: 'Is it too much to hope that the Welsh warring factions within this tiny land will lay aside their grievances and disputes and work together for the common good and ultimate peace and prosperity, not only of Wales but of the whole of the United Kingdom?'[113] George Thomas confidently proclaimed the answer: 'We shall forget all our differences and unite in saluting our own Prince.'[114]

Nationalist opponents disagreed, rejecting the investiture and its construction of Welshness on nearly every count. Rather than a meaningful connection between Prince and

---

[112] *Western Mail*, 30 June 1969.
[113] *Denbighshire Free Press*, 5 July 1969.
[114] *Western Mail*, 30 June 1969.

people, they equated the ceremony with mere political stratagem. In the words of a student protesting in Aberystwyth, 'The Prince is being used as a political puppet by Harold Wilson and his associates' to quell the political disquiet in Wales.[115] At the St David's Day rally, demonstrators were told that the Prince was being thrust upon them in an attempt to win back their loyalty to the government at Westminster.[116] In the Welsh-language newspaper *Baner*, a columnist explained: 'To an English party like the Labour Party, that sees Wales slipping through its fingers, the investiture was an excellent opportunity (though costly) to try to tie Wales closer to London.'[117] Contrary to popular views on the non-controversial nature of the monarchy, nationalist critics of the investiture regarded the presence and function of the Royal Family in Wales as actively and provocatively political. 'If the Prince is non-political in English politics, in Welsh politics an English prince is as much a supporter of one side as Cledwyn Hughes himself', wrote Plaid's youth chairman Dafydd Elis Thomas: 'He is as biased politically as if his mother were a paid up member of the Labour Party.'[118] The political nature of the Royal Family in Wales justified the opposition to its presence. 'The invitation to the prince to attend the Eisteddfod Genedleathol yr Urdd a month before the investiture was a political act', argued T. Emyr Pritchard: 'Thus, the political protest that was had at the time was totally appropriate and fair.'[119]

To critics, the benefits of the investiture were crassly materialistic, fleeting and outweighed by the cost. According to the *Carmarthen Times*, opponents viewed the investiture and its affiliated events, 'not as an honour and distinction for which Wales should be truly thankful, but as an overdose of propaganda aimed at boosting the tourist economy'.[120] In his 1968 poem 'Loyalties', R. S. Thomas was moved to ask of the investiture:

---

[115] *Western Mail*, 6 November 1967.
[116] *Western Mail*, 17 March 1969.
[117] *Baner ac Amserau Cymru*, 12 June 1969.
[118] *I'r Gad*, spring 1968.
[119] *Baner ac Amserau Cymru*, 12 June 1969.
[120] *Carmarthen Times*, 26 July 1968.

And where does it lead to

Anyway? Behind the counters

The shopkeepers are all attention[121]

Meanwhile, valuable resources were thought to be diverted by the 'pantomime' from the real problems of Wales. On a controversial BBC programme, a Plaid Cymru county councillor complained: 'There are vital projects which you would like to do – social services, education, health, and so on – which year after year we have got to shelve because we haven't got the money; and yet they can go and throw the money away on a thing like this – which is no good at all.'[122] Cymdeithas yr Iaith described the Wilson government as a: 'slobbering socialistic government insisting on spending a half million on pageantry at the expense of not being able to build houses, nor to increase pensions and throwing thousands out of work.'[123] A leaflet by the Anti-Investiture Campaign Committee exclaimed: 'This country is being dragged down by depopulation, unemployment, rail closures, pit closures, lack of good roads, etc. etc. and then to crown these achievements of misrule, we are to have an investiture in the great and wonderful tradition of silly English pageantry!'[124]

To the talk of the 'Prince and his people', opponents of the investiture retorted that the Prince was not a Prince of Wales at all but a foreign aristocrat, alien to Wales and Welsh life in every respect. The anti-investiture campaign held that the ethnicity of Prince Charles disqualified him from a legitimate investiture as the Prince of Wales. Demonstrators often referred to the 'Alien Prince' and popular placard slogans included 'No Englishman will be Prince of Wales', 'No English Charlie', and 'God Keep the Prince in England'. The investiture ceremony itself was dismissed as either an 'English ritual' or merely the product of the unprincipled political opportunism

[121] *Observer Magazine*, 22 June 1969.
[122] Extract from '24 Hours', recorded from transmission BBC 1 2220, 28 February 1969, PREM 13/2505, PRO.
[123] *Tafod y Ddraig*, June 1969.
[124] Leaflet, 1282 Fund, Anti-Investiture Campaign Committee, Tŷ Cenedl 1 AI/5, NLW.

of David Lloyd George.[125] Deriding both his princely status and his claims to ordinariness, opponents often referred to the Prince as 'Charles Windsor'. Contesting the prince's image as a young man 'just like us', Dafydd Iwan's 'Carlo' portrayed Prince Charles as a youth of alien ways, isolated from others of his generation by his perfect manners, impeccable appearance, aristocratic upbringing and fondness for polo.[126] Appearing in *Tafod y Ddraig*, a series of satirical letters 'From the Queen' highlighted the contradictions of the royal embrace of ordinariness and Welshness. Through its simultaneous portrayal of Queen Elizabeth as a Welsh mam and as an English plutocrat, it ridiculed the Royal Family's pretensions to be all things to all people. Blending the barriers of class and nationality, protest signs declared: 'No English Blueblood for the Red Dragon of Wales.'

The prince's study and apparent mastery of the Welsh language presented a serious challenge to those who would reject his Welshness. Language activists were placed in the uncomfortable position of having to dethrone the language as the primary criterion of Welsh nationality in preference to a more ambiguous amalgam of birth, blood and belonging. T. Emyr Pritchard protested in the *Baner*:

> It is true that the prince showed in his speech in the eisteddfod that he could utter the Welsh language well. But that was irrelevant, and his speech was a fraud. This Prince of Wales is an Englishman; an Englishman with a heritage of the English crown ... He cannot be white-washed overnight into a Welshman by giving a Welsh lecture at the Eisteddfod Genedlaethol yr Urdd, nor by attending a one term course at the College in Aberystwyth.[127]

Similar reasoning was repeated in Cymdeithas yr Iaith's journal, *Tafod y Ddraig*, which argued that Charles was a 'Prince' not a 'Tywysog' and could never be placed in the succession of the true Princes of Wales.[128] At the Cymdeithas yr Iaith rally at Cilmery, Emyr Llewelyn Jones insisted that 'more was needed

[125] *Western Mail*, 21 October 1968; *Liverpool Daily Post*, 3 March 1969.
[126] Dafydd Iwan, *Holl Ganeuon Dafydd Iwan* (Tal-y-bont, 1992), p. 58.
[127] *Baner ac Amserau Cymru*, 12 June 1969.
[128] *Tafod y Ddraig*, January 1968.

than the empty bottle of language' to change an alien prince into a Prince of Wales.[129]

Because of its political nature, the prince's support of Welsh culture and nationhood was only to be ridiculed and lampooned. In the hands of the satirist, Prince Charles became an ultra-nationalist. In *Tafod y Ddraig*, the Queen stops Prince Charles from trooping off to Caerphilly to campaign for Plaid Cymru. 'I am the Prince of Wales', he retorts, 'I bet you that Owain Glyndŵr's mam didn't scold him for doing his part for his country.'[130] A cartoon by Tegwyn Jones portrayed the prince wearing the uniform of the Free Wales Army and vandalizing Buckingham Palace with a can of spray paint. In 'Carlo', Dafydd Iwan sang of the Prince's enthusiasm for everything Welsh:

> Bob wythnos mae e'n darllen y Cymro a Herald,
> Mae e'n darllen Dafydd ap Gwilym yn ei wely bob nos,
> Mae dyfodol y wlad a'r iaith yn agos at 'i gallon [*sic*] fach e
> A mae nhw'n dweud 'i fod e'n perthyn i'r FWA! [131]

> Every week he is reading the Cymro and the Herald
> He is reading Dafydd ap Gwilym in his bed every night
> The future of the land and the language is near to his little heart
> And what they say is that he belongs to the FWA!

Such satire highlighted the inherent contradiction and political nature of the prince's position. It rejected the idea that Welshness could be acquired and questioned the motivation for the prince's much publicized commitment to Wales.

Countering Charles's claim to the title of the Prince of Wales, anti-investiture activists held up the medieval figure of Llywelyn, the 'last true prince of Wales'. Llywelyn the Last was presented as the greatest of Welsh leaders and heroes, the embodiment of the independent sovereignty of the Welsh people. Anti-investiture propaganda, however, did not focus so much on the heroism of his life as on the circumstances of his death at Cilmery in 1282. Directly countering the festive textual image of 'Croeso 69', simple black placards and banners extolled the faithful to remember and mourn '1282'. Emyr

---

[129] *Baner ac Amsersau Cymru*, 3 July 1969.
[130] *Tafod y Ddraig*, August 1969.
[131] Iwan, *Holl Ganeuon*, p. 58.

Llewelyn Jones asked Welsh-language activists: 'How can anyone forget that the blood of Llywelyn is on the crown that is to be placed on the head of the Prince?'[132] Anti-investiture propaganda produced highly coloured accounts of Llywelyn's death, dwelling on the grisly and atrocious details of how the prince was stabbed in the back by the English while taking a drink from a stream, how his head was cut off, mocked with a crown of ivy and displayed on a spike in London.[133] This emphasis on the death, dismemberment, and humiliation of the body of the last true Prince of Wales at the hands of the English king personified the destruction of the Welsh body politic itself by the British state. In one leaflet by the Patriotic Front, a crude drawing of Llywelyn's severed head weeps tears of blood, the corpse transferring the focus of mourning back onto the nation itself. The same image and theme was expressed later in a more notable and artistic form in 'Fy Ngwlad', the pre-eminent poem from Gerallt Lloyd Owen's collection that won him the chair at the 1969 Urdd Eisteddfod. Surveying the scenes of adulation for Prince Charles in Wales, Owen exhorts the dead prince:

> Wylit, wylit Lywelyn,
> Wylit waed pe gwelit hyn . . .[134]
>
> Weep, weep Llywelyn,
> Weep blood when you see this . . .

The paramilitaries and Cymdeithas yr Iaith competed for the honour of claiming the memorial at Cilmery as the central symbolic site of anti-investiture protest. For both groups, the major rite at Cilmery was the mourning of Llywelyn and the corresponding loss of the Welsh nation's sovereignty. As an effective counterpoint to Caernarfon Castle, Cymdeithas yr Iaith also employed Dolbadarn Castle, a fortress constructed and held by the native Welsh princes until its capture by the English in the year of Llywelyn's death. King Edward I was cast as the ultimate villain, a sadist and rapist. Following the death of Llywelyn, commentators focused on Edward's oppression of

[132] *Baner ac Amserau Cymru*, 3 July 1969.
[133] 'Remember Llywelyn: No Englishman for Prince of Wales', leaflet, Tŷ Cenedl 1 AI/5, NLW.
[134] *Cerddi'r Gadair* (Urdd Genedlaethol Cymru, 1969), p. 4.

the Welsh people, when 'hangings and castrations were the order of the day for all those who opposed English rule'.[135] Edward's appropriation of the title 'Prince of Wales' from the slain Llywelyn was an usurpation, the manner of his bestowing it upon his infant son a trick to humiliate the conquered Welsh. 'Symbolically and in the spiritual realm, there is no Prince for us but the one whose rights and the sovereignty of his lineage were broken at Cilmery', declared *Tafod y Ddraig*.[136]

Rather than a celebration of the existence of the Welsh nation, nationalist opponents cast the investiture as a calculated insult to Welsh nationhood. Instead of an imperial partner, Wales was cast as colonized victim. Revisiting its origin myth and emphasizing the destruction of the native line of Welsh princes, opponents reconstructed the investiture as a celebration of the nation's defeat by a gloating English state. Maintaining that 'The investiture is merely a celebration of the fact that Wales was conquered by England', the Llywelyn Society was formed 'to fight the degrading insult to our nation of having the son of an English Sovereign as the Prince of Wales'.[137] An article in Plaid Cymru's *Welsh Nationalist* put forth a novel spin on the origins of the prince's motto, relating how Edward I held up his infant son and declared to the Welsh chiefs:

> 'Eich dyn – this is your man'. Edward I had the coarse speech of a soldier and liked to humiliate his defeated enemies and we may be sure he did not overlook the resemblance of the words to 'Eich tin' (tr. Your ass). In 1301, when Edward of Caernarfon was invested as the first English Prince of Wales at Lincoln, these words were chosen as his motto. No doubt Edward I laughed heartily at his joke.[138]

To one dissident church body in Carmarthenshire, the investiture was a 'symbol of our nation's inferior status'.[139] Adopting the slogan 'Insult 69', the Patriotic Front's Anti-Investiture Campaign Committee defined the investiture as the 'greatest insult to Wales this century'.[140] Gwyneth Morgan told

[135] Leaflet, Anti-Investiture Committee, Tŷ Cenedl 1 AI/5, NLW.
[136] *Tafod y Ddraig*, September 1968.
[137] *Western Mail*, 8 January 1968.
[138] *Welsh Nationalist*, December 1967.
[139] *Western Mail*, 24 May 1968.
[140] Statement of the People of Wales, 12 October 1968, Anti-Investiture

Cymdeithas yr Iaith demonstrators that it was 'some cheek' and 'an insult to the memories of the true Princes' to push an English Prince on Wales. It was 'the last kick of English imperialism – a kick that the countries of Africa would never accept'.[141]

Enunciated in Welsh-language periodicals and on the platform of Cymdeithas yr Iaith rallies, the most fully developed theory opposing the investiture came from J. R. Jones, a celebrated professor of philosophy at UCW Swansea and a noted language activist. In his influential 1967 essay 'Need the Language Divide Us?', Jones argued that the Welsh language was the only basis for the separate identity of the Welsh nation. Rather than seeing Welsh merely as a means of communication, he pointed to 'the way in which it becomes, after being spoken over the generations by the inhabitants of the same region, a vessel to collect and store the past, and through that a means to form them into a People'.[142] Following this reasoning, J. R. Jones tied the Welsh language to the various strands of anti-investiture rhetoric to form a coherent theory regarding a destructive symbolism of union implicit in the ceremony of investiture. Jones recognized that British union could appear as the conjoining of three equal nations, but rejected the idea as wilful deceit. The true, hidden purpose of union was to destroy the separate identity of the Welsh and to amalgamate the English and Welsh into one 'British' nation. The Prince of Wales and his investiture were a hidden symbol of 'the defeat of our existence as a nation': 'Our independence ended with the death of Llywelyn; his title was handed over along with his power to England and nothing from then on was to better our subjugated condition.' Jones argued that underneath peaceful, patronizing gestures, the 'Crown of London is a covert symbol that will assimilate us and devour our separate identity'. Through 'perpetual brainwashing', the conquest of Wales would be forgotten and with it the proper tongue and national identity of the Welsh people. English was the medium of the British union and the land of Wales would be nothing more

Campaign Committee, Tŷ Cenedl 1 AI/5, NLW; 1282 Fund, Anti-Investiture Campaign Committee, Tŷ Cenedl 1 AI/5 NLW.
[141] *Y Cymro*, 6 March 1969.
[142] Reprinted in translation in *Planet*, January 1980.

than a part of England once the Welsh people lost their language. The battle against the investiture was thus equated to the fight for the Welsh language and ultimately for the sovereignty and existence of Wales itself.

In this struggle, J. R. Jones maintained that symbols and memory were the most potent of weapons. Those fighting on behalf of union employed the destructive and hidden symbolism of the British monarchy:

> In the battle for the existence of the Welsh speaking nation, the Crown is being used as a weapon against it. It is going to be used in this castle in July as a symbol of this unity, of the secret union that is wearing us down unmercifully. In going to battle – either we wake up, or we get blotted out of existence.[143]

Pennar Davies reinforced this idea when he told the rally at Dolbadarn: 'The main aim of the investiture of the son of the Queen of England in Caernarfon this year is to try to enthrone Britishness rather than Welshness in the consciousness of the Welsh people.'[144] In like manner, the Anti-Investiture Campaign Committee declared: 'The investiture will be the cross on the grave of Wales.'[145] J. R. Jones provided the memory of the old princes as a sword and shield for those fighting on behalf of Welsh language and identity. As Emyr Llewelyn Jones argued: 'The reason that the Welsh language is important to each of us is that through it we can understand the meaning of 1282.'[146] When the last of the old princes died, Jones maintained, sovereignty passed back to the Welsh people not to the throne of England. Princeship over Wales was thus at the discretion of the 'Welsh-speaking nation' alone. A hunger striker at Aberystwyth explained that the edge of Insult 69 came from the fact that 'Prince Charles was an alien prince imposed on us without consent'.[147]

In the view of its opponents, the investiture was forced on the Welsh nation by the armed might of the British state. The

---

[143] *Y Cymro*, 6 March 1969; *Baner ac Amserau Cymru*, 3 July 1969; *Tafod y Ddraig*, September 1968.
[144] *Y Cymro*, 6 March 1969.
[145] Leaflet, Anti-Investiture Campaign Committee, Tŷ Cenedl 1 AI/5, NLW.
[146] *Baner ac Amserau Cymru*, 3 July 1969.
[147] *Western Mail*, 2 June 1968.

extensive security measures provoked by paramilitary activity certainly helped foster the image of a police state in Wales. The Patriotic Front's Anti-Investiture Campaign Committee declared: 'England has delivered Wales an ultimatum and it is "we shall crown Charley Windsor at all costs".'[148] In another leaflet, the AICC drew an image of the state sponsored coercion behind the investiture:

> We shall show the world what we think of a nation that forces onto us their royalty – AT GUNPOINT! Yes, gunpoint. Our wonderful British police have rented rooftops (every other one is the rumour) in Caernarfon, and they are to post an armed man on every one. The town will be virtually sealed off a fortnight before the pantomime, and passes will be needed to enter the town. The bootlickers say that there will be fewer soldiers for this investiture than at the last effort in 1912 but even if there are less this time they will be used for a completely different purpose.[149]

Deliberately provoked by the bombing campaign of the MAC, such images directly served the agenda of the paramilitaries and were echoed by Julian Cayo-Evans and other members of the FWA. In 1968, Cayo-Evans said that he would be delighted if he was arrested, as: 'The Whitehall Gestapo would then show that we had won.'[150] Reflecting several years later on the activities of the Patriotic Front, Gethin ap Iestyn declared victory. 'We had said that the only way the Investiture would take place was under siege conditions and this was what in fact happened', he recounted: 'It was clear to all that Wales was an occupied country with a foreign prince being imposed upon it by military force.'[151] Abetted by speculation and rumour, there can be no doubt that the extraordinary presence and heightened activities of police and security forces in the summer of 1969 helped to sustain an image of an occupied nation, at least for those who were inclined to see it. Consequently, the idea of Wales as a police state was not confined to paramilitaries but broadly employed among nationalists. Surveying the security

[148] Leaflet, Anti-Investiture Campaign Committee, no date, Tŷ Cenedl 1 AI/5, NLW.
[149] Leaflet, Number One, Anti-Investiture Campaign Committee, no date, Tŷ Cenedl 1 AI/5, NLW.
[150] *Daily Mirror*, 11 September 1968.
[151] 'Seize the Time', *Penderyn*, clipping, Tŷ Cenedl 1 AI/5, NLW.

arrangements on the eve of the prince's study at the University of Wales, *Barn* declared 'Caernarfon and Aberystwyth are garrison towns once again'. As Wales was now regarded as a 'hostile colony', Britain was free to engage in a show of force.[152] A poster produced by the Lolfa press featured a malevolent image of 'a policeman at work in Wales' and warned 'If You're Welsh You're Watched'.[153] At Cymdeithas yr Iaith's St David's Day rally, Gwyneth Morgan told the demonstrators that their country was being turned into a police state under their noses and that: 'Before long we will have no right to open our mouths without facing "bed and breakfast" in Cardiff.'[154] Often reviled and ridiculed by more mainstream nationalists before their arrest, the FWA men were accorded broader sympathy during their trial. Carrying placards in support of the defendants, the wives and relatives of the jailed FWA men were received with great respect by Cymdeithas yr Iaith at its rally at Cilmery.[155] Although admitting that the FWA was a 'fantasy without a bit of substance', Saunders Lewis rallied to the defence of the men in the dock in his address:

> I had not a bit of sympathy with tricksters Mr. Cayo-Evans and Mr. Coslett until the day of their arrest ... Their imprisonment made them hostages, hostages for any nationalist who opposed in any way the investiture in Caernarfon. They were thrown into solitary confinement for twenty three hours of every day ... The people of Arfon and Mon began to realize that they knew through further experience what it was to live in a state similar to Greece or Czechoslovakia, police states. The nine Welsh nationalists in Swansea were hostages in the hands of policemen until the afternoon of the investiture. Hostages for us, each one of us who loath the investiture and are eager to supplant the English government in Wales. For us was their pain, for us they are imprisoned lest we cause worry to the little Queen over there and to her government that had them held for five long months. Welsh hostages in the English prison, that is what they were, that is what they are. Never mind, therefore, about their earlier follies; from the minute they were thrown into prison, our hostages, our fellow nationalists, our fellow Welsh they were and are ... We

[152] *Barn*, March 1969.
[153] 'If You're Welsh You're Watched', poster, Tŷ Cenedl 1 AI/5, NLW.
[154] *Y Cymro*, 6 March 1969.
[155] *Western Mail*, 30 June 1969.

know now by experience that oppression and power is the answer of the English government to the rights of the Welsh nation. Through English prisons, not through Westminster, will come self-government for Wales. That is the definite lesson of July 1, 1969.[156]

Even Gwynfor Evans, a staunch critic of the FWA, was moved to proclaim that 'the police state manner' of the arrest was 'repugnant' and that keeping the men in solitary confinement while in prison was 'utterly abhorrent'. Claiming the prosecution was conducted to discredit the nationalist movement in Wales, Evans attacked the political 'show trial' of the FWA as setting 'a dangerous precedent against which Welsh men and others who cherish the right of freedom of speech must be on their guard'.[157]

Rather than pride in a new-found sense of nationhood, acceptance of the investiture was a sign of the degeneration of the Welsh nation, a manifestation of Welsh servility and a cause of abject shame. The Patriotic Front declared that if the investiture was allowed to happen, it would reveal that 'the Welsh nation has lost all pride and dignity and self respect in itself as a people'.[158] A cartoon in the Welsh newspaper *Baner* depicted the investiture in terms of middle-aged Welshmen and women lining up to kiss the prince's feet beneath a banner labelled 'Serfdom'.[159] Claiming that 'Our servility was the mark of our inferiority', J. R. Jones told protestors that they had all come to the Cymdeithas rally at Cilmery 'to be sure of ourselves' and to 'regain our self-respect'.[160] From the same platform, the Revd D. Jacob Davies intoned a dramatic 'Psalm of Shame':

> I bow my head in sadness because I am ashamed that I belong to a nation that has fallen into the disgrace of heavy servility.
>
> I am ashamed of a nation with its towns and villages swathed in the decoration of foreign glory and rejoicing at their own death.
>
> I am ashamed of a nation that gives empty cups to its children on the day of the investiture when the bowl of its past was so full of rare treasure.

[156] In translation, *Barn*, August 1969.
[157] *Western Mail*, 3 July 1969.
[158] Transcript of film on Welsh nationalism, Tŷ Cenedl 1 AI/4, NLW.
[159] In translation, *Baner ac Amserau Cymru*, June 12 1969.
[160] In translation, ibid., 3 July 1969.

I am ashamed of a nation that sold its backbone for thirty borrowed words of Welsh . . .[161]

Earlier that year at the anti-investiture rally at Dolbadarn, the Revd Davies gave his wholehearted support to Cymdeithas yr Iaith's effort to 'purify our country from the rottenness of its servitude' and condemned those who were 'grovelling on their bellies before the foreigner'. 'Do not bow, boys! Stand on your feet!' he exclaimed.[162] In the celebrated anti-investiture poem 'Fy Ngwlad', Gerallt Lloyd Owen depicted the Welsh as an 'enslaved', 'safely servile' people without roots nor bonds of nationality, 'looking for favours' with 'meek smiles'.[163] Tellingly, this popular poem would be republished in 1972 in a volume of poetry entitled *Cerddi'r Cywilydd* (Songs of Shame).

Defining the ceremony as an insult to Welsh nationhood, the anti-investiture movement seized upon the word 'bradwr' (traitor) to describe those Welsh who actively supported the ceremony and the prince. The entire protest campaign was infused with the imagery and language of treason. Placards reading 'Brad 1282' recalled the 'treason' of Llywelyn's death, likening the Welsh allies of Edward I to Welsh supporters of the investiture. When Prince Charles addressed the Urdd Eisteddfod, protestors held up signs reading, 'Bradychwyd yr Urdd' (The Urdd has been betrayed). A columnist in the *Baner* explained the significance of the word:

> 'Brad' was on the posters of some of the protestors in Aberystwyth. That, in one word, is the investiture, if you happen to believe that Wales is a nation and should be permitted to live as a nation. Because the nation-state of Wales has not existed for centuries, the word 'brad' has lost much of its meaning for us . . . When we come to understand the meaning of the word 'brad' once again, there will be hope for us as a nation.[164]

At Dolbadarn, Cymdeithas yr Iaith members were reminded that 'there are still traitors in Wales' and that the investiture was being pushed upon them by 'John Bull and his little servant Dic Sion Dafydd'. 'Every Welshman of the right sort must push

---

[161] In translation, ibid.
[162] In translation, *Y Cymro*, 6 March 1969.
[163] In translation, *Cerddi'r Gadair*, p. 4.
[164] In translation, *Baner ac Amserau Cymru*, 12 June 1969.

back against this attempt to make captive and to contaminate the minds of our people.'¹⁶⁵ The Anti-Investiture Campaign Committee went so far as to claim:

> All those who assist in the preparations or attend the insult or any of the local celebrations must be regarded as traitors, quislings, and lackeys, and must expect the just deserts of such scum on the day of the revolution . . . Everyone who is loyal to the Dragon Flag and freedom, will oppose this degradation to the nation.¹⁶⁶

Anti-investiture opponents held that, in contradistinction to the course attempted by Plaid Cymru, everyone must make a clear and conscious decision on the matter of the ceremony. 'No one can remain neutral over a question of such magnitude', said the AICC: 'You are either a loyal patriot or a traitor!'¹⁶⁷ 'Many were compelled, the great and the small, to show their side concerning Welsh matters and to show of what stuff they are made' mused the *Baner*.¹⁶⁸ Of course, the allegation of treason was most vociferously aimed at Welsh leaders of the Labour Party. Cledwyn Hughes and George Thomas were constantly vilified as traitors. In particular, George Thomas became the epitome of servility, snobbery and treachery in the nationalist imagination. Those targeted were clearly alarmed by the accusation of treason and were anxious to deny it. In response, there was much talk of good Welshmen, born and bred. Cledwyn Hughes sputtered, 'I believe and have always believed I hope I am a good Welshman and as good a patriot as anyone in the land, despite being called a traitor by some'. T. Glynne Davies sadly wrote of the investiture: 'It is easy in Wales to be a traitor, and easy to feel you are one.'¹⁶⁹

Labour and the English language press countered the image of the 'bradwr' with that of the 'extremist', a youth characterized by fanaticism, intolerance and violence. Excessively used in public statements from the Welsh Office and anti-investiture press coverage, the word 'extremist' was a mantra meant to

---

¹⁶⁵ In translation, *Y Cymro*, 6 March 1969.
¹⁶⁶ Leaflet, Number One, Anti-Investiture Campaign Committee, Tŷ Cenedl 1 AI/4, NLW.
¹⁶⁷ Ibid.
¹⁶⁸ In translation, *Baner ac Amserau Cymru*, 12 June 1969.
¹⁶⁹ *New Statesmen*, 30 May 1969; as quoted in Philip Butt, *The Welsh Question* (Cardiff, 1975), p. 245.

define and marginalize the anti-investiture movement. Rather than a principled opposition, anti-investiture campaigners were portrayed as 'the scruffy fringe that hangs around these days waiting for a chance to protest against nothing in particular and everything in general'.[170] In the words of Prince Philip, their protests were 'mob activity' with 'chanted arguments' devoid of reason.[171] The *Daily Mirror* described investiture opponents as a 'lunatic fringe which is not particularly Welsh or Celtic – just lunatic'.[172] In contrast to the clean cut image of the youthful Prince of Wales, the Welsh extremist was 'irresponsibly young, untidy, long haired and thoroughly unrepresentative'.[173] Opponents of the investiture were 'narrow minded', and 'inward looking'.[174] Their rejection of the prince was explained as a form of 'border hatred' and racism. *Liverpool Daily Post* columnist Charles Quant provocatively observed:

> I see no reports of students of UCW hunger striking against the residence there of African or Asian students, whose knowledge of Wales and Welsh can be no better than that of Prince Charles. Indeed, I imagine that they would get short shrift under the Race Relations Act if they did. Why then can some inhospitable, intolerant students proclaim a doctrine which smacks of Welsh-English race hatred? Would they do this if his face were black – and if they did, would they get away with it? Just what must Charles Windsor, Prince of Wales, do to be accepted in Wales? Learn Welsh? That he is trying to do and at the end of his efforts he will probably know more Welsh than most of the three quarters of the native population of Wales whose first and only language is English. Learn about Wales? That, too, he is trying to do. Work in Wales? He already has one small task in Wales, and surely will have more. Will he ever be accepted in Wales without racial prejudice? I fear not.[175]

Dafydd Iwan's 'Carlo' was memorably characterized by a letter to the editor as a 'hymn of hate' sung in the tones of the 'love agonies of a sick seal'.[176] 'I do not agree with Dafydd Iwan

[170] *South Wales Argus*, 3 March 1969.
[171] *Western Mail*, 22 February 1969.
[172] *Daily Mirror*, 1 July 1969.
[173] *Carmarthen Times*, 6 December 1968.
[174] *The Times*, 28 January 1969; *Western Mail*, 19 December 1968.
[175] *Liverpool Daily Post*, 4 February 1969.
[176] *Caernarfon & Denbighshire Herald*, 28 February 1969.

preaching hate', 'Cymraes' declared to the *Cymro*: 'We must live together and respect the English people.'[177] While citing the positive qualities of an 'enlightened Welsh nationalism', the Anglican Archbishop of Wales warned that it 'must at all costs be free from the intolerant bitterness of some of its supporters'.[178] George Thomas went further, exclaiming that: 'The extremists stand condemned' by the people of Wales who rejected a nationalism based on 'a hatred of the English or of anyone who is not of their kith or kin.'[179] Extremist violence and violent rhetoric were unjustifiable acts of an irrational fanaticism. In the opinion of the *Sun*:

> Set against the realities of life, the violence to which a few Welshmen have turned seems pathetically meaningless and wrong headed beyond understanding . . . Violence is the refuge of scoundrels or of good men oppressed beyond bearing and with no other means of protest. In that sense, Wales is not oppressed. She is free to follow freedom. To pretend otherwise is not to face reality but to live in the shadows of evil make-believe.[180]

Emphasizing the inherent absurdity of Welsh political violence against British 'oppression', the *Daily Mail* repeated erroneous rumours that the Abergele men had been killed on their way to blow up a social security office. 'What could be less of a symbol of harsh oppression than an office which sees to old age pensions?', it asked.[181]

In contrast to the modern and forward looking spirit of the investiture, the extremists were condemned for their dangerous fixation on the distant past. The *South Wales Evening Post* spoke disapprovingly of: 'efforts to substitute Llewelyn [sic], a long gone ghost, for a personable, 20 year old, 20th century flesh and blood prince in the affections of the people of Wales . . .'[182] The *South Wales Echo* admitted that:

> The opposition is understandable if you have a sense of history, for the investiture can then be seen as a symbol of subjection . . . Yet these objections cut little ice with the majority of the Welsh people, who

[177] In translation, *Y Cymro*, 13 March 1969.
[178] *Western Mail*, 26 May 1969.
[179] *Western Mail*, 30 June 1969.
[180] *Sun*, 2 July 1969.
[181] *Daily Mail*, 2 July 1969.
[182] *South Wales Evening Post*, 22 January 1969.

have no interest whatsoever in the quarrel of ancient princes. And, indeed, it's only fair to ask whether the 20th century should be dragged kicking and screaming into the morass of medieval politics. I think one must strike a balance. We should be aware of our history without becoming prisoners of the past ... You can't rub out 700 years of history by shouting insults at Prince Charles, and the majority of Welsh men and women undoubtedly feel more attachment to the House of Windsor than the Princes of Gwynedd and Powys ... We will appear a bad tempered, inhospitable nation, obsessed by ancient wrongs if all those boycotts and patriotic posturing continues.[183]

Somewhat more neutrally, Prince Charles himself observed in an interview that among some in Wales '1282 and the death of Llewelyn [sic] is yesterday'.[184] 'What avails us today to remember that when he was killed in 1282 Edward I cut his head off and sent it on show to his army in Anglesey, and to his citizens in London?', asked crowned bard and Welsh-language litterateur Caradog Pritchard: 'The Prince is dead. Long live the Prince!'[185]

The pro-investiture campaign rejected the actions, behaviour and attitudes of the extremists as being fundamentally antithetical to Welshness. 'They are aliens of a foreign nature with an insane desire to destroy and besmirch the land they profess to belong to', wrote one investiture supporter: 'They don't belong to us or the land of Wales.'[186] The violence associated with the anti-investiture movement conflicted with the popular idea of the Welsh as an inherently pacifist nation. On the subject of the bombings, the *Western Mail* lectured:

> These irresponsible actions contravene the whole spirit of Welsh history as it has developed in the last six or seven centuries. Any political paths which the Welsh people may choose to take now or in the future will be trod peaceably and constitutionally. They will not be pushed into alien ways by publicly self styled commandants or by secret saboteurs.[187]

The warm reception received by the prince in Wales established the alien nature of the extremist, the jubilant crowds assembled

---

[183] *South Wales Echo*, 4 January 1969.
[184] *Western Mail*, 6 June 1969.
[185] *Daily Telegraph*, 1 July 1969.
[186] *Western Mail*, 2 July 1969.
[187] *Western Mail*, 3 December 1968.

outside Caernarfon showing that: 'Wales was not a land of bombs, but the land of song.'[188] Perhaps even worse than their violence was the extremist's much commented upon boorishness. Welsh hospitality, manners, and innate kindness were regarded as treasured national traits. For the nation's reputation to be sullied by rude young extremists was regarded as inexcusable. Commentators attacked the 'ignorant discourtesy' of 'inconsiderate elements' and reminded the protestors that 'Good manners cost nothing'.[189] The Anglican Archbishop of Wales presumed to speak for the nation when he said: 'We feel particularly hurt that the natural courtesy of the Welsh people seems to be set at naught by people who go out of their way to be offensive and rude.'[190] Recognizing the Welsh people had a reputation 'for friendship and hospitality', the *Western Mail* implicitly warned: 'If they do not now take Prince Charles, their own Prince, to their hearts they will deserve to lose that reputation.'[191] Violence and rudeness were simply 'not in keeping with Welsh tradition or dignity' and were 'totally in conflict with the real character and attitudes of the vast majority of Welshmen'.[192]

Investiture supporters argued that the actions of the extremists did nothing to defend Wales but brought only harm, disgrace and division to the Welsh nation. Commentators described Wales as being 'ashamed', 'embarrassed', 'disgusted' and 'dishonoured' by the protests. Because of the high profile of the investiture, the nation's humiliation was significantly compounded by the resulting international coverage of the 'political turmoil' surrounding the ceremony. George Thomas opened a commercial display of Welsh products in London with a statement carrying an implicit warning: 'Wales has never been more conscious that the world is watching her as she is at the moment.'[193] A Welsh American wrote to the *Western Mail* to complain:

---

[188] *Belfast Telegraph*, 1 July 1969.
[189] *Cambrian News*, 6 June 1969; *Daily Sketch*, 29 September 1969.
[190] *Western Mail*, 26 September 1968.
[191] *Western Mail*, 2 June 1969.
[192] *Western Mail*, 2 July, 1 July 1969.
[193] *Western Mail*, 27 June 1969.

> I am very much ashamed when I see articles in our papers here in America telling about how his life is threatened and how threats are being made to sabotage his investiture... These threats are probably being made by a minority group, but all Welsh people are being held responsible. What happened to make my people so vindictive? It seems to me that they are hurting their own cause. The eyes of the world are on Wales now, and if it wants to gain the respect of the world its people must change its attitudes. I have heard people who have planned to go over next summer to the National Gymanfa Ganu and to the investiture express some fear of going in case of trouble.[194]

The Welsh Office cautioned that the disgraceful conduct of the extremists could result in wasted opportunities and significant material damage to the Welsh nation. During the summer of 1969, the press was rife with tales of foreign tourists cancelling their vacation plans in Wales. 'It would be an enormous tragedy for Wales if the potential benefits of the investiture were lost because of misguided – and dangerous – acts of violence', said the *South Wales Echo*.[195] George Thomas spoke of industrialists and financiers ready to invest in the Welsh economy, but cautioned:

> They are more likely to be interested in Wales if they get a picture of its people as happy, contented workers, lovers of song and welcoming hosts. At the present time, carping critics, parsimonious councillors, anti-Royalists and cranky nationalists are doing their best to poison minds and turn people against the investiture. If they succeed, we will lose a chance of developing our country and ensuring our future prosperity.[196]

Condemning the obstruction of Cymdeithas yr Iaith, the chairman of Croeso 69 reinforced this message. D. J. Davies claimed that:

> Considerable damage may be done to the economy if an image of 'lawlessness' was created in Wales by a small minority during celebrations for the investiture of the Prince of Wales. Mounting efforts to secure fresh capital investment and create more employment could be seriously jeopardized by illegal and irresponsible acts.[197]

[194] *Western Mail*, 14 February 1969.
[195] *South Wales Echo*, 18 December 1968.
[196] *Merthyr Express*, 24 October 1968.
[197] *South Wales Echo*, 18 December 1968.

The damage caused by extremism was not confined to the economy but hindered the spiritual cause of Welsh nationalism by dividing Wales against itself. The *South Wales Echo* characterized the controversy over the investiture as 'a running and bitter battle . . . largely between Welshmen' from which 'Wales could gain nothing'.[198] With an eye to Cymdeithas's anti-investiture and sign painting campaigns, the Bishop of St David's asserted that extremists 'have deliberately tried to create a feeling of hostility between those who can speak Welsh and those who can't'.[199] Commentators condemned the extremists for harming the causes of the Welsh language and devolution. Poet Caradog Pritchard attacked the extremists as 'spiritual deserters who would turn Wales into a desert'.[200] Incredibly, even the sympathetic newspaper *Baner ac Amserau Cymru* instructed investiture opponents on the day of the investiture to 'stop creating a fuss among our brothers and conflict among ourselves' and to 'remember that we are one nation'.[201]

Like the bruised feelings of investiture supporters over nationalist allegations of treason, many investiture opponents were stung by their sharp characterization in the press as a rude, violent and racist faction of an irresponsible youth. Not all opponents of the investiture were young, violent or rude, yet they were often lumped together under the 'extremist' label and image. Professor Gareth Jones of the University College of Wales, Swansea, defended the St David's Day rally held by Cymdeithas yr Iaith:

> It seems that any voice raised in protest is to be equated with rebellion and lack of dignity . . . Any positive protest has been met with accusations of youthful disrespect and has earned the disfavour of newspaper columns throughout the land. Let us remember that last Saturday's protest was addressed by university professors, lecturers, teachers and the like – people of substance who would think twice before making fools of themselves. Even if their views are not the views of us all, they deserve our respect. Due prominence should be given to them, lest a new kind of extremism, under a cloak of

---

[198] *Carmarthen Times*, 13 June 1969.
[199] *Daily Telegraph*, 1 July 1969.
[200] In translation, *Baner ac Amserau Cymru*, 12 June 1969.
[201] *Western Mail*, 5 March 1969.

journalistic respectability, should be allowed to blind us all to the problems which are at hand.[202]

'Let the fact not be overlooked that under the circumstances the protest at the Urdd Eisteddfod was lodged with politeness', urged one investiture opponent.[203] Murray Jenkins, a member of Cymdeithas yr Iaith, became infamous in the press as 'the man who yelled at Prince Charles' during the 1968 smoke bomb protest in Cardiff. In the *Western Mail*, he defended himself by claiming: 'I did not go out of my way to be rude to Prince Charles and had no intention of doing so. My opposition is not to him personally but to his investiture as the Prince of Wales.'[204]

Anti-investiture campaigners were at pains to demonstrate that their opposition to the investiture was not based on a personal antipathy to Charles, much less to racial hatred. At the Cilmery rally in March 1969, members of Cymdeithas yr Iaith were instructed not to indulge in 'hatred for the Prince' or to commit violent acts in opposition to the investiture. Fred Francis, a student hunger striker from Aberystwyth, told the crowd: 'We should not personally hate Prince Charles, but we must oppose his investiture, which is a symbol of English domination.'[205] Similar sentiments were expressed by a host of anti-investiture activists, including Dafydd Iwan, J. R. Jones, Emyr Llewelyn Jones and Owain Williams. Even paramilitary leaders Julian Cayo-Evans, Gethin ap Iestyn and John Jenkins denied any animosity for the Prince or desire to harm him personally.[206] Amongst the placards condemning the 'English prince', protest signs read 'Not against you, Charles – Just the way you'll earn your living in 1969' and 'We admire your guts, but not your position'.[207] However, the difficulty of separating the person of the prince from his office was not lost on investiture opponents, one of whom reasonably surmised:

[202] *Western Mail*, 4 June 1969.
[203] *Western Mail*, 5 July 1968.
[204] *Western Mail*, 17 March 1968.
[205] *Y Cymro*, 6 March 1969; Extract from '24 Hours', recorded from transmission BBC 1 2220, 28 February 1969, PREM 13/2505, PRO.
[206] *Guardian*, 29 June 1968; *Western Mail*, 29 June 1968.
[207] *Baner ac Amserau Cymru*, 12 June 1969.

It is impossible to protest against the investiture without protesting about the Prince of Wales. How can one protest impersonally against a prince who is a person? He is the prince. Without him there would be no investiture.[208]

Contrasting images of '*bradwyr*' and 'extremists' were a part of a wider struggle to establish who truly spoke for the Welsh nation and, by extension, who was and was not Welsh. Supported by polling information on public opinion, the pro-investiture faction contrasted the volume and enthusiasm of support in Wales for the investiture with the numerically marginal nature of the opposition. Newspapers and Labour politicians spoke of the 'vast majority' and the 'overwhelming proportion' of the Welsh people who would give the Prince a 'warm and overwhelming welcome' or a 'tremendous reception'. In defiance of nationalist protest, George Thomas expressed his absolute confidence that the Welsh people would 'turn out in their tens of thousands' to greet the prince.[209] 'Every time it has the chance', Thomas declared, 'Wales shows its loyalty and affection for the Royal Family'.[210] Triumphal declarations were used to belittle dissent. The *Daily Mirror* wrote of the investiture:

> Today, Prince Charles Philip Arthur George of Buckingham Palace, England, patted the Welsh Dragon on its head, cordially challenging it to lick or bite. We, in Caernarfon, and the odd five hundred million looking on, endured the universal apprehension that this roaring and most eloquent sore head might grill Charles rigid and fork tongue him back from whence he came. Instead, there for all the world to see was the Dragon blissfully swishing its tail, melodiously chanting a thousand Hallelujahs towards Mount Snowdon and beyond . . . [The Prince] did not take Wales. Wales claimed him.[211]

In contrast to the images of support, those who opposed the investiture were described as an inconsequential 'fringe', a 'few lunatics' and a 'small and vociferous minority' who thought that 'if they created enough noise and caused enough violence

[208] Transcript of soundtrack of film on Welsh nationalism, Tŷ Cenedl 1 AI/4, NLW.
[209] *Western Mail*, 18 December 1969.
[210] *Daily Mirror*, 2 July 1969.
[211] *Western Mail*, 26 September 1968.

we might be persuaded to drop the ceremony'.[212] Protestors made up only a 'handful' of individuals and their demonstrations amounted to nothing more than an 'angry puff', 'isolated booing', or a 'murmur of dissent' to be 'squashed', 'overwhelmed' and 'drowned' by the cheers of thousands who welcomed the prince. Dramatically, the eruption of cheers during the prince's procession in Caernarfon prompted Richard Baker to triumphantly exclaim on BBC television: 'Here's an answer to those who were opposed to the investiture!'[213] Supporters hoped that the anti-investiture faction would be crushed by the sheer numerical weight of Welsh support for the ceremony.

Meant to marginalize and silence the opposition, the image of the 'extremist' actually came to appeal to young nationalists themselves. After all, the youth culture of the 1960s was primarily motivated by a sense of alienation from conventional society and a rejection of orthodox methods of political activity. Accelerated by increasingly intrusive security measures, the 'extremist' label served to excite the feeling of alienation felt among some sections of Welsh youth and added to the glamour and romance of 1960s style rebellion. By 1969, the anti-investiture campaign had dropped its pretension of representing the majority of Welsh popular opinion in favour of projecting the moral authority of militancy and minority status. At a rally held by Cymdeithas yr Iaith, Emyr Llewelyn Jones compared anti-investiture militants to Mahatma Gandhi and Martin Luther King. There was no value in maintaining the peace, he extolled, until injustice is removed. 'Only when they raise their swords will the minority be heard at all!' he exclaimed.[214] Rankled by the prince's plea for tolerance, Dafydd Iwan skillfully turned the tables on the British state:

> As for the tolerance he speaks of, I'm sure he does not advocate the tolerating of injustice; and we in Wales have tolerated injustice for far too long. We have tolerated seeing Welsh reduced from the language of practically the whole of Wales to the language of a decreasing minority; tolerated English as the only official language of Wales for centuries; tolerated seeing English only on public signs and official

[212] *Daily Mirror*, 2 July 1969.
[213] *Baner ac Amserau Cymru*, 3 July 1969.
[214] *Western Mail*, 23 June 1969.

documents, tolerated a schooling system which introduced the 'Welsh Not' and used English as the only medium of education and which made Welsh a foreign tongue in its own country; tolerated seeing young Welshmen and women gaoled for insisting on their right to use Welsh in Wales. But this we cannot tolerate any more, and will not.[215]

Rather than marginalizing it, the anti-investiture campaign was all the more righteous for the fact that it was only a minority of the Welsh nation that took up the fight. The Patriotic Front's Anti-Investiture Campaign Committee implicitly compared anti-investiture militants to the eighteen guards of Prince Llywelyn who stood alone and were eventually overwhelmed by the fury of the English army at the medieval battle of Irfon Bridge. 'The whole world could be on the other side of the bridge, but the eighteen will not fail me . . .' Llywelyn is made to proclaim proudly.[216] At Dolbadarn rally, Emyr Llewelyn Jones made a similar comparison between the youths of Cymdeithas yr Iaith and Llywelyn's small band of defenders. 'The Welsh youth are ready now for the great conclusive battle', he declared.[217] Popular support for this battle was irrelevant, for the extremists represented the true national conscious in a land of shameful degenerates and *bradwyr*. Like Llywelyn himself, the 'extremists' became the 'true princes' of Wales, for it was the job of a prince to lead the people and to defend their culture and national self-respect.[218] In contrast, the patriotism of investiture supporters was suspect. Urdd poet Gerallt Lloyd Owen referred in 'Fy Ngwlad' to the 'Britishized' as those of 'moderate emotion', the 'mild patriots' and the 'extreme international men'.[219]

The battle over who spoke for the Welsh nation was not to be determined solely by the strength of poll majorities, the volume of cheering or jeering, or the ardency of declarations.

[215] Leaflet, Anti-Investiture Campaign Committee, Tŷ Cenedl 1 AI/5, NLW.
[216] *Y Cymro*, 6 March 1969.
[217] *Y Cymro*, 6 March 1969; *Baner ac Amserau Cymru*, 3 July 1969
[218] In translation, *Cerddi'r Gadair*, p. 4.
[219] 'Charles Windsor Shall Not Pass', leaflet, Patriotic Front, Tŷ Cenedl 1 AI/5, NLW; Leaflet, Anti-Investiture Campaign Committee, Tŷ Cenedl 1 AI/5, NLW.

Given the contested nature of the event, the belligerents were very conscious of the crucial, independent role the media played in representing the investiture and in constructing its meaning. Both pro- and anti-investiture forces played to the media in hopes of seeking positive attention and attacked the press for what they regarded as grossly slanted coverage favouring the other side. The Patriotic Front spoke of the 'English television cameras and Sais controlled press' and their attempts to 'brainwash our people into blind acceptance of this investiture of an Englishman as Prince of Wales'. In particular, they condemned the *Western Mail*, 'the so called and self styled National Newspaper of Wales', for its support of the investiture and its unfair coverage.[220] Given that 'the most powerful propaganda machine in the modern world has been at it to brainwash us', Dr R. Tudur Jones told Cymdeithas demonstrators in Cilmery that 'the miracle is that we are not in Caernarfon'.[221] Indeed, the Welsh Office was in fact actively seeking to influence the nature of press coverage, inviting the editors of the *Western Mail*, the *Liverpool Daily Post*, the *South Wales Echo* and the *Newport Argus* to meet with the Secretary of State 'over a glass of sherry' to discuss how the government could assist the papers in providing a 'better image' for the investiture.[222] The editors of the *Western Mail* and the *Liverpool Daily Post* even served on the Investiture Committee.

On the other hand, the Welsh Office was beside itself with frustration over the seemingly continuous press reports on extremist actions and opinions. Investiture supporters alleged that coverage of extremist activities was totally out of proportion to their numbers and gave a false impression of the true state of Welsh public opinion. They complained that the fanatics 'made the noise and the headlines' and that press coverage magnified the strength of the opposition while ignoring the feelings of the majority of the Welsh people.[223] Just before the prince arrived to take up his studies, the *Cambrian*

---

[220] *Baner ac Amserau Cymru*, 3 July 1969.
[221] Jack Parker to Idris Evans, 15 January 1969, BD 67/69, PRO.
[222] *Daily Telegraph*, 2 July 1969; *Western Mail*, 29 June 1969, 20 June 1969, 16 December 1968, 18 November 1967.
[223] *Cambrian News*, 18 October 1968.

News charged that press reports had headlined the actions and comments of 'minority groups' to such an extent that an inaccurate 'picture of violence' depicting Aberystwyth as 'a hot bed of anti-Prince feeling' had been painted.[224] 'An image is being created of an unstable society on the verge of armed revolt', complained the *Western Mail*: 'Nothing could be further from the truth.'[225]

Backed by the Welsh Office, investiture supporters focused their ire on the 'irresponsible reporting' and the 'calculated anti-Investiture tone' of BBC and ITV news broadcasts.[226] In February 1969, the Welsh Office complained to the BBC about its four consecutive nights of covering four students on hunger strike in Aberystwyth. The Permanent Undersecretary told the BBC that: 'It was interesting that your people did not interview one single student belonging to the majority who are, I understand, prepared to welcome the Prince.'[227] However, the storm really broke later that month in connection to a segment on the BBC news programme '24 Hours'. Focusing on anti-investiture sentiment in Caernarfon, the segment included interviews with several investiture opponents and a conductor whose youth band had voted 'unanimously' to boycott the celebrations. It also featured footage of dilapidated homes in Caernarfon and a dramatic final scene depicting young school boys smashing commemorative mugs bearing the image of Prince Charles.[228] All together, the programme gave the impression that the town was seriously divided in its attitude to the investiture. This caused an instant uproar in Caernarfon against 'the continual anti-Investiture propaganda put out by the BBC and ITV which seems to go on unabashed on that medium'.[229] Indignant letters to newspaper editors, an anti-BBC petition and a resolution from Caernarfon Royal Borough Council condemned

[224] *Western Mail*, 3 December 1968.
[225] Mrs G. M. Griffiths to George Thomas, 3 March 1969, BD 67/12, PRO; *Western Mail*, 3 March 1969.
[226] Idris Evans to John Rowley, 10 February 1969, BD 67/52, PRO.
[227] Extract from '24 Hours', Recorded from transmission BBC 1 2220, 28 February 1969, PREM 13/2505, PRO.
[228] Lt Col Sidney Goodchild to Dr Goronwy Jones, 11 March 1969, BD 67/52, PRO.
[229] *Western Mail*, 25, 31 March 1969; Megan Bonner Pritchard to Director General BBC, 12 March 1969, BD 67/52, PRO.

what one councillor described as a 'put up job'.[230] 'We resent the regular propagation by the BBC and ITV of a nationalist element's hate', wrote one supporter to *The Times*.[231] The Welsh Office conducted its own investigation and found the circumstances incriminating. Not only was Owain Williams, of MAC fame, a paid consultant for the piece, he actually accompanied the BBC crew through most of the filming. The 'unanimous' vote of the youth band against the investiture turned out to be anything but unanimous, the badly divided musical group disbanding over the issue shortly after the broadcast. The town clerk claimed that the footage of dilapidated homes was not even taken in Caernarfon. Most provocatively, the youths captured on film smashing investiture mugs were recruited to perform the act expressly for the camera. The schoolboys turned out to be the children of a Plaid Cymru councillor from Anglesey with well-known anti-investiture views who also happened to be the father-in-law of one of the FWA defendants then on trial. The mugs themselves were fabricated by the children's mother for the purpose of smashing them for the BBC crew.[232] George Thomas wrote to a clearly annoyed prime minister: 'There is no doubt at all that the BBC team in this case has behaved abominably and I confidently anticipate that Lord Hill will feel obliged to offer an apology.'[233] In his letter to the BBC chairman, Thomas claimed:

> There is certainly prima facie evidence that the BBC directed its attention to well known minority opponents of the Investiture. It would be possible for any slanted programme which concentrated on minority groups to give a completely distorted and untrue picture of the feelings of a community on any subject. I have an overwhelming impression from the evidence that has come to me that those responsible for the production of this programme had one intention only, to produce an anti-Investiture programme . . . I trust that when you have collected your evidence, you will feel able to make a public statement. I think the BBC will be very fortunate if it avoids severe Parliamentary criticism based on what appears to be firm evidence

---

[230] As quoted in *Western Mail*, 3 March 1969.
[231] Memorandum on '24 Hours', PREM 13/2505, PRO.
[232] George Thomas to prime minister, 13 March 1969, PREM 13/2505, PRO.
[233] George Thomas to Lord Hill of Luton, 13 March 1969, PREM 13/2505, PRO.

showing partiality on this question. In view of the strength of feeling in Wales, I have no option but to make public the fact that I am asking for this enquiry.[234]

A 'top level inquiry' was in fact ordered by the BBC but no public apology or statement on its findings was ever released.[235]

In truth, the media was divided in its orientation to the investiture. Led by the *Western Mail*, English-language newspapers in Wales largely cooperated with the Welsh Office in providing positive depictions of the investiture and in actively marginalizing the opposition. Welsh-language newspapers were more ambiguous in their approach to the investiture, but with significant papers like *Y Cymro* and *Y Baner ac Amserau Cymru* clearly in sympathy with anti-investiture sentiment. The wider British press and television news, including the BBC and ITV, featured positive coverage of the investiture but were equally attracted to the story of its opponents. Alongside the press releases of the Welsh Office, the Palace and their own largely pro-investiture editorial pages, British dailies and television provided heavy coverage of anti-investiture opinions and activities. The frequency and volume of such coverage no doubt exaggerated the prevalence of anti-investiture opinion in Wales. Evoking the struggle to influence and direct media coverage of the event, a frustrated member of the Investiture Committee noted that 'The editor of the *Carnarvon & Denbighshire Herald* does his very best to whip up enthusiasm for the Investiture, and renders a very great service thereby', but complained that 'his work is of little avail against the combined efforts of broadcasters who seemingly are pledged to misrepresent true public opinion'.[236]

As attested by opinion polls, the pro-investiture campaign clearly succeeded in winning over public opinion in Wales but

---

[234] The BBC holds files on the investigation but they are sealed. In a personal communication, the BBC Written Archive Centre has confirmed that they have no record of a public statement on the inquiry being made. For the announcement of the investigation, see *The People*, 16 March 1969.

[235] Lt Col Sidney Goodchild to Dr Goronwy Jones, 11 March 1969, BD 67/52, PRO.

[236] *Sun*, 1 July 1969.

it was the image of the investiture as an object of controversy that ultimately prevailed in the British press. Rather than a proud nation welcoming its prince in unison, Wales was seen as a divided nation at odds with itself over its own national identity and at war over the place of the Welsh nation within the United Kingdom. Press coverage of the investiture was dualistic, positive news of the investiture inevitably accompanied by reports of opposition and violence. Stories anticipating the grand pageantry of the ceremony were illustrated with photographs of police searching instrument cases and viewing stands, marching in columns by the castle and laying the boom in the harbour.[237] Above front page headlines hailing the investiture in Caernarfon appeared a series of photographs of the 'flight, pursuit, and capture' of a Welsh extremist in the crowd.[238] If the timing of the verdicts in the Free Wales Army trial was in fact manipulated by authorities to discredit the opposition, the tactic backfired dramatically because it insured that the investiture itself would share the front page with the paramilitary opposition. The events were conjoined in lines like: 'Three members of the Free Wales Army were jailed at Swansea yesterday while, at Caernarfon, Prince Charles was being invested as Prince of Wales.'[239] A similar effect was achieved as a by-product of the explosion at Abergele, coverage of the festivities inescapably opening with recognition that the day had begun with violence and death. The night after the investiture, the BBC broadcast in prime time a film on the Free Wales Army, replete with footage of fighting between protestors and police, images of bomb damage and a step-by-step explanation of how to blow up a pipeline. It was immediately followed by enthusiastic coverage of the first day of the prince's post-investiture tour.[240] Journalists were often inspired to wax poetic on the contested nature of the event. In Caernarfon, 'Seagulls and security men perched equally watchfully on rain washed roofs' on a day where 'There were bomb blasts as well as fanfares in the Principality'.[241] Even in reporting on the

[237] *Scotsman*, 2 July 1969.
[238] *Daily Mirror*, 2 July 1969.
[239] *Daily Telegraph and Morning Post*, 3 July 1969.
[240] *Daily Telegraph*, 2 July 1969; *Daily Mail*, 2 July 1969.
[241] *Daily Mail*, 2 July 1969.

ceremony itself, press coverage was not free of the imagery of opposition and violence. 'Heraldic banners cracked like pistol shots in the breeze', reported the *Daily Mail*, 'some of them bearing the arms of Welsh princes who would cheerfully rise from the grave to slaughter the Saesneg lot of us'.[242] In defining and presenting the story of the investiture, a narrative of dichotomy was too compelling a pattern for British journalists to resist. The cumulative effect was to foster a conceptual parity between the investiture and its discontents, no matter the actual state of popular opinion in Wales.

At one level, coverage of the anti-investiture campaign was astute and reflected an awareness of what was going on in Wales among an active if small minority of people. However, the imagination of the British press was clearly captivated by and receptive to the idea of the Welsh extremist. Indeed, the language of the Welsh Office's diatribes against extremists may have actually encouraged the interest of the press in them. Rather than being the antithesis of Welshness as projected by investiture supporters, the sullen, resentful, and fanatical extremist confirmed long held English stereotypes of the parochial, irrational and joyless nature of the Welsh. With paeans to the memory of a medieval prince and colourful figures like Julian Cayo-Evans and Denis Coslett, the anti-investiture campaign seemed to be the very embodiment of Matthew Arnold's Celtic revolt against the despotism of fact. In contrast to the Welsh Office's projection of a modern, forward looking nation, this was a Wales that was in accord with the Celticist image of the Welsh held by many in England. Some commentary could not avoid the temptation to fix 'extremism' on the inherent insularity and obstinacy of an unchanging Welsh character:

> God was good to the Welsh. He gave them fine looks, a beautiful land of mountains and valleys, a love of music and poetry and grand voices with which to express themselves. It was only natural, then, that they should be content to stay where they were, treat the rest of the world as though it did not exist and kick up merry hell when people like the Romans and English tried to boss them around. For centuries, after the Romans had failed, the English tried to bring the Welsh under control. They pleaded. They threatened. But it was no use. So the English built a chain of castles across Wales in an attempt

---

[242] *Business Visitor to Britain*, autumn/winter 1968.

to tame the wild Celts. But the Welsh burned down most of the castles and went on singing.[243]

A script for a film conflating the history of Wales and the investiture spoke of the Welsh as 'traditional seceders' and 'professional nonconformists', who 'went religious but never went peaceful'.[244] In vetting an article for the editors, the Welsh Office had to explain to the *National Geographic* magazine that 'The Welsh are no moodier as a people than any other, nor more introspective', and that 'Welshmen like other men may cry in circumstances of personal grief and tragedy but not generally or frequently, and certainly not in relation to Wales' political status'.[245] The image of the fawning and servile 'bradwr' cultivated by the anti-investiture campaign and epitomized in the figure of George Thomas also struck a familiar chord in the English imagination. For the British media, the contest between the 'extremist' and the 'bradwr' was a comfortable pairing of Welsh stereotypes. From their vantage point outside of Wales, English commentators could regard the feud amongst the neighbouring Taffys with alternating degrees of condescension, amusement and alarm.

Supporters and opponents of the investiture alike ultimately rejected the idea of the 1969 Investiture as a meaningless, anachronistic ceremony. They were diametrically opposed, however, in their construction of the ceremony's meaning. Labour regarded the investiture as a celebration of Welsh nationhood and recognition of a great national reawakening in Wales. Contrarily, anti-investiture propaganda defined the ceremony as a calculated insult to Wales signifying the domination and eventual destruction of Welsh nationhood. For supporters, the Prince of Wales enjoyed a special relationship with the people and culture of the principality and was himself a dignified physical link between the Welsh nation, the Crown and the British state. For opponents, the prince was a foreign, alien presence imposed by force upon the people of Wales by the power of an imperialistic British power. Redolent of

[243] Outline script, 'The Proud Dragon', Shirley Cobham Productions, 17 September 1968, BD 67/60, PRO.
[244] Comments to National Geographic, Idris Evans, BD 67/120, PRO.
[245] *Merthyr Express*, 24 October 1968.

national identity fostered in south Wales, the investiture projected the multicultural idea of an aspirational Welshness defined in terms of national service and attachment. This was countered by opponents rooted in a rural north, who defined Welsh national identity in more essential terms, predicated not only upon language but upon birth and belonging. In contrast to the optimistic vision of a progressive, social democratic and forward looking Wales implied by the investiture, opponents presented the image of a fallen and degenerate Wales that was in danger of forgetting its past and discarding its nationhood. The investiture's rhetoric of national pride and triumph was shadowed by images of national decline, shame and regret. In the debate over the investiture, both sides laid special claim to the youth of the nation. Images of investiture supporters as 'bradwyr' characterized by servility and treason were countered by the construction of 'extremist' opponents described in terms of irrationality and hate. In the end, the investiture clearly carried the day in terms of garnering popular support. However, opponents were equally successful in projecting an image of the investiture as an object of division, compromising the ideal of national unity central to the investiture project.

13
Whither the prince?

In the immediate aftermath of the ceremony, the 1969 Investiture appeared to be a triumphant success. The vast majority of the Welsh people had welcomed their prince in a ceremony that projected to the world an image of a contemporary and revitalized Wales. According to the *Daily Mail*:

> The investiture of Prince Charles has done more for Wales than all the nationalist slogans put together. For it has reminded the world of the splendour of Welsh song, the lilt of her language, the beauty of her landscapes and castles. The youth of the Prince has fired the memories of the old Wales with the hopes of the new.[1]

The investiture was broadly seen as a triumph not only for the Welsh nation but for the British union. Nationalist schemes to break up the United Kingdom were supposedly foiled by the resurgent support of the Welsh people for a prince who was imagined to have a special attachment and concern for Wales. The Palace's public relation's campaign to introduce the prince to the broader British public was deemed a success. Having cultivated an image of Prince Charles as a model of youth and citizenship, the Palace believed that the prince's future progress would be watched by the British public with warmth and support. Despite lower attendance than anticipated in Caernarfon, the investiture seemed to have fulfilled its economic promise as well. As the *Western Mail* described the scene:

> Shops tinkled continuously as money cascaded across the counters in a silver stream, and drooping assistants, feet pinching and backs aching, tried to keep up with the endless demand for cigarettes, ice cream, chocolate and souvenirs.[2]

[1] *Daily Mail*, 2 July 1969.
[2] *Western Mail*, 1 July 1969.

A few months after the investiture, George Thomas was able to congratulate the Wales Tourist Board that through their 'difficult and sometimes thankless task' they had 'put Wales securely on the map as a tourist country' and had established tourism as a 'successful Welsh industry' and as a 'new dimension to our economy'.[3] As for the role of the Welsh Office in the investiture, George Thomas received numerous letters of congratulations conflating his work on the ceremony, his victory over 'the more evil forms of nationalism', and his shoring up of electoral support for Labour in Wales.[4]

Yet, there were omens that this victory may have been hollow. Rather than being universal and uncontroversial, the opposition to the investiture highlighted the cultural division and identity crisis amongst the Welsh and delineated the fractures in British national identity. There were also signs that the practical and material returns on the investiture were shallow or illusory. Tellingly, the result of the much publicized investiture souvenir competition proved to be a disappointment. Lord Snowdon admitted that some of the designs submitted to the competition were 'really terrible, worse than one would expect'. To add insult to injury, only eleven of the 60 manufacturers who submitted winning designs were from Welsh firms.[5] In the weeks after the ceremony, the quarrymen that had produced the slate dais for the investiture were thrown out of work, the railway line that had carried the Queen to north Wales was closed and the bridge that had been constructed in Caernarfon to accommodate guest traffic was dismantled as a mere temporary solution to a long-standing demand.[6] Beneath the hubris and triumphalism of the investiture, it is not difficult to detect the general sense of disillusionment that was casting its shadow across the Wilson government in 1969.

The political impact of the investiture on the relationship between Labour and nationalism was ambiguous. Although the ceremony explicitly celebrated Welsh membership in the

[3] Speech by the Secretary of State for Wales at Meeting of the Wales Tourist Board Directors, 10 October 1969, BD 67/20, PRO.
[4] See correspondence in #895, Viscount Tonypandy Papers, NLW.
[5] *The Times*, 2 January 1968.
[6] *Welsh Nationalist*, August 1969.

United Kingdom, it should be recognized that the investiture was in no way inherently hostile to devolution per se. Indeed, with its emphasis on the prince's special connections to the principality and with the primacy of the Welsh Office in its planning and implementation, the ceremony was to a large extent predicated upon the principle of devolution. The subsequent course of Welsh parliamentary politics certainly calls into question the extent to which popular support for the investiture reflected the ascendancy of centralists and the defeat of nationally conscious devolutionists within the ranks of Labour. Although it would remain the strongest party in Welsh politics, Labour lost five Welsh seats in its 1970 general election defeat. Following closely on the heels of the investiture, this was a painful reminder that its hegemony as the 'Party of Wales' continued to be under threat. If the investiture was meant to bolster unionist sympathy, it appeared that it had done little to stem the ebb flow of Labour support in Wales. Subsequently, the party only managed to secure a little under 50 per cent of the Welsh vote in the general elections of 1974 and 1979. Plaid Cymru had suffered in the 1970 election as well, having lost its only parliamentary seat. Yet, in the same election, the nationalist party had secured its largest overall vote. Rather than being forced back into political irrelevance, Plaid Cymru would not only put Gwynfor Evans back in office but would increase its parliamentary seats to three by 1974. In response to these electoral trends, Labour opted for more rather than less devolution, the party giving its official support to the demand for a Welsh parliament in 1972. This reversal in policy was poignantly underscored in 1974 upon the return of Labour to government when Wilson unceremoniously dropped George Thomas as his Secretary of State for Wales. As a concession to the stunned and demoralized Thomas, Wilson encouraged him to pursue the honorary position of the Speaker of the House, a post he took up in 1976.

Clearly, Labour's support of a devolved Welsh assembly was informed by a belief in the need to address national sentiments and to counter the potential electoral threat of nationalism. The Labour government, however, was unprepared for the extent to which opposition to devolution would be manifest amongst Welsh Labour supporters. Pitting Labour centralists against an alliance of Labour devolutionists and nationalists, the 1979 government-backed referendum campaign in favour of devolution effectively reopened the wounds of 1969. Paralleling the investiture's margin of support, devolution was rejected in Wales by four to one. Although it continued to command political support in Wales, the Labour Party was removed from government by the Conservative victory in the 1980 British general election shortly thereafter. However, declarations that the debacle of 1979 represented the final defeat of devolution or even the end of Welsh national history were premature. Over a decade of Conservative rule based on an English parliamentary majority would provide Labour supporters in Wales with a harsh lesson in the democratic deficit of the centralized political system. When the opposing sides of Labour joined battle over the issue of devolution once again in the mid 1990s, the centralist wing was publicly supported by an aging George Thomas, now Lord Tonypandy and a celebrated former Speaker of the House. In yet another Labour government-backed referendum in favour of Welsh devolution, the 'Yes' campaign ultimately defeated the 'No' campaign in 1997. Yet, the rejuvenated support for Welsh devolution resulted in a margin of victory of less than 1 per cent. When the Welsh National Assembly was finally opened in 1999, it was clear that the complexities and divisions of Welsh national identity delineated by the 1969 Investiture were continuing to define and bedevil Welsh politics some thirty years later.

Rather than its popularity burying nationalist protest culture, the 1969 Investiture helped to establish and define what proved to be the flowering of extra-parliamentary nationalism in Wales. In the 1970s, young Welsh-language activists and nationalists increasingly came to adopt the 'extremist' label as their own, transforming what was constructed as a badge of shame into a title of honour. Reflecting the increasing cultural value of the term, Ned Thomas referred specifically to the anti-investiture campaign in his 1973 manifesto *The Welsh Extremist* when he wrote:

> I had grown up with the word extremist almost constantly in my newspaper – Kenya, Cyprus, Israel, Malaya, Aden; very often the word changed to terrorist and then one day the words would

disappear and the head of a new independent state would arrive in London to meet the Queen.[7]

Expanding upon the direct action and sabotage tactics first introduced during the investiture, Cymdeithas yr Iaith increasingly attracted sympathy rather than disgust from the general Welsh-language population. With the dramatic expansion of its membership, the 1970s would prove to be the society's most active and successful era. In stark contrast to its controversial image during the investiture, Cymdeithas yr Iaith would come to enjoy a status of established respectability during the 1980s. Dafydd Iwan would go on to become remembered as the leader of Cymdeithas yr Iaith in its glory years and would receive a hallowed place in contemporary Welsh-language culture as an iconic figure, established entertainer and successful entrepreneur. Dafydd Elis Thomas, who had attracted the ire of the party leadership for leading the rearguard anti-investiture campaign of Plaid's youth branch in 1969, was elected as Plaid Cymru's second Member of Parliament in 1974. Ten years later, Dafydd Elis Thomas secured the presidency of Plaid Cymru in a heated contest with none other than Dafydd Iwan. Somewhat ironically, Elis Thomas went on to become Plaid's first member of the House of Lords in 1992 and then the presiding officer of the Welsh National Assembly at its inception in 1999. As for Dafydd Iwan, he succeeded in his goal of winning the party's presidency in 2003. On the cultural front, the critically acclaimed anti-investiture poetry of Gerallt Lloyd Owen had by the 1990s become a celebrated part of the Welsh-language cannon and a common element in the curriculum of Welsh elementary schools. The nationalist extreme of the 1960s had become the national mainstream by the millennium's end.

Other elements of the anti-investiture movement hung on to an existence on the extreme margins of political life. In the immediate wake of the investiture, the trials and imprisonment of the FWA and MAC leadership disrupted and deflated the Welsh paramilitary movement. The rise of the 'Troubles' in Northern Ireland further discredited the ideology of nationalist violence in Wales but the Cilmery rallies continued to be held by

[7] Ned Thomas, *The Welsh Extremist* (Tal-y-bont, 1973), p. 9.

small groups of radical republicans. There were no immediate successors to the dismantled Mudiad Amddiffyn Cymru, Free Wales Army, and Patriotic Front, yet their influence proved to be surprisingly resilient. During the 1980s, a general nostalgia for the youth culture of the 1960s coupled with rising political frustrations helped romanticize the old paramilitaries and spawn emulation. A popular and celebratory account of the FWA and the MAC was published by Lolfa Press in 1980 and in 1981 a rally was held to commemorate the deaths of the 'Abergele martyrs' of 1969 by 300 Welsh republicans, some marching in makeshift paramilitary uniforms.[8] With the nationalist loss of the 1979 devolution campaign, the escalating cost of housing in rural Wales and the acceleration of coal and steel closures during the long decade of Conservative rule, the environment in Wales was conducive to a paramilitary revival. In December 1979 and extending through the mid-1990s, nationalist violence reignited in the form of an arson campaign targeting English owned holiday homes. A 1980 BBC television programme on the arson attacks featured an interview with John Jenkins in which he made the improbable claim that the MAC was still in existence and had been quietly waiting for the right time to strike. The programme then aired a supposedly official statement from the MAC that directly linked the paramilitary organization to the arson campaign. Later that year, a letter maintaining that the 'MAC was alive and burning' was sent to the press in conjunction with an attempt to set alight the home of the Conservative Secretary of State for Wales. However, the supposed involvement of the MAC turned out to be a ruse, the arson campaign actually being conducted by a new organization known as Meibion Glyndŵr. Rather than physically surviving, the memory of the MAC was being drawn upon by a new generation of paramilitaries for publicity value and dramatic effect. Attacks on rural holiday homes were complemented by a series of bombing attacks on government installations conducted by the Workers Army of the Welsh Republic (WAWR) in 1981–2. This led to a series of arrests and conspiracy trials in 1983. Among those arrested was John Jenkins, although it became apparent in trial

[8] Roy Clews, *To Dream of Freedom* (Tal-y-bont, 1980); John Osmond, *Police Conspiracy* (Tal-y-bont, 1984), p. 29.

that he was scarcely involved. A lack of evidence and police overreaching assured not guilty verdicts for the defendants.[9]

The commandants of the Free Wales Army and the Patriotic Front continued to be quite active in nationalist circles. Enjoying a status somewhere between semi-comic celebrities and folk heroes, Julian Cayo-Evans and Denis Coslett emerged as public symbols of an uncompromising and explicitly republican nationalism in Thatcher's Wales. At the 1993 Cilmery rally, the 55-year-old Cayo-Evans spoke out in support of the renewed campaign of nationalist violence. He bestowed a medal upon the mother of Sion Aubrey Roberts, a man associated with Meibion Glyndŵr then awaiting trial for the attempted letter bombing of Conservative politicians. With the Llywelyn Monument as a backdrop, the rally culminated when a masked man (rumoured to be none other than Gethin ap Iestyn) set alight a bloodied effigy of Prince Charles's head and burned a portrait of the Queen.[10] The FWA thus returned to public discourse in dramatic fashion. The deaths of Cayo-Evans in 1998 and Coslett in 2004 produced press obituaries alternatively praising and ridiculing the paramilitary commandants. In 2001, a Cardiff pub was named the 'Cayo Arms' in honour of the FWA leader. Reputedly, this prompted progressive playwright Dic Edwards to pen the drama *Franco's Bastard*, a thinly veiled and scathing depiction of Cayo-Evans as a fascist named 'Carlo'. This in turn inspired nationalist protest, press attacks on the playwright and, in one notable incident featuring Gethin ap Iestyn, the physical disruption of the play's production.[11] In 2004, Cayo-Evans appeared among the list of the nation's 100 all-time heroes in a poll conducted by Culturenet Cymru, an arts body receiving funding from the new Welsh National Assembly. Coming in at number 33 in the poll, Julian Cayo-Evans actually beat out Dafydd Iwan at number 63. Notably, George Thomas and Prince Charles failed to make the cut. Shortly after these results were announced, a former programmer for the project accused the poll of being fixed, alleging that votes for the Labour socialist and centralist Aneurin Bevan were artificially raised to the

[9] Osmond, *Police Conspiracy*, pp. 17, 36–40.
[10] *Wales on Sunday*, 12 December 1993.
[11] *Western Mail*, 6 May 2002.

number 1 slot while those for Cayo-Evans were fraudulently discounted in order to exclude him from the list of the top twenty Welsh heroes. Subsequent calls were made on the floor of the Welsh Assembly for an investigation into possible poll rigging.[12] Certainly, the continued legend and controversy surrounding the paramilitary opponents of the investiture highlights the extent to which the issues of 1969 remain a raw nerve in Wales today.

While the stature of the investiture's opponents has grown with time in Wales, the same cannot be said of the prince himself. Once the investiture was over, the project to form a particular, lasting and meaningful connection between Prince and Principality was all but abandoned. Tellingly, the Palace requested that the Welsh Office's monthly bulletin to the prince on Welsh affairs be discontinued in the spring of 1971.[13] With the ceremony behind him, Prince Charles refocused his characteristic commitment and enthusiasm on his next series of challenges, responsibilities and interests. As the prince had candidly admitted in a radio interview before the investiture, his ultimate focus was on his duties not as the Prince of Wales per se but as the heir-apparent to the throne of the United Kingdom and British Commonwealth. Contrary to the assertions of the Welsh Office and press, the prince's summer romance with Wales turned out to be a mere temporary dalliance along the long path to the British throne. Prince Charles's subsequent relationship with the principality was characterized through his charitable organizations and occasional visits, but these activities were largely devoid of any specifically Welsh content or national meaning. With few exceptions in the 1970s and 1980s, he ceased to use the Welsh-language or to engage meaningfully with Welsh national and cultural developments. Rather than reflecting a specifically Welsh connection, the fortunes of his popularity in the principality tended to mirror that of the United Kingdom as a whole.

[12] *Western Mail,* 14 July 2004: An interview with the computer programmer who made the allegations was published online in September 2004 in 'What's Wrong with Wales', *http://walesontheweb. blogspot.com/2004/09/culturenet-not-quite-right.html,* accessed on 27 November 2005.

[13] Idris Evans to Mervyn Lloyd, 25 March 1971, BD 67/52, PRO.

The commemoration of the twenty-fifth anniversary of the investiture in 1994 was so low key it was practically a non-event. It did, however, provide an opportunity for soundings on public opinion and for the prince to defend his record on a BBC Wales television broadcast. A poll conducted by the programme found that public opinion had shifted dramatically since 1969. The prince's performance in service to Wales was deemed a failure by 52 per cent compared to 40 per cent who regarded it as a success. In an accompanying interview, Prince Charles rationalized his strained relationship with Wales by pointing to his many obligations as heir to the throne. Asked if his son, Prince William, would take up the Welsh language at an earlier date than himself, Prince Charles indicated that it was possible but referred to the difficulties of fitting everything into a child's education. Unenthused by the suggestion, he noted that the young prince would 'have enough difficulties as it is'. Truthful and candid, perhaps, but these were not the words to reassure demoralized Welsh royalists. Pointedly, the television programme concluded by noting that the Investiture Fountain, inaugurated amongst much fanfare in Cardiff in 1969, had gone dry and was indefinitely closed for repairs.[14] Welsh anti-monarchical opinion reasserted itself in the late 1990s in a form strikingly redolent of 1969. In 1996, a boisterous Cymdeithas yr Iaith protest forced the Queen to abandon a visit to open new additions at the National Library of Wales and the University of Wales in Aberystwyth.[15] Meanwhile, notable Welsh intellectuals and policy think tanks began to pontificate on the replacement of the Prince of Wales with an elected honoree.[16] Prince Charles's apparent reawakening of interest in Welsh matters in the late 1990s was often dismissed by cynical commentators as an attempt to compete with the more popular figure of his estranged wife, Diana, whose popularity had risen in the principality by her habit of attending Welsh international

[14] '25 Years On', BBC Wales Today, BBC 1, AM 1099/03, National Screen and Sound Archive, NLW.
[15] *Western Mail*, 30 May–1 June 1995.
[16] Jan Morris, *The Princeship of Wales* (Llandysul, 1995); Russell Deacon and Steve Belzak, '*God Bless the Prince of Wales*': *Wales' Royal Prerogative – Do We Still Need a Prince of Wales?* (Cardiff, 2000).

rugby matches. Although Diana's death in 1997 was mourned with an ardour similar to that found elsewhere in the United Kingdom, there was little that was specifically Welsh in those expressions of grief. Beyond the Welsh Guards carrying her casket, her funeral made few connections between the princess and the principality. Indeed, the most distinctly Welsh response to the funeral seems to have been resentment over Elton John's identification of the princess as 'England's Rose'.[17] The opportunity for the monarchy to reconnect with the Welsh nation upon the inauguration of the Welsh National Assembly was further dimmed by a series of allegations made on the eve of the devolution referendum in 1997. In what was described as a 'humiliating snub', the press detailed an alleged dispute between the Palace and the Labour government over the reputed refusal by the Queen and the Prince of Wales to open the assembly if it were in fact approved by the upcoming referendum. The Palace and prime minister were quick to characterize the reports as nonsense, but George Thomas welcomed the supposed development and characterized the invitation to open such an assembly as 'an insult to the Queen' on the part of 'someone who would reduce the status of the monarchy'.[18] Overall, the incident promoted the image of a monarchy opposed to the prospect of devolution and hostile to Welsh national sentiment.

What, then, will be the fate of the ceremony and what is the prospect for a third investiture to be held in Wales? Given the fluidity of the ceremony and the political complications surrounding it, it is difficult to say. However, factors and developments which impinge on the question of a future investiture and its relationship to the principality are worth noting. As in 1969, there can be little doubt that an investiture would attract the attention of the world's media and once again put Wales on the global map. The potential advantages of such a ceremony to the material welfare and international stature of Wales would no doubt be a major consideration but it would have to be weighed against the potential for disruption and embarrassment caused by likely opposition. The extent, form and potential success of opposition may be difficult to determine, but it is

[17] Jane Thomas, *Diana's Mourning: A People's History* (Cardiff, 2002); *Western Mail*, 5 September 1997.
[18] *Western Mail*, 30 July–2 August 1997; *Guardian*, 30 July 1997.

not hard to imagine that a third investiture held in Wales would attract resistance. This opposition would no doubt draw inspiration and legitimacy from the example and rhetoric of 1969. Attitudes are far less deferential to the monarchy than they were in the 1960s and opposition would probably find credibility and support beyond that enjoyed by the campaign against the investiture of Prince Charles. As in 1969, such opposition would no doubt attempt to confound the intended message of the investiture and contest the model of national identity on which it is based. The British monarchy could very easily be dragged into another donnybrook over the nature of Welsh national identity. It is conceivable that the Crown could avoid this danger by simply abandoning the public ceremony all together, plausibly dismissing it as a modern creation that had outworn its usefulness. While this would probably be accepted by the public without a great outcry, this would be a difficult decision for the Crown to make as it would be tantamount to an admission of defeat for an institution that must constantly prove its relevance and worth to contemporary British life. More importantly, it would be a clear, perhaps critical setback for the vitality of a British national identity increasingly defined in multinational terms.

In fact, there have been tantalizing signs that the Crown has no such retreat in mind. With greater and more consistent royal attention and patronage in the Welsh cultural scene in recent years, Prince Charles himself has redeveloped and publicized his reawakened interest in Wales. The spotlight in Wales also seems to be increasingly shifting from Charles to the popular figure of Prince William, the young and attractive heir to his father's Welsh title. Reminiscent of Prince Charles's coming of age in 1969, the young prince confined his public appearances in conjunction with his twenty-first birthday to a visit to north Wales. More significantly, news reports following the establishment of the Welsh National Assembly in 1999 explicitly indicated that Prince William was learning Welsh in order to prepare for his own eventual investiture. Additional reports made in 2003 further claimed that the young prince would emulate his father by spending six months learning the language at Aberystwyth sometime following the completion of his university course at St Andrews in 2005.[19] In contrast to Prince Charles's own crash course in Welshness, such early and prolonged measures of preparation and visibility for the young prince might help foster the growth of a more organic relationship between prince and people in Wales.

The Palace too seems eager to re-establish its relationship with the Welsh nation. Despite disputed initial accounts to the contrary, the royal family apparently relished the opportunity to open the National Assembly in 1999. For the occasion, the Queen, Prince Philip and Prince Charles visited the principality together for the first time since the 1969 Investiture. Without the slightest hint of irony, they were received and welcomed to the assembly building by none other than Dafydd Elis Thomas in his capacity as presiding officer. The Queen and the Prince of Wales presided over the formal opening of the assembly, the prince brushing off his training from 1969 to provide a notable address in the Welsh language. Afterwards, the royal family marked the historic occasion by attending the 'Voice of the Nation' extravaganza held in the new Millennium Stadium. In protest against the royal presence, the Welsh rock group the Manic Street Preachers declined their invitation to perform at the event, but they were the notable exception. Featuring the leading lights in contemporary Welsh culture and entertainment, the televised celebration effectively integrated the monarchy into a grand evocation of Welsh national identity. Much the same effect was achieved by the state opening of the assembly's new ultramodern home, the Senedd, on St David's Day 2006. Attended by the Queen, Prince Charles, Prince Philip and the Duchess of Cornwall, the ceremony featured an address by the Queen, fly-pasts, twenty-one-gun salutes, and bilingual poetry. On the streets outside, it attracted a modicum of protest as well as cheers. These opening celebrations of the assembly may very well provide viable models for a future investiture.

Certainly, the existence of the Welsh National Assembly would ensure that Prince William would be invested in circumstances far different from that of his father. Like the investiture's relationship with the Welsh Office in 1969, the National

[19] *BBC News*, 1 August 1999, 23 September 2001, 6 June 2003, http://news.bbc.co.uk.

Assembly of Wales would inevitably become the central institution behind the event and a major actor in the ceremony itself. Indeed, the hyperactive international attention that would assuredly be garnered by an investiture would provide an attractive opportunity to relaunch the assembly yet again, this time on a truly global scale. Such a ceremony would have the potential to effectively define, crystallize and project the evolving relationship between the Welsh nation and the multinational United Kingdom in front of the eyes of the world in a way that devolution and the advent of the assembly has thus far failed to do. A third investiture would be a temptation that many politicians and statesmen would find difficult to resist.

Whether a future investiture will ultimately provide more grounds for national consensus than conflict is unclear. History suggests, however, that the reception for such a ceremony will depend less on the person or actions of the prince and more on the extent to which the deep fissures within Welsh and British national identity revealed in 1969 are still present in a post devolution Wales.

Conclusion

The 'invented tradition' of the Investiture of the Prince of Wales has often been dismissed as a largely insignificant bit of pageantry adorning the historical record of Wales in the twentieth century. However, contemporaries regarded the performance of the royal ceremonies in 1911 and 1969 as events imbued with deep meaning and of great historical importance for Wales and the United Kingdom. This meaning and significance can be recovered and understood by setting the ceremonies within the political, cultural and social context of Wales in the early and mid twentieth century. Conducted at times of crisis when concepts and structures of nation and people were in flux, the ceremonies actively engaged with the issues of their day and sought to articulate and fix the identity of the Welsh nation and its relationship to the British state. The political projects underlying the 1911 and 1969 Investitures can be reconstructed by examining the process of creating the ceremonies and by identifying the role and agenda of their organizers. The construction of ceremonial meaning, however, was not confined to the private deliberations and decisions of the ceremony's creators but was equally determined through an open process of public discourse engaged by newspapers, propagandists, and political actors with varying and often conflicting views. By identifying the themes of consensus and conflict inherent within commentary on the ceremonies, the investitures can be explored as historical events significant in their own right and as pieces of historical evidence that cast light on the complexities of politics, culture and Welsh national identity in the twentieth century. Although the context and meaning of the investitures in 1911 and 1969 were widely different, similar patterns in the organization, implementation and function of the ceremonies are readily apparent.

The 1911 and 1969 Investitures were performed at critical junctures where political hegemony was being challenged by changing social and cultural circumstances. Wales is distinctive in the modern history of Britain in that its politics has been characterized by long eras of overwhelming support for a single political party. The Liberal Party in the Edwardian period and the Labour Party in the late 1960s enjoyed such political ascendancies in Wales. With good reason, these parties saw themselves as the political voice of the Welsh nation, encapsulating Welsh national sentiment and commanding the allegiance of the Welsh electorate. However, the hegemony of these parties did not go unchallenged. In an industrialized Edwardian Wales, Liberal ascendancy was compromised by an increasingly resentful and militant working class, represented politically by the nascent Labour Party. Opposition to the traditional landed elite no longer effectively bound the working class to Welsh-speaking middle-class leadership. The cultural and social changes of industrial Wales undermined the rural, nonconformist populism that girded Liberal power. In the late 1960s, a similar crisis was faced by the Labour Party, whose support had expanded from its original working class base to encompass a broad section of the population, including the Welsh-speaking middle class. Initial enthusiasm for Labour as the 'Party of Wales', however, turned to bitter disappointment over the critical decline of the Welsh language and the dismantling of the traditional socio-economic structure of Welsh mining and farming communities. In these circumstances, Labour's claims to represent the Welsh nation were besieged by the criticism of a resurgent nationalist movement. Embodied in the political party of Plaid Cymru, popular extraparliamentary organizations like Cymdeithas yr Iaith and small paramilitary bodies like the MAC and FWA, this nationalism drew on the support of alienated segments of the Welsh-language population and a politically mobilized Welsh youth. Electorally marginal, opponents of the political hegemonies of 1911 and 1969 found outlet for their frustration through campaigns of direct action and political violence. This took the form of working class rioting in the Edwardian coal field and the sign painting, paramilitary and bombing campaigns of the 1960s. Collectively, these extraparliamentary actions challenged political hegemony and compelled both pragmatic and

CONCLUSION

ideological responses from both the Welsh political establishment and the British state.

The 1911 and 1969 Investitures rearticulated the nature of Welsh national identity in direct response to the historical transformations and challenges of the period in which they were performed. Political stability was being undermined by changing cultural and social structures and a corresponding dislocation of national identity in Wales. Through royal ceremony, organizers of the 1911 and 1969 Investitures hoped to provide a vehicle for stabilizing and reconstructing Welsh national identity. Although the bodies that organized and implemented the investiture were composed of diverse individuals of different political and social backgrounds, the governing party clearly exercised a large degree of control over ceremony planning. While the Liberals of 1911 buttressed their own position by establishing grounds of consensus and cooperation with the Anglican Church and the Welsh landed elite, the 1969 Investiture reflected the postwar consensus over economic planning and the welfare state under the auspices of the Labour Party. The form of the investiture and the positive commentary in the media that it provoked helped define the investitures, articulating a set of meanings for the ceremony that supported the respective political projects of Welsh Liberalism and Labour respectively.

The investitures ultimately hinged on questions of identity: what composed Welshness? Whom did the Welsh nation embrace and, by implication, who did it exclude? What was the character of the relationship between the Welsh nation and the British state? To borrow from discourse theory, the ceremony's response to these questions involved the employment of a 'logic of difference' in which elements previously excluded from Welshness were incorporated into a revised sense of identity that emphasized consensus and marginalized division. In the mind of ceremony organizers, the existence of the Welsh nation was realized through the unity of the nation's reception of the prince. For the Liberals in 1911, the investiture provided an opportunity to reassert a vision of Wales that transcended class and whose existence and value as a nation was explicitly acknowledged by the state. Populist and democratic imagery was paired with rhetoric that reconciled the formerly alienated landed elite with a nation under middle class auspices. In the face of traditional denials of Welsh nationhood, the 1911 Investiture asserted the reality of the Welsh nation through state recognition manifest in the participation of the British monarchy. The ceremony acknowledged the Welsh nation's worth and right to exist by setting it within the context of Liberal notions of a multinational British state and empire. For Labour in 1969, the investiture was a vehicle for reconciling an estranged ethnic and linguistically based patriotism with a civic sense of Welsh identity aligned to social democracy. Modelled after the historical experience of south Wales, this civically based Welshness incorporated diverse populations based on ideals of national service and the welfare of its people. Welsh national sentiment was effectively joined with programmes of economic modernization and the values of social democracy, traits ultimately grounded in the Welsh nation's organic connection to a progressive British state. Set against a background of internal division and conflict, the investitures of 1911 and 1969 asserted and celebrated the image of a unified and indivisible Welsh nation, in turn unified and indivisible with the larger British state of which it was a part.

Opposition to the investitures in 1911 and 1969 contested the meaning of the ceremonies and the models of national identity upon which they were based. In the process, opponents of the investiture defined their own sense of Welsh national identity, articulating alternative constellations of elements designed to refute the political project of the ceremony's creators and to establish their own alternative order of national belonging. In what discourse theorists have termed a 'logic of equivalence', anti-investiture rhetoric and imagery reassigned the elements of Welsh national identity so as to emphasize difference and polarity where once was imagined unity. Through their opposition to the 1911 Investiture, the socialists of the Labour Party ascribed the authentic Welsh nation to the common, working people of Wales in opposition to a new conceptual category of national oppressors that equated the Welsh-speaking middle class, the landed British elite and the capitalist British Empire as the enemies of the Welsh people. Conversely, the 1969 Investiture provoked rhetoric of nationalist opposition that pitted Welsh-speaking activists and

CONCLUSION

English-speaking republicans against those who would betray and destroy the political sovereignty and cultural foundation of the Welsh nation. In constructing this category of national enemies, nationalists effectively equated a hostile British state with the supposedly de-nationalized and collaborationist Welsh socialists of the Labour Party. The investitures thus not only established and promulgated the national vision of their creators but reified and fixed the alternative models of national identity in Wales expressed by the opposition. A minority opinion during the investitures themselves, these oppositional constructions of Welshness would become increasingly significant and influential in the articulation of Welsh national identity in the decades following the 1911 and 1969 Investitures.

Meant to foster an image of national unity and reconciliation, the 1911 and 1969 Investitures ultimately highlighted the fault lines and fissures of Welsh and British national identity. The debate over the investitures reflected an antagonism between supporters and opponents where the presence of the 'Other' blocked each side from fully realizing their identities as Welsh people. In 1911, the claim of the Welsh-speaking middle class to leadership of a classless Welsh nation was undermined by the presence of a defiant, vocal and growing industrial working class. From the socialist perspective, the Welsh language and nonconformist culture of conventional Edwardian Welsh nationalism served to question the Welshness of an emerging working class culture characterized by the predominance of English language culture and internationalism. To a large degree, this conflict over national identity was expressed in geographic terms pitting the pure 'Welsh' of the north against a south whose nationality was suspect. The same antagonism was largely at the root of the controversy over the 1969 Investiture, only with the relative positions of support and opposition reversed.

Despite its setting, the 1969 Investiture was a celebration primarily emanating from the industrial south against an opposition largely but not exclusively grounded in the Welsh-speaking north. Labour was frustrated in its attempts to transform the popular political faith of the people of Wales into the national voice of Wales, its claims to Welshness limited by the vocal presence and linguistic credentials of Welsh language-activists. In a parallel fashion, Labour's mutual embrace of both Welsh and British identities was effectively questioned by the political orientation of nationalists who focused their political loyalty on Wales alone. Conversely, claims to an essential and critical Welshness embodied in the language and, to a lesser extent, in an unqualified support for Welsh sovereignty were foiled by the popular support and democratic mandate of the Labour Party in Wales. Labour's dual identity as both Welsh and British obstructed nationalist attempts to fully realize their more concentrated vision of Welshness. The primary weapons in this antagonism were symbols, the investiture chief amongst them. Through their mutually opposed orientation and constructions of the investiture, each side attempted to project their own sense of Welsh national identity while denying the Welsh identity of their opponents. Ultimately, the controversies over the investitures in 1911 and 1969 were less conflicts between the British state and the Welsh nation than quarrels amongst the people of Wales over who and what constituted Welshness.

Select bibliography

Manuscripts

Borough of Caernarfon Gwynedd Record Office, Caernarfon
Papers: Correspondence regarding the Investiture 1911
College of Arms, London
Papers: 1969 Investiture of the Prince of Wales; Vincent 151
National Library of Wales, Aberystwyth
Papers: Lord Cledwyn; J. Glynn Davies; David Lloyd George; William George; James Griffiths; Owen Rhoscomyl; Viscount Tonypandy; Tŷ Cenedl
Miscellaneous Volumes: ex 566; ex 1669; ex 1975–85
National Screen and Sound Archive: *Everyone Held their Breath,* Air Date: BBC 1, 1 July 1994, AM 1099/03; '25 Years On', BBC Wales Today, BBC 1, AM 1099/03; Various other television and film related to the 1969 Investiture
Public Records Office, London
Papers: Cabinet 164–165; Home Office 287, 290, 325; Prime Minister's Papers 13; Treasury 227; Welsh Office 25, 67

Newspapers and periodicals 1910–11

Baner ac Amserau Cymru
Birmingham Post
Cambrian News
Carnarvon & Denbighshire Herald
Cork Examiner
Daily Chronicle
Daily Express
Daily Mail
Daily Telegraph
Evening Standard

INVESTITURE

Freeman's Journal
Glasgow Herald
Goleuad, Y
Gwyliedydd Newydd
Holyhead Chronicle
Irish Freedom
Irish Times
Lady's Realm
Llais Llafur
Llan a'r Dywysogaeth
Lloyd's News
Manchester Dispatch
Manchester Guardian
Merthyr Pioneer
Morning Advertiser
Morning Leader
Morning Post
Newcastle Chronicle
New York Evening Post
North Wales Chronicle
Pall Mall Gazette
Seren Cymru
South Wales Daily News
Standard
Times, The
Tyst
Wales
Western Mail
Young Wales

Newspapers and periodicals 1967–69

Baner ac Amserau Cymru
Barn
Belfast Telegraph
Business Visitor to Britain
Cambrian News
Cardigan & Tivy Side Advertiser
Caernarvon & Denbighshire Herald

SELECT BIBLIOGRAPHY

Cymro
Daily Express
Daily Mirror
Daily Sketch
Daily Telegraph and Morning Post
Daily Telegraph Magazine
Denbighshire Free Press
Evening Post
Evening Standard
Glasgow Herald
Guardian
Herald of Wales
Holyhead & Anglesey Mail
I'r Gad
Liverpool Daily Post
Llanelli Star
Lol
Merthyr Express
National Geographic
News of the World
Observer
Observer Magazine
Plastics and Rubber Weekly
Rhyl & Prestatyn Gazette
Scotsman
Sheffield Star
South Wales Argus
South Wales Echo
South Wales Evening Post
Sun
Sunday Express
Sunday Observer
Sunday Telegraph
Sunday Times
Tafod y Ddraig
Times, The
Welsh Nationalist
Western Mail
Wrexham Leader

INVESTITURE

1911 Investiture: miscellaneous printed sources

Anon., *Illustrated Programme of the Investiture of the Prince of Wales* (Carnarvon, 1911)
Anon., *The Investiture of H. R. H. The Prince of Wales at Carnarvon: Handbook and Official Programme of Festivities* (Liverpool, 1911)
Anon., *Investiture of H. R. H. The Princes of Wales: Medals and Souvenirs Designed & Manufactured by Fattorini & Sons Ltd* (Bradford, 1911)
Anon., *Ceremonial to be Observed at the Investiture of his Royal Highness the Prince of Wales, K.G.*, July 1911 (London, 1911)
Anon., *Wales and her Prince: The Investiture and All About It: With a Programme of the Tour of the King and Queen. Copious illustrations and portraits* (London, 1911)
Anon., *Invitation to the Investiture of H. R. H. the Prince of Wales* (1911)
Archbishop of Wales, *Memories* (London, 1927)
Edwards, J. Hugh, *The Life of David Lloyd George with a Short History of the Welsh People* (London, 1918)
Evans, Beriah Gwynfe, *Glyndŵr: Tywysog Cymru – The Welsh Historical Investiture Play* (Caernarfon, 1911)
Rhoscomyl, Owen, *The Book of the Investiture* (Cardiff, 1911)
——, *Flame-Bearers of Welsh History* (Merthyr Tydfil, 1905)
Windsor, Edward, *A King's Story: The Memoirs of H. R. H. The Duke of Windsor K.G.* (London, 1951)
Welsh Housing Association, 'Souvenir of the Investiture of His Royal Highness the Prince of Wales, K.G., at Carnarvon Castle on the 13th of July, 1911' (1911)
Abraham H. Thomas, 'Urddwisgiad ei uchelder Brfeninol Twysog Cymru yn Nghaernarfon, 1911' (Llansamlet, 1911)

1969 Investiture: miscellaneous printed sources

Anon., *The Wedding of Her Royal Highness the Princess Margaret and Mr. Antony Armstrong-Jones, Westminster Abbey 6 May 1960* (London, 1960)

Hughes, Emrys, *The Prince, the Crown and the Cash* (London, 1969)
Owen, Gerallt Lloyd, *Cerddi'r Gadair* (Aberystwyth, 1969)
——, *Cerddi'r Cywilydd* (Rhosbodrual, 1972)
Thomas, Ned, *The Welsh Extremist* (Tal-y-bont, 1973)
Welsh Office, *Wales, the Way Ahead* (Cardiff, 1967)

Secondary sources

Anderson, Benedict, *Imagined Communities: Reflections on the Origin and Spread of Nationalism* (London, 1991)
Bell, Catherine, *Ritual Theory, Ritual Practice* (Oxford, 1992)
Bradford, Sarah, *Elizabeth: A Biography of Her Majesty the Queen* (London, 1996)
Butt, Phillip, *The Welsh Question* (Cardiff, 1975)
Cannadine, David, *The Decline and Fall of the British Aristocracy* (New Haven and London, 1990)
——, 'The Context, Performance and Meaning of Ritual: The British Monarchy and the Invention of Tradition, c.1820–1977', in Eric Hobsbawm and Terrence Ranger (eds), *Invention of Tradition* (Cambridge, 1983)
Chapman, Malcolm, *The Celts: The Construction of a Myth* (New York, 1992)
Clews, Roy, *To Dream of Freedom: The Struggle of the M. A. C. and the Free Wales Army* (Tal-y-bont, 1980)
Colley, Linda, *Britons: Forging the Nation 1707–1837* (New Haven and London, 1992)
Coopey, Richard, Steven Fielding and Nick Tiratsoo (eds), *The Wilson Governments 1964–1970* (London and New York, 1993)
Cragoe, Matthew, *Culture, Politics and National Identity in Wales 1832–1886* (Oxford, 2004)
Creiger, Don M., *Bounder from Wales: Lloyd George's Career before the First World War* (Columbia and London, 1976)
Cunningham, Hugh, 'The Conservative Party and Patriotism', in Robert Colls and Phillip Dodd (eds), *Englishness: Politics and Culture 1880–1920* (London, 1986)
Daunton, M. J., *Coal Metropolis: Cardiff 1870–1914* (London, 1977)

Davidoff, Leonore and Catherine Hall, *Family Fortunes: Men and Women of the English Middle Class 1780–1850* (London, 1987)

Davies, D. Hywel, *The Welsh Nationalist Party 1925–1945: A Call to Nationhood* (Cardiff, 1983)

Davies, John, *A History of Wales* (London, 1990)

——, 'Victoria and Victorian Wales', in Geraint H. Jenkins and J. Beverley Smith (eds), *Politics and Society in Wales, 1840–1922* (Cardiff, 1988)

——, 'Wales in the Nineteen-sixties', *Llafur*, 4 (1987), 78–82

——, 'Aristocratic town-makers and the coal metropolis: the Marquesses of Bute and the growth of Cardiff, 1776 to 1947', in David Cannadine (ed.), *Patricians, Power and Politics in Nineteenth Century Towns* (New York, 1982)

Davies, W. Watkin, *Lloyd George 1863–1914* (London, 1939)

Deacon, Russell Martin, *The Governance of Wales: The Welsh Office and the Policy Process 1964–99* (Cardiff, 2002)

——, Deacon, Russell and Steve Belzak, *'God Bless the Prince of Wales': Wales' Royal Prerogative Do We Still Need a Prince of Wales?* (Cardiff, 2000)

Edwards, Andrew and Duncan Tanner, 'Defining or Dividing the Nation? Opinion Polls, Welsh Identity and Devolution, 1966–1979', *Contemporary Wales*, 18 (2006), 54–71

Edwards, Hywel Teifi and E. G. Millward, *Jiwbilî y Fam Wen Fawr: Fictoria 1887–1897* (Llandysul, 2002)

——, 'Pasiant Cenedlaethol Caerdydd 1909', *Codi'r Hen Wlad Yn Ei Hôl* (Swansea, 1989)

Edwards, J. Goronwy, *The Principality of Wales 1267–1967: A Study in Constitutional History* (Caernarvonshire, 1969)

Ellis, John S., 'A Pacific People – A Martial Race: Pacifism, Militarism and Welsh National Identity' in Matthew Cragoe and Chris Williams (eds), *Wales at War: Society, Politics and Religion in the Nineteenth and Twentieth Centuries* (Cardiff, 2006)

——, 'Celt versus Teuton: Race, Character and British National Identity, 1850–1918', *Irish German Studies* (2001/2002), 13–27

——, 'The "Methods of Barbarism" and the "Rights of Small Nations": War Propaganda and British Pluralism,' *Albion*, 30(1) (spring 1998), 49–75

——, 'Reconciling the Celt: Identity, Empire and the 1911 Investiture of the Prince of Wales', *Journal of British Studies*, 37 (1998), 391–418.

——, 'The Prince and the Dragon: Welsh National Identity and the 1911 Investiture of the Prince of Wales', *Welsh History Review*, 18 (1996), 272–94.

Erfyl, Gwyn, 'Tryweryn: The Drowning of a Valley', *Planet*, 73 (1989), 49–53.

Evans, Neil, '"A Nation in a Nutshell": The Swansea Disestablishment Demonstration of 1912 and the Political Culture of Edwardian Wales', in R. R. Davies and Geraint H. Jenkins (eds), *From Medieval to Modern Wales: Historical Essays in Honour of Kenneth O. Morgan and Ralph A. Griffiths* (Cardiff, 2004)

——, 'The Welsh Victorian City: Middle Class and Civic and National Consciousness in Cardiff, 1850–1914', *Welsh History Review*, 12(3) (1985), 350–87

Faverty, Frederic E., *Matthew Arnold: The Ethnologist* (Evanston, 1951)

Field, H. John, *Toward a Programme of Imperial Life: The British Empire at the Turn of the Century* (Westport, 1982)

Fielding, Stephen and John W. Young (eds), *The Labour Governments 1964–70*, vol. 1–3 (Manchester and New York, 2003)

Formisano, Ronald P., 'The Concept of Political Culture', *Journal of Interdisciplinary History*, 31 (winter 2001), 393–426

Geertz, Clifford, *The Interpretation of Cultures* (New York, 1973)

Gilbert, Bentley Birkenhoff, *David Lloyd George: A Political Life: The Architect of Change 1863–1912* (London, 1987)

Gordon, Stewart, *Robes and Honour: The Medieval World of Investiture* (Basingstoke, 2000)

Grigg, John, *Lloyd George: The People's Champion 1902–1911* (London, 1978)

Dafydd Gwynn, 'Arwisgiad 1969: Yr Ymateb Gwleidyddol', *Cof Cenedl*, XV (2000), 163–91

Hayden, Ilse, *Symbol and Privilege: The Ritual Context of British Royalty* (Tuscon, 1987)
Hobsbawm, Eric J., *Nations and Nationalism Since 1780* (New York, 1990)
——, 'Introduction: Inventing Traditions', Eric Hobsbawm and Terrence Ranger (eds), *The Invention of Tradition* (Cambridge, 1983)
—— and Terrence Ranger (eds), *The Invention of Tradition* (Cambridge, 1983)
Hoey, Brian, *Snowdon: Public Figure, Private Man* (Thrupp, 2005)
Holden, Anthony, *Charles: A Biography* (London, 1998)
Howarth, David and Yannis Stavrakakis, 'Introducing Discourse Theory and Political Analysis', in David Howarth, Aletta J. Norval and Yannis Stavrakakis (eds), *Discourse Theory and Political Analysis: Identities, Hegemonies and Social Change* (Manchester and New York, 2000)
Howell, Lyn, *The Wales Tourist Board: The Early Years* (Cardiff, 1988)
Iwan, Dafydd, *Holl Ganeuon Dafydd Iwan* (Tal-y-bont, 1992)
——, *Dafydd Iwan* (Caernarfon, 1981)
Jenkins, Geraint H., *The University of Wales: An Illustrated History* (Cardiff, 1993)
Jones, Aled Gruffydd, *Press, Politics and Society: A History of Journalism in Wales* (Cardiff, 1993)
Jones, Francis, *The Princes and Principality of Wales* (Cardiff, 1969)
Jones, Goronwy J., *Wales and the Quest for Peace* (Cardiff, 1969)
Jones, J. B., 'The Development of Welsh Territorial Institutions: Modernization Theory', *Contemporary Wales*, 2 (1988), 47–61
Jones, R. Merfyn and Ioan Rhys Jones, 'Labour and the Nation', in Duncan Tanner, Chris Williams and Deian Hopkins (eds), *The Labour Party in Wales 1900–2000* (Cardiff, 2000)
Keay, Douglas, *Elizabeth II: Portrait of a Monarch* (London, 1991)
Kertzer, David I., *Ritual, Politics and Power* (London and New Haven, 1988)

Kuhn, William, *Democratic Royalism: The Transformation of the British Monarchy, 1861–1914* (New York, 1996)
Levin, Bernard, *The Pendulum Years: Britain and the Sixties* (London, 1979)
——, *Run it Down the Flagpole: Britain in the Sixties* (New York, 1970)
Loughlin, James, *The British Monarchy and Ireland* (Cambridge, 2007)
MacDougall, Hugh, *Racial Myth in English History* (Hanover, 1982)
Marwick, Arthur, *The Sixties: Cultural Revolution in Britain, France, Italy, and the United States, c.1958–1974* (Oxford, 1998)
McKie, David and Chris Cook, *The Decade of Disillusionment: British Politics in the Sixties* (London and Basingstoke, 1972)
Mellor, David Alan and Laurent Gervereau Dorléac, *The Sixties: Britain and France, 1962–1973: The Utopian Years* (London, 1997)
Mock, Wolfgang, 'The Function of Race in Imperialist Ideologies: The Example of Joseph Chamberlain', in Paul Kennedy and Anthony Nicholls (eds), *Nationalist and Racialist Movements in Britain and Germany Before 1914* (Oxford, 1981)
Morgan, Kenneth O., *The Red Dragon and the Red Flag: The Cases of James Griffiths and Aneurin Bevan* (Aberystwyth, 1989)
——, 'Peace Movements in Wales, 1899–1945', *Welsh History Review* (1982), 234–56
——, *Rebirth of a Nation: Wales 1880–1980* (Oxford, 1981)
——, *Keir Hardie: Radical and Socialist* (London, 1975)
——, *Freedom or Sacrilege: A History of the Campaign for Welsh Disestablishment* (Penarth, 1966)
——, *Wales in British Politics 1868–1922* (Cardiff, 1963)
Morgan, Prys, 'Early Victorian Wales and its Crisis of Identity', in Laurence Brockliss and David Eastwood (eds.), *A Union of Multiple Identities: The British Isles, c.1750–1850* (Manchester and New York, 1997)

——, 'The Gwerin of Wales – Myth and Reality', in I. Hume and W. T. R. Pryce (eds), *The Welsh and their Country* (Swansea, 1986)
——, 'The Clouds of Witnesses: The Welsh Historical Tradition', in R. Brinley Jones (ed.), *Anatomy of Wales* (Peterston-Super-Ely, 1972)
Morris, Jan, *The Princeship of Wales* (Llandysul, 1995)
Murphy, James H., *Abject Loyalty: Nationalism and Monarchy in Ireland during the Reign of Queen Victoria* (Washington DC, 2001)
Nairn, Tom, *The Enchanted Glass* (London, 1988)
Nelmes, Graham V., 'Stuart Rendel and Welsh Liberal Political Organization in the Late Nineteenth Century', *Welsh History Review*, 9 (1978/79), 468–85
O'Day, Alan, 'Irish Home Rule and Liberalism', in Alan O'Day (ed.) *The Edwardian Age: Conflict and Stability 1900–1914* (London and Basingstoke, 1979)
O'Leary, Paul, 'The Languages of Patriotism in Wales 1840–1880', in Geraint H. Jenkins (ed.), *The Welsh Language and its Social Domains 1801–1911* (Cardiff, 2000)
——, 'Religion, Nationality and Politics: Disestablishment in Ireland and Wales, 1868–1914', in John R. Guy and W. G. Neely, *Contrasts and Comparisons: Studies in Irish and Welsh Church History* (Cardiff, 1999)
Osmond, John, *Police Conspiracy* (Tal-y-bont, 1984)
Owen, Bryn, *Owen Rhoscomyl and the Welsh Horse* (Caernarfon, 1990)
Parry, Adrian John, 'Welsh Politics and the Investiture of the Prince of Wales, in 1969' (MA, University of Wales, Aberystwyth, 1981).
Paseta, Senia, 'Nationalist Responses to Two Royal Visits to Ireland, 1900 and 1903', *Irish Historical Studies*, 124 (1999), 488–504.
Phillips, Dylan, 'The History of the Welsh Language Society, 1962–1998', in Geraint H. Jenkins and Mari A. Williams (eds), *'Let's Do Our Best for the Ancient Tongue': The Welsh Language in the Twentieth Century* (Cardiff, 2000)
——, *Trwy Ddulliau Chwyldro . . .? Hanes Cymdeithas yr Iaith Gymraeg, 1962–1992* (Llandysul, 1998)

Pimlott, Ben, *The Queen: A Biography of Elizabeth II* (London, 1996)
Pittock, Murray G. H., *Celtic Identity and the British Image* (Manchester, 2000)
——, *Inventing and Resisting Britain: Cultural Identities in Britain and Ireland, 1685–1789* (New York, 1997)
Price, Emyr, *Lord Cledwyn of Penrhos* (Pen-y-groes, 1990)
Ramon, Hunston, *Order! Order!: A Biography of the Right Honourable George Thomas* (Basingstoke, 1981)
Randall, P.J., 'Wales in the Structure of Central Government', *Public Administration 50* (1972), 353–369.
Roberts, Gwyneth Tyson, *The Language of the Blue Books: The Perfect Instrument of Empire* (Cardiff, 1998)
——, '"Under the Hatches" English Parliamentary Commissioners Views of the People and Language of Mid-Nineteenth Century Wales', in Bill Schwartz (ed.), *The Expansion of England: Race, Ethnicity and Cultural History* (London, 1996)
Robertson, E. H., *George: A Biography of Viscount Tonypandy* (London, 1993)
Rose, Sonya O., *Limited Livelihoods: Gender and Class in Nineteenth Century England* (Berkeley and Los Angeles, 1992)
Rowlands, E., 'The Politics of Regional Administration: The Establishment of the Welsh Office', *Public Administration*, 50 (1972), 331–51
Rowlands, Ted, *Something Must Be Done: South Wales vs Whitehall 1921–1951* (Merthyr Tydfil, 2000)
Schwarz, Bill, 'Politics and Rhetoric in the Age of Mass Culture', *History Workshop Journal*, 46 (1998), 129–59
Smith, Dai, *Aneurin Bevan and the World of South Wales* (Cardiff, 1993)
——, *Wales? Wales!* (London, 1984)
Smyth, Gerry, 'The Natural Course of Things: Matthew Arnold, Celticism and the English Poetic Tradition', *Victorian Studies*, 1 (1996)
Stead, Peter, 'The Labour Party and the Claims of Wales', in John Osmond (ed.), *The National Question Again: Welsh Political Identity in the 1980s* (Llandysul, 1985)

——, 'The Language of Edwardian Politics', in David Smith (ed.), *A People and a Proletariat* (London, 1980)
Stephens, Meic, 'Lord Cledwyn of Penrhos (1916–2001)', *Planet*, 146 (2001), 95
Taylor, Antony, *'Down with the Crown': British Anti-monarchism and Debates about Royalty since 1790* (London, 1999)
Thomas, Einion, *Capel Celyn: Deng Mlynedd o Chwalu: 1955–1965* (Abertawe, 1997)
Thomas, George, *George Thomas, Mr. Speaker: The Memoirs of Viscount Tonypandy* (London, 1985)
Thomas, Ian, *The Creation of the Welsh Office: Conflicting Purposes in Institutional Change* (Glasgow, 1981)
Thomas, Jane, *Diana's Mourning: A People's History* (Cardiff, 2002)
Tyler, Neil Purvey, 'Lloyd George, the Bishop of St. Asaph and the Disestablishment Controversy', in Judith Loades (ed.), *The Life and Times of David Lloyd George* (Bangor, 1991)
Vaughan-Thomas, Wynford, *The Princes of Wales* (Kingswood, 1982)
Vlastos, Stephen, 'Tradition Past/Present Culture and Modern Japanese History' in Stephen Vlastos (ed.), *Mirror of Modernity: Invented Traditions of Modern Japan* (California, 1998)
Ward, Paul, *Britishness since 1870* (London and New York, 2004)
Weight, Richard, *Patriots: National Identity in Britain, 1940–2000* (London, 2002)
Williams, Emyr W., 'Liberalism in Wales and the Politics of Welsh Home Rule 1886–1910', *The Bulletin of the Board of Celtic Studies* 37 (1980), 191–207.
Williams, Gareth, *Valleys of Song: Music and Society in Wales 1840–1914* (Cardiff, 2003)
——, *1905 and All That* (Llandysul, 1991)
Williams, Gwyn A., *When Was Wales?* (London, 1985)
——, 'Imperial Wales', in Gwyn A. Williams, *The Welsh and Their History* (London, 1980)
Williams, J. Gwynn, *The University Movement in Wales* (Cardiff, 1993)

Index

Aberfan 137, 138, 141
Abergele martyrs 234–5, 240, 286
Aberystwyth, 198–200
   Prince Charles as student 249
   security precautions 230
Abraham, William 'Mabon' 87–8
Acts of Union 40–1
Ambassador
   investiture issue 168
Anderson, Benedict
   nationalism, on 10
Anglican Church 24–6, 54, 77–9, 81–5
   Welsh nationalism, and 81–2
Anglo-Saxonism 21–2, 26, 102–3, 120–1
ap Iestyn, Gethin 212, 214, 218–19, 225, 227–9, 291
ap Rhobart, Euryn
   surveillance of 225
Armstrong-Jones, Antony 149–50
   see also Lord Snowdon
Arnold, Matthew 102, 300
Asquith, H. H. 5, 54
   home rule, and 34–5
   Imperial Conference 1911 111–12

Baden-Powell, R. S. S. 111
battle of the sites 59–62, 69–72
BBC
   allegations of bias 295–9
Bevan, Aneurin 128, 309–10
Black Prince 41
Boer War 30, 33–4, 110–11
bombings 226, 210–11, 234–7

Bosworth, Battle of 44
Botha, Louis 34
   invitation to 1911 Investiture 111
Boy scouts 107
'Bradwr' 283–4, 292, 301
British Empire 109–13
   nature of 22–3, 91, 118
British family
   model for British state, as 104
British national identity
   pluralist construction 113, 252–3
Brooke, Henry
   Prince of Wales, on 146

Caernarfon 3–4, 59–62, 205
   Celtic image, and 103
   Constable of 75, 155
   planned occupation 218–19
   security arrangements 231–2
   security of transport routes 233–4
   slate docks 72–3
Caernarfon Castle 47, 56, 92–3, 206, 218, 231, 255
   construction of 39–40
   symbolism 92–3

Callaghan, Jim 222–4
Cannadine, David
   aristocracy, on 82–3
Cardiff 59–62, 69–72, 145–6
   cultivation of inclusive sense of nationality 79
   unofficial capital, as 68–70
   urban middle class 68–9, 71–2

INDEX

Cayo-Evans, Julian 211–12, 214–15, 219, 224, 226–8, 280, 291, 300, 309
    death of 309
Celticism 21–2, 42, 95–6, 102–3, 106, 118, 258, 300
Checketts, David 151, 154
Churchill, Winston 5
    Tonypandy riots, and 83
Cilmery 206, 216–17, 238, 255, 276, 281, 308
class division
    Investiture of 1911, and 86–8
Clwyd, Anne
    Welsh language, on 186
coal industry
    contraction of 137
    English immigrants, and 32
    revitalization of coal field 166
College of Arms 14, 148, 149, 155–7, 159–60
Colley, Linda
    national identity, on 10
Commonwealth Games 1958 145
Conservative government 1895–1906 29–30
Conservative Party
    investiture of 1969, and 192
    Irish home rule, and 101–2
    national unity, and 22
    'unity in diversity', and 100
Cool Cymru 261–2
Coslett, Denis 212, 215, 218, 224, 227–9, 300, 309
Countryside Act 1968 173
Cox, Ian
    injury to 236–7, 240
Crécy, Battle of
    ostrich device, and 43
    wearing of leek, and 43
Croeso 69 175–7, 201, 204
Croeso conference 1967 175
cultural revolution of 1960s 134–5

custom 37–47
Cymdeithas yr Iaith 139, 199, 200, 204–8, 217, 306–7
    complicated position of 206–7
    investiture of 1969, and 204–8
    rallies 205–6
    sign painting campaign 182
    support for 307
Cymru Fydd 29, 31, 33

Daniel, G. H. 153, 155
design 156–7, 168–71, 256–8
devolution 26, 29, 31, 35, 118, 140–1, 180–2, 251, 305–6, 314–15
Duke of Windsor
    memoirs 1951 52–3

Earl Marshall 62–3, 148, 152
    see also Norfolk, Duke of
Ebbw Vale
    steelworks 166
economic reform 164–80
Edward I 38–40
Edward VII 34, 92–3, 121, 255, 268, 276–8
    death of 35
Edward VIII
    visit to Wales 127–8
Edward of Caernarfon 40
Edwards, A. G. 57, 60, 63
    investiture of 1911, and 54, 65
Edwards, Sir Ifan ab Owen 154, 201–4
Eisteddfod
    royal patronage 45
Elis Thomas, Dafydd 272, 307
    investiture of 1969, on 197–8
Elizabeth II 145–8, 152, 250–1
Ellis, Thomas E. 28, 57
Evans, Beriah Gwynfe 94
Evans, Gwyndaf 207
Evans, Gwynfor 282
    attitude to 1969 Investiture 196–7

INDEX

election as MP 142, 193
Evans, Myrddin
   British League, on 70
Evans, R.T.
   nationalism, on 117–18
extremist 284, 292–5, 301, 306

Festival of Wales 1948 145–6, 174
First World War 125–6
Fishlock, Trevor
   Aberystwyth, on 200
   coal industry, on 166
Free Wales Army 208, 307–9
   armed revolt, plan for 218
   arrest of leaders 219, 226
   international connections 213–14
   nature of 211–12, 213
   origin 211
   Patriotic Front, and 215
   training camp 219, 226
   trial 227–9, 281, 299
future investiture 312–15

Geertz, Clifford
   royal ceremonies, on 13
gender roles 103–4
   feminine characterization of Wales 104–5
   masculinity 105–7
general election 1922 128
George V 3–5, 51, 53–4, 57, 111–12, 126, 148
   coronation 35
   masculinity, image of 106
Gibson-Watt, David 191
Gladstone, W. E.
   Welsh nationhood, and 27–8
Glyndŵr: Tywysog Cymru 94
Gorsedd of Bards 14, 37, 74
Griffiths, James 143
Griggs, John
   Lloyd George, on 53

gwerin 67–89
   elements of 76–7

Hen Wlad fy Nhadau 5
Henry, Prince
   investiture 41
Henry III 39
Henry VII 44, 94–5
Heseltine, William 249
   role as Queen's press secretary 150–1
Hobsbawm, Eric
   invented tradition, on 9, 11, 37
Holyhead 3, 5, 234
House of Lords veto controversy 34–5
Hughes, Cledwyn 141, 143, 165, 184, 189, 284
   planning of 1969 Investiture, and 147–8, 152
   Prince Charles, and 247
Hughes, Emrys
   opposition to 1969 Investiture 190–1

Imperial Conference 1911 111–12
Imperial Durbar 112
Imperial unity 22–3, 110–13
Imperialism 22–3, 109–13, 118
India 113, 120
Invented tradition 9–17, 317
   anti-democratic origins 11
   term of analysis, as 12
invention of investiture 49–66
investiture
   history of 41–7
   invented tradition, as 9–17
   iuxta morem 41
   modernization 256–8
   Welsh national identity, and 13–14, 15
Investiture of 1911 3–5, 21–47
   Boer War, and 110–11

337

INDEX

celebration of Welsh nationhood, as 67
Celticism, and 102
costume 53
democracy, and 74–5
image of Wales as united nation 88–9
Imperial backdrop 110–11
Investiture of 1969
  distinguished 6–7
miner's attitude to 87
monarchy, and 38
National Committee 62–6
nature of British State, and 99
new ceremony, as 49
official consent of King 62
process of invention 66
publicity 91–2
scarcity of documentation 14
selection of site 60–1
significance 15
spirit of nationalism, and 98–9
Welsh national identity, and 67–8
Welsh soldiers 107–9
youthful masculinity, image of 105–6
Investiture of 1969 5–6
  'Alien Prince' 273–4
  apparent success of 303–4
  arguments as to design 156–7
  arrest of demonstrators 236
  breadth of opposition to 238–9
  committee structure 153
  construction of ceremony's meaning 301–2
  cost of 157–60, 272–3
  criticism of 245–6
  decline of monarchy, and 164
  democracy, and 248–9
  denial of hostility to Prince Charles 291–2
  design, and 257
  design ethos 169–71
  documentation 14–15
  Earl Marshal, and 148
  economic policies of Labour government, and 164
  effect on Welsh Labour Party 304–6
  equality of language 183
  extra-parliamentary nationalism, and 306–7
  extremism, criticism of 285–9
  financial venture, as 179–80
  gold coronet 170
  hostile incidents July 1969 236
  image of Welsh, and 258
  insult to Welsh nationhood, characterisation as 277–8
  integration of United Kingdom, and 252–3
  Investiture Committee 154–5
  Investiture of 1911, and 155–6, 247–8
Investiture of 1911
  distinguished 6–7
Labour Party, and 163
Labour's image of Wales, and 245, 251–2
media coverage and bias 298–301
military, and 258–60
Officials Committee 154–5
opposition to 115–24, 189
origin myth 255
origins of 145–7
personal relationship with Prince of Wales 246–7
planning infrastructure 153–5
political impact 304–5
political implications 272
popular opinion polls 239–41
popular support for 241, 242–3
post-investiture events 260–1
potential economic benefits 289–90

INDEX

Prince Charles, image of 262–3, 265
Prince Charles as Welsh ambassador 266–7
propaganda, and 295–6
Psalm of Shame 282–3
public relations potential 179
role of Royal Family in planning 149
rugby, and 260
security network 223
security precautions 220–1, 229–34
significance 15
souvenir competition 304
surveillance campaign 224–5
television, and 296–8
unification of Welsh nation, and 270
Wales as police state 279–81
Welsh infrastructure, and 171–2
Welsh pride, and 256
Welsh social democracy, and 253–4
youth, emphasis on 262, 263–5
Ireland
  Celticism, atmosphere of 97
  home rule 27–35, 101–2, 126
  parallel with Wales 96
  Royal family's visit 1911 96–8
Iwan, Dafydd 194, 242, 275
  Carlo 199, 205, 241–2, 274, 285, 291, 309
  opposition to 1969 Investiture 205, 208
  Welsh language, on 293–4

James, Edward
  Owen Rhoscomyl, on 57
Jenkins, John 209–10, 234, 235–7, 291, 308
Jenkins, Roy
  cost of 1969 Investiture, and 157–8, 159, 160

John, Goscombe 67
Jones, Alwyn 234
Jones, Frances 54, 149
  Welsh language, on 183
Jones, Gareth
  demonstrations, on 290–1
Jones, J. R.
  opposition to investiture 278–9, 282, 291
Jones, R. H. 153
Jones, Tegid 230
Jones, Tegwyn 199, 202, 275, plate 2
Jones, Tom 263

Keir Hardie, James 32, 115, 191
  attack on investiture of 1911 120
  death of 125–6
  Germanic associations of Royal Family, on 120–1
  May Day, on 116–17
  nationalism, on 118–19
  opposition to 1911 Investiture 115–20
  Welsh Liberals, on 119
Kuhn, William
  democratic royalism, on 12
  invented traditions, on 37

Labour government
  policies in Wales, and 163–4, 168, 171, 182, 186–7
Labour governments 1964–70 133–6
  expectations 135
  modernist spirit 135
Labour Party
  1922 general election 128–9
  centralists 122–4, 128, 140–1, 305–6
  challenges to 318
  devolutionists 124, 140–1, 129, 305

339

dominance of 139–40
monarchy, and 189–90
nationalism, and 122–3, 129
Welsh national aspirations, and 139–40, 165, 187, 219, 305
Letters Patent
  reading in Welsh 183–4
Lewis, Anthony 214, 227
Lewis, Saunders 127
  FWA, on 281–2
  Welsh language, on 139
Liberal government 1906–14 33–5
Liberal Party 21–47
  1906 election 31
  1916 split 126
  1922 election 127
  Irish home rule, and 101
  national recognition, attitude to 100
  political hegemony 31
  Welsh nationalism, and 27
  Welsh Parliamentary Party 28
Llantrisant
  royal mint 165
Llewelyn, Sir David
  investiture of 1969, on 192
Llewelyn Jones, Emyr 206, 209, 225, 291, 293–4
Llewelyn Williams, W. 74–5, 126
Lloyd George, David
  background of 50–1
  close links to investiture 51–3, 60, 64–7, 76, 112
  coalition government 126
  criticism of 126–7
  democracy, and 75
  empire, on 112
  Investiture of 1911, and 49–52
  People's Budget 1909 34, 51
  populism, and 75
Lloyd Owen, Gerallt
  Fy Ngwlad 203–4, 276, 283, 294–5

Llywelyn the Great 39
Llywelyn the Last 38–40, 122, 215–16, 252, 255, 264, 275–7, 279, 283, 286–7, 294
Lol 194–5
Loyalty Address of the Welsh People 109

MacMillan, Harold 145–6
Marquess of Bute 79
May Day
  Merthyr celebrations 116–17
Meibion Glyndŵr 308
Merthyr Tydfil
  May Day celebrations 1911 116
military and militarism 5, 43, 107–9, 126–7, 196, 232, 234–5, 258–60, 264–5
Millward, Edward
  Cymdeithas yr Iaith, on 207
  tutor of Prince Charles 186, 197, 268–9
Mudiad Amddiffyn Cymru (MAC) 208, 307–9
  arrest of 237–8
  bomb on A5 235
  bombings 210–11
  campaign against investiture 210
  formation 209
  Investiture of 1969, and 234
  music 5, 73–4, 261–2

Nairn, Tom
  monarchy, on 113
National Committee 62–6
  Asquith and 64
  Lloyd George and 64–5
  membership 63
  secrecy 64, 65
National Library of Wales

INDEX

creation 29
National Museum of Wales
  creation 29
  investiture exhibitions 257
National Pageant 1909 38
national unity
  essential element, as 84–5
New Imperialism 29–30
Nicholas, Revd T. E.
  Investiture of 1911, on 121–2
Nonconformist middle class
  political dominance 83
  radicals, influence of 84
Nonconformity 24–6, 77–8
Norfolk, Duke of (15th) 148
Norfolk, Duke of (16th) 148–9, 155, 159–60, 177

pacifism 107, 117, 258–9, 264–5, 287
pageantry 3–7
  development of 37–8
paramilitary organizations 208–24
  aims 208–9
  demonstrations 216–17
  prosecutions 227–9
  revival 307–9
  seriousness of threat posed by 221–2
  voice of radical discontent, as 220
Parliament Bill 1910 34
Patriotic Front 208, 276
  Anti-Investiture Campaign Committee 280
  arrest of leaders 219
  demonstrations 216–17
  FWA, and 215
  Investiture of 1969, and 215–16
  origin 214
  umbrella organization, as 214–15

Pembrey nail bombing 226
People's Budget 1909 34, 51
Plaid Cymru 193–200, 305
  conference 1968 198, 216
  division on investiture issue 198–9
  formation of 127
  growth of 142, 305
  policy on 1969 Investiture 193–200
  Welsh-language youth culture, and 194
  youth branch 197–8
Plymouth, Lord
  planning of investiture 65–6
poetry 73–4, 200, 203–4, 206, 272–3, 276, 283, 294–5
political hegemony
  challenges to 317–18
populism 26, 31, 74–5
Port Talbot Trade Council
  opposition to 1969 Investiture 192
Powel, David
  Historie of Cumbria 47
prince
  meaning 38–9
Prince Charles 5–6
  creation as Prince of Wales 146
  Cymricization of 254–5, 268–9
  Labour Party policy, on 168
  reawakened interest in Wales 313–14
  Rhondda, visit to 166
  role in planning 1969 investiture 151–2
  since the investiture 310–12
  temporary dalliance with Wales 310–11
  visit to retraining and employment centres 164–5
  Welsh descent 254–5
  Welsh language, and 184–6, 274–5

INDEX

Prince Edward 4–5, 52–3, 74, 106–7, 151
Prince of Wales
  creation of 40–1
  creation of Prince Charles as 146
  origins and meaning 38–41
  youthful masculinity, image of 105–6
Prince protection squad 223–4
Prince William 314–15
Princess Diana
  death of 311–12
Princess Margaret 149, 231
publicity 176–9

Quant, Charles
  extremism, on 285–6

regional division of Wales
  Investiture of 1911, and 85–6
reinventing the investiture 145–62
religion 24–6
  Investiture of 1911, and 77
Rhondda 166
  riots (Tonypandy) 32, 38, 86–8
  support for 1969 Investiture 243
Rhoscomyl, Owen 50, 54–60
  background 54–5
  Boer War 55
  Caernarfon, and 60–1
  call for Welsh to return to Wales 109
  Cardiff, and 59–60, 71
  Flame-Bearers of Welsh History 56
  form of ceremony, on 59
  Gorsedd of Bards 59
  Investiture of 1911, and 50, 54–60
  Lord Howard de Walden, and 57

Matter of Wales, The 56
  movement to revive investiture, and 60
  Rhwysg 58
  Welsh nationalism, on 110
  Welsh past, on 92
  Welsh patriot, as 55–6
  Western Mail article 58
royal ceremonies 9–10
  Celtic periphery, and 11
  effect of 10
Royal Family
  film 250–1
  presented image of 150–1, 164, 249–50
  re-establishing relationship with Wales 314
  Welsh connection 94–5
royal visits 44–5
rural Wales
  transformation during 1960s 137–8

St Asaph, Bishop of 49, 50
  see also Edwards, A. G.
St David's Day 38
Saxon
  images of 102–3
Secretary of State for Wales
  creation of office 140–1
  role in the Investiture 152, 155
Seeley, John Robert
  Expansion of England, The 22–3
Siop y Pethe 199
Snowdon, Lord 149–50, 152, 155–7, 160, 257, 304
  costume 171
  design ethos 169–71
  'theatre in the round' 170
socialism 115, 247
  egalitarianism and social democracy 247–8

INDEX

internationalism 116–17
nationalism 117–20, 122–4
republicanism 116, 120–1, 189–92
South Africa 30, 53–4, 110–11
souvenir industry 167–8, 169
Staniforth, J. M. 85, 104
Stephens, Meic 195
'Swinging Britain' 136

Taylor, A. J. P.
  education of Prince Charles, on 192–3
Taylor, George 235
technology 135–6, 168, 257
television coverage 177–8
Temple of Peace 204, 210, 221
Thomas, George 143–4, 191–2, 203, 218, 235, 252, 259, 269, 284, 288, 295–8, 301, 304–6
  cost of 1969 Investiture, and 158–1
  'invisible' benefits, on 179
  Labour's image of Wales, and 251–2
  learning Welsh 183–4
  Welsh nationalism, on 123–4
  Welshness, on 267, 269, 271
Thomas, Ned 306
Thomas, R. S. 272–3
Tithe War 29
Tonypandy riots 83
tourism 167, 172–6, 178–82, 289, 303–4
traditions
  'chosen' 12
Treason of the Blue Books 25
Tryweryn
  flooding of 138, 145, 208, 211, 214
Tudor dynasty 44, 94–5

unity 84–6, 270–1

University of Wales 184, 192–3, 211, 247–8, 313
  Chancellor 45–6
  creation 29
  symbolism 80
Urdd Gobaith Cymru 201–4
Urdd Youth Eisteddfod 203

Victoria, Queen
  Boadicea rediviva, as 42
Vlastos, Stephen
  invented traditions, on 13

Wagner, Sir Anthony 159–60
Wales: The Way Ahead
  White Paper 163–4
Wales Tourist Board 173–6
  cost of investiture, on 180
  development of 180–1
  funding of 180–1
  nature of investiture, and 174–5
Webb, Harri 198
  Welsh republicanism, and 195
Weight, Richard
  post-imperial Britain, on 136
Welsh coal industry
  contraction during 1960s 137
Welsh disestablishment 26, 29, 33–5, 126
Welsh gentry and aristocracy 24–6, 78
  acceptance of 79
  cultural and educational institutions, and 80
  decline of 82
  image of 81
  university movement, and 80
Welsh home rule 26, 29, 31, 35, 118
Welsh Housing Association 95–6
Welsh identity 319–22
Welsh language 182
  decline of 138–9

in 1911 Investiture 73–4
in 1969 Investiture 182–6
'Living Welsh' 186
press 23–4, 298–9
proposed destruction of 25
revival of 73
use in Investiture 184–6
Welsh identity, and 22–5,
  267–8, 274, 320–1
Welsh Language Act 1967 182
Welsh military service 43–4
Welsh National Assembly 314–15
Welsh nationalism 21–47
  coal industry, and 32
  cracks in alliance 31–2
  cultural identity 24–5
  denial of Welsh nationhood
    21
  ethnic divisions 24–5
  growth in nineteenth century
    26
  growth of democratic politics,
    and 26–7
  industrial and rural
    disturbances, and 24
  industrial expansion, and 29
  Liberal Party, and 27
  political power during
    Edwardian period 33
  populism, and 26
  rising spirit of 28–9
  socialism, relationship with
    115–16
  success during late Victorian
    period 31
  Wales as industrial centre 24
  Wales dismissed as rural
    backwater 23
Welsh Office 129, 251
  creation of 140–1
  development of 142–3, 164
  mediation between Labour
    government and investiture
    of 1969 159
  planning of 1969 investiture,
    and 152–4, 160–2
Welsh Parliamentary Party 28
Welsh royalist tradition 42–3,
    193–4
Welsh Rugby Union
  adoption of Prince of Wales's
    icon 42
Welsh Sunday Closing Act 1881
  29
Wheatley, J. L.
  Cardiff, on 70–1
White, Eirene 156
  Welshness, on 267–8
Williams, Christopher 74
Williams, D. J. 127, 206
Williams, Llewelyn
  University of Wales, on 46
Williams, Owain 209, 218
  arrest of 225–6
Williams, Waldo 206
Wilson, Harold 133–6
  cost of 1969 Investiture, and
    161
  monarchy, and 189–90
  paramilitary organizations, on
    222–3
Wilson, Jock 224, 226, 229, 231,
    239
Workers Army of the Welsh
  Republic 308–9
Wynne, Robert 216, 224

Y Lolfa 194, 199
Y Tyst 77
youth 105–7, 262–5
  youth protest culture 194–5,
    199–204, 220